2008
First
Bus Handbook

British Bus Publishing

Body codes used in the Bus Handbook series:

Type:

A	Articulated vehicle
B	Bus, either single-deck or double-deck
BC	Interurban - high-back seated bus
C	Coach
M	Minibus with design capacity of 16 seats or less
N	Low-floor bus (*Niederflur*), either single-deck or double-deck
O	Open-top bus (CO = convertible - PO = partial open-top)

Seating capacity is then shown. For double-decks the upper deck quantity is followed by the lower deck.

Door position:-

C	Centre entrance/exit
D	Dual doorway.
F	Front entrance/exit
R	Rear entrance/exit (no distinction between doored and open)
T	Three or more access points

Equipment:-

T	Toilet	TV	Training vehicle.
M	Mail compartment	RV	Used as tow bus or engineers' vehicle.
L	Lift for wheelchair (post 2005 express coaches are fitted with lifts as standard)		

Allocation:-

t	Training bus
u	out of service or strategic reserve; refurbishment or seasonal requirement
w	Vehicle is withdrawn and awaiting disposal.

e.g. - B32/28F is a double-deck bus with thirty-two seats upstairs, twenty-eight down and a front entrance/exit.
N43D is a low-floor bus with two or more doorways.

Re-registrations:-
Where a vehicle has gained new index marks the details are listed at the end of each fleet showing the current mark, followed in sequence by those previously carried starting with the original mark.

Annual books are produced for the major groups:

The Stagecoach Bus Handbook
The First Bus Handbook
The Arriva Bus Handbook
The Go-Ahead Bus Handbook
The National Express Coach Handbook (bi-annual)
Some editions for earlier years are available. Please contact the publisher.

Regional books in the series:

The Scottish Bus Handbook
The Welsh Bus Handbook
The Ireland & Islands Bus Handbook
English Majors: Smaller Groups
English Majors: Notable Independents
English Majors: Coaches

Associated series:

The Hong Kong Bus Handbook
The Malta Bus Handbook
The Leyland Lynx Handbook
The Postbus Handbook
The Mailvan Handbook
The Toy & Model Bus Handbook - Volume 1 - Early Diecasts
The Fire Brigade Handbook (fleet list of each local authority fire brigade)
The Police Range Rover Handbook

Some earlier editions of these books are still available. Please contact the publisher on 01952 255669.

Contents

In 2004 First announced *ftr,* a hybrid mode that is a cross between a traditional light-rail tram system and a traditional bus service. The concept, *ftr*, is the texting shorthand for 'future', while the vehicles are called 'StreetCar', articulated single-deck vehicles based on Volvo B7LA chassis. 19020, YJ07LVM, is seen in York Street, Leeds. *Richard Godfrey*

2008 First Bus Handbook

The 2008 First Bus Handbook is a special edition of the Bus Handbook series. It contains the various vehicles of First plc's European operations which form a single fleet number system. The Bus Handbook series is published by *British Bus Publishing*, an independent publisher of quality books for the industry and bus enthusiasts. Further information on these books may be obtained from the address below.

Quality photographs for inclusion in the series are welcome, for which a fee is payable. Unfortunately, the publishers cannot accept responsibility for any loss and they require that you show your name on each picture or slide. High-resolution digital images of six megapixels or higher are also welcome on CD or DVD discs.

To keep the fleet information up to date the publishers recommend the Ian Allan magazine *Buses* published monthly, or for more detailed information, the PSV Circle monthly news sheets.

The writer and publisher would be glad to hear from readers should any information be available which corrects or enhances that given in this publication.

Editorial team: Stuart Martin and Bill Potter

Acknowledgments:
We are grateful to David Donati, Tom Johnson, Malcolm Jones, Mark Lyons, Simon Nicholas, the PSV Circle and the management and officials of First companies for their kind assistance and co-operation in the compilation of this book. The front cover picture is by Mark Lyons with fronticepiece by Mark Doggett.

Earlier Editions are available from the orderline, 01952 255669, or the web site www.britishbus.co.uk.

ISBN 9781904875185
Published by British Bus Publishing Ltd
16 St Margaret's Drive, Wellington, Telford, TF1 3PH
© British Bus Publishing Ltd, July 2008

e-mail: Orders@britishbuspublishing.co.uk
internet: http://www.britishbuspublishing.co.uk

Introduction

FirstGroup plc ('First') is the UK's largest surface transportation company with a turnover of over £3 billion a year and some 74,000 employees throughout the UK and North America. The Group is Britain's largest bus operator running more than one in five of all local bus services. A fleet of some 9,000 buses carries over 2.8 million passengers a day in more than forty major towns and cities from Aberdeen to Penzance. The Group is the UK's largest train operator with four passenger franchises First Great Western, First Capital Connect, First TransPennine Express and First ScotRail, and one open access operator Hull Trains. The Group operates one quarter of the UK passenger rail network with a balanced portfolio of intercity, commuter and regional services, carrying over 250 million passengers each year. The group operates freight services through GB Railfreight. The Group operates the Croydon Tramlink network which carries over twenty million passengers a year. In North America the Group has three operating divisions: First Student (yellow school buses), First Transit (contracting and management services) and First Services (vehicle maintenance and ancillary services). With headquarters in Cincinnati, the businesses operate across the US and Canada. First Student is the second largest provider of student transportation in North America with a fleet of over 21,000 yellow school buses carrying nearly 2 million students every day across the uS and Canada. First's vision is to Transform Travel – providing public transport services that are safe, reliable, high quality, personal and accessible. The company was formed in 1995 as FirstBus plc from the merger of two listed companies, Badgerline Group plc, based in Weston-super-Mare, and GRT Bus Group plc based in Aberdeen. The name was changed to FirstGroup plc in December 1997 to reflect the further diversity of the business into rail and airport management. First works closely with Government and local authorities to develop buses as an integral part of a sustainable transport policy. The Group is at the forefront of developments to create a new vision for bus transport across the UK. The bus division alone employs over 25,000 people. First is committed to innovation and developing new marketing initiatives designed to encourage more people to think about taking the bus for some journeys. In 1999, First launched 'The Overground' in Glasgow. This is a simple, easy to use bus network with frequent and reliable services, offering colour-coded routes and interchange points. 'Overground' and 'Metro' networks have now been introduced in over thirty towns and cities across the UK. First is continuing to develop satellite-based tracking systems that provide improved real-time passenger information at bus stops, and direct to customers' mobile telephones using SMS technology. First is at the forefront in the introduction of Guided Busways. Four schemes are in operation in North and East Leeds, Bradford and Ipswich. In February 2002 First brought the highly successful

First is one of the operators to provide buses for TfL's heritage service. Routemaster 39876, 776DYE, is seen at Charing Cross while displaying its bonnet number RM1776. *Richrd Godfrey*

American-style yellow school bus concept to the UK. The first scheme was introduced in Hebden Bridge in West Yorkshire using genuine US-built 'Blue Bird' yellow school buses. Since then further schemes have been introduced in Runnymede in Surrey, Wrexham in North Wales, Wokingham and Windsor in Berkshire, Bristol, Aberdeen, Northampton and Liverpool. The American-style yellow school bus services have the same driver every day with the same safety and security features that First uses in the United States to carry one million children to school each day. Some of the drivers are mothers with children at the schools – a tradition copied from the USA. The success of the initiative has seen local authorities develop their own schemes, often using yellow school buses owned by First to operate the services under contract to them. Up to 2005 new low-floor buses carried a different livery from older vehicles. First continues to lead the industry with its commitment to the environment through the use of environmentally friendly fuels. First is actively involved in trials of alternative fuels with initiatives such as gas buses and hybrid engines and is committed to running all of its buses on ultra-low sulphur diesel. As the UK's largest bus operator, First is ideally placed to make a significant contribution to reducing levels of pollution in our towns and cities by encouraging greater use of public transport.

The 2008 First Bus Handbook

First has entered into several contracts with local authorities, including the provision of *Park and Ride* services, for which local liveries have been introduced. Illustrating the Norwich scheme is Volvo 69010, AU05DMY. Since the picture was taken, this vehicle has moved to Great Yarmouth. *Mark Doggett*

In 2004 First announced *ftr,* a hybrid mode that is a cross between a traditional light-rail tram system and a traditional bus service. *ftr*, the texting shorthand for 'future', is a partnership between First and local authorities who want to demonstrate their commitment to reducing traffic congestion in their towns and cities, but where the option of a light-rail tramway system may not be appropriate. In the *ftr* partnership First provides the vehicle and the local authority provides the *ftr* 'track'. The vehicle has been designed by the Wright Group with close involvement by First. The vehicle is called 'StreetCar' and is an articulated single-deck vehicle based on a Volvo B7LA chassis. The 'track' will see local authorities providing more priority traffic lights, more car restraint measures in city centres, and more priority roadspace to ensure that *ftr* services bring their passengers to their destination without being caught in the usual traffic congestion. *ftr* is a first class example of the way in which First is working in partnership with local authorities to make public transport more attractive to more people. The first *ftr* scheme started in York during 2006 and Leeds in 2007. First are evaluating plans for further schemes in cities such as Sheffield, Swansea, Reading, Bath and Glasgow. For more information about First go to www.firstgroup.com. For more information about ftr go to www.goftr.com.

First Potteries Ltd   First Potteries   Second Avenue, Crewe   CW

Names, depot addresses and codes

Company legal name as holder of O licence	Group company name	Registered operating centres	code
First Aberdeen Ltd	First in Aberdeen	King Street, Aberdeen	AB
G E Mair Hire Services Ltd	First in Aberdeen	King Street, Aberdeen	ABM
Midland Bluebird Ltd	First Edinburgh	Dunmore Street, Balfron	BF
Midland Bluebird Ltd	First Edinburgh	Cowie Road, Bannockburn	BK
Midland Bluebird Ltd	First Edinburgh	Stirling Road, Larbert	LT
Midland Bluebird Ltd	First Edinburgh	High Street, Linlithgow	LW
Midland Bluebird Ltd	First Edinburgh	Stirling Street, Galashiels	GS
First Edinburgh Ltd	First Edinburgh	The Mall, Musselburgh	MU
First Edinburgh Ltd	First Edinburgh	Eskbank Road, Dalkeith	DK
First Edinburgh Ltd	First Edinburgh	Deans Road, Livingston	LV
First Glasgow (No 1) Ltd	First in Glasgow	South Street, Scotstoun, Glasgow	SN
First Glasgow (No 1) Ltd	First in Glasgow	Victoria Road, Glasgow (Larkfield)	LF
First Glasgow (No 1) Ltd	First in Glasgow	Tollcross Road, Glasgow (Parkhead)	PH
First Glasgow (No 2) Ltd	First in Glasgow	Blantyre	B
First Glasgow (No 2) Ltd	First in Glasgow	Birch Road, Dumbarton	DU
First Glasgow (No 2) Ltd	First in Glasgow	Warner Street, Stevenston	SV
First Glasgow (No 2) Ltd	First in Glasgow	Glencryan Road, Cumbernauld	CD
First Manchester Ltd	First in North West	Knowsley	KW
First Manchester Ltd	First in North West	Weston Street, Bolton	BN
First Manchester Ltd	First in North West	Rochdale Road, Bury	BY
First Manchester Ltd	First in North West	Melverley Street, Wigan	WN
First Manchester Ltd	First in North West	Queen's Road, Manchester	QS
First Manchester Ltd	First in North West	Wallshaw Street, Oldham	OM
First Manchester Ltd	First in North West	Wigan Enterprise Park, Ince, Wigan	IN
First Manchester Ltd	First in North West	Broadway, Dukinfield, Tameside	TE
First Potteries Ltd	First Potteries	Dividy Road, Adderley Green	AG
First Potteries Ltd	First Potteries	Liverpool Road, Newcastle-under-Lyme	NE
First Potteries Ltd	First Potteries	Station Road, Chester	CC
First Potteries Ltd	First Potteries	Liverpool Road, Chester	CH
First Potteries Ltd	First Potteries	New Chester Road, Rock Ferry	BH
First Potteries Ltd	First Potteries	Second Avenue, Crewe	CW
First West Yorkshire Ltd	First in Leeds	Hunslet Park, Leeds	HP
First West Yorkshire Ltd	First in Leeds	Headconner Lane, Bramley, Leeds	BM
First West Yorkshire Ltd	First in Leeds	Cherry Row, Mabgate, Leeds	CR
First West Yorkshire Ltd	First in Bradford	Bowling Back Lane, Bradford	BD
First West Yorkshire Ltd	First in Huddersfield	Old Fieldhouse Lane, Huddersfield	HU
First West Yorkshire Ltd	First in Halifax	Skircoat Lane, Halifax	HX
First York Ltd	First in York	James Street, York	YK
First South Yorkshire Ltd	First in South Yorkshire	Midland Road, Rotherham	RO
First South Yorkshire Ltd	First in South Yorkshire	Olive Grove, Sheffield	OG
First South Yorkshire Ltd	First in South Yorkshire	Duke Street, Doncaster	DN
Leicester CityBus Ltd	First in Leicester	Abbey Lane, Leicester	LE
Northampton Transport Ltd	First in Northampton	St James Road, Northampton	NN
First Midland Red Buses Ltd	First in Wyvern	Island Drive, Kidderminster	KD
First Midland Red Buses Ltd	First in Wyvern	Friar Street, Hereford	HD
First Midland Red Buses Ltd	First in Wyvern	Padmore Street, Worcester	WR
First Midland Red Buses Ltd	First in Wyvern	Plymouth Road, North Redditch	RH
First Eastern Counties Buses Ltd	First in the Eastern Counties	Vancouver Avenue, King's Lynn	KL
First Eastern Counties Buses Ltd	First in the Eastern Counties	Caister Road, Great Yarmouth	YA
First Eastern Counties Buses Ltd	First in the Eastern Counties	Foundation Street, Ipswich	IP

The 2008 First Bus Handbook

Company	Fleetname	Location	Code
First Eastern Counties Buses Ltd	First in the Eastern Counties	Gas Works Road, Lowestoft	LO
First Eastern Counties Buses Ltd	First in the Eastern Counties	Roundtree Way, Norwich	NR
First Eastern Counties Buses Ltd	First in the Eastern Counties	Vulcan Road, Norwich	VN
First Essex Buses Ltd	First Essex	Westway, Chelmsford	CM
First Essex Buses Ltd	First Essex	Queen Street, Colchester	CO
First Essex Buses Ltd	First Essex	Telford Road, Clacton	CN
First Essex Buses Ltd	First Essex	Springfield Ind Est, Braintree	BR
First Essex Buses Ltd	First Essex	Station Approach, Harwich	HA
First Essex Buses Ltd	First Essex	Cherrydown East, Basildon	BS
First Essex Buses Ltd	First Essex	London Road, Hadleigh	HH
First Capital East Ltd	First in London	Chequers Lane, Dagenham	DG
First Capital North Ltd	First in London	Marsh Lane, Northumberland Park	NP
First Capital North Ltd	First in London	Lea Interchange, Leyton	L
Centrewest London Buses Ltd	First in London	Bakers Road, Uxbridge	UX
Centrewest London Buses Ltd	First in London	Great Western Road, Westbourne Park	X
Centrewest London Buses Ltd	First in London	Greenford Road, Greenford	G
Centrewest London Buses Ltd	First in London	Ealing Road, Alperton	ON
Centrewest London Buses Ltd	First in London	Isleworth	IS
Centrewest London Buses Ltd	First in London	Rigby Lane, Hayes	HY
First Beeline Buses Ltd	First in London	Market Street, Bracknell	BL
First Beeline Buses Ltd	First in London	Stoke Road, Slough	SH
First Hampshire & Dorset Ltd	First in Hampshire & Dorset	London Road, Hilsea, Portsmouth	HI
First Hampshire & Dorset Ltd	First in Hampshire & Dorset	Gosport Road, Hoeford, Fareham	HO
First Hampshire & Dorset Ltd	First in Hampshire & Dorset	Portswood Road, Southampton	SO
First Hampshire & Dorset Ltd	First in Hampshire & Dorset	Edward Street, Weymouth	WH
First Hampshire & Dorset Ltd	First in Hampshire & Dorset	West Street, Bridport	BP
First Cymru Buses Ltd	First Coaches	Pentregethin Road, Ravenhill, Swansea	RAC
First Cymru Buses Ltd	First Cymru	Pentregethin Road, Ravenhill, Swansea	RA
First Cymru Buses Ltd	First Cymru	Inkerman Street, Llanelli	LL
First Cymru Buses Ltd	First Cymru	Dolgwili Road, Carmarthen	CA
First Cymru Buses Ltd	First Cymru	Withybush Ind Est, Haverfordwest	HV
First Cymru Buses Ltd	First Cymru	Tawe Terrace, Pontardawe	PD
First Cymru Buses Ltd	First Cymru	Acacia Avenue, Sandfields, Port Talbot	PT
First Cymru Buses Ltd	First Cymru	Aneurin Bevan Avenue, Bridgend	BG
First Bristol Ltd	First in Bristol	Lawrence Hill, Bristol	LH
First Bristol Ltd	First in Bristol	Muller Road, Bristol	MR
First Bristol Ltd	First in Bristol	Hengrove, Bristol	HG
First Somerset & Avon Ltd	First Somerset & Avon	Lawrence Hill, Bristol	MS
First Somerset & Avon Ltd	First Somerset & Avon	Searle Crescent, Weston-super-Mare	WS
First Somerset & Avon Ltd	First Somerset & Avon	Western Island, Bath	BA
First Somerset & Avon Ltd	First Somerset & Avon	East Quay, Bridgwater	BW
First Somerset & Avon Ltd	First Somerset & Avon	Hamilton Road, Taunton	TN
First Somerset & Avon Ltd	First Somerset & Avon	Reckleford, Yeovil	YV
First Coaches Ltd	First Coaches	Lawrence Hill, Bristol	LHC
First Devon & Cornwall Ltd	First Devon & Cornwall	Chelson Meadow, Plymouth	PL
First Devon & Cornwall Ltd	First Devon & Cornwall	Coney Avenue, Barnstaple	BB
First Devon & Cornwall Ltd	First Devon & Cornwall	Union Street, Camborne	CE
First Devon & Cornwall Ltd	First Devon & Cornwall	Newham Ind Est, Truro	TR
First Northern Ireland	First Northern Ireland	Belfast International Airport, Belfast	BT
Aircoach Ltd	Aircoach	Airport Business Park, Dublin Airport	D
FirstGroup Rhein-Neckar GmnH	First	Heinkelstrsse, Speyer	SP
FirstGroup Rhein-Neckar GmnH	First	Hatschekstrasse, Heidleberg	HB
FirstGroup Rhein-Neckar GmnH	First	Pitterstrasse, Langen	LN

Depot codes

AB	King Street, Aberdeen	KD	Island Drive, Kidderminster
AG	Dividy Road, Adderley Green, Stoke-on-Trent	KL	Vancouver Avenue, King's Lynn
B	Blantyre	L	Lea Interchange, Leyton
BA	Western Island, Bath	LA	Luton Airport
BB	Coney Avenue, Barnstaple	LE	Abbey Lane, Leicester
BD	Bowling Back Lane, Bradford	LF	Victoria Road, Larkfield, Glasgow
BE	Cotton Lane, Bury St Edmunds	LH	Lawrence Hill, Bristol
BF	Dunmore Street, Balfron	LHC	Lawrence Hill, Bristol (First Coaches)
BG	Aneurin Bevan Avenue, Bridgend	LL	Inkerman Street, Llanelli
BH	New Chester Road, Rock Ferry	LN	Pitterstrasse, Langen
BK	Cowie Road, Bannockburn	LO	Gas Works Road, Lowestoft
BL	Market Street, Bracknell	LT	Stirling Road, Larbert
BM	Headconner Lane, Bramley, Leeds	LV	Deans Road, Livingston
BN	Weston Street, Bolton	MR	Muller Road, Bristol
BP	West Street, Bridport	MS	Marlborough Street, Bristol
BR	Springfield Ind Est, Braintree	MU	The Mall, Musselburgh
BS	Cherrydown East, Basildon	NB	Tantallon Road, North Berwick
BT	Belfast International Airport	NE	Liverpool Road, Newcastle-under-Lyme
BW	East Quay, Bridgwater	NN	St James Road, Northampton
BX	Bristol Airport	NP	Marsh Lane, Northumberland Park
BY	Rochdale Road, Bury	NR	Roundtree Way, Norwich
CA	Dolgwili Road, Carmarthen	OG	Olive Grove, Sheffield
CC	Station Road, Chester	OM	Wallshaw Street, Oldham
CD	Glencryan Road, Cumbernauld	ON	Ealing Road, Alperton
CE	Union Street, Camborne	PD	Tawe Terrace, Pontardawe
CH	Liverpool Road, Chester	PH	Tollcross Road, Parkhead, Glasgow
CM	Westway, Chelmsford	PL	Chelson Meadow, Plymouth
CN	Telford Road, Clacton	PT	Acacia Avenue, Sandfields, Port Talbot
CO	Queen Street, Colchester	QS	Queen's Road, Manchester
CR	Cherry Row, Mabgate, Leeds	RA	Pentregethin Road, Ravenhill, Swansea
CW	Second Avenue, Crewe	RAC	Pentregethin Road, Swansea (coach unit)
D	Airport Business Park, Dublin	RH	Plymouth Road, North Redditch
DG	Chequers Lane, Dagenham	RO	Midland Road, Rotherham
DK	Eskbank Road, Dalkeith	SH	Stoke Road, Slough
DN	Duke Street, Doncaster	SN	South Street, Scotstoun
DU	Birch Road, Dumbarton	SO	Portswood Road, Southampton
G	Greenford Road, Greenford	SP	Heinkelstrasse, Speyer
GS	Stirling Street, Galashiels	TE	Broadway, Dukinfield, Tameside
HA	Station Approach, Harwich	TN	Hamilton Road, Taunton
HB	Hatschekstrasse, Heidelberg	TR	Newham Industrial Estate, Truro
HD	Friar Street, Hereford	UX	Bakers Road, Uxbridge
HG	Hengrove, Bristol	VN	Vulcan Road, Norwich
HH	London Road, Hadleigh	WH	Edward Street, Weymouth
HI	London Road, Hilsea, Portsmouth	WJ	Station Road, Willesden Junction
HO	Gosport Road, Hoeford, Fareham	WN	Melverley Street, Wigan
HP	Hunslet Park, Leeds	WR	Padmore Street, Worcester
HU	Old Fieldhouse Lane, Huddersfield	WS	Searle Crescent, Weston-super-Mare
HV	Withybush Ind Est, Haverfordwest	X	Great Western Road, Westbourne Park
HX	Skircoat Lane, Halifax	YA	Caister Road, Great Yarmouth
IN	Wigan Enterprise Park, Ince, Wigan	YK	James Street, York
IP	Foundation Street, Ipswich	YV	Reckleford, Yeovil
IS	Isleworth		

Fleet at June 2008

10000-10014 Volvo B10BLA Wright Fusion AN50D 1999

10000	BN	S111FML	**10004**	BN	S995UJA	**10008**	BN	T509JNA	**10012** BN T513JNA
10001	BN	S992UJA	**10005**	BN	T506JNA	**10009**	BN	T510JNA	**10013** BN T514JNA
10002	BN	S993UJA	**10006**	BN	T507JNA	**10010**	BN	T511JNA	**10014** BN T515JNA
10003	BN	S994UJA	**10007**	BN	T508JNA	**10011**	BN	T512JNA	

10015	SN	Y151ROT	Volvo B7LA	Wright Eclipse Fusion	AN55D	1999
10016	SN	Y152ROT	Volvo B7LA	Wright Eclipse Fusion	AN55D	1999
10017	BN	X401CSG	Scania L94UA	Wrightbus Solar Fusion	AN58D	2001

10018-10032 Volvo B10BLA Wright Fusion AN55D 1999

10018	HP	T101VWU	**10022**	HP	T105VWU	**10026**	HP	T109VWU	**10030** HP V113LVH
10019	HP	T102VWU	**10023**	HP	T106VWU	**10027**	HP	T110VWU	**10031** HP V114LVH
10020	HP	T103VWU	**10024**	HP	T107VWU	**10028**	HP	T211VWU	**10032** HP V115LVH
10021	HP	T104VWU	**10025**	HP	T108VWU	**10029**	HP	V112LVH	

10033-10043 Volvo B7LA Wright Eclipse Fusion AN56D 2000

10033	SN	W116CWR	**10036**	YK	W119CWR	**10039**	YK	W122DWX	**10042** YK W129DWX
10034	SN	W117CWR	**10037**	YK	W122CWR	**10040**	YK	W128DWX	**10043** YK W126DWX
10035	YK	W118CWR	**10038**	YK	W127DWX	**10041**	YK	W124DWX	

10044	SN	V601GGB	Volvo B10BLA	Wright Fusion	AN53D	1999
10045	SN	V602GGB	Volvo B10BLA	Wright Fusion	AN53D	1999
10046	AB	K1GRT	Mercedes-Benz O405G	Alexander Cityranger	AB60T	1992

Articulated buses have been employed in several towns and cities by First and, while they have an expensive initial outlay, they have some advantages over the double-deck bus. Pictured on the York *Park & Ride* service is 10040, W128DWX, which has a Volvo B7LA chassis. *Mark Lyons*

Carrying an orange livery for the Bath University scheme is Wright Eclipse Fusion-bodied Volvo 10175, WX55HWA. Further articulated buses are at Bolton, Bury, Aberdeen, Leeds and Glasgow, with new examples on order for Dublin and Swansea once major street works are complete. *Mark Lyons*

10047-10052 — Volvo B7LA — Wright Eclipse Fusion — AN56D — 2000

| 10047 | AB | W2FAL | 10049 | AB | W4FAL | 10051 | AB | W6FAL | 10052 | AB | W7FAL |
| 10048 | AB | W3FAL | 10050 | AB | W5FAL | | | | | | |

10103-10110 — Volvo B10BLA — Wright Fusion — AN55D — 1999

| 10103 | SN | V603GGB | 10105 | SN | V605GGB | 10107 | SN | V607GGB | 10109 | SN | V609GGB |
| 10104 | SN | V604GGB | 10106 | SN | V606GGB | 10108 | SN | V608GGB | 10110 | SN | V610GGB |

10131-10149 — Volvo B7LA — Wrightbus Eclipse Fusion — AN56D — 2000-01

10131	SN	W131WPO	10136	SN	X136FPO	10141	SN	X141FPO	10146	SN	X146FPO
10132	SN	W132WPO	10137	SN	X137FPO	10142	SN	X142FPO	10147	SN	Y147ROT
10133	SN	W133WPO	10138	SN	X138FPO	10143	SN	X143FPO	10148	SN	Y148ROT
10134	SN	X134FPO	10139	SN	X139FPO	10144	SN	X144FPO	10149	SN	Y149ROT

10151	BA	Y644AVV	Volvo B7LA		Wrightbus Eclipse Fusion	AN42D	2001
10152	BA	Y642AVV	Volvo B7LA		Wrightbus Eclipse Fusion	AN42D	2001
10153	BA	Y643AVV	Volvo B7LA		Wrightbus Eclipse Fusion	AN42D	2001

10154-10173 — Volvo B7LA — Wrightbus Eclipse Fusion — AN56D — 2005

10154	AB	SV05DXA	10159	AB	SV05DXG	10164	AB	SV05DXM	10169	AB	SV05DXT
10155	AB	SV05DXC	10160	AB	SV05DXH	10165	AB	SV05DXN	10170	AB	SV05DXU
10156	AB	SV05DXD	10161	AB	SV05DXJ	10166	AB	SV05DXP	10171	AB	SV05DXW
10157	AB	SV05DXE	10162	AB	SV05DXK	10167	AB	SV05DXR	10172	AB	SV05DXX
10158	AB	SV05DXF	10163	AB	SV05DXL	10168	AB	SV05DXS	10173	AB	SV05DXY

10174-10183 — Volvo B7LA — Wrightbus Eclipse Fusion — AN56D — 2005

10174	BA	WX55HVZ	10177	BA	WX55HWC	10180	BA	WX55HWF	10182	BA	WX55HWH
10175	BA	WX55HWA	10178	BA	WX55HWD	10181	BA	WX55HWG	10183	SN	SF05KUH
10176	BA	WX55HWB	10179	BA	WX55HWE						

The Mercedes-Benz Citaro O530G was selected for Transport for London (TfL) contracts and has been chosen by several operators who provide services in the capital. Seen in Acton's High Street, while working to Shepherds Bush, is 11041, LK05FDC, which, like all the vehicles based in London, has a local prefix, in this example EA. *Mark Lyons*

11000	WJ	BX54EBC	Mercedes-Benz Citaro O530G	Mercedes-Benz	AN49T	2003	Evobus demonstrator, 2006

11001-11032

Mercedes-Benz Citaro O530G — Mercedes-Benz — AN49T — 2003

11001	WJ	LK53FAA	11009	WJ	LK53FBC	11017	WJ	LK53FBN	11025	WJ	LK53FCD
11002	WJ	LK53FAF	11010	WJ	LK53FBD	11018	WJ	LK53FBU	11026	WJ	LK53FCE
11003	WJ	LK53FAJ	11011	WJ	LK53FBE	11019	WJ	LK53FBV	11027	WJ	LK53FCM
11004	WJ	LK53FAM	11012	WJ	LK53FBF	11020	WJ	LK53FBX	11028	WJ	LK53FCN
11005	WJ	LK53FAO	11013	WJ	LK53FBG	11021	WJ	LK53FBY	11029	WJ	LK53FCO
11006	WJ	LK53FAU	11014	WJ	LK53FBJ	11022	WJ	LK53FBZ	11030	WJ	LK53FCP
11007	WJ	LK53FBA	11015	WJ	LK53FBL	11023	WJ	LK53FCA	11031	WJ	LK53FCU
11008	WJ	LK53FBB	11016	WJ	LK53FBO	11024	WJ	LK53FCC	11032	WJ	LK53FCV

11033-11038

Mercedes-Benz Citaro O530G — Mercedes-Benz — AN38T* — 2002-04 — 11038-11028 are AN27T

11033	D	02D74688	11035	D	02D76812	11037	D	04D62405	11038	D	04D62423
11034	D	02D76210	11036	D	04D62404						

11039-11065

Mercedes-Benz Citaro O530G — Mercedes-Benz — AN49T — 2005

11039	IS	LK54FKW	11046	IS	LK05FDG	11053	IS	LK05FCO	11060	IS	LK05FCZ
11040	IS	LK54FKX	11047	IS	LK05FDL	11054	IS	LK05FCP	11061	IS	LK05FDA
11041	IS	LK05FDC	11048	IS	LK05EZW	11055	IS	LK05FCU	11062	IS	LK05FBZ
11042	IS	LK05FDD	11049	IS	LK05EZX	11056	IS	LK05FCV	11063	IS	LK05FCA
11043	IS	LK05FDE	11050	IS	LK05EZZ	11057	IS	LK05FBY	11064	IS	LK05FCD
11044	IS	LK05FDF	11051	IS	LK05FCM	11058	IS	LK05FCX	11065	IS	LK05FCC
11045	IS	LK05FDJ	11052	IS	LK05FCN	11059	IS	LK05FCY			

11066-11069

Mercedes-Benz Citaro O530G — Mercedes-Benz — AN49T — 2002 — Stagecoach London, 2006

11066	WJ	LV52VFW	11067	WJ	LV52VFX	11068	WJ	LV52VFY	11069	WJ	LV52VFZ

11070	TR	AN02EDN	Mercedes-Benz Citaro O530	Mercedes-Benz	AN53T	2006	Truronian, 2008
11071	TR	BN02EDN	Mercedes-Benz Citaro O530	Mercedes-Benz	AN53T	2006	Truronian, 2008
11072	TR	CN02EDN	Mercedes-Benz Citaro O530	Mercedes-Benz	AN53T	2006	Truronian, 2008

11073-11083

Mercedes-Benz Citaro O530G — Mercedes-Benz — AN38T — 2008 — On order for Dublin

11073	D	08D	11076	D	08D	11079	D	08D	11082	D	08D
11074	D	08D	11077	D	08D	11080	D	08D	11083	D	08D
11075	D	08D	11078	D	08D	11081	D	08D			

During recent months the Streetcar model has been introduced at Luton Airport following the award of a service contract. In contrast, seen passing the Corn Exchange in Leeds is 19024, YJ07LVS, which is allocated to the Pudsey service. *Richard Godfrey*

11101-11115			Mercedes-Benz Citaro O530G		Mercedes-Benz		AN-d	2008	On order for York
11101	YK	-	11105	YK	-	11109	YK	-	11113	YK	-
11102	YK	-	11106	YK	-	11110	YK	-	11114	YK	-
11103	YK	-	11107	YK	-	11111	YK	-	11115	YK	-
11104	YK	-	11108	YK	-	11112	YK	-			

12001-12018			Scania OmniCity CN94UA		Scania		AN48D	2005
12001	BY	YN05GYA	12006	BY	YN05GYD	12011	BY	YN05GYO	12015	BY	YN05GYR
12002	BY	YN05GYB	12007	BY	YN05GYE	12012	BY	YN05GYV	12016	BY	YN05GYS
12003	BY	YN05GYH	12008	BY	YN05GYF	12013	BY	YN05GYU	12017	BY	YN05GYT
12004	BY	YN05GYJ	12009	BY	YN05GYG	12014	BY	YN05GYP	12018	BY	YN05GYW
12005	BY	YN05GYC	12010	BY	YN05GYK						

19001-19038			Volvo B7LA		Wrightbus StreetCar		AN40D	2006-07
19001	YK	YK06AOU	19011	YK	YK06AUC	19021	BM	YJ07LVN	19030	LA	CU57AJV
19002	YK	YK06ATV	19012	BM	YJ06XLR	19022	BM	YJ07LVO	19031	LA	YS07LVX
19003	YK	YK06ATU	19013	BM	YJ06XLS	19023	BM	YJ07LVR	19032	LA	CU57AJX
19004	YK	B7FTR	19014	BM	YJ05EAA	19024	BM	YJ07LVS	19033	RA	YN07SYJ
19005	YK	YK06ATX	19015	BM	YJ05EAC	19025	BM	YJ07LVT	19034	LA	CU57AJY
19006	YK	OO06FTR	19016	BM	YJ05EAE	19026	BM	YJ07LVU	19035	RA	CU57AKG
19007	YK	YK06ATY	19017	BM	YJ05EAF	19027	BM	YJ07LVV	19036	RA	CU57AKJ
19008	YK	YK06ATZ	19018	BM	YJ05EAG	19028	BM	YJ07LVW	19037	RA	CU57AKN
19009	YK	YK06AUL	19019	BM	YJ07LVL	19029	YK	YK06EKT	19038	RA	CU57AKK
19010	YK	YK06AUA	19020	BM	YJ07LVM						

20008	AB	542GRT	Scania K124IB4	Irizar Century 12.35	C49FT	1998
20009	ABM	M106PKS	Scania K113CRB	Van Hool Alizée HE	C49FT	1995
20011	ABM	2GRT	Volvo B10M-62	Plaxton Expressliner 2	C49FT	1994
20012	ABM	N1GRT	Volvo B10M-62	Plaxton Première 350	C48FT	1996
20013	ABM	J11GRT	Volvo B10M-60	Jonckheere Deauville P599	C49FT	1992
20014	ABM	LSK570	Volvo B10M-60	Jonckheere Deauville P599	C49FT	1993
20015	ABM	LSK571	Volvo B10M-60	Jonckheere Deauville P599	C47FT	1993

As well as providing vehicles for several National Express diagrams, First also uses coaches on longer services many of which are now fitted with wheelchair lifts. Seen passing through Acle, en route for Peterborough, is 20119, N619APU, which carries a Plaxton Première 320 body. *Richard Godfrey*

20016	AB	PSU627	Scania K124IB4	Irizar Century 12.35	C49FT	1998	
20017	AB	PSU628	Scania K113CRB	Irizar Century 12.35	C51FT	1997	
20018	AB	PSU629	Scania K113CRB	Irizar Century 12.35	C51FT	1997	
20019	ABM	M1GRT	Volvo B10M-62	Plaxton Expressliner 2	C44FT	1994	
20020	ABM	M11AFC	Volvo B10M-62	Plaxton Expressliner 2	C44FT	1994	
20021	AB	FC52AFC	Volvo B12B	Jonckheere Mistral	C38FT	2003	
20027	ABM	LSK530	Dennis Javelin 8.5m	Plaxton Paramount 3200 III	C35F	1988	Dewar, Falkirk, 1992
20029	ABM	TSU651	Volvo B10M-60	Jonckheere Deauville P599	C51FT	1989	
20036	ABs	PSU314	Scania K113CRB	Plaxton Paramount 3500 III	Classroom	1990	
20044	CE	GIL2967	Volvo B10M-61	Van Hool Alizée	C50FT	1988	Allisons, Dunfermline, 1994
20050	CE	UHW661	Volvo B10M-61	Van Hool Alizée	C50FT	1987	
20052	PL	UWB183	Volvo B10M-61	Van Hool Alizée	C50FT	1987	
20053	CE	XFF283	Volvo B10M-61	Van Hool Alizée	C44FT	1987	
20055	BP	NTL655	Volvo B10M-62	Plaxton Première 350	C53F	1996	
20088	TR	HWV885Y	Volvo B10M-61	Plaxton Paramount 3200	C53F	1983	Truronian, 2008
20094	u	JIL7904	Volvo B10M-60	Plaxton Paramount 3200 III	C49FT	1990	Truronian, 2008

20102-20119 Volvo B10M-62   Plaxton Première 320   C53F   1995-96

20101	u	N601APU	20106	KL	N606APU	20111	LO	N611APU	20116	LT	N616APU
20102	CO	N602APU	20107	LO	N607APU	20112	KL	N612APU	20117	LO	N617APU
20103	LO	N603APU	20109	KL	N609APU	20114	LO	N614APU	20118	KL	N618APU
20104	LO	N604APU	20110	CO	N610APU	20115	u	N615APU	20119	LO	N619APU
20105	KL	N605APU									

20120	LO	P330RVG	Volvo B10M-62	Plaxton Première 320	C53F	1997
20121	LO	P731NVG	Volvo B10M-62	Plaxton Première 320	C53F	1996
20122	IPt	P732NVG	Volvo B10M-62	Plaxton Première 320	C53F	1996
20123	LO	P733NVG	Volvo B10M-62	Plaxton Première 320	C53F	1996
20124	LO	P734NVG	Volvo B10M-62	Plaxton Première 320	C53F	1996

20125-20131 Volvo B10M-62   Plaxton Première 320   C55F*   1997   *seating varies

20125	NRt	P765XHS	20127	LO	P767XHS	20129	YAt	P769XHS	20131	LO	P771XHS
20126	YA	P766XHS	20128	NRt	P768XHS	20130	u	P770XHS			

20141	KL	R841DVF	Volvo B10M-62	Plaxton Première 320	C53F	1998	
20142	KL	R842DVF	Volvo B10M-62	Plaxton Première 320	C53F	1998	
20144	CE	S314SRL	Volvo B10M-62	Plaxton Interurban	BC51F	1999	
20145	CE	S315SRL	Volvo B10M-62	Plaxton Interurban	BC51F	1999	

20201-20207 Volvo B12T Plaxton Excalibur C51F 1999

20201	CM	T701JLD	20203	CM	T703JLD	20205	AB	T705JLD	20207	AB	T707JLD
20202	CM	T702JLD	20204	AB	T704JLD	20206	AB	T706JLD			

20300	LHC	WX54ZHM	Volvo B7R	Plaxton Profile	C53F	2005	
20301	LHC	WX54ZHN	Volvo B7R	Plaxton Profile	C53F	2005	
20302	LHC	WX54ZHO	Volvo B7R	Plaxton Profile	C53F	2005	
20303	LHC	WM03BYD	Volvo B7R	TransBus Profile	C53F	2003	
20304	u	T104JBC	Volvo B7R	Plaxton Prima	C49F	1999	
20305	PL	T105JBC	Volvo B7R	Plaxton Prima	C49F	1999	
20306	PL	T106JBC	Volvo B7R	Plaxton Prima	C49F	1999	
20307	LHC	WX05OZF	Volvo B7R	Plaxton Profile	C53F	2005	

20321-20327 Volvo B7R Plaxton Profile C70F 2007

20321	RAC	YN57BVU	20323	RAC	YN57BVW	20325	RAC	YN57BVY	20327	RAC	YN57BWU
20322	RAC	YN57BVV	20324	RAC	YN57BVX	20326	RAC	YN57BVZ			

20351-20374 Volvo B7R Plaxton Profile C49F 2005

20351	BB	WA05UNG	20357	LV	CV55ABK	20363	RAC	CV55ACZ	20369	BL	CV55AMU
20352	BB	WA05UNF	20358	RAC	CV55ACO	20364	DK	CV55AFE	20370	GS	CV55AGY
20353	BB	WA05UNE	20359	RAC	CV55ACU	20365	RAC	CV55AHA	20371	GS	CV55AMX
20354	LV	CU05LGJ	20360	RAC	CV55ACX	20366	BL	CV55AFF	20372	BL	CV55ANF
20355	LV	CU05LGK	20361	RAC	CV55ACY	20367	BL	CV55AGX	20373	BL	CV55ANP
20356	DK	CV55ABN	20362	RAC	CV55AFA	20368	RAC	CV55AGZ	20374	BL	CV55AOO

20404	LVt	R304JAF	Volvo B10M-62	Plaxton Expressliner 2	C44FT	1998	
20405	BKt	R305JAF	Volvo B10M-62	Plaxton Expressliner 2	C44FT	1998	
20407	HUs	R307JAF	Volvo B10M-62	Plaxton Expressliner 2	C46FT	1998	
20408	PLt	R308JAF	Volvo B10M-62	Plaxton Expressliner 2	C44FT	1998	
20409	HUs	R309JAF	Volvo B10M-62	Plaxton Expressliner 2	C44FT	1998	
20410	PLt	R310JAF	Volvo B10M-62	Plaxton Expressliner 2	C44FT	1998	
20411	RAC	S311SCV	Volvo B10M-62	Plaxton Expressliner 2	C49FT	1998	
20412	CEt	S312SCV	Volvo B10M-62	Plaxton Expressliner 2	C44FT	1998	
20413	CEt	S313SCV	Volvo B10M-62	Plaxton Expressliner 2	C44FT	1998	
20416	CE	WSV408	Volvo B10M-62	Plaxton Expressliner 2	C44FT	1999	
20417	SOt	P177NAK	Volvo B10M-62	Plaxton Première 350	C53F	1997	Waugh, Greenhead, 1998
20418	HOt	P176NAK	Volvo B10M-62	Plaxton Première 350	C49FT	1997	Waugh, Greenhead, 1998
20421	CE	P521PRL	Volvo B10M-62	Van Hool Alizée HE	C44FT	1996	
20424	RAC	T64BHY	Volvo B10M-62	Plaxton Expressliner 2	C44FT	1999	
20426	TR	280ERY	Volvo B10M-62	Caetano Algarve 2	C49FT	1994	Truronian, 2008
20428	RAC	T948UEU	Volvo B10M-62	Plaxton Expressliner 2	C44FT	1999	
20436	PL	M92BOU	Volvo B10M-62	Plaxton Expressliner 2	C46FT	1994	
20437	WH	M41FTC	Volvo B10M-62	Plaxton Expressliner 2	C44FT	1995	
20438	LVt	M413DEU	Volvo B10M-62	Plaxton Expressliner 2	C44FT	1995	
20439	BP	M439FHW	Volvo B10M-62	Plaxton Expressliner 2	C53F	1995	
20440	WH	M440FHW	Volvo B10M-62	Plaxton Expressliner 2	C53F	1995	
20441	PL	M301BRL	Volvo B10M-62	Plaxton Expressliner 2	C46FT	1994	
20442	PL	M302BRL	Volvo B10M-62	Plaxton Expressliner 2	C46FT	1994	
20443	CE	M303BRL	Volvo B10M-62	Plaxton Expressliner 2	C48FT	1994	
20454	WH	P944RWS	Volvo B10M-62	Plaxton Expressliner 2	C49FT	1996	
20455	TN	P945RWS	Volvo B10M-62	Plaxton Expressliner 2	C49FT	1996	
20456	TN	P946RWS	Volvo B10M-62	Plaxton Expressliner 2	C49FT	1996	
20457	SOt	R813HWS	Volvo B10M-62	Plaxton Expressliner 2	C49FT	1997	
20458	LHC	R814HWS	Volvo B10M-62	Plaxton Expressliner 2	C49FT	1997	
20459	LHC	R943LHT	Volvo B10M-62	Plaxton Expressliner 2	C44FT	1998	
20460	LHC	T310AHY	Volvo B10M-62	Plaxton Expressliner 2	C44FT	1999	
20461	YK	X191HFB	Volvo B10M-62	Plaxton Expressliner 2	C44FT	2000	
20462	YK	X192HFB	Volvo B10M-62	Plaxton Expressliner 2	C44FT	2000	
20463	CM	X193HFB	Volvo B10M-62	Plaxton Expressliner 2	C44FT	2000	
20464	WH	X194HFB	Volvo B10M-62	Plaxton Expressliner 2	C44FT	2000	
20471	TR	R1TRU	Volvo B10M-62	Van Hool T9 Alizée	C49FT	1998	Truronian, 2008
20472	TR	T2TRU	Volvo B10M-62	Plaxton Excalibur	C49FT	1999	Truronian, 2008
20473	TR	W3TRU	Volvo B10M-62	Plaxton Panther	C49FT	2000	Truronian, 2008
20474	TR	Y5TRU	Volvo B10M-62	Plaxton Panther	C49FT	2001	Truronian, 2008
20498	TR	X192HFB	Volvo B12M	Jonckheere	C51FT	2005	*On loan to First*
20499	TR	N3GPD	Volvo B12M	Plaxton	C49FT	2003	*On loan to First*

20500-20509 — Volvo B12M — Plaxton Paragon — C53F — 2002

20500	KL	AO02RBX	20503	KL	AO02RCF	20506	KL	AO02RCX	20508	KL	AO02RCZ
20501	KL	AO02RBY	20504	KL	AO02RCU	20507	KL	AO02RCY	20509	KL	AO02RDU
20502	KL	AO02RBZ	20505	KL	AO02RCV						

20510-20513 — Volvo B12M — Plaxton Paragon — C49FT — 2001

20510	LHC	WX51AJV	20511	LHC	WX51AJU	20512	RAC	WX51AJY	20513	RAC	WX51AKY

20514-20517 — Volvo B12M 12.8m — Plaxton Paragon — C49FT — 2002

20514	BA	WV02EUP	20515	BA	WV02EUR	20516	BA	WV02EUT	20517	BA	WV02EUU

20518-20524 — Volvo B12M — Plaxton Paragon — C49FT — 2002

20518	CE	WK02UMA	20520	CE	WK02UMC	20522	CE	WV52FAO	20524	CE	WV52HSX
20519	CE	WK02UMB	20521	RAC	WV52FAM	20523	CE	WV52FCX			

20525-20533 — Volvo B12M — Plaxton Paragon — C49FT — 2002 — *20525-7 are 12.8m

20525	BA	WV52KTJ	20528	CE	WK52SVU	20530	CE	WV52HTT	20532	CE	WV52HVF
20526	BA	WV52KTK	20529	CE	WK52SVV	20531	CE	WV52HVE	20533	LHC	WV52AKY
20527	BA	WV52KTL									

20534-20549 — Volvo B12M — TransBus Paragon — C44FT — 2003-04

20534	RAC	WX03ZFG	20538	RAC	CU03AVC	20542	RAC	WX53WFA	20546	CE	WX53WGG
20535	CE	WM03BXP	20539	RAC	CU03AVD	20543	RAC	WX53WEW	20547	CE	WX53WGF
20536	CE	WK03EKX	20540	CE	WX53PFJ	20544	RAC	WX53WFP	20548	CE	CU53AEG
20537	CE	WK03EKW	20541	CE	WX53PFG	20545	CE	WX53WGJ	20549	RAC	CU53AFZ

20550	RAC	CU04AYP	Volvo B12B	TransBus Paragon	C44FT	2004	
20551	RAC	CU04AYS	Volvo B12B	TransBus Paragon	C44FT	2004	
20556	TR	TT04TRU	Volvo B12B	Plaxton Panther	C49FT	2004	Truronian, 2008
20557	TR	TT05TRU	Volvo B12B	Plaxton Panther	C50FT	2005	Truronian, 2008
20558	TR	TT55TRU	Volvo B12B 12.8m	Plaxton Panther	C48FT	2005	Truronian, 2008
20559	TR	TT55TRU	Volvo B12B	Plaxton Panther	C49FT	2006	Truronian, 2008
20560	TR	TT06NEX	Volvo B12B	Plaxton Panther	C49FT	2006	Truronian, 2008
20561	TR	TX06NEX	Volvo B12B	Plaxton Panther	C49FT	2006	Truronian, 2008
20603	D	05G501	Volvo B12B	Jonckheere Mistral 50	C49FT	2005	On loan from Volvo
20604	D	05G504	Volvo B12B	Jonckheere Mistral 50	C49FT	2005	On loan from Volvo
20610	D	07D73994	Volvo B12B	Plaxton Panther	C49FT	2007	On loan from Volvo
20611	BL	LK07CDE	Volvo B12B	Plaxton Panther	C49F	2007	
20612	BL	LK07CDF	Volvo B12B	Plaxton Panther	C49F	2007	
20613	BL	LK07CDN	Volvo B12B	Plaxton Panther	C49F	2007	

20651-20669 — Volvo B12B — Jonckheere SSV — C--F — 2008 — On order for Aircoach

20651	D	-	20656	D	-	20661	D	-	20656	D	-
20652	D	-	20657	D	-	20662	D	-	20657	D	-
20653	D	-	20658	D	-	20663	D	-	20658	D	-
20654	D	-	20659	D	-	20664	D	-	20659	D	-
20655	D	-	20660	D	-	20665	D	-			

Reading rail station is the location for this view of rear-engined Volvo B12B 20613, LK07CDN. This Plaxton Panther-bodied coach is one of a trio that plies between the station and Heathrow Airport. *Richard Godfrey*

20701	D&C	FN06FLC	Volvo B12B	Caetano Levante	C49FT	2006	Swans, Chadderton, 2008
20702	D&C	FN06FLD	Volvo B12B	Caetano Levante	C49FT	2006	Swans, Chadderton, 2008
21006	RAt	L6BMS	Dennis Javelin 12m	Plaxton Première 320	C49FT	1994	
21008	RAt	L8BMS	Dennis Javelin 12m	Plaxton Première 320	C49FT	1994	
21014	RAC	L14BMS	Dennis Javelin 12m	Plaxton Première 350	C49FT	1994	
21032	BW	J732KBC	Dennis Javelin 11m	Plaxton Paramount 3200 III	C53F	1982	Jones, Login, 1998,
21053	WSt	RIL1053	Dennis Javelin 12m	Plaxton Paramount 3200 III	TV	1989	Beeline, Warminster, 1996
21064	YVt	J864WSX	Dennis Javelin 12m	Plaxton Paramount 3200 III	TV	1992	
21090	DG	M290FAE	Dennis Javelin GX 12m	Plaxton Expressliner 2	C49FT	1995	
21097	RAC	R297AYB	Dennis Javelin GX 12m	Plaxton Expressliner 2	C49FT	1998	
21098	CA	R298AYB	Dennis Javelin GX 12m	Plaxton Expressliner 2	C53F	1998	
21099	CA	R299AYB	Dennis Javelin GX 12m	Plaxton Expressliner 2	C53F	1998	
21109	RAC	M109PWN	Dennis Javelin GX 12m	Plaxton Expressliner 2	C51F	1995	
21110	RAC	M110PWN	Dennis Javelin GX 12m	Plaxton Expressliner 2	C51F	1995	
21111	RAt	M111PWN	Dennis Javelin GX 12m	Plaxton Expressliner 2	C51F	1995	
21112	CA	N112EWJ	Dennis Javelin GX 12m	Plaxton Expressliner 2	C53F	1996	
21113	LL	N113VWN	Dennis Javelin GX 12m	Plaxton Expressliner 2	C44FT	1996	
21114	RAC	N114VWN	Dennis Javelin GX 12m	Plaxton Expressliner 2	C44FT	1996	
21115	RAC	N115VWN	Dennis Javelin GX 12m	Plaxton Expressliner 2	C44FT	1996	
21119	RAC	N319NHY	Dennis Javelin GX 12m	Plaxton Expressliner 2	C49FT	1995	
21120	WH	N320NHY	Dennis Javelin GX 12m	Plaxton Expressliner 2	C46FT	1995	
21121	DG	N821KWS	Dennis Javelin GX 12m	Plaxton Expressliner 2	C46FT	1996	
21122	DG	N822KWS	Dennis Javelin GX 12m	Plaxton Expressliner 2	C49FT	1995	
21123	CA	N322NHY	Dennis Javelin GX 12m	Plaxton Expressliner 2	C49FT	1995	
21127	RAC	N472KHU	Dennis Javelin GX 12m	Plaxton Expressliner 2	C49FT	1995	
21132	RAC	N232WFJ	Dennis Javelin GX 12m	Plaxton Expressliner 2	C44FT	1996	
21133	RAC	N233WFJ	Dennis Javelin GX 12m	Plaxton Expressliner 2	C44FT	1996	
21135	RAC	P235CTA	Dennis Javelin GX 12m	Plaxton Expressliner 2	C53F	1997	
21136	RAC	P236CTA	Dennis Javelin GX 12m	Plaxton Expressliner 2	C53F	1997	
21145	RAC	R175VWN	Dennis Javelin GX	Plaxton Première 350	BC70F	1998	
21146	RAC	R176VWN	Dennis Javelin GX	Plaxton Première 350	BC70F	1998	
21147	RAC	R177VWN	Dennis Javelin GX	Plaxton Première 350	BC70F	1998	
21148	RAC	R178VWN	Dennis Javelin GX	Plaxton Première 350	C44FT	1998	
21150	RAC	S116RKG	Dennis Javelin GX	Plaxton Expressliner 2	C44FT	1999	
21151	LL	T101XDE	Dennis Javelin GX	Plaxton Expressliner 2	C44FT	1999	
21152	RAC	T102XDE	Dennis Javelin GX	Plaxton Expressliner 2	C44FT	1999	
21153	AB	T103XDE	Dennis Javelin GX	Plaxton Expressliner 2	C44FT	1999	
22045	WSt	G115JBO	Leyland Tiger TRCTL11/3ARZM	Plaxton Paramount 3500 III	TV	1990	Hill's of Tredegar, 1991

23008-23015

Scania K114IB — Irizar Century Capacity 12.35 — C53F — 2003-04

23008	BL	YV03UBA	23010	BL	YV03UBC	23012	BL	YV03UBE	23014	BL	YN04AJX
23009	BL	YV03UBB	23011	BL	YV03UBD	23013	BL	YN04AJU	23015	BL	YN04AJV

23016-23021

Scania K114IB — Irizar Century Capacity 12.35 — C53F — 2004

23016	BL	YN54APO	23018	BL	YN54APV	23020	LHC	YN54APK	23021	LHC	YN54APF
23017	BL	YN54APU	23019	LHC	YN54APX						

23126	B	P26RFS	Scania L94IB	Irizar InterCentury 12.32	C55F	1997

23201-23204

Scania K114IB — Irizar Century 12.35 — C44FT — 2004 — 23016-8 are C49F

23201	LHC	YN04YHY	23202	LHC	YN04YHW	23203	LHC	YN04YHX	23204	LHC	YN04YHZ

23205-23208

Volvo B12B — Plaxton Panther — C49FT — 2004

23205	RAC	WM04NYV	23206	RAC	WM04NYW	23207	RAC	WM04PHK	23208	CE	WM04NZU

23301-23314

Scania K114EB — Irizar PB — C49FT — 2004

23301	LHC	YN54NXM	23305	LHC	YN54NXX	23309	LHC	YN54NXR	23312	LHC	YN54NYT
23302	LHC	YN54NXU	23306	LHC	YN54NXY	23310	LHC	YN54NXT	23313	LHC	YN54NYU
23303	LHC	YN54NXV	23307	LHC	YN54NXZ	23311	LHC	YN54NYR	23314	LHC	YN54NYV
23304	LHC	YN54NXW	23308	LHC	YN54NXO						

23315-23320

Scania K114EB — Irizar PB — C49FT — 2005

23315	LHC	YN55PXF	23317	LHC	YN55PXH	23319	LHC	YN55PXK	23320	LHC	YN55PXL
23316	LHC	YN55PXG	23318	LHC	YN55PXJ						

23321-23325

Scania K114EB — Irizar PB — C49FT — 2006

23321	LHC	YN06CGU	23323	LHC	YN06CGX	23324	LHC	YN06CGY	23325	LHC	YN06CGZ
23322	LHC	YN06CGV									

Most of the coaches now supplied for National Express services use Scania chassis, the latest carrying either Caetano Levante bodywork or Spanish-built Irizar products. Seen arriving in the city from Bristol Airport is 23021, YN54APF, which has an Irizar Century Capacity body. *Mark Lyons*

23331	D	06D71429	Scania K114EB	Irizar Century PB	C53FT	2006
23401	AB	SV54FRZ	Scania K114EB	Irizar Century 12.35	C49FT	2004
23402	AB	SV54FTA	Scania K114EB	Irizar Century 12.35	C49FT	2004

23501-23504 — Scania K340EB — Caetano Levante — C49FT — 2006

| 23501 | RAC | FJ56OBO | 23502 | RAC | FJ56PFG | 23503 | RAC | FJ56PFK | 23504 | RAC | FJ56PFN |

| 24000 | D | 05D62327 | Setra S315 GT-HD | Setra | C49F | 2005 | Evobus demonstrator, 2006 |

24017-24028 — Setra S415HD — Setra — C45F* — 2003 — *24027/28 are C38F

24017	D	03D31562	24020	D	03D36557	24023	D	03D36574	24028	D	03D37476
24018	D	03D36551	24021	D	03D36559	24024	D	03D36585	24027	D	03D46738
24019	D	03D36555	24022	D	03D36569	24025	D	03D36588	24028	D	03D46750

24029-24048 — Setra S415HD — Setra — C44F — 2004

24029	D	04D22632	24034	D	04D22820	24039	D	04D22841	24044	D	04D22855
24030	D	04D22816	24035	D	04D22821	24040	D	04D22842	24045	D	04D22871
24031	D	04D22817	24036	D	04D22822	24041	D	04D22843	24046	D	04D34312
24032	D	04D22818	24037	D	04D22823	24042	D	04D22844	24047	D	04D34313
24033	D	04D22819	24038	D	04D22824	24043	D	04D22845	24048	D	04D34316

30029-30038 — Leyland Olympian ONCL10/1RZ — Leyland — B47/29F* — 1989 — *seating varies

| 30029 | CW | G753XRE | 30031 | CW | G755XRE | 30034 | CW | G758XRE | 30037 | CH | G761XRE |
| 30030 | CW | G754XRE | 30033 | CW | G757XRE | 30035 | CW | G759XRE | 30038 | CW | G762XRE |

30060	CH	A162VDM	Leyland Olympian ONLXB/1R	Eastern Coach Works	B45/32F	1984	
30065	TR	A167VDM	Leyland Olympian ONLXB/1R	Eastern Coach Works	B45/32F	1984	
30069	CW	F160XYG	Leyland Olympian ONCL10/1RZ	Northern Counties	B45/29F	1988	
30072	CH	B181BLG	Leyland Olympian ONLXB/1R	Eastern Coach Works	B45/32F	1984	Crosville, 1990
30074	CH	B188BLG	Leyland Olympian ONLXB/1R	Eastern Coach Works	B45/32F	1985	Crosville, 1990
30077	CH	B200DTU	Leyland Olympian ONLXB/1R	Eastern Coach Works	BC42/32F	1985	Crosville, 1990
30078	CH	B201DTU	Leyland Olympian ONLXB/1R	Eastern Coach Works	BC42/32F	1985	Crosville, 1990

Great Yarmouth depot currently operates the batch of tri-axle Olympians that were new to New World First Bus in Hong Kong. They were re-imported to Britain during the time that operation was part of the First Group. 30103, K487EUX, is seen in the town. *Mark Doggett*

30097-30106
Leyland Olympian ON3R49C18Z4 Alexander RH   B53/31F   1993

30097	YA	K481EUX	30100	YA	K484EUX	30103	YA	K487EUX
30098	YA	K482EUX	30101	YA	K485EUX	30104	YA	K488EUX
30099	YA	K483EUX	30102	YA	K486EUX			

30105	YA	K489EUX
30106	YA	K480EUX

30107   PH   K174EUX   Volvo Olympian   Alexander RH   B42/32F   1994

30216-30220
Leyland Olympian ON2R56C16Z4 Northern Counties Palatine   B44/32F   1992

30216	DK	K601LAE	30218	OM	K603LAE	30219	OM	K604LAE
30217	DK	K602LAE						

30220   OM   K605LAE

30221-30227
Leyland Olympian ON2R50C13Z4 Northern Counties Palatine   B47/30F   1992

30221	OM	K888TTT	30223	OM	K888TWY	30225	OM	K888PFD
30222	OM	K888ELR	30224	OM	K888LAD	30226	OM	K888BFG

30227   OM   K888BWU

30228	OM	K888TKS	Leyland Olympian ON2R50C13Z4 Northern Counties Palatine II	B46/29F	1993
30229	HU	G176JYG	Leyland Olympian ONCL10/1RZ	Northern Counties	B47/29F	1990
30230	LHC	G177JYG	Leyland Olympian ONCL10/1RZ	Northern Counties	B47/29F	1990
30231	HU	G178JYG	Leyland Olympian ONCL10/1RZ	Northern Counties	B47/29F	1990
30234	OM	J154YRM	Leyland Olympian ON2R50C13Z4	Leyland	B47/29F	1991
30235	KL	J155YRM	Leyland Olympian ON2R50C13Z4	Leyland	B47/29F	1991
30236	OM	J156YRM	Leyland Olympian ON2R50C13Z4	Leyland	B47/29F	1991

30238-30247
Volvo Olympian   Alexander Royale   B43/29F   1998

30238	BM	S654NUG	30241	BM	S657NUG	30244	BM	S660NUG
30239	BM	S655NUG	30242	BM	S658NUG	30245	BM	S661NUG
30240	BM	S656NUG	30243	BM	S659NUG			

30246	BM	S662NUG
30247	BM	S663NUG

30340-30349
Volvo Citybus B10M-50   Northern Counties   B45/31F*   1991-92   *30348/9 are B45/26F

30340	PH	H701GVM	30343	PH	H704GVM	30346	PH	H707GVM
30341	PH	H702GVM	30344	PH	H705GVM	30347	PH	H708GVM
30342	PH	H703GVM	30345	PH	H706GVM			

30348	PH	J709ONF
30349	PH	J710ONF

Another batch of buses with Chinese connections is the 1992 intake of Leyland Olympians with Northern Counties bodywork. Purchased new for Hong Kong-owned Capital Citybus in London, all the index marks contain lucky 888 numbers. Now allocated to Oldham, 30227, K888BWU, is seen in Ashton-under-Lyne's bus station. *Richard Godfrey*

30350-30379   Volvo Citybus B10M-50   Alexander RV   B47/37F   1989

30350	HU	F792LSU	30359	HU	G282OGE	30366	HU	G296OGE	30379	HU	G523RDS
30358	GS	G281OGE	30365	HU	G293OGE	30377	HU	G698PNS			

30386	ROp	3156WE	Leyland Titan PD2/30	Roe	B33/26R	1958

30546-30552   Volvo Olympian   Northern Counties Palatine II   B43/29F   1995

30546	OG	N301JBV	30548	OG	N303JBV	30550	OG	N305JBV	30552	OG	N312JBV
30547	OG	N302JBV	30549	OG	N304JBV	30551	OG	N311JBV			

30553-30557   Volvo Olympian   Northern Counties Palatine   B47/27D*   1996   *30553/5/6 are B47/31F

30553	OG	N244CMP	30555	OG	P245HMD	30556	OG	P248HMD	30557	OG	P249HMD
30554	OG	P243HMD									

30558	CO	P181TGD	Volvo Olympian	Alexander RL	B47/32F	1996
30559	DG	P183TGD	Volvo Olympian	Alexander RL	B47/32F	1996
30560	CO	P190TGD	Volvo Olympian	Alexander RL	B47/32F	1996
30561	OG	X856UOK	Volvo B7TL	Alexander ALX400	N49/29F	2001
30562	OG	X857UOK	Volvo B7TL	Alexander ALX400	N49/29F	2001
30563	OG	X858UOK	Volvo B7TL	Alexander ALX400	N49/29F	2001

30564-30578   Volvo B7TL   Alexander ALX400   N49/29F   2002

30564	OG	WU02KVE	30568	OG	WU02KVJ	30572	OG	WU02KVO	30576	OG	WU02KVT
30565	OG	WU02KVF	30569	OG	WU02KVK	30573	OG	WU02KVP	30577	OG	WU02KVV
30566	OG	WU02KVG	30570	OG	WU02KVL	30574	OG	WU02KVR	30578	OG	WU02KVW
30567	OG	WU02KVH	30571	OG	WU02KVM	30575	OG	WU02KVS			

30579-30588   Dennis Arrow   Northern Counties Palatine II   B49/33F   1996-97   *30586-8 are B49/35F

30579	IN	P401PLE	30582	IN	P409PLE	30585	IN	P412PLE	30587	IN	P414MTW
30580	IN	P407PLE	30583	IN	P410PLE	30586	IN	P413MTW	30588	IN	P416MTW
30581	IN	P408PLE	30584	IN	P411PLE						

Leeds is the location for this view of 30835, S655FWY. This Volvo Olympian which carries an Alexander Royale body is from a batch new to Yorkshire Rider. The Royale was built by Alexander's alongside the RL and RH models, and competed with the Northern Counties Palatine II model. *Richard Godfrey*

30627-30646

Leyland Olympian ONLXB/1R   Roe   B47/29F   1984

| 30627 | BD | A120KUM | 30640 | BD | B134RWY | 30643 | BD | B137RWY | 30646 | BD | B501RWY |

30651	BD	C146KBT	Leyland Olympian ONLXB/1R	Optare		CO47/29F	1985
30652	BD	C148KBT	Leyland Olympian ONLXB/1R	Optare		B47/29F	1985
30654	BD	C150KBT	Leyland Olympian ONLXB/1R	Optare		B47/29F	1985

30655-30671

Leyland Olympian ONCL10/1RZ   Northern Counties   B45/29F*   1988   *30661 is B43/29F

30655	HX	F157XYG	30660	HX	F164XYG	30664	HX	F168XYG	30668	HX	F172XYG
30657	HX	F161XYG	30661	HX	F165XYG	30665	HX	F169XYG	30669	HX	F173XYG
30658	HX	F162XYG	30662	HX	F166XYG	30666	HX	F170XYG	30670	HX	F174XYG
30659	HX	F163XYG	30663	HX	F167XYG	30667	HX	F171XYG	30671	HX	F175XYG

30672-30678

Leyland Olympian ONCL10/1RZ   Northern Counties   B47/29F   1990

| 30672 | BD | G179JYG | 30674 | BD | G181JYG | 30676 | BD | G183JYG | 30678 | BD | G185JYG |
| 30673 | BD | G180JYG | 30675 | BD | G182JYG | 30677 | BD | G184JYG | | | |

30685-30707

Leyland Olympian ONCL10/1RZ   Alexander RL   B47/32F*   1990   *30692-8 are B47/30F

30685	BD	G623OWR	30691	BD	G606OWR	30697	BD	G612OWR	30703	BD	G618OWR
30686	BD	G601OWR	30692	BD	G607OWR	30698	BD	G613OWR	30704	BD	G619OWR
30687	BD	G602OWR	30693	BD	G608OWR	30699	BD	G614OWR	30705	BD	G620OWR
30688	BD	G603OWR	30694	BD	G609OWR	30700	BD	G615OWR	30706	BD	G621OWR
30689	BD	G604OWR	30695	BD	G610OWR	30701	BD	G616OWR	30707	BD	G622OWR
30690	BD	G605OWR	30696	BD	G611OWR						

30709-30720

Leyland Olympian ON2R50C13Z4   Leyland   B47/29F   1991

30709	BM	J141YRM	30713	BM	J145YRM	30716	BM	J138YRM	30719	BM	J146YRM
30710	BM	J142YRM	30714	BM	J136YRM	30717	BM	J139YRM	30720	BM	J148YRM
30712	BM	J144YRM	30715	BM	J247YRM	30718	BM	J140YRM			

30722	HXs	B49PJA	Leyland Olympian ONLXB/1R	Northern Counties	B43/30F	1985	
30730	HU	J129YRM	Leyland Olympian ON2R50C13Z4	Northern Counties	B47/30F	1991	
30731	HU	J130YRM	Leyland Olympian ON2R50C13Z4	Northern Counties	B47/30F	1991	
30734	HU	H131FLX	Leyland Olympian ON2R50C13Z4	Northern Counties	B47/30F	1990	
30735	HU	L25GAN	Leyland Olympian ON2R50C13Z4	Alexander RH	B45/29F	1993	
30736	HU	L26GAN	Leyland Olympian ON2R50C13Z4	Alexander RH	B45/29F	1993	
30737	HX	L306PWR	Volvo Olympian	Northern Counties Palatine	B47/29F	1994	
30738	HX	L312PWR	Volvo Olympian	Northern Counties Palatine	B47/29F	1994	
30739	HX	L313PWR	Volvo Olympian	Northern Counties Palatine	B47/29F	1994	

30740-30751 Volvo Olympian   Alexander RL   B47/32F 1996

30740	BK	P192TGD	30743	BK	P195TGD	30746	DK	P198TGD	30749	DK	P202TGD
30741	BK	P193TGD	30744	DK	P196TGD	30747	DK	P199TGD	30750	BK	P203TGD
30742	DK	P194TGD	30745	DK	P197TGD	30748	DK	P201TGD	30751	BK	P204TGD

30752	HU	L888TTT	Volvo Olympian	Northern Counties Palatine II	B47/29F	1993	
30753	HU	L888YTT	Volvo Olympian	Northern Counties Palatine II	B47/29F	1993	

30754-30758 Volvo Olympian   Northern Counties Palatine   B47/29F 1994

30754	BD	L401PWR	30756	BD	L403PWR	30757	BD	L404PWR	30758	BD	L405PWR
30755	BD	L402PWR									

30761	BD	B143RWY	Leyland Olympian ONLXB/1R	Roe	B47/29F	1984	
30762	BD	B144RWY	Leyland Olympian ONLXB/1R	Roe	B47/29F	1984	

30781-30785 Volvo Olympian   Northern Counties Palatine   B47/29F 1994

30781	BD	L601PWR	30783	BD	L603PWR	30784	BD	L604PWR	30785	BD	L605PWR
30782	BD	L602PWR									

30786-30815 Volvo Olympian   Alexander Royale   B43/29F 1997-98

30786	HP	R606JUB	30794	HP	R614JUB	30802	BH	R622JUB	30809	BM	R629JUB
30787	HP	R607JUB	30795	HP	R615JUB	30803	BH	R623JUB	30810	HP	R630JUB
30788	HP	R608JUB	30796	HP	R616JUB	30804	BH	R624JUB	30811	HP	R631JUB
30789	HP	R609JUB	30797	HP	R617JUB	30805	BH	R625JUB	30812	HP	R632JUB
30790	HP	R610JUB	30798	HP	R618JUB	30806	BH	R626JUB	30813	HP	R633JUB
30791	HP	R611JUB	30799	HP	R619JUB	30807	BH	R627JUB	30814	HP	R634JUB
30792	HP	R612JUB	30800	HP	R620JUB	30808	BM	R176HUG	30815	HP	R636JUB
30793	HP	R613JUB	30801	HP	R621JUB						

30816-30839 Volvo Olympian   Alexander Royale   B43/29F 1998-99

30816	HU	R636HYG	30822	HU	R642HYG	30828	LT	R648HYG	30834	HP	S654FWY
30817	HU	R637HYG	30823	HU	R643HYG	30829	MU	R649HYG	30835	HP	S655FWY
30818	HU	R638HYG	30824	HU	R644HYG	30830	MU	R650HYG	30836	HP	S656FWY
30819	HU	R639HYG	30825	HU	R645HYG	30831	MU	R651HYG	30837	HP	S657FWY
30820	HU	R640HYG	30826	LT	R646HYG	30832	MU	R652HYG	30838	HP	S658FWY
30821	HU	R641HYG	30827	MU	R647HYG	30833	LT	R653HYG	30839	HP	S659FWY

30840-30845 Volvo Olympian   Alexander Royale   B43/29F 1999

30840	HU	T660VWU	30842	HU	T662VWU	30844	HX	T664VWU	30845	HU	T665VWU
30841	HU	T661VWU	30843	HU	T663VWU						

30846-30870 Volvo B7TL   Alexander ALX400   N49/29F 2000

30846	HP	W701CWR	30853	HP	W708CWR	30859	CR	W714CWR	30865	CR	W668CWT
30847	HP	W702CWR	30854	HP	W709CWR	30860	CR	W715CWR	30866	CR	W721CWR
30848	HP	W703CWR	30855	CR	W667CWT	30861	CR	W716CWR	30867	CR	W722CWR
30849	HP	W704CWR	30856	CR	W711CWR	30862	CR	W717CWR	30868	CR	W723CWR
30850	HP	W705CWR	30857	CR	W712CWR	30863	CR	W718CWR	30869	CR	W724CWR
30851	HP	W706CWR	30858	CR	W713CWR	30864	CR	W719CWR	30870	CR	W726CWR
30852	HP	W707CWR									

30871-30915 Volvo B7TL · Alexander ALX400 · N49/29F · 2000

30871	DN	W726DWX	30883	DN	W738DWX	30894	BD	X749VUA	30905	DN	W776DWX
30872	DN	W727DWX	30884	DN	W739DWX	30895	BD	W773DWX	30906	DN	W761DWX
30873	DN	W728DWX	30885	BD	W772DWX	30896	BD	W751DWX	30907	DN	W762DWX
30874	DN	W729DWX	30886	VN	W741DWX	30897	BD	W752DWX	30908	BD	X763VUA
30875	DN	W771DWX	30887	NR	W742DWX	30898	BD	W753DWX	30909	BD	X764VUA
30876	RO	W731DWX	30888	VN	W743DWX	30899	DN	W754DWX	30910	BD	W778DWX
30877	RO	W732DWX	30889	VN	W744DWX	30900	NR	W774DWX	30911	BD	X766VUA
30878	RO	W733DWX	30890	BD	W745DWX	30901	NR	W756DWX	30912	BD	X767VUA
30879	RO	W734DWX	30891	BD	W746DWX	30902	VN	W757DWX	30913	BD	W768DWX
30880	RO	W735DWX	30892	BD	W747DWX	30903	VN	W758DWX	30914	BD	W769DWX
30881	DN	W736DWX	30893	BD	W748DWX	30904	DN	W759DWX	30915	BD	X779VUA
30882	DN	W737DWX									

30916-30938 Volvo B7TL · Alexander ALX400 · N49/29F · 2000

30916	HP	W771KBT	30922	CR	W788KBT	30928	CR	X796NWR	30934	CR	X354VWT
30917	HP	W772KBT	30923	CR	X791NWR	30929	CR	X797NWR	30935	CR	X356VWT
30918	HP	W773KBT	30924	CR	X792NWR	30930	CR	X798NWR	30936	CR	X357VWT
30919	HP	W774KBT	30925	CR	X793NWR	30931	CR	X351VWT	30937	CR	X358VWT
30920	HP	W787KBT	30926	CR	X794NWR	30932	CR	X352VWT	30938	CR	X359VWT
30921	HP	W776KBT	30927	CR	X795NWR	30933	CR	X353VWT			

30939-30965 Volvo B7TL · Alexander ALX400 · N49/27F · 2001-02

30939	BD	Y794XNW	30946	BM	YJ51RRO	30953	BM	YJ51RSU	30960	YK	YJ51RDU
30940	BD	Y795XNW	30947	BM	YJ51RRU	30954	YK	YJ51RDO	30961	YK	YJ51RDV
30941	BM	Y796XNW	30948	BM	YJ51RRV	30955	YK	YJ51RCU	30962	YK	YJ51RDX
30942	BM	Y797XNW	30949	BM	YJ51RRX	30956	YK	YJ51RCV	30963	YK	YJ51RDY
30943	BM	Y798XNW	30950	BM	YJ51RRY	30957	YK	YJ51RCX	30964	YK	YJ51RAU
30944	BM	YJ51RPY	30951	BM	YJ51RRZ	30958	YK	YJ51RCZ	30965	YK	YJ51RAX
30945	BM	YJ51RPZ	30952	BM	YJ51RSO	30959	YK	YJ51RCO			

31080	CC	G803JYG	Scania N113DRB	Alexander RH	B47/33F	1990
31084	CC	H807TWX	Scania N113DRB	Northern Counties	B47/33F	1990

31088-31113 Scania N113DRB · Alexander RH · B47/31F · 1991

31088	CC	H611VNW	31092	BM	H615VNW	31096	BM	H619VNW	31110	CC	H633VNW
31089	CC	H612VNW	31093	CR	H616VNW	31097	BM	H620VNW	31113	CC	H636VNW
31090	CR	H613VNW									

31121	OM	J158YRM	Leyland Olympian ON2R50C13Z4	Leyland	B47/29F	1991
31127	HU	G298OGE	Volvo Citybus B10M-50	Alexander RV	B47/37F	1989

31129-31148 Volvo B7TL · Alexander ALX400 · N49/29F · 2003

31129	OG	YU52VYE	31134	OG	YU52VYK	31140	OG	YU52VYR	31145	CR	YU52VYX
31130	OG	YU52VYF	31135	OG	YU52VYL	31141	OG	YU52VYS	31146	CR	YU52VYY
31131	OG	YU52VYG	31137	OG	YU52VYN	31142	CR	YU52VYT	31147	CR	YU52VYZ
31132	OG	YU52VYH	31138	OG	YU52VYO	31143	CR	YU52VYV	31148	OG	YU52VZA
31133	OG	YU52VYJ	31139	OG	YU52VYP	31144	CR	YU52VYW			

31150	HU	L24GAN	Leyland Olympian ON2R50C13Z4	Alexander RH	B45/29F	1993
31151	HU	L27GAN	Leyland Olympian ON2R50C13Z4	Alexander RH	B45/29F	1993
31152	HU	L28GAN	Leyland Olympian ON2R50C13Z4	Alexander RH	B45/29F	1993
31198	CM	L163UNS	Leyland Olympian ON2R50C13V3	Alexander RL	B47/31F	1993
31200	B	R152EHS	Volvo Olympian	Alexander Royale	B42/29F	1997

31269-31285 Volvo Citybus B10M-50 · Alexander RV · B47/37F · 1989

31269	HU	F91JYS	31270	HU	F92JYS	31284	HU	G303OGE	31285	PH	G304OGE

31297-31320 Volvo Citybus B10M-50 · Alexander RV · B47/37F · 1989-90

31297	HU	G527RDS	31313	CE	G686PNS	31315	HU	G693PNS	31318	PH	G696PNS
31300	PH	G531RDS	31314	PH	G692PNS	31317	PH	G695PNS	31320	PH	G702PNS
31310	PH	G544RDS									

The 2008 First Bus Handbook

Also seen in Leeds, and operating from Bramley depot, is 30950, YJ51RRY. This is a Volvo B7TL with an Alexander ALX400 body, a combination bought in numbers by First around the millennium. *Richard Godfrey*

31373-31413

Leyland Olympian ON2R50C13V3   Alexander RL   B47/31F   1993

31373	BS	L160UNS	31382	LF	L170UNS	31396	LF	L184UNS	31405	LF	L193UNS
31374	BS	L161UNS	31383	LF	L171UNS	31397	LF	L185UNS	31406	LF	L194UNS
31375	BS	L162UNS	31384	LF	L172UNS	31398	LF	L186UNS	31407	LF	L195UNS
31376	HH	L164UNS	31385	LF	L173UNS	31399	LF	L187UNS	31408	LF	L196UNS
31377	HA	L165UNS	31386	LF	L174UNS	31400	LF	L188UNS	31410	LF	L198UNS
31378	HA	L165UNS	31392	LF	L180UNS	31401	LF	L189UNS	31411	LF	L199UNS
31379	HA	L165UNS	31393	LF	L181UNS	31402	LF	L190UNS	31412	LF	L201UNS
31380	RH	L168UNS	31394	LF	L182UNS	31403	LF	L191UNS	31413	LF	L202UNS
31381	LF	L169UNS	31395	LF	L183UNS	31404	LF	L192UNS			

31414-31420

Volvo Olympia   Alexander Royale   B45/29F   1994

31414	CD	L827YGA	31416	CD	L829YGA	31419	CD	L832YGA	31420	CD	L833YGA
31415	CD	L828YGA	31418	CD	L831YGA						

31421-31428

Volvo Olympian   Alexander Royale RL   B47/32F   1994

31421	B	M834DUS	31423	CD	M836DUS	31426	CD	M839DUS	31428	CD	M841DUS
31422	CD	M835DUS	31425	CD	M838DUS	31427	CD	M840DUS			

31429	PH	M939EYS	Volvo Olympian	Alexander Royale	B45/29F	1995
31430	PH	M940EYS	Volvo Olympian	Alexander Royale	B45/29F	1995
31431	SN	M941EYS	Volvo Olympian	Northern Counties Palatine II	B47/30F	1995
31432	SN	M942EYS	Volvo Olympian	Northern Counties Palatine II	B47/30F	1995

31433-31462

Volvo Olympian   Alexander RL   B47/32F   1996

31433	CD	N944SOS	31440	SN	N951SOS	31447	SN	N958SOS	31457	PL	N968SOS
31434	CD	N945SOS	31441	SN	N952SOS	31448	SN	N959SOS	31458	CE	N969SOS
31435	CD	N946SOS	31442	SN	N953SOS	31449	SN	N960SOS	31459	PL	N970SOS
31436	CD	N947SOS	31443	SN	N954SOS	31450	SN	N961SOS	31460	CE	N971SOS
31437	CD	N948SOS	31444	SN	N955SOS	31452	WR	N963SOS	31461	CE	N972SOS
31438	SN	N949SOS	31445	SN	N956SOS	31454	NN	N965SOS	31462	HH	N973SOS
31439	SN	N950SOS	31446	SN	N957SOS	31456	HH	N967SOS			

31468-31495   Volvo Olympian   Alexander Royale   B42/29F   1997

31468	CD	P595WSU	31475	PH	P603WSU	31482	PH	P618WSU	31489	SN	R146EHS
31469	SN	P596WSU	31476	PH	P604WSU	31483	B	P619WSU	31490	SN	R147EHS
31470	CD	P597WSU	31477	PH	P605WSU	31484	PH	P620WSU	31491	B	R148EHS
31471	CD	P598WSU	31478	PH	P606WSU	31485	PH	R139EHS	31492	B	R149EHS
31472	B	P599WSU	31479	PH	P607WSU	31486	PH	R143EHS	31493	B	R150EHS
31473	PH	P601WSU	31480	PH	P608WSU	31487	CD	R144EHS	31494	B	R151EHS
31474	PH	P602WSU	31481	PH	P617WSU	31488	SN	R145EHS	31495	B	R153EHS

31496-31505   Volvo Olympian   Northern Counties Palatine II   B43/29F   1997

31496	CD	R654DUS	31499	SN	R657DUS	31501	SN	R659DUS	31504	SN	R662DUS
31497	CD	R655DUS	31500	SN	R658DUS	31503	SN	R661DUS	31505	SN	R663DUS
31498	SN	R656DUS									

31506-31515   Volvo B7TLT   East Lancs Nordic   N55/40F   2003

31506	PH	SA52DVR	31509	PH	SA52DVV	31512	PH	SA52DVY	31514	PH	SA52DWC
31507	PH	SA52DVT	31510	PH	SA52DVW	31513	PH	SA52DVZ	31515	PH	SA52DWD
31508	PH	SA52DVU	31511	PH	SA52DVX						

31516	B	M846DUS	Leyland Olympian		Alexander Royale RL	BC47/28F	1994
31517	CD	WLT408	Volvo Olympian		Alexander Royale RL	B47/32F	1994

31518-31522   Volvo Olympian   Alexander Royale RL   BC47/28F   1994

31518	CW	M847DUS	31520	B	WLT741	31521	B	WLT770	31522	CW	M848DUS
31519	CW	M849DUS									

31523	CD	WLT976	Volvo Olympian	Alexander Royale RL	BC47/28F	1994
31524	LFs	KGG142Y	Leyland Olympian ONTL11/1R	Eastern Coach Works	B--/--F	1982
31528	ABp	URS318X	Leyland Atlantean AN68C/1R	Alexander AL	O45/29D	1982
31529	ABp	CRG325C	Daimler CVG6	Alexander B	B37/29R	1965
31531	CE	A102FSA	Leyland Olympian ONLXB/1R	Alexander RH	B47/24D	1984
31534	CE	A105FSA	Leyland Olympian ONLXB/1R	Alexander RH	B47/26D	1984
31536	CE	A107FSA	Leyland Olympian ONLXB/1R	Alexander RH	B47/26D	1984
31539	CE	B112MSO	Leyland Olympian ONLXB/1RV	Alexander RH	B47/26D	1985
31542	CE	B115MSO	Leyland Olympian ONLXB/1RV	Alexander RH	B47/26D	1985
31547	AB	B121MSO	Leyland Olympian ONLXB/1RV	Alexander RH	B47/24D	1985

31548-31557   Leyland Olympian ONCL10/2RZ   Alexander RH   B49/29D*   1988   *31548/9 BC47/33F

31548	AB	E122DRS	31551	AB	E125DRS	31553	AB	E127DRS	31556	AB	E130DRS
31549	AB	E123DRS	31552	AB	E126DRS	31554	AB	E128DRS	31557	AB	E131DRS
31550	AB	E124DRS									

31558-31563   Volvo B7TL   Alexander ALX400   N42/29F   2001

31558	AB	X132NSS	31560	AB	X103NSS	31562	AB	X136NSS	31563	AB	X137NSS
31559	AB	X771NSO	31561	AB	X104NSS						

31569	LT	R301LKS	Volvo Olympian	Alexander Royale	B42/29F	1998
31570	LT	R422YMS	Volvo Olympian	Alexander Royale	B42/29F	1998
31571	LT	P589WSU	Volvo Olympian	Alexander Royale	B42/29F	1997
31572	GS	P594WSU	Volvo Olympian	Alexander Royale	B42/29F	1997
31577	AB	XSS344Y	Leyland Atlantean AN68D/1R	Alexander AL	B--/--F	1983

31634-31654   Volvo Olympian   Alexander Royale   B42/29F   1998

31634	DK	R302LKS	31640	DK	R308LKS	31645	LV	R313LKS	31650	DK	R418YMS
31635	LV	R303LKS	31641	DK	R309LKS	31646	DK	R314LKS	31651	DK	R419YMS
31636	DK	R304LKS	31642	LT	R310LKS	31647	LT	R315LKS	31652	DK	R420YMS
31637	MU	R305LKS	31643	DK	R311LKS	31648	LV	R416YMS	31653	DK	R421YMS
31638	DK	R206LKS	31644	DK	R312LKS	31649	LT	R417YMS	31654	LT	R423YMS
31639	DK	R307LKS									

31655-31669   Volvo Olympian   Alexander Royale   B42/29F   1998-89

31655	GS	S924AKS	31659	LV	S928AKS	31663	MU	S932AKS	31667	MU	S936AKS
31656	LV	S925AKS	31660	GS	S929AKS	31664	MU	S933AKS	31668	MU	S937AKS
31657	LV	S926AKS	31661	MU	S930AKS	31665	MU	S934AKS	31669	MU	S938AKS
31658	u	S927AKS	31662	MU	S931AKS	31666	MU	S935AKS			

Spring in Galashiels and Olympian 31572, P594WSU, with Alexander Royale bodywork leaves the town on the local service to West Langlee. *Richard Godfrey*

31670-31680

Volvo Olympian   Alexander Royale   B42/29F   1997

31670	MU	R140EHS	31673	HP	P609WSU	31676	HP	P612WSU	31679	LT	P615WSU
31671	MU	R141EHS	31674	HP	P610WSU	31677	HP	P613WSU	31680	LT	P616WSU
31672	MU	R142EHS	31675	LV	P611WSU	31678	LV	P614WSU

31681-31688

Volvo Olympian   Alexander Royale   B42/29F   1997

31681	LT	P585WSU	31683	HP	P587WSU	31685	HP	P590WSU	31687	GS	P592WSU
31682	LT	P586WSU	31684	GS	P588WSU	31686	HP	P591WSU	31688	GS	P593WSU

31727-31731

Leyland Olympian ON2R50C13V3 Alexander RL   B47/31F   1993

31727	BF	K350SDS	31729	BF	L552USU	31730	BF	L553USU	31731	BF	L554USU
31728	BF	L551USU

31732	BF	L156UNS	Leyland Olympian ON2R50C13V3	Alexander RL	B47/31F	1993
31733	BF	L157UNS	Leyland Olympian ON2R50C13V3	Alexander RL	B47/31F	1993
31734	BF	L158UNS	Leyland Olympian ON2R50C13V3	Alexander RL	B47/31F	1993
31735	BF	L159UNS	Leyland Olympian ON2R50C13V3	Alexander RL	B47/31F	1993

31737-31740

Leyland Olympian ON2R50C13Z4 Northern Counties   B47/30F   1990

31737	HX	H133FLX	31738	HX	H134FLX	31739	HU	H138FLX	31740	HX	H143FLX

31760-31775

Volvo Olympian   Alexander RH   B47/25D   1997-98   London United, 2003

31760	HP	R921WOE	31764	HP	R925WOE	31768	HP	R932YOV	31772	HP	R937YOV
31761	HP	R922WOE	31765	HP	R926WOE	31769	HP	R933YOV	31773	HP	R938YOV
31762	HP	R923WOE	31766	HP	R930WOE	31770	HP	R934YOV	31774	HP	R939YOV
31763	HP	R924WOE	31767	HP	R931WOE	31771	HP	R935YOV	31775	HP	R940YOV

31776-31786

Volvo B7TL   TransBus ALX400   N49/27F   2003

31776	DN	YN53EOA	31779	DN	YN53EOD	31782	OG	YN53EOG	31785	OG	YN53EOK
31777	DN	YN53EOB	31780	DN	YN53EOE	31783	OG	YN53EOH	31786	OG	YN53EOL
31778	DN	YN53EOC	31781	OG	YN53EOF	31784	OG	YN53EOJ

31787-31804 — Volvo B7TL — Wrightbus Eclipse Gemini — N45/29F — 2003

31787	OG	YN53EFE	31792	OG	YN53EFK	31797	OG	YN53EFR	31801	OG	YN53EFW
31788	OG	YN53EFF	31793	OG	YN53EFL	31798	OG	YN53EFT	31802	OG	YN53EFX
31789	OG	YN53EFG	31794	OG	YN53EFM	31799	OG	YN53EFU	31803	OG	YN53EFZ
31790	OG	YN53EFH	31795	OG	YN53EFO	31800	OG	YN53EFV	31804	OG	YN53EGC
31791	OG	YN53EFJ	31796	OG	YN53EFP						

31805-31808 — Volvo Olympian — Alexander RH — B47/25D — 1997-98 — London United, 2003

31805	HP	R927WOE	31806	HP	R928WOE	31807	HP	R929WOE	31808	HP	R936YOV

31811-31818 — Volvo Olympian — Alexander RH — B47/25D — 1997 — London United, 2005

31811	HP	XDZ5911	31813	HP	XDZ5913	31815	HP	XDZ5915	31818	HP	R918WOE
31812	HP	XDZ5912	31814	HP	XDZ5914	31816	HP	XDZ5916			

31820-31830 — Volvo Olympian — Northern Counties Palatine — B47/27D — 1997 — London General, 2005

31820	SO	P920RYO	31825	SO	P925RYO	31828	SO	P908RYO	31830	SO	P930RYO
31821	SO	P921RYO	31826	SO	P926RYO						

31836	SO	R336LGH	Volvo Olympian	Northern Counties Palatine	B47/27D	1998	London General, 2005
31841	WS	R241LGH	Volvo Olympian	Northern Counties Palatine II	BC47/31F	1998	Ensign, Purfleet, 2005
31846	WS	R246LGH	Volvo Olympian	Northern Counties Palatine II	BC47/31F	1998	London General, 2005
31877	SO	R277LGH	Volvo Olympian	Northern Counties Palatine	B47/27D	1998	London General, 2005
31878	SO	R278LGH	Volvo Olympian	Northern Counties Palatine II	B47/27D	1998	London General, 2005

31902-31915 — Dennis Arrow — Northern Counties Palatine 2 — B47/33F* — 1996 — *31915 is B47/35F

31902	IN	P402PLE	31904	IN	P404PLE	31906	IN	P406PLE	31915	IN	P415MTW
31903	IN	P403PLE	31905	IN	P405PLE						

31917-31926 — Dennis Arrow — East Lancs Pyoneer — B49/31F — 1997

31917	IN	P417PVW	31920	WN	P420PVW	31923	WN	P423PVW	31925	TE	P425PVW
31918	WN	P418PVW	31921	WN	P421PVW	31924	WN	P424PVW	31926	IN	R426SOY
31919	IN	P419PVW	31922	WN	P422PVW						

31927-31954 — Dennis Arrow — East Lancs Pyoneer — B49/31F — 1998

31927	TE	R427ULE	31935	TE	R435ULE	31942	IN	R442ULE	31949	TE	R449ULE
31928	IN	R428ULE	31936	TE	R436ULE	31943	IN	R443ULE	31950	TE	R450ULE
31929	TE	R429ULE	31937	TE	R437ULE	31944	IN	R844YLC	31951	WN	S451SLL
31930	TE	R430ULE	31938	TE	R438ULE	31945	IN	R445ULE	31952	WN	S452SLL
31932	WN	R432ULE	31939	TE	R439ULE	31946	IN	R446ULE	31953	IN	S453SLL
31933	WN	R433ULE	31940	TE	R440ULE	31947	IN	R447ULE	31954	IN	S454SLL
31934	WN	R434ULE	31941	IN	R441ULE	31948	IN	R448ULE			

Vehicles transferred from London provide useful mid-life buses in the provinces. Pictured in Southampton is an example that joined the depot strength from London General. Olympian 31836, R336LGH, retains its dual-door configuration.
Paul Gainsbury

32001-32024   Volvo B7TL   Alexander ALX400   N49/29F   2000

32001	LH	W801PAE	32007	LH	W807PAE	32014	LH	W814PAE	32019	LH	W819PAE
32002	LH	W802PAE	32008	LH	W808PAE	32015	LH	W815PAE	32021	LH	W821PAE
32003	HG	W803PAE	32009	LH	W809PAE	32016	LH	W816PAE	32022	LH	W822PAE
32004	HG	W804PAE	32011	LH	W811PAE	32017	LH	W817PAE	32023	LH	W823PAE
32005	HG	W805PAE	32012	LH	W812PAE	32018	LH	W818PAE	32024	LH	W824PAE
32006	LH	W806PAE	32013	LH	W813PAE						

32031-32046   Volvo B7TL   Alexander ALX400   N49/29F   2000

32031	SO	W801EOW	32035	SO	W805EOW	32039	SO	W809EOW	32044	SO	W814EOW
32032	SO	W802EOW	32036	SO	W806EOW	32041	SO	W811EOW	32045	SO	W815EOW
32033	SO	W803EOW	32037	SO	W807EOW	32042	SO	W812EOW	32046	SO	W816EOW
32034	SO	W804EOW	32038	SO	W808EOW	32043	SO	W813EOW			

32052	ON	X578RJW	Volvo B7TL 10.2m		East Lancs Vyking		N41/22D	2000

32053-32065   Volvo B7TL   Alexander ALX400   N49/29F   2000

32053	LE	W213XBD	32056	LE	W216XBD	32059	LE	W219XBD	32063	LE	W223XBD
32054	LE	W214XBD	32057	LE	W217XBD	32061	LE	W221XBD	32064	LE	W224XBD
32055	LE	W215XBD	32058	LE	W218XBD	32062	LE	W422SRP	32065	LE	W425SRP

32066-32099   Volvo B7TL   Alexander ALX400   N49/29F   2002

32066	LE	KP51VZO	32075	LE	KP51WAO	32084	LE	KP51WBU	32092	LE	KP51WCN
32067	LE	KP51VZR	32076	LE	KP51WAU	32085	LE	KP51WBV	32093	LE	KP51WCO
32068	LE	KP51VZS	32077	LE	KP51WBD	32086	LE	KP51WBY	32094	LE	KP51WCR
32069	LE	KP51VZT	32078	LE	KP51WBG	32087	LE	KP51WBZ	32095	LE	KP51WCW
32070	LE	KP51VZW	32079	LE	KP51WBJ	32088	LE	KP51WCA	32096	LE	KP51WCX
32071	LE	KP51VZX	32080	LE	KP51WBK	32089	LE	KP51WCF	32097	LE	KP51WCY
32072	LE	KP51VZY	32081	LE	KP51WBL	32090	LE	KP51WCG	32098	LE	KP51WDD
32073	LE	KP51VZZ	32082	LE	KP51WBO	32091	LE	KP51WCJ	32099	LE	KP51WDE
32074	LE	KP51WAJ	32083	LE	KP51WBT						

32100-32112   Volvo B7TL 10m   Plaxton President 4.4m   N39/20D   2002

32100	X	LT02ZCJ	32104	X	LT02ZCO	32107	X	LT02ZCY	32110	X	LT02ZDJ
32101	X	LT02ZCK	32105	X	LT02ZCU	32108	X	LT02ZCZ	32111	X	LT02ZDK
32102	X	LT02ZCL	32106	X	LT02ZCV	32109	X	LT02ZDH	32112	X	LT02ZDL
32103	X	LT02ZCN									

Leicester's allocation of vehicles are all now from the Volvo catalogue, with the B7TL double-deck dominating. 32087, KP51WBZ from the 2002 intake, is seen heading for the General Hospital.
Richard Godfrey

First's buses in London had their own version of the willow-leaf livery based on red but this is being replaced on repaint with a simple all-red scheme to meet TfL requirements. Pictured passing Marble Arch on route 10 is 32263, LT52WWJ, a Volvo B7TL with Alexander bodywork. *Richard Godfrey*

32200-32228

Volvo B7TL 10.6m | Plaxton President 4.4m | N42/23D | 2002

32200	ON	LT52WTE	32208	ON	LT52WTO	32215	ON	LT52WTY	32222	NP	LT52WUG
32201	ON	LT52WTF	32209	ON	LT52WTP	32216	ON	LT52WTZ	32223	NP	LT52WUH
32202	ON	LT52WTG	32210	ON	LT52WTR	32217	ON	LT52WUA	32224	NP	LT52WUJ
32203	ON	LT52WTJ	32211	ON	LT52WTU	32218	ON	LT52WUB	32225	NP	LT52WUK
32204	ON	LT52WTK	32212	ON	LT52WTV	32219	ON	LT52WUC	32226	NP	LT52WUL
32205	ON	LT52WTL	32213	ON	LT52WTW	32220	ON	LT52WUD	32227	NP	LT52XAL
32206	ON	LT52WTM	32214	ON	LT52WTX	32221	NP	LT52WUE	32228	NP	LT52XAM
32207	ON	LT52WTN									

32249-32276

Volvo B7TL 10.6m | Alexander ALX400 4.4m | N45/21D | 2003

32249	X	LT52WVM	32256	X	LT52WWB	32263	X	LT52WWJ	32270	X	LT52WWR
32250	X	LT52WVN	32257	X	LT52WWC	32264	X	LT52WWK	32271	X	LT52WWS
32251	X	LT52WVO	32258	X	LT52WWD	32265	X	LT52WWL	32272	X	LT52WWU
32252	X	LT52WVP	32259	X	LT52WWE	32266	X	LT52WWM	32273	X	LT52WXC
32253	X	LT52WVY	32260	X	LT52WWF	32267	X	LT52WWN	32274	X	LT52WXD
32254	X	LT52WVZ	32261	X	LT52WWG	32268	X	LT52WWO	32275	X	LT52WXE
32255	X	LT52WWA	32262	X	LT52WWH	32269	X	LT52WWP	32276	X	LT52WXF

32277	LE	KP51WDF	Volvo B7TL		Alexander ALX400 4.4m	N49/29F	2002
32278	HG	YU52VYM	Volvo B7TL		Alexander ALX400 4.4m	N49/29F	2003

32279-32292

Volvo B7TL 11.2m | TransBus ALX400 4.4m | N49/27F | 2003

32279	HG	WR03YZL	32283	HG	WR03YZS	32287	HG	WR03YZW	32290	HG	WX53UKL
32280	HG	WR03YZM	32284	HG	WR03YZT	32288	HG	WR03YZX	32291	HG	WR03ZBC
32281	HG	WR03YZN	32285	HG	WR03YZU	32289	HG	WX53UKK	32292	HG	WR03ZBD
32282	HG	WR03YZP	32286	HG	WR03YZV						

32294-32327 — Volvo B7TL 10.6m — TransBus President 4.4m — N44/21D — 2003

32294	NP	LK03NGJ	32303	NP	LK03NHC	32312	NP	LK03NHN	32320	NP	LK03NJF
32295	NP	LK03NGN	32304	NP	LK03NHD	32313	NP	LK03NHP	32321	NP	LK03NJJ
32296	NP	LK03NGU	32305	NP	LK03NHE	32314	NP	LK03NHT	32322	NP	LK03NJN
32297	NP	LK03NGV	32306	NP	LK03NHF	32315	NP	LK03NHV	32323	NP	LK03NJV
32298	NP	LK03NGX	32307	NP	LK03NHG	32316	NP	LK03NHX	32324	NP	LK03NJX
32299	NP	LK03NGY	32308	NP	LK03NHH	32317	NP	LK03NHY	32325	NP	LK03NJY
32300	NP	LK03NGZ	32309	NP	LK03NHJ	32318	NP	LK03NHZ	32326	NP	LK03NJZ
32301	NP	LK03NHA	32310	NP	LK03NHL	32319	NP	LK03NJE	32327	NP	LK03NKA
32302	NP	LK03NHB	32311	NP	LK03NHM						

32328-32348 — Volvo B7TL 10.6m — Wrightbus Eclipse Gemini — N41/24D — 2003-04

32328	ON	LK53LYH	32334	ON	LK53LYU	32339	ON	LK53LYZ	32344	ON	LK53LZE
32329	ON	LK53LYJ	32335	ON	LK53LYV	32340	ON	LK53LZA	32345	ON	LK53LZF
32330	ON	LK53LYO	32336	ON	LK53LYW	32341	ON	LK53LZB	32346	ON	LK53LZG
32331	ON	LK53LYP	32337	ON	LK53LYX	32342	ON	LK53LZC	32347	ON	LK53LZH
32332	ON	LK53LYR	32338	ON	LK53LYY	32343	ON	LK53LZD	32348	ON	LK53LZL
32333	ON	LK53LYT									

32349-32370 — Volvo B7TL 10.1m — Wrightbus Eclipse Gemini — N38/21D — 2004

32349	ON	LK53LZM	32355	ON	LK53LZU	32361	X	LK04HYN	32366	X	LK04HYY
32350	ON	LK53LZN	32356	ON	LK53LZV	32362	X	LK04HYM	32367	X	LK04HYA
32351	ON	LK53LZO	32357	ON	LK53LZW	32363	X	LK04HYW	32368	X	LK04HYS
32352	ON	LK53LZP	32358	ON	LK53LZX	32364	X	LK04HYT	32369	X	LK04HYU
32353	ON	LK53LZR	32359	ON	LK53MBF	32365	X	LK04HYX	32370	X	LK04HYV
32354	ON	LK53LZT	32360	ON	LK04HYP						

32371-32430 — Volvo B7TL 10.1m — Wrightbus Eclipse Gemini — N38/21D — 2004

32371	X	LK04HZA	32386	X	LK04HZU	32401	X	LK04HXL	32416	X	LK04JBY
32372	X	LK04HZB	32387	X	LK04HZV	32402	X	LK04HXM	32417	X	LK04JBZ
32373	X	LK04HZC	32388	X	LK04HZW	32403	X	LK04HXN	32418	X	LK04JCJ
32374	X	LK04HZD	32389	X	LK04HZX	32404	X	LK04HXP	32419	X	LK04JCU
32375	X	LK04HZE	32390	X	LK04HZY	32405	X	LK04HXR	32420	X	LK04JCV
32376	X	LK04HZF	32391	X	LK04HZZ	32406	X	LK04HXS	32421	X	LK04JCX
32377	X	LK04HZG	32392	X	LK04HXA	32407	X	LK04HXT	32422	X	LK04HYZ
32378	X	LK04HZH	32393	X	LK04HXB	32408	X	LK04HXU	32423	X	LK04JCZ
32379	X	LK04HZJ	32394	X	LK04HXC	32409	X	LK04HXV	32424	X	LK04HYB
32380	X	LK04HZL	32395	X	LK04HXD	32410	X	LK04HXW	32425	X	LK04HYC
32381	X	LK04HZM	32396	X	LK04HXE	32411	X	LK04HXX	32426	X	LK04HYF
32382	X	LK04HZN	32397	X	LK54FNO	32412	X	LK04JBE	32427	X	LK04HYG
32383	X	LK04JBU	32398	X	LK54FNP	32413	X	LK04HZP	32428	X	LK04HYH
32384	X	LK04HZS	32399	X	LK04HXH	32414	X	LK04JBV	32429	X	LK04HYJ
32385	X	LK04HZT	32400	X	LK04HXJ	32415	X	LK04JBX	32430	X	LK04HYL

32431-32473 — Volvo B7TL 10.1m — Wrightbus Eclipse Gemini — N45/28F — 2004

32431	BM	K1YRL	32442	BM	YJ04FYN	32453	BM	YJ04FZA	32464	BM	YJ04FZN
32432	BM	YJ04FYB	32443	BM	YJ04FYP	32454	BM	YJ04FZB	32465	BM	YJ04FZP
32433	BM	YJ04FYC	32444	BM	YJ04FYR	32455	BM	YJ04FZC	32466	BM	YJ04FZR
32434	BM	YJ04FYD	32445	BM	YJ04FYS	32456	BM	YJ04FZD	32467	BM	YJ04FZS
32435	BM	YJ04FYE	32446	BM	YJ04FYT	32457	BM	YJ04FZE	32468	BM	YJ04FZT
32436	BM	YJ04FYF	32447	BM	YJ04FYU	32458	BM	YJ04FZF	32469	BM	YJ04FZU
32437	BM	YJ04FYG	32448	BM	YJ04FYV	32459	BM	YJ04FZG	32470	BM	YJ04FZV
32438	BM	YJ04FYH	32449	BM	YJ04FYW	32460	BM	YJ04FZH	32471	BM	YJ04FZX
32439	BM	YJ04FYK	32450	BM	YJ04FYX	32461	BM	YJ04FZK	32472	BM	YJ04FZY
32440	BM	YJ04FYL	32451	BM	YJ04FYY	32462	BM	YJ04FZL	32473	BM	YJ04FZZ
32441	BM	YJ04FYM	32452	BM	YJ04FYZ	32463	BM	YJ04FZM			

32475-32494 — Volvo B7TL 10.7m — TransBus ALX400 4.3m — N49/27F — 2003

32475	VN	AU53HJJ	32480	YA	AU53HJX	32485	YA	AU53HKC	32490	IP	AU53HKH
32476	VN	AU53HJK	32481	YA	AU53HJY	32486	VN	AU53HKD	32491	IP	AU53HKJ
32477	VN	AU53HJN	32482	YA	AU53HJZ	32487	IP	AU53HKE	32492	IP	AU53HKK
32478	VN	AU53HJO	32483	YA	AU53HKA	32488	IP	AU53HKF	32493	IP	AU53HKL
32479	VN	AU53HJV	32484	YA	AU53HKB	32489	IP	AU53HKG	32494	IP	AU53HKM

32495-32502 Volvo B7TL 10.1m Wrightbus Eclipse Gemini N38/21D 2004

32495	ON	LK54FLA	32497	ON	LK54FLC	32499	ON	LK54FLE	32501	ON	LK54FLG
32496	ON	LK54FLB	32498	ON	LK54FLD	32500	ON	LK54FLF	32502	ON	LK54FLH

32503-32542 Volvo B7TL 10.7m Wrightbus Eclipse Gemini N45/28F 2004

32503	HU	YJ54XTO	32513	HX	YJ54XUB	32523	HX	YJ54XUO	32533	HX	YJ54XVA
32504	HU	YJ54XTP	32514	HX	YJ54XUC	32524	HX	YJ54XUP	32534	HX	YJ54XVB
32505	HU	YJ54XTR	32515	HX	YJ54XUD	32525	HX	YJ54XUR	32535	HX	YJ54XVC
32506	HU	YJ54XTT	32516	HX	YJ54XUE	32526	HX	YJ54XUT	32536	HX	YJ54XVD
32507	HU	YJ54XTU	32517	HX	YJ54XUF	32527	HX	YJ54XUU	32537	HX	YJ05VUX
32508	HU	YJ54XTV	32518	HX	YJ54XUG	32528	HX	YJ54XUV	32538	HX	YJ05VUW
32509	HX	YJ54XTW	32519	HX	YJ54XUH	32529	HX	YJ54XUW	32539	HX	YJ05VWG
32510	HX	YJ54XTX	32520	HX	YJ54XUK	32530	HX	YJ54XUX	32540	HX	YJ05VWF
32511	HX	YJ54XTZ	32521	HX	YJ54XUM	32531	HX	YJ54XUY	32541	HX	YJ05VWF
32512	HX	YJ54XUA	32522	HX	YJ54XUN	32532	HX	YJ05VUY	32542	HX	YJ05VWH

32543-32626 Volvo B7TL 10.7m Wrightbus Eclipse Gemini N45/28F 2004-05

32543	SN	SF54OSD	32564	SN	SF54OTE	32585	LF	SF54OUE	32606	LF	SF54TKJ
32544	SN	SF54OSE	32565	SN	SF54OTG	32586	LF	SF54OUG	32607	LF	SF54TKK
32545	SN	SF54OSG	32566	LF	SF54OTH	32587	LF	SF54OUH	32608	LF	SF54TKO
32546	SN	SF54OSJ	32567	LF	SF54OTJ	32588	LF	SF54OUJ	32609	LF	SF54TKN
32547	LF	SF54OSK	32568	LF	SF54OTK	32589	LF	SF54OUK	32610	LF	SF54TKT
32548	SN	SF54OSL	32569	SN	SF54OTL	32590	SN	SF54OUL	32611	CD	SF54TKU
32549	SN	SF54OSM	32570	SN	SF54OTM	32591	SN	SF54OUM	32612	CD	SF54TKV
32550	SN	SF54OSN	32571	SN	SF54OTN	32592	SN	SF54OUN	32613	CD	SF54TKX
32551	SN	SF54OSO	32572	SN	SF54OTP	32593	SN	SF54THV	32614	CD	SF54YKY
32552	SN	SF54OSP	32573	SN	SF54OTR	32594	SN	SF54THX	32615	CD	SF54TKZ
32553	SN	SF54OSR	32574	SN	SF54OTT	32595	SN	SF54THZ	32616	CD	SF54TLJ
32554	SN	SF54OSU	32575	SN	SF54OTU	32596	SN	SF54TJO	32617	CD	SF54TLK
32555	SN	SF54OSV	32576	SN	SF54OTV	32597	SN	SF54TJU	32618	CD	SF54TLN
32556	SN	SF54OSW	32577	SN	SF54OTW	32598	SN	SF54TJV	32619	CD	SF54TLO
32557	SN	SF54OSX	32578	SN	SF54OTX	32599	SN	SF54TJX	32620	CD	SF54TLU
32558	SN	SF54OSY	32579	SN	SF54OTY	32600	SN	SF54TJY	32621	CD	SF54TLX
32559	SN	SF54OSZ	32580	LF	SF54OTZ	32601	SN	SF54TJZ	32622	CD	SF54TLY
32560	SN	SF54OTA	32581	LF	SF54OUA	32602	SN	SF54THA	32623	CD	SF54TLZ
32561	SN	SF54OTB	32582	LF	SF54OUB	32603	LF	SF54TKC	32624	CD	SF54TMO
32562	SN	SF54OTC	32583	LF	SF54OUC	32604	LF	SF54TKD	32625	CD	SF54TMU
32563	SN	SF54OTD	32584	LF	SF54OUD	32605	LF	SF54TKE	32626	CD	SF54TMV

32627-32650 Volvo B7TL 10.7m Wrightbus Eclipse Gemini N45/28F 2005

32627	LE	KP54KAO	32633	LE	KP54LAE	32639	LE	KP54AZA	32645	LE	KP54AZJ
32628	LE	KP54KAU	32634	LE	KP54LAO	32640	LE	KP54AZB	32646	LE	KP54AZL
32629	NN	KP54KAX	32635	LE	KX05MGV	32641	LE	KP54AZC	32647	LE	KP54AZN
32630	NN	KP54KBE	32636	WS	WX05UAF	32642	LE	KP54AZD	32648	LE	KP54KBK
32631	LE	KP54KBF	32637	WS	WX05UAG	32643	LE	KP54AZF	32649	LE	KP54KBN
32632	LE	KP54KBJ	32638	WS	WX05UAH	32644	LE	KP54AZG	32650	LE	KP54KBO

32651-32656 Volvo B7TL 10.7m ADL ALX400 N47/27F 2005

32651	VN	AU05MUO	32653	VN	AU05MUV	32655	VN	AU05MUY	32656	VN	AU05MVA
32652	VN	AU05MUP	32654	VN	AU05MUW						

32657-32668 Volvo B7TL 10.7m Wrightbus Eclipse Gemini N41/21D 2005

32657	DG	LK55ACO	32660	DG	LK55AAF	32663	DG	LK55AAU	32666	DG	LK55AAY
32658	DG	LK55ACU	32661	DG	LK55AAJ	32664	DG	LK55AAV	32667	DG	LK55AAZ
32659	DG	LK55AAE	32662	DG	LK55AAN	32665	DG	LK55AAX	32668	DG	LK55ABF

32669-32683 Volvo B7TL 10.7m Wrightbus Eclipse Gemini N45/28F 2005

32669	DK	SN55HDZ	32673	DK	SN55HFA	32677	DK	SN55HFE	32681	DK	SN55HFJ
32670	DK	SN55HEJ	32674	DK	SN55HFB	32678	DK	SN55HFF	32682	DK	SN55HFK
32671	DK	SN55HEU	32675	DK	SN55HFC	32679	DK	SN55HFG	32683	DK	SN55HFL
32672	DK	SN55HEV	32676	DK	SN55HFD	32680	DK	SN55HFH			

East Lancs Coachbuilders of Blackburn have supplied several small batches of buses to First, mostly on Dennis chassis. Seen in *Tamar Link* livery is 32758, WA54OLT, which features the Myllennium Lolyne body. *Tamar Link* receives support from both Cornwall County Council and Caradon District Council with the vehicles carying this pink livery. *Mark Lyons*

32684-32697

Volvo B7TL 10.7m   Wrightbus Eclipse Gemini   N45/28F*   2006   *32692-7 are N45/27F

32684	BA	WX56HJZ	32688	BA	WX56HKD	32692	CR	YJ06XLK	32695	CR	YJ06XLN
32685	BA	WX56HKA	32689	BA	WX56HKE	32693	CR	YJ06XLL	32696	CR	YJ06XLO
32686	BA	WX56HKB	32690	BA	WX56HKF	32694	CR	YJ06XLM	32697	CR	YJ06XLP
32687	BA	WX56HKC	32691	BA	WX56HKG						

32701-32717

Dennis Trident   East Lancs Lolyne   N49/30F   2000

32701	HG	V701FFB	32705	HG	W705PHT	32709	PL	W709RHT	32714	PL	W714RHT
32702	HG	W702PHT	32706	HG	W706PHT	32711	PL	W711RHT	32715	PL	W715RHT
32703	HG	W703PHT	32707	HG	W707PHT	32712	PL	W712RHT	32716	PL	W716RHT
32704	HG	W704PHT	32708	HG	W708PHT	32713	PL	W713RHT	32717	PL	W717RHT

32751-32754

Dennis Trident   East Lancs Lolyne   N49/30F   2000

| 32751 | BB | X501BFJ | 32752 | BB | X502BFJ | 32753 | BB | X503BFJ | 32754 | BB | X504BFJ |

| 32755 | BB | WK52SYE | Dennis Trident | | East Lancs Myllennium Lolyne N49/30F | | | 2002 | | | |

32756-32768

Dennis Trident 9.9m   East Lancs Myllennium Lolyne   NC49/27F   2005

32756	PL	WA54OLO	32760	PL	WA54OLR	32763	PL	WJ55CSF	32766	BB	WJ55CSV
32757	PL	WA54OLP	32761	PL	WJ55CRX	32764	BB	WJ55CSO	32767	BB	WJ55CTE
32758	PL	WA54OLT	32762	PL	WJ55CRZ	32765	BB	WJ55CSU	32768	BB	WJ55CTF
32759	PL	WA54OLN									

32801-32822

Dennis Trident 9.9m   Plaxton President 4.4m   N39/20D*   1999   *seating varies

32801	X	T801LLC	32807	ONt	T807LLC	32813	NP	T813LLC	32818	H	T818LLC
32802	PL	T802LLC	32808	PL	T808LLC	32814	NP	T814LLC	32819	PL	T819LLC
32803	PL	T803LLC	32809	G	T809LLC	32815	NP	T815LLC	32820	CD	T820LLC
32804	NP	T804LLC	32810	X	T810LLC	32816	NP	T816LLC	32821	CD	T821LLC
32805	CD	T805LLC	32811	CD	T811LLC	32817	PL	T817LLC	32822	DGt	T822LLC
32806	DGt	T806LLC	32812	PL	T812LLC						

Plaxton President bodywork was built in Wigan following the acquisition of Northern Counties by the Scarbourough-based business. Several batches of Dennis Tridents with this bodywork were supplied to First's London operation with 32898, V898HLH, illustrated here in High Street, Cranford. *Mark Lyons*

32823-32853
Dennis Trident 9.9m   Plaxton President 4.4m   N39/20D*   1999   *seating varies

32823	CD	T823LLC	32831	CD	T831LLC	32839	NP	T839LLC	32847	NP	T847LLC
32824	CD	T824LLC	32832	CD	T832LLC	32840	NP	T840LLC	32848	CD	T848LLC
32825	CD	T825LLC	32833	CD	T833LLC	32841	NP	T841LLC	32849	NP	T849LLC
32826	CD	T826LLC	32834	CD	T834LLC	32842	NP	T842LLC	32850	NP	T850LLC
32827	CD	T827LLC	32835	CD	T835LLC	32843	NP	T843LLC	32851	NP	T851LLC
32828	CD	T828LLC	32836	CD	T836LLC	32844	NP	T844LLC	32852	NP	T852LLC
32829	CD	T829LLC	32837	CD	T837LLC	32845	NP	T845LLC	32853	NP	T853LLC
32830	CD	T830LLC	32838	NP	T838LLC	32846	PL	T846LLC			

32854-32887
Dennis Trident 9.9m   Plaxton President 4.4m   N39/20D   1999

32854	NP	T854KLF	32863	NP	V863HBY	32872	NP	V872HBY	32880	NP	T880KLF
32855	NP	V855HBY	32864	NP	T864KLF	32873	NP	T873KLF	32881	NP	T881KLF
32856	NP	V856HBY	32865	NP	V865KLF	32874	NP	V874HBY	32882	NP	V882HBY
32857	NP	V857HBY	32866	NP	T866KLF	32875	NP	T875KLF	32883	NP	T883KLF
32858	NP	V858HBY	32867	NP	V867HBY	32876	NP	T876KLF	32884	NP	T884KLF
32859	NP	V859HBY	32868	NP	T868KLF	32877	NP	V877HBY	32885	NP	T885KLF
32860	NP	V860HBY	32869	NP	V869HBY	32878	NP	T878KLF	32886	NP	V886HBY
32861	NP	V861HBY	32870	NP	T870KLF	32879	NP	T879KLF	32887	NP	V887HBY
32862	NP	V862HBY	32871	NP	T871KLF						

32888-32930
Dennis Trident 9.9m   Plaxton President 4.4m   N43/24D   2000

32888	UX	V988HLH	32899	G	V899HLH	32910	IS	W895VLN	32921	IS	W921VLN
32889	UX	V889HLH	32900	X	V990HLH	32911	IS	W896VLN	32922	IS	W922VLN
32890	UX	V890HLH	32901	X	W901VLN	32912	IS	W912VLN	32923	IS	W923VLN
32891	UX	V891HLH	32902	X	W902VLN	32913	IS	W913VLN	32924	IS	W924VLN
32892	UX	V892HLH	32903	X	W903VLN	32914	IS	W914VLN	32925	IS	W925VLN
32893	UX	V893HLH	32904	X	W904VLN	32915	IS	W915VLN	32926	IS	W926VLN
32894	NP	V894HLH	32905	X	W905VLN	32916	IS	W916VLN	32927	IS	W927VLN
32895	UX	V895HLH	32906	IS	W906VLN	32917	IS	W917VLN	32928	IS	W928VLN
32896	UX	V896HLH	32907	UX	W907VLN	32918	IS	W918VLN	32929	IS	W929VLN
32897	G	V897HLH	32908	IS	W908VLN	32919	IS	W919VLN	32930	UX	W899VLN
32898	G	V898HLH	32909	IS	W909VLN	32920	IS	W897VLN			

While the Alexander-bodied batch of Tridents has now been transferred to Glasgow's Parkhead depot, most of the Plaxton Presidents remain in London. Pictured in Acton is 32984, Y984NLP, the first from a 2001 batch that incorporated additional luggage space. *Mark Lyons*

32931-32952
Dennis Trident 9.9m   Alexander ALX400 4.4m   N45/24D   2000

32931	PH	W931ULL	32937	PH	W937ULL	32942	PH	W942ULL	32949	PH	W949ULL
32934	PH	W934ULL	32939	PH	W939ULL	32946	PH	W946ULL	32950	PH	W132VLO
32935	PH	W935ULL	32940	PH	W840VLO	32947	PH	W947ULL	32951	PH	W951ULL
32936	PH	W936ULL	32941	PH	W941ULL	32948	PH	W948ULL	32952	PH	W952ULL

32954-32983
Dennis Trident 9.9m   Plaxton President 4.4m   N39/23D   2001

32954	G	X954HLT	32962	X	X962HLT	32970	NP	X613HLT	32977	NP	X977HLT
32955	G	X611HLT	32963	X	X963HLT	32971	NP	X971HLT	32978	NP	X978HLT
32956	G	X956HLT	32964	X	X964HLT	32972	NP	X972HLT	32979	NP	Y224NLF
32957	NP	X957HLT	32965	X	X965HLT	32973	NP	X973HLT	32980	NP	X614HLT
32958	X	X958HLT	32966	X	X966HLT	32974	NP	X974HLT	32981	NP	X981HLT
32959	X	X959HLT	32967	NP	X967HLT	32975	NP	X975HLT	32982	NP	Y346NLF
32960	X	X612HLT	32968	NP	X968HLT	32976	NP	Y223NLF	32983	NP	Y344NLF
32961	X	X961HLT	32969	NP	X969HLT						

32984-33000
Dennis Trident 9.9m   Plaxton President 4.4m   N39/20D   2001

32984	G	Y984NLP	32989	G	Y989NLP	32993	G	Y993NLP	32997	G	Y997NLP
32985	G	Y985NLP	32990	G	Y932NLP	32994	G	Y994NLP	32998	G	Y998NLP
32986	G	Y986NLP	32991	G	Y991NLP	32995	G	Y995NLP	32999	G	Y933NLP
32987	G	Y987NLP	32992	G	Y992NLP	32996	G	Y996NLP	33000	G	Y934NLP
32988	G	Y988NLP									

33001-33036
Dennis Trident 10.5m   Plaxton President 4.4m   N42/23D   2001

33001	NP	LK51UZO	33011	L	LK51UZJ	33020	L	LK51UYX	33029	DG	LK51UYL
33002	NP	LK51UZP	33012	L	LK51UZL	33021	L	LK51UYY	33030	DG	LK51UYM
33003	NP	LK51UZS	33013	L	LK51UZM	33022	L	LK51UYZ	33031	DG	LK51UYN
33004	NP	LK51UZT	33014	L	LK51UZN	33023	L	LK51UZA	33032	DG	LK51UYO
33006	L	LK51UZD	33015	L	LK51UYS	33024	L	LK51UZB	33033	L	LK51UYP
33007	L	LK51UZE	33016	L	LK51UYT	33025	L	LK51UYF	33034	L	LK51UYR
33008	L	LK51UZF	33017	L	LK51UYU	33026	L	LK51UYG	33035	L	LK51UYD
33009	L	LK51UZG	33018	L	LK51UYV	33027	L	LK51UYH	33036	DG	LK51UYE
33010	L	LK51UZH	33019	L	LK51UYW	33028	L	LK51UYJ			

33037-33071   Dennis Trident 9.9m   Plaxton President 4.4m   N39/20D   2001

33037	UX	LN51DWA	33047	DG	LN51DVM	33056	DG	LN51GKP	33064	DG	LN51GKY
33039	DG	LN51DWD	33048	DG	LN51GKD	33057	DG	LN51GJJ	33065	DG	LN51GKZ
33040	X	LN51DWE	33049	DG	LN51GKE	33058	DG	LN51GJK	33066	DG	LN51GLF
33041	DG	LN51DWF	33050	UX	LN51GKF	33059	UX	LN51GJO	33067	DG	LN51GLJ
33042	DG	LN51DWG	33051	DG	LN51GKG	33060	DG	LN51GJU	33068	NP	LN51GLK
33043	DG	LN51DVG	33052	DG	LN51GKJ	33061	DG	LN51GKU	33069	DG	LN51GLV
33044	DG	LN51DVH	33053	DG	LN51GKK	33062	DG	LN51GKV	33070	DG	LN51GLY
33045	DG	LN51DVK	33054	DG	LN51GKL	33063	DG	LN51GKX	33071	DG	LN51GKA
33046	G	LN51DVL	33055	DG	LN51GKO						

33072-33099   Dennis Trident 10.5m   Plaxton President 4.4m   N42/23D   2002

33072	DG	LN51GOC	33079	DG	LN51GNK	33086	DG	LN51GMG	33093	NP	LN51NRJ
33073	DG	LN51GOE	33080	DG	LN51GNP	33087	DG	LN51GMO	33094	DG	LN51NRK
33074	DG	LN51GOH	33081	DG	LN51GNU	33088	DG	LN51GMU	33095	X	LN51NRL
33075	DG	LN51GOJ	33082	DG	LN51GNV	33089	X	LN51GMV	33096	L	LN51GNY
33076	DG	LN51GOK	33083	DG	LN51GNX	33090	L	LN51GMX	33097	L	LN51GNZ
33077	DG	LN51GNF	33084	DG	LN51GME	33091	DG	LN51GMY	33098	NP	LN51GOA
33078	DG	LN51GNJ	33085	DG	LN51GMF	33092	DG	LN51GMZ	33099	DG	LN51GLZ

33113-33129   Dennis Trident 9.9m   Plaxton President 4.4m   N39/20D   2002

33113	NP	LT02NVX	33118	NP	LT02NWA	33122	NP	LT02NVL	33126	NP	LT02NVO
33114	NP	LT02NVW	33119	NP	LT02NWB	33123	NP	LT02NVK	33127	NP	LT02NVP
33115	NP	LT02NVV	33120	NP	LT02NWC	33124	NP	LT02NVM	33128	NP	LT02NVR
33116	NP	LT02NVU	33121	NP	LT02NWD	33125	NP	LT02NVN	33129	NP	LT02NVS
33117	NP	LT02NVZ									

33131-33140   Dennis Trident 10.5m   Plaxton President 4.4m   N42/23D   2002

33131	UX	LT02ZBX	33134	UX	LT02ZCA	33137	UX	LT02ZFJ	33139	UX	LT02ZFL
33132	UX	LT02ZBY	33135	UX	LT02ZCE	33138	UX	LT02ZFK	33140	UX	LT02ZFM
33133	UX	LT02ZBZ	33136	UX	LT02ZCF						

33141-33154   Dennis Trident 9.9m   Plaxton President 4.4m   N39/20D   2002

33141	G	LR02LWW	33145	G	LR02LXA	33149	G	LR02LXH	33152	G	LR02LXL
33142	G	LR02LWX	33146	G	LR02LXB	33150	G	LR02LXJ	33153	G	LR02LXM
33143	G	LR02LWY	33147	G	LR02LXC	33151	X	LR02LXK	33154	G	LR02LXN
33144	G	LR02LWZ	33148	G	LR02LXG						

33155-33199   Dennis Trident 9.9m   Plaxton President 4.4m   N39/20D   2002

33155	G	LR02LXO	33167	G	LR02LYF	33178	X	LR02LYX	33189	X	LT52WVE
33156	G	LR02LXP	33168	G	LR02LYG	33179	X	LR02LYY	33190	X	LT52XAA
33157	G	LR02LXS	33169	G	LR02LYJ	33180	X	LR02LYZ	33191	X	LT52XAB
33158	G	LR02LXT	33170	G	LR02LYK	33181	X	LR02LZA	33192	X	LT52XAC
33159	G	LR02LXU	33171	G	LR02LYO	33182	X	LR02LZB	33193	X	LT52XAD
33160	G	LR02LXV	33172	G	LR02LYP	33183	X	LR02LZC	33194	X	LT52XAE
33161	G	LR02LXW	33173	G	LR02LYS	33184	X	LR02LZD	33195	X	LT52XAF
33162	G	LR02LXX	33174	G	LR02LYT	33185	X	LR02LZE	33196	X	LT52XAG
33163	G	LR02LXZ	33175	G	LR02LYU	33186	X	LT52WVB	33197	X	LT52XAH
33164	G	LR02LYA	33176	G	LR02LYV	33187	X	LT52WVC	33198	X	LT52XAJ
33165	G	LR02LYC	33177	G	LR02LYW	33188	X	LT52WVD	33199	X	LT52XAK
33166	G	LR02LYD									

33229-33248   Dennis Trident 9.9m   Plaxton President 4.4m   N39/20D   2002-03

33229	X	LT52WXG	33234	X	LT52WWX	33239	X	LT52WVH	33245	X	LT52WUW
33230	X	LT52WXH	33235	X	LT52WWY	33240	X	LT52WVJ	33246	X	LT52WUX
33231	X	LT52WXJ	33236	X	LT52WWZ	33242	X	LT52WVL	33247	X	LT52WUY
33232	X	LT52WXK	33237	X	LT52WVF	33244	X	LT52WUV	33248	X	LT52WVA
33233	X	LT52WWV	33238	X	LT52WVG						

33277-33293   Dennis Trident 9.9m   Plaxton President 4.4m   N39/20D   2003

33277	G	LK03NKC	33282	G	LK03NKP	33286	G	LK03NKU	33290	G	LK03NLA
33278	G	LK03NKD	33283	G	LK03NKR	33287	G	LK03NKW	33291	G	LK03NLC
33279	G	LK03NKE	33284	G	LK03NKS	33288	G	LK03NKX	33292	G	LK03NLP
33280	G	LK03NKF	33285	G	LK03NKT	33289	G	LK03NKZ	33293	G	LK03NLR
33281	G	LK03NKG									

Alexander Dennis introduced a new body for the Trident 2 chassis. This is the Enviro 400, currently available on Scania and Volvo chassis in addition to the Trident 2. Nine for Plymouth depot were supplied in 2006, represented here by 33418, WA56FTT, seen in the North Cross area of the city. *Mark Lyons*

33328-33342

TransBus Trident 9.9m   TransBus President 4.4m   N39/20D   2003

33328	UX	LK03UFD	33332	UX	LK03UFL	33336	UX	LK03UFR	33340	UX	LK03UFV
33329	UX	LK03UFE	33333	UX	LK03UFM	33337	UX	LK03UFS	33341	UX	LK03UFW
33330	UX	LK03UFG	33334	UX	LK03UFN	33338	UX	LK03UFT	33342	UX	LK03UFX
33331	UX	LK03UFJ	33335	UX	LK03UFP	33339	UX	LK03UFU			

33343-33386

TransBus Trident 10.5m   TransBus ALX400 4.4m   N42/21D   2003

33343	X	LK53EZV	33354	X	LK53FDA	33365	X	LK53EYF	33376	X	LK53EYV
33344	X	LK53EZW	33355	X	LK53EXT	33366	X	LK53EYG	33377	X	LK53EYW
33345	X	LK53EZX	33356	X	LK53EXU	33367	X	LK53EYH	33378	X	LK53EYX
33346	X	LK53EZZ	33357	X	LK53EXV	33368	X	LK53EYJ	33379	X	LK53EYY
33347	X	LK53FCF	33358	X	LK53EXW	33369	X	LK53EYL	33380	X	LK53EYZ
33348	X	LK53FCG	33359	X	LK53EXX	33370	X	LK53EYM	33381	X	LK53EZA
33349	X	LK53FCJ	33360	X	LK53EXZ	33371	X	LK53EYO	33382	X	LK53EZB
33350	X	LK53FCL	33361	X	LK53EYA	33372	X	LK53EYP	33383	X	LK53EZC
33351	X	LK53FCX	33362	X	LK53EYB	33373	X	LK53EYR	33384	X	LK53EZD
33352	X	LK53FCY	33363	X	LK53EYC	33374	X	LK53EYT	33385	X	LK53EZE
33353	X	LK53FCZ	33364	X	LK53EYD	33375	X	LK53EYU	33386	X	LK53EZF

33401-33405

TransBus Trident 10.7m   TransBus ALX400 4.4m   N47/27F   2004

33401	RH	VX54MTV	33403	RH	VX54MTZ	33404	RH	VX54MUA	33405	RH	VX54MUB
33402	RH	VX54MTY									

33411-33472

ADL Trident 2 11m   ADL Enviro 400   NC39/32F   2006 and on order

33411	PL	WA56FUB	33414	PL	WA56FTK	33417	PL	WA56FTP	33470	D&C	-
33412	PL	WA56FUD	33415	PL	WA56FTN	33418	PL	WA56FTT	33471	D&C	-
33413	PL	WA56FUE	33416	PL	WA56FTO	33419	PL	WA56FTU	33472	D&C	-

The 2008 First Bus Handbook

A batch of Enviro 400-bodied Trident 2s is currently entering service in London. These vehicles are the longer model as shown by 33502, LK57EJO, seen in Wapping shortly after entering service. *Mark Lyons*

33501-33543   ADL Trident 2 11m   ADL Enviro 400   N47/27F   2007-08

33501	DG	LK57EJN	33512	X	LK08LMU	33523	-	LK08	33534	-	LK08
33502	DG	LK57EJO	33513	X	LK08LMV	33524	-	LK08	33535	-	LK08
33503	DG	LK08FNE	33514	X	LK08LMX	33525	-	LK08	33536	-	LK08
33504	DG	LK08	33515	X	LK08LMY	33526	-	LK08	33537	-	LK08
33505	DG	LK08	33516	X	LK08LMZ	33527	-	LK08	33538	-	LK08
33506	DG	LK08	33517	X	LK08FNA	33528	-	LK08	33539	-	LK08
33507	DG	LK08	33518	X	LK08FNC	33529	-	LK08	33540	-	LK08
33508	DG	LK08	33519	X	LK08FND	33530	-	LK08	33541	-	LK08
33509	X	LK08LMA	33520	-	LK08	33531	-	LK08	33542	-	LK08
33510	X	LK08LMO	33521	-	LK08	33532	-	LK08	33543	-	LK08
33511	X	LK08LMP	33522	-	LK08	33533	-	LK08			

34001-34004   Volvo Olympian   Northern Counties Palatine   BC39/30F   1993

34001	BB	K801ORL	34002	PL	K802ORL	34003	BB	K803ORL	34004	BB	K804ORL

34006-34010   Volvo Olympian   Northern Counties Palatine II   B43/29F   1995

34006	MR	N306JBV	34008	MR	N308JBV	34009	MR	N309JBV	34010	MR	N310JBV
34007	MR	N307JBV									

34011-34040   Volvo Olympian   Northern Counties Palatine   B49/33F*   1996   Stagecoach, 2003
*34021/2/33 are B47/27D; 34023/8/9/31/5/7-40 are B49/30F

34011	BS	P551EFL	34017	HO	P537EFL	34023	KW	P533HMP	34036	KW	P536HMP
34012	BS	P552EFL	34018	CO	P546EFL	34028	KW	P528HMP	34037	KW	P537HMP
34013	CO	P553EFL	34019	KW	P529EFL	34029	KW	P529HMP	34038	KW	P538HMP
34014	CO	P554EFL	34020	WH	P530EFL	34031	KW	P531HMP	34039	KW	P539HMP
34015	BK	P535EFL	34021	HO	P541HMP	34033	SO	P543HMP	34040	KW	P540HMP
34016	HO	P536EFL	34022	HO	P542HMP	34035	KW	P535HMP			

34041-34055   Volvo Olympian   Northern Counties Palatine II   B43/27F   1996

34041	MR	P241UCW	34045	MR	P245UCW	34049	MR	P249UCW	34053	OG	P253UCW
34042	MR	P242UCW	34046	MR	P246UCW	34050	MR	P250UCW	34054	OG	P254UCW
34043	MR	P243UCW	34047	MR	P247UCW	34051	MR	P251UCW	34055	OG	P255UCW
34044	MR	P244UCW	34048	MR	P248UCW	34052	MR	P252UCW			

The 2008 First Bus Handbook

A batch of Olympians from 1999 has recently been transferred to Doncaster where most have been converted to single-door during refurbishment. Special destination blinds that fit the London style aperture have been incorporated as shown on 34097, T897KLF. *Richard Godfrey*

34056-34083

Volvo Olympian   Northern Counties Palatine   B49/33F   1996   Stagecoach, 2003
*34080 is B49/30F

34056	CO	P556EFL	34062	WH	P562EFL	34069	KW	P569EFL	34076	BK	P576EFL
34057	KW	P547EFL	34063	TN	P563EFL	34070	KW	P570EFL	34078	SO	P578EFL
34058	KW	P548EFL	34064	TN	P564EFL	34071	HO	P571EFL	34079	SO	P579EFL
34059	SO	P559EFL	34066	BK	P566EFL	34072	HO	P572EFL	34080	KW	P530HMP
34060	HO	P550EFL	34067	BK	P567EFL	34073	BK	P573EFL	34082	KW	P532EFL
34061	KW	P561EFL	34068	SO	P568EFL	34075	BK	P575EFL	34083	BK	P533EFL

34088-34107

Volvo Olympian   Northern Counties Palatine   B47/31F*   1999   *34096 is B47/27D

34088	DN	T988KLF	34093	DN	T893KLF	34098	DN	T898KLF	34103	DN	T903KLF
34089	DN	T889KLF	34094	DN	T894KLF	34099	DN	T899KLF	34104	DN	T904KLF
34090	DN	T890KLF	34095	DN	T895KLF	34100	DN	T990KLF	34105	DN	T905KLF
34091	DN	T891KLF	34096	DN	T896KLF	34101	DN	T901KLF	34106	DN	T906KLF
34092	DN	T892KLF	34097	DN	T897KLF	34102	DN	T902KLF	34107	DN	T907KLF

34108-34114

Volvo Olympian   Alexander Royale   BC43/29F   2000   Blazefield, Yorkshire, 2005-06

34108	BA	W435CWX	34110	BA	W437CWX	34112	BA	W432CWX	34114	BA	W434CWX
34109	BA	W436CWX	34111	BA	W431CWX	34113	BA	W433CWX			

34115	BB	L815CFJ	Volvo Olympian	Northern Counties Palatine	B47/29F	1993	
34116	BB	L816CFJ	Volvo Olympian	Northern Counties Palatine	B47/29F	1993	
34117	BB	L817CFJ	Volvo Olympian	Northern Counties Palatine	B47/29F	1993	
34128	SO	P828FEF	Volvo Olympian	Northern Counties Palatine	B49/33F	1996	Stagecoach, 2003
34129	SO	P829FEF	Volvo Olympian	Northern Counties Palatine	B49/33F	1996	Stagecoach, 2003
34130	SO	P830FEF	Volvo Olympian	Northern Counties Palatine	B49/33F	1996	Stagecoach, 2003

34131-34154

Volvo Olympian   Northern Counties Palatine II   B47/29F   1993-94

34131	MR	L631SEU	34137	LH	L637SEU	34143	LH	L643SEU	34149	BW	L649SEU
34132	MR	L632SEU	34138	LH	L638SEU	34144	LH	L644SEU	34151	BA	L651SEU
34133	MR	L633SEU	34139	LH	L639SEU	34145	LH	L645SEU	34152	BA	L652SEU
34134	LH	L634SEU	34140	LH	L640SEU	34146	LH	L646SEU	34153	MS	L653SEU
34135	LH	L635SEU	34141	LH	L641SEU	34147	LH	L647SEU	34154	WS	L654SEU
34136	LH	L636SEU	34142	LH	L642SEU	34148	LH	L648SEU			

34155-34164 — Volvo Olympian — Northern Counties Palatine II — B43/29F — 1997

34155	MS	P655UFB	34158	MS	P658UFB	34161	LH	R661NHY	34163	LH	R663NHY
34156	MS	P656UFB	34159	MS	P659UFB	34162	LH	R662NHY	34164	LH	R664NHY
34157	MS	P657UFB	34160	MS	P660UFB						

34165-34187 — Volvo Olympian — Northern Counties Palatine II — B43/29F — 1998

34165	WS	S665AAE	34172	BW	S672AAE	34178	BW	S678AAE	34183	MR	S683AAE
34167	WS	S667AAE	34173	TN	S673AAE	34179	BW	S679AAE	34184	MR	S684AAE
34168	WS	S668AAE	34174	TN	S674AAE	34180	BW	S680AAE	34185	MR	S685AAE
34169	WS	S669AAE	34175	TN	S675AAE	34181	MR	S681AAE	34186	LH	S686AAE
34170	WS	S670AAE	34176	TN	S676AAE	34182	MR	S682AAE	34187	LH	S687AAE
34171	WS	S671AAE	34177	TN	S677AAE						

34188-34191 — Volvo Olympian — Northern Counties Palatine II — BC47/29F — 1998

34188	WS	S688AAE	34189	WS	S689AAE	34190	WS	S690AAE	34191	WS	S691AAE

34192	CE	530OHU	Volvo Olympian	Alexander Royale	BC43/22F	1995	National Express, 2004
34193	CE	VJT738	Volvo Olympian	Alexander Royale	BC43/22F	1995	National Express, 2004
34194	CE	481FPO	Volvo Olympian	Alexander Royale	BC43/22F	1995	National Express, 2004
34195	CE	TJI4838	Volvo Olympian	Alexander Royale	BC43/22F	1995	National Express, 2004
34196	CE	OWB243	Volvo Olympian	Alexander Royale	BC43/22F	1995	National Express, 2004
34197	CE	HVJ716	Volvo Olympian	Alexander Royale	BC43/22F	1995	National Express, 2004
34198	PL	UKT552	Volvo Olympian	Alexander Royale	BC43/22F	1995	National Express, 2004
34199	CE	NER621	Volvo Olympian	Alexander Royale	BC43/22F	1995	National Express, 2004
34200	CE	VOO273	Volvo Olympian	Alexander Royale	BC43/22F	1995	National Express, 2004
34202	BA	M922UYG	Volvo Olympian	Alexander Royale	BC45/27F	1995	Blazefield, Keighley, 2005
34203	BA	M923UYG	Volvo Olympian	Alexander Royale	BC45/27F	1995	Blazefield, Keighley, 2005
34205	BA	M925UYG	Volvo Olympian	Alexander Royale	BC45/27F	1995	Blazefield, Keighley, 2005

34206-34222 — Volvo Olympian — Northern Counties Palatine — B47/31F* — 1998 — *34215/6/8 are B47/27D

34206	RO	S206LLO	34211	RO	S211LLO	34215	DG	S215LLO	34219	RO	S219LLO
34207	RO	S207LLO	34212	RO	S212LLO	34216	DG	S216LLO	34220	RO	S220LLO
34208	RO	S208LLO	34213	RO	S213LLO	34217	RO	S217LLO	34221	RO	S221LLO
34209	RO	S209LLO	34214	DN	S214LLO	34218	NP	S218LLO	34222	RO	S422LLO
34210	RO	S210LLO									

34223-34238 — Volvo Olympian — Alexander RH — B47/25D — 1997

34223	BH	P223MPU	34227	BH	P227MPU	34231	BH	P231MPU	34236	BH	P236MPU
34224	BH	P224MPU	34228	BH	P228MPU	34232	BH	P232MPU	34237	BH	P237MPU
34225	BH	P225MPU	34229	BH	P229MPU	34233	BH	P233MPU	34238	HP	P238MPU
34226	BH	P226MPU	34230	BH	P230MPU	34234	HP	P234MPU			

34239-34247 — Volvo Olympian — Northern Counties Palatine — B47/31F — 1996

34239	RO	P239HMD	34241	OG	N241CMP	34246	OG	P246HMD	34247	RO	N247CMP
34240	RO	P240HMD	34242	RO	P242HMD						

34249-34261 — Volvo Olympian — Northern Counties Palatine — B47/30F* — 1995 — Go-Ahead London, 2004-05
*seating varies; 34258 is PO47/27D

34249	SO	N547LHG	34253	BN	M403RVU	34256	BY	M406RVU	34259	SO	N533LHG
34251	BN	M401RVU	34254	BN	M404RVU	34257	BY	M407RVU	34260	BY	N536JHG
34252	BN	M402RVU	34255	BY	M405RVU	34258	WH	N528LHG	34261	SO	N542LHG

34262	BY	N412JBV	Volvo Olympian	Northern Counties Palatine	B43/30F	1995	Go-Ahead London, 2005
34263	BY	N423JBV	Volvo Olympian	Northern Counties Palatine	B43/30F	1995	Go-Ahead London, 2005
34264	BN.	M264SGY	Volvo Olympian	Alexander Royale	B45/29F	1995	Ensign Bus, 2005
34265	BN	M86MYM	Volvo Olympian	Alexander Royale	B45/29F	1995	Go-Ahead London, 2005

34274-34290 — Volvo Olympian — Alexander RL — B47/32F — 1996

34274	SH	P174TGD	34278	BL	P178TGD	34284	HA	P184TGD	34288	HA	P188TGD
34275	SH	P175TGD	34279	SH	P179TGD	34285	HA	P185TGD	34289	WR	P189TGD
34276	BL	P176TGD	34280	HA	P180TGD	34286	HA	P186TGD	34290	CO	P191TGD
34277	BL	P177TGD	34282	HA	P182TGD	34287	NN	P187TGD			

34291-34296 — Volvo Olympian — Northern Counties Palatine — B47/30F — 1996

34291	KW	P291KPX	34293	KW	P293KPX	34295	KW	P295KPX	34296	KW	P296KPX
34292	KW	P292KPX	34294	KW	P294KPX						

34301-34315 — Volvo Olympian YN2RV18Z4 — Northern Counties Palatine — B47/29F — 1994

34301	CO	L301PWR	34304	CO	L304PWR	34308	CO	L308PWR	34311	CO	L311PWR
34302	CO	L302PWR	34305	CO	L305PWR	34309	CO	L309PWR	34314	CO	L314PWR
34303	CO	L303PWR	34307	CO	L307PWR	34310	CO	L310PWR	34315	CO	L315PWR

34329-34345 — Leyland Olympian ON2R50C13Z4 — Northern Counties — B47/30F — 1990-91

34329	DG	H129FLX	34333	NR	H132FLX	34337	YA	H137FLX	34342	WH	H142FLX
34330	DG	H130FLX	34334	DK	J134YRM	34339	DG	H139FLX	34344	WH	H144FLX
34331	DGt	J131YRM	34335	WH	J135YRM	34340	DG	H140FLX	34345	DGt	H145FLX
34332	DK	J132YRM	34336	WH	H136FLX	34341	DG	H141FLX			

34346	LMt	J135PVC	Leyland Olympian ON2R50C13Z4	Leyland		B47/25D	1991	Volvo demonstrator, 1991
34349	PD	J149YRM	Leyland Olympian ON2R50C13Z4	Leyland		B47/29F	1991	
34350	PD	J150YRM	Leyland Olympian ON2R50C13Z4	Leyland		B47/29F	1991	
34351	PD	J151YRM	Leyland Olympian ON2R50C13Z4	Leyland		B47/29F	1991	
34355	u	L155UNS	Leyland Olympian ON2R50C13V3	Alexander RL		B47/31F	1993	
34502	WH	JHU902X	Leyland Olympian ONLXB/1R	Roe		B47/29F	1982	
34509	BP	JHU909X	Leyland Olympian ONLXB/1R	Roe		B47/29F	1982	
34540	WH	NTC140Y	Leyland Olympian ONLXB/1R	Roe		B47/29F	1983	
34541	WH	NTC141Y	Leyland Olympian ONLXB/1R	Roe		B47/29F	1983	

34606-34630 — Leyland Olympian ON2R56C16Z4 — Northern Counties Palatine — B44/32F — 1993

34606	BD	K606LAE	34613	BD	K613LAE	34619	BD	K619LAE	34625	MR	K625LAE
34607	BD	K607LAE	34614	BD	K614LAE	34620	BD	K620LAE	34626	MR	K626LAE
34608	BD	K608LAE	34615	BD	K615LAE	34621	BD	K621LAE	34627	MR	K627LAE
34609	BD	K609LAE	34616	BD	K616LAE	34622	MR	K622LAE	34628	MR	K628LAE
34610	BD	K610LAE	34617	BD	K617LAE	34623	MR	K623LAE	34629	MR	K629LAE
34611	BD	K611LAE	34618	BD	K618LAE	34624	MR	K624LAE	34630	MR	K630LAE
34612	BD	K612LAE									

34709	CE	A809THW	Leyland Olympian ONLXB/1R	Roe		CO47/29F	1984	
34710	CE	A810THW	Leyland Olympian ONLXB/1R	Roe		CO47/29F	1984	
34713	CE	D513HUB	Leyland Olympian ONTL11/1R	Optare		B43/27F	1987	
34714	CE	D514HUB	Leyland Olympian ONTL11/1R	Optare		B43/27F	1987	
34719	u	C819BYY	Leyland Olympian ONLXB/1RH	Eastern Coach Works		B42/30F	1986	Truronian, 2008
34724	u	C24CHM	Leyland Olympian ONLXB/1RH	Eastern Coach Works		B42/26D	1986	Truronian, 2008

34750-34755 — Leyland Olympian ONLXB/1R — Eastern Coach Works — BC44/32F* — 1983 — *34750 is O44/32F

34750	CEs	A750VAF	34752	CE	A752VAF	34754	CE	A754VAF	34755	CE	A755VAF
34751	CE	A751VAF	34753	CE	A753VAF						

34787	u	C87CHM	Leyland Olympian ONLXB/1RH	Eastern Coach Works		B42/26D	1986	Truronian, 2008

34807-34818 — Leyland Olympian ONLXB/1R — Eastern Coach Works — BC42/30F — 1986

34807	CM	C407HJN	34812	PL	C412HJN	34814	WH	C414HJN	34817	PL	C417HJN
34809	PL	C409HJN	34813	PL	C413HJN	34815	CM	C415HJN	34818	CM	C418HJN
34810	WH	C410HJN									

34822	KL	F102AVG	Leyland Olympian ONLXB/1RZ	Northern Counties		B40/35F	1989	
34825	LO	F105AVG	Leyland Olympian ONLXB/1RZ	Northern Counties		B40/35F	1989	
34826	u	F106AVG	Leyland Olympian ONLXB/1RZ	Northern Counties		B40/35F	1989	
34858	CE	F158XYG	Leyland Olympian ONCL10/1RZ	Northern Counties		B45/29F	1988	
34872	IP	F172LBL	Leyland Olympian ONCL10/1RZ	Northern Counties		B45/29F	1988	
34873	IP	F173LBL	Leyland Olympian ONCL10/1RZ	Northern Counties		B45/29F	1988	
34876	LO	F176LBL	Leyland Olympian ONCL10/1RZ	Northern Counties		B45/29F	1988	

34901-34904 — Leyland Olympian ON2R50G13Z4 — Leyland — B45/32F — 1990

34901	KL	H101KVX	34902	NR	H102KVX	34903	NR	H103KVX	34904	KL	H104KVX

34921-34928 — Leyland Olympian ONCL10/1RZ — Alexander RL — B47/33F — 1990

34921	LO	G121YEV	34923	u	G123YEV	34926	LO	G126YEV	34928	IP	G128YEV
34922	LO	G122YEV	34925	IP	G125YEV						

34933	IP	G133ATW	Leyland Olympian ONCL10/1RZ	Northern Counties		B45/30F	1989	

34946-34955 — Leyland Olympian ONCL10/1RZ — Alexander RL — B47/28F — 1989

34946	u	G46XLO	34950	LO	G50XLO	34952	LO	G52XLO	34955	KL	G55XLO
34948	LO	G48XLO	34951	KL	G51XLO						

34961-34970

Leyland Olympian ONCL10/1RZ Leyland B47/31F* 1989 *34969/70 are BC43/29F

34961	CE	G901TWS	34965	CE	G905TWS	34967	YV	G907TWS	34969	CE	G909TWS
34962	CE	G902TWS	34966	YV	G906TWS	34968	CE	G908TWS	34970	CE	G910TWS
34964	CE	G904TWS									

34972	LO	J622BVG	Leyland Olympian ON2R50G13Z4	Leyland	B47/31F	1991
34973	LO	J623BVG	Leyland Olympian ON2R50G13Z4	Leyland	B47/31F	1992
34989	SO	E289HRV	Leyland Olympian ONLXB/1RH	East Lancs	BC43/27F	1987
34990	SO	E290HRV	Leyland Olympian ONLXB/1RH	East Lancs	BC43/27F	1987

35001-35004

Wrightbus/VDL Bus integral Wrightbus N / D 2008 On order for London

35001	-	-	35002	-	-	35003	-	-	35004	-	-

36001-36006

Scania N94UD East Lancs OmniDekka NC43/26F 2004-05

36001	WH	YN04GNV	36003	WH	YN04GNY	36005	WH	YN04GLV	36006	WH	YN05HGA
36002	WH	YN04GNX	36004	WH	YN04GNZ						

36007-36030

Scania N94UD East Lancs OmniDekka N43/26F 2005

36007	LV	SN05HWW	36013	LV	SN05HWL	36019	LV	SN05HWH	36025	LV	SN05HWS
36008	LV	SN05HWX	36014	LV	SN05HWK	36020	LV	SN05HWE	36026	LV	SN05HWU
36009	LV	SN05HWY	36015	LV	SN05HWO	36021	LV	SN05HWP	36027	LV	SN05HWV
36010	LV	SN05HWZ	36016	LV	SN05HWM	36022	LV	SN05HWF	36028	LV	SN05HWT
36011	LV	SN05HXA	36017	LV	SN05HWJ	36023	LV	SN05HWD	36029	LV	SN55KKE
36012	LV	SN05HXB	36018	LV	SN05HWG	36024	LV	SN05HWR	36030	LV	SN55KKF

36922	BM	F422GWG	Scania N113DRB	Alexander RH	B43/33F	1988	Black Prince, 2005
36925	u	F425GWG	Scania N113DRB	Alexander RH	B47/33F	1988	Black Prince, 2005
36930	BM	G379NRC	Scania N113DRB	Alexander RH	B47/33F	1989	Black Prince, 2005
36932	BM	H232LOM	Scania N113DRB	Alexander RH	B47/31F	1990	Black Prince, 2005
36935	u	H235LOM	Scania N113DRB	Alexander RH	B47/31F	1990	Black Prince, 2005
36936	u	H236LOM	Scania N113DRB	Alexander RH	B47/31F	1990	Black Prince, 2005
36938	u	H237LOM	Scania N113DRB	Alexander RH	B47/31F	1990	Black Prince, 2005
36950	u	J810HMC	Scania N113DRB	Alexander RH	B47/31F	1990	Black Prince, 2005
36951	u	J821HMC	Scania N113DRB	Alexander RH	B47/31F	1990	Black Prince, 2005

37001-37020

Volvo B7TL Wrightbus Eclipse Gemini N45/29F 2005

37001	HG	WX55VHK	37006	HG	WX55VHP	37011	HG	WX55VHW	37016	HG	WX55VJD
37002	HG	WX55VHL	37007	HG	WX55VHR	37012	HG	WX55VHY	37017	HG	WX55VJE
37003	HG	WX55VHM	37008	HG	WX55VHT	37013	HG	WX55VHZ	37018	HG	WX55VJF
37004	HG	WX55VHN	37009	HG	WX55VHU	37014	HG	WX55VJA	37019	HG	WX55VJG
37005	HG	WX55VHO	37010	HG	WX55VHV	37015	HG	WX55VJC	37020	HG	WX55VJJ

Interesting additions to the First fleet at Weymouth and Livingston are semi-integral Scania double-decks. These were completed at East Lancs under the OmniDekka name, a product subsequently built in integral form in Poland. Pictured in Edinburgh is 36008, SN05HWX.
Mark Lyons

The current standard double-deck for First is the Volvo B9TL with Wrightbus Eclipse Gemini bodywork of which some 400 are on order for the coming months. One of five recent arrivals at Southampton is 37162, HY07FSV. *Mark Lyons*

37021-37062 Volvo B7TL Wrightbus Eclipse Gemini N45/27F 2006

37021	CR	YJ06XKK	37032	CR	YJ06XKX	37043	BD	YJ06XLT	37053	BD	YJ06XMD
37022	CR	YJ06XKL	37033	CR	YJ06XKY	37044	BD	YJ06XLU	37054	BD	YJ06XME
37023	CR	YJ06XKM	37034	CR	YJ06XKZ	37045	BD	YJ06XLV	37055	BD	YJ06XMF
37024	CR	YJ06XKN	37035	CR	YJ06XLA	37046	BD	YJ06XLW	37056	BD	YJ06XMG
37025	CR	YJ06XKO	37036	CR	YJ06XLB	37047	BD	YJ06XLX	37057	BD	YJ06XMH
37026	CR	YJ06XKP	37037	CR	YJ06XLC	37048	BD	YJ06XLY	37058	BD	YJ06XMK
37027	CR	YJ06XKS	37038	CR	YJ06XLD	37049	BD	YJ06XLZ	37059	BD	YJ06XML
37028	CR	YJ06XKT	37039	CR	YJ06XLE	37050	BD	YJ06XMA	37060	BD	YJ06XMM
37029	CR	YJ06XKU	37040	CR	YJ06XLF	37051	BD	YJ06XMB	37061	BD	YJ06XMO
37030	CR	YJ06XKV	37041	CR	YJ06XLG	37052	BD	YJ06XMC	37062	BD	YJ06XMP
37031	CR	YJ06XKW	37042	CR	YJ06XLH						

37063-37132 Volvo B9TL Wrightbus Eclipse Gemini N45/27F 2007-08

37063	BD	YK57EZS	37081	BD	YJ08GVT	37099	BD	YJ08GWP	37116	HP	YK07AYP
37064	BD	YK57EZT	37082	BD	YJ08GVU	37100	BD	YJ08GWU	37117	HP	YK07AYS
37065	BD	YK57EZU	37083	BD	YJ08GVV	37101	BD	YJ08GWV	37118	HP	YK07AYT
37066	BD	YK57EZV	37084	BD	YJ08GVW	37102	BD	YJ08GWW	37119	HP	YK07AYU
37067	BD	YK57EZW	37085	BD	YJ08GVX	37103	HP	YK07AYA	37120	HP	YK07AYV
37068	BD	YK57EZX	37086	BD	YJ08GVY	37104	HP	YK07AYB	37121	HP	YK07AYW
37069	BD	YK57EZZ	37087	BD	YJ08GVZ	37105	HP	YK07AYC	37122	HP	YK07AYX
37070	BD	YK57FAA	37088	BD	YJ08GWA	37106	HP	YK07AYD	37123	HP	YK07AYY
37071	BD	YJ08GVE	37089	BD	YJ08GWC	37107	HP	YK07AYE	37124	HP	YK07AYZ
37072	BD	YJ08GVF	37090	BD	YJ08GWD	37108	HP	YK07AYF	37125	HP	YK57CJF
37073	BD	YJ08GVG	37091	BD	YJ08GWE	37109	HP	YK07AYG	37126	HP	YK57CJJ
37074	BD	YJ08GVK	37092	BD	YJ08GWF	37110	HP	YK07AYH	37127	HP	YK57CJO
37075	BD	YJ08GVL	37093	BD	YJ08GWG	37111	HP	YK07AYJ	37128	HP	YK57CJU
37076	BD	YJ08GVM	37094	BD	YJ08GWK	37112	HP	YK07AYL	37129	HP	YK57CJV
37077	BD	YJ08GVN	37095	BD	YJ08GWL	37113	HP	YK07AYM	37130	HP	YK57CJX
37078	BD	YJ08GVO	37096	BD	YJ08GWM	37114	HP	YK07AYN	37131	HP	YK57CJY
37079	BD	YJ08GVP	37097	BD	YJ08GWN	37115	HP	YK07AYO	37132	HP	YK57CJZ
37080	BD	YJ08GVR	37098	BD	YJ08GWO						

37133-37145   Volvo B9TL   Wrightbus Eclipse Gemini   N45/27F   2007

37133	GS	SN57HDH	37137	LV	SN57HCV	37140	LV	SN57HCZ	37143	LV	SN57HDD
37134	GS	SN57HDJ	37138	LV	SN57HCX	37141	LV	SN57HDA	37144	LV	SN57HDE
37135	LW	SN57HCP	37139	LV	SN57HCY	37142	LV	SN57HDC	37145	LV	SN57HDF
37136	LV	SN57HCU									

37146-37155   Volvo B7TL   Wrightbus Eclipse Gemini   N45/27F   2006

37146	VN	YN06UPZ	37149	OG	YN06URC	37152	OG	YN06URF	37154	OG	YN06URH
37147	OG	YN06URA	37150	OG	YN06URD	37153	OG	YN06URG	37155	OG	YN06URJ
37148	OG	YN06URB	37151	OG	YN06URE						

37156-37165   Volvo B7TL   Wrightbus Eclipse Gemini   N45/27F   2007

37156	VN	AU07DXS	37159	VN	AU07DXW	37162	SO	HY07FSV	37164	SO	HY07FSU
37157	VN	AU07DXT	37160	VN	AU07DXX	37163	SO	HY07FSZ	37165	SO	HY07FSX
37158	VN	AU07DXV	37161	SO	HY07FTA						

37166-37185   Volvo B7TL   Wrightbus Eclipse Gemini   N45/27F   2007

37166	LF	SF07FCP	37171	LF	SF07FDA	37176	LF	SF07FDJ	37181	LF	SF07FDO
37167	LF	SF07FCV	37172	LF	SF07FDC	37177	LF	SF07FDK	37182	LF	SF07FDP
37168	LF	SF07FCX	37173	LF	SF07FDD	37178	LF	SF07FDL	37183	LF	SF07FDU
37169	LF	SF07FCY	37174	LF	SF07FDE	37179	LF	SF07FDM	37184	LF	SF07FDV
37170	LF	SF07FCZ	37175	LF	SF07FDG	37180	LF	SF07FDN	37185	LF	SF07FDX

37186-37227   Volvo B9TL   Wrightbus Eclipse Gemini   N45/27F   2007

37186	LF	SF07FDY	37197	LF	SF07FEM	37208	LF	SF57MKG	37218	LF	SF57MKX
37187	LF	SF07FDZ	37198	LF	SF07FEO	37209	LF	SF57MKJ	37219	LF	SF57MKZ
37188	LF	SF07FCC	37199	LF	SF07FCL	37210	LF	SF57MKK	37220	LF	SF57MLE
37189	LF	SF07FCD	37200	LF	SF07FEP	37211	LF	SF57MKL	37221	LF	SF57MLJ
37190	LF	SF07FCE	37201	LF	SF07FCM	37212	LF	SF57MKM	37222	LF	SF57MKK
37191	LF	SF07FCG	37202	LF	SF07FCO	37213	LF	SF57MKN	37223	LF	SF57MLL
37192	LF	SF07FCJ	37203	LF	SF07FET	37214	LF	SF57MKO	37224	LF	SF57MLN
37193	LF	SF07FEG	37204	LF	SF07FEU	37215	LF	SF57MKP	37225	LF	SF57MLO
37194	LF	SF07FEH	37205	LF	SF57MKA	37216	LF	SF57MKU	37226	LF	SF57MLU
37195	LF	SF07FEJ	37206	LF	SF57MKC	37217	LF	SF57MKV	37227	LF	SF57MLV
37196	LF	SF07FEK	37207	LF	SF57MKD						

37228-37265   Volvo B9TL   Wrightbus Eclipse Gemini   N45/29F   2007-08

37228	DN	YN57RJU	37238	DN	YN08LCT	37248	RO	YN07MKF	37257	u	YN07MKX
37229	DN	YN08LCJ	37239	DN	YN08LCU	37249	RO	YN07MKG	37258	RO	YN07MKZ
37230	DN	YN08LCK	37240	DN	YN08LCV	37250	RO	YN07MKJ	37259	RO	YN07MLE
37231	DN	YN08LCL	37241	DN	YN08LCW	37251	RO	YN07MKK	37260	RO	YN07MLF
37232	DN	YN57RJZ	37242	DN	YN08LCY	37252	RO	YN07MKL	37261	RO	YN07MLJ
37233	RO	YN57RKA	37243	DN	YN08LCZ	37253	RO	YN07MKM	37262	RO	YN07MLK
37234	DN	YN08LCM	37244	DN	YN08LDA	37254	RO	YN07MKO	37263	RO	YN07MLL
37235	DN	YN08LCO	37245	DN	YN08LDC	37255	RO	YN07MKP	37264	RO	YN07MLO
37236	DN	YN57RKJ	37246	RO	YN07MKD	37256	RO	YN07MKV	37265	RO	YN07MLU
37237	DN	YN08LCP	37247	RO	YN07MKE						

37266-37278   Volvo B9TL   Wrightbus Eclipse Gemini   N45/29F*   2008   *37264-6 are NC / F

37266	LW	SN57HDG	37269	LW	SN57JBE	37272	LW	SN57JBV	37275	BL	
37267	LW	SN57JAO	37270	LW	SN57JBO	37273	LW	SN57JBX	37276	BL	
37268	LW	SN57JAU	37271	LW	SN57JBU	37274	BL		37278	DN	YN08LDD

37279-37314   Volvo B9TL   Wrightbus Eclipse Gemini   N45/29F   2007

37279	QS	MX07BPY	37288	QS	MX07BSZ	37297	QS	MX07BUE	37306	WN	MX07BVA
37280	QS	MX07BPZ	37289	QS	MX07BTE	37298	QS	MX07BUF	37307	WN	MX07BVC
37281	QS	MX07BRF	37290	QS	MX07BTF	37299	BY	MX07BUH	37308	WN	MX07BVD
37282	QS	MX07BRV	37291	QS	MX07BTO	37300	BY	MX07BUJ	37309	WN	MX07BVE
37283	QS	MX07BRZ	37292	QS	MX07BTU	37301	BY	MX57HDZ	37310	WN	MX07BVF
37284	QS	MX07BSO	37293	QS	MX07BTV	37302	BN	MX57HEJ	37311	WN	MX07BVG
37285	QS	MX07BSU	37294	QS	MX07BTY	37303	BN	MX07BUU	37312	WN	MX07BVJ
37286	QS	MX07BSV	37295	QS	MX07BTZ	37304	BN	MX07BUV	37313	WN	MX07BVK
37287	QS	MX07BSY	37296	QS	MX07BUA	37305	BN	MX07BUW	37314	WN	MX07BVL

Bristol's Lawrence Hill depot received a large batch of Volvo B9TLs in 2007, including 37353, WX57HLP, pictured in Hanham while working route 45. As we go to press the type is being supplied to Aberdeen and South Wales with a Manchester order to follow. *Mark Lyons*

37315-37359 Volvo B9TL   Wrightbus Eclipse Gemini   N45/27F   2007

37315	WS	WX57HJO	37327	LH	WX57HKH	37338	LH	WX57HKW	37349	LH	WX57HLK
37316	WS	WX57HJU	37328	LH	WX57HKJ	37339	LH	WX57HKY	37350	LH	WX57HLM
37317	WS	WX57HJV	37329	LH	WX57HKK	37340	LH	WX57HKZ	37351	LH	WX57HLN
37318	LH	WX57HJY	37330	LH	WX57HKL	37341	LH	WX57HLA	37352	LH	WX57HLO
37319	LH	WX57HJZ	37331	LH	WX57HKM	37342	LH	WX57HLC	37353	LH	WX57HLP
37320	LH	WX57HKA	37332	LH	WX57HKN	37343	LH	WX57HLD	37354	LH	WX57HLR
37321	LH	WX57HKB	37333	LH	WX57HKO	37344	LH	WX57HLE	37355	LH	WX57HLU
37322	LH	WX57HKC	37334	LH	WX57HKP	37345	LH	WX57HLF	37356	LH	WX57HLV
37323	LH	WX57HKD	37335	LH	WX57HKT	37346	LH	WX57HLG	37357	LH	WX57HLW
37324	LH	WX57HKE	37336	LH	WX57HKU	37347	LH	WX57HLH	37358	LH	WX57HLY
37325	LH	WX57HKF	37337	LH	WX57HKV	37348	LH	WX57HLJ	37359	LH	WX57HLZ
37326	LH	WX57HKG									

37360-37440 Volvo B9TL   Wrightbus Eclipse Gemini   N45/27F   2008   On order

37360	BD		37381	-	MX	37401	-	MX	37421	-	MX
37361	BD		37382	-	MX	37402	-	MX	37422	-	MX
37362	BD		37383	-	MX	37403	-	MX	37423	-	MX
37363	BD		37384	-	MX	37404	-	MX	37424	-	MX
37364	BD		37385	-	MX	37405	-	MX	37425	-	MX
37365	BD		37386	-	MX	37406	-	MX	37426	-	MX
37366	BD		37387	-	MX	37407	-	MX	37427	-	MX
37367	-	MX	37388	-	MX	37408	-	MX	37428	-	MX
37368	-	MX	37389	-	MX	37409	-	MX	37429	-	MX
37369	-	MX	37390	-	MX	37410	-	MX	37430	-	MX
37370	-	MX	37391	-	MX	37411	-	MX	37431	-	MX
37371	-	MX	37392	-	MX	37412	-	MX	37432	-	MX
37372	-	MX	37393	-	MX	37413	-	MX	37433	-	MX
37373	-	MX	37394	-	MX	37414	-	MX	37434	-	MX
37374	-	MX	37395	-	MX	37415	-	MX	37435	-	MX
37375	-	MX	37396	-	MX	37416	-	MX	37436	-	MX
37376	-	MX	37397	-	MX	37417	-	MX	37437	-	MX
37377	-	MX	37398	-	MX	37418	-	MX	37438	-	MX
37378	-	MX	37399	-	MX	37419	-	MX	37439	-	MX
37379	-	MX	37400	-	MX	37410	-	MX	37440	-	MX
37380	-	MX									

37441-37471 — Volvo B9TL — Wrightbus Eclipse Gemini — N45/29F — 2008 — On order for Manchester

37441	-	37449	-	37457	-	37465	-
37442	-	37450	-	37458	-	37466	-
37443	-	37451	-	37459	-	37467	-
37444	-	37452	-	37460	-	37468	-
37445	-	37453	-	37461	-	37469	-
37446	-	37454	-	37462	-	37470	-
37447	-	37455	-	37463	-	37471	-
37448	-	37456	-	37464	-		

37472-37529 — Volvo B9TL — Wrightbus Eclipse Gemini — N45/29F — 2008 — On order for South Yorkshire

37472	OG	YN08NLL	37487	OG	YN08NMK	37502	-	-	37516	-	-
37473	OG	YN08NLM	37488	OG	YN08NMO	37503	-	-	37517	-	-
37474	OG	YN08NLO	37489	OG	YN08NMU	37504	-	-	37518	-	-
37475	OG	YN08NLP	37490	OG	YN08NMV	37505	-	-	37519	-	-
37476	OG	YN08NLR	37491	OG	YN08NMX	37506	-	-	37520	-	-
37477	OG	YN08NLT	37492	OG	YN08NMY	37507	-	-	37521	-	-
37478	OG	YN08NLU	37493	-	-	37508	-	-	37522	-	-
37479	OG	YN08NLV	37494	-	-	37509	-	-	37523	-	-
37480	OG	YN08NLX	37495	-	-	37510	-	-	37524	-	-
37481	OG	YN08NLY	37496	-	-	37511	-	-	37525	-	-
37482	OG	YN08NLZ	37497	-	-	37512	-	-	37526	-	-
37483	OG	YN08NMA	37498	-	-	37513	-	-	37527	-	-
37484	OG	YN08NME	37499	-	-	37514	-	-	37528	-	-
37485	OG	YN08NMF	37500	-	-	37515	-	-	37529	-	-
37486	OG	YN08NMJ	37501	-	-						

37530-37544 — Volvo B9TL — Wrightbus Eclipse Gemini — N45/29F — 2008 — On order for Glasgow

37530	-	-	37534	-	-	37538	-	-	37542	-	-
37531	-	-	37535	-	-	37539	-	-	37543	-	-
37532	-	-	37536	-	-	37540	-	-	37544	-	-
37533	-	-	37537	-	-	37541	-	-			

37580-37586 — Volvo B9TL — Wrightbus Eclipse Gemini — N45/29F — 2008 — On order for Hampshire

37580	-	-	37582	-	-	37584	-	-	37586	-	-
37581	-	-	37583	-	-	37585	-	-			

37633-37644 — Volvo B9TL — Wrightbus Eclipse Gemini — N45/29F — 2008

37633	AB	SV08FXP	37636	AB	SV08FXU	37639	AB	SV08FXX	37642	AB	SV08FYA
37634	AB	SV08FXS	37637	AB	SV08FXV	37640	AB	SV08FXY	37643	AB	SV08FYB
37635	AB	SV08FXT	37638	AB	SV08FXW	37641	AB	SV08FXZ	37644	AB	SV08FYC

38000-38082 — Volvo Citybus B10M-50 — Alexander RV — BC47/35F* — 1987 — *38000-6 are O47/35F

38000	CE	D700GHY	38004	CE	D704GHY	38007	TR	D707GHY	38010	HGs	D710GHY
38001	CE	D701GHY	38005	CE	D705GHY	38008	TR	D708GHY	38016	PL	E216BTA
38002	CE	D702GHY	38006	CE	D706GHY	38009	TR	D709GHY	38082	NN	LSU717

38083	NN	F83XBD	Volvo Citybus B10M-50	Alexander RV	BC47/35F	1987
38085	WR	F85XBD	Volvo Citybus B10M-50	Alexander RV	BC47/35F	1989
38089	DK	H289VRP	Volvo Citybus B10M-55	Alexander RV	BC47/35F	1990
38091	GS	H291VRP	Volvo Citybus B10M-55	Alexander RV	BC47/35F	1990
38092	GS	H292VRP	Volvo Citybus B10M-55	Alexander RV	BC47/35F	1990

38095-38099 — Volvo Citybus B10M-50 — Alexander RV — BC47/35F — 1991

38096	GS	J296GNV	38097	WR	J297GNV	38098	NN	J298GNV	38099	NN	J299GNV

38121	NN	K121URP	Volvo Citybus B10M-50	Alexander RV	BC47/35F	1992
38122	NN	WSU481	Volvo Citybus B10M-50	East Lancs Pyoneer (1998)	BC49/39F	1992

38123-38132 — Volvo Citybus B10M-50 — Alexander RV — BC47/35F — 1992-93

38123	KD	K123URP	38126	RH	K126URP	38128	OM	K128URP	38130	PH	K130GNH
38124	RH	K124URP	38127	OM	K127URP	38129	LTt	K129GNH	38132	LFt	K132GNH
38125	KD	K125URP									

While most of the Routemasters operated by First are in London, three remain at Great Yarmouth where they sport different liveries. Seen in the former Great Yarmouth Transport colours is 39717, SMK717F.
Mark Doggett

38790	CMs	KOO790V	Bristol VRT/SL3/6LXB	Eastern Coach Works	B43/31F	1978
38844	PLs	LFJ844W	Bristol VRT/SL3/6LXB	Eastern Coach Works	B43/31F	1980
39167	LEt	G667FKA	Dennis Dominator DDA1024	East Lancs	TV	1990

39442-39735

			AEC Routemaster R2RH1	Park Royal	B40/32R	1965-67

39442	LHC	JJD442D	**39623**	YA	NML623E	**39717**	YA	SMK717F	**39735**	Xs	SMK735F
39480	YA	JJD480D								

39804	X	204CLT	AEC Routemaster R2RH	Park Royal/Marshall	B36/28R	1962	LBL, 2005
39809	Xs	SSL609	AEC Routemaster R2RH	Park Royal	O36/28R	1959	LBPG, Cobham, 1999
39810	Xs	510CLT	AEC Routemaster R2RH1	Park Royal	O36/28R	1962	London Buses, 2004
39813	X	ALD913B	AEC Routemaster R2RH	Park Royal/Marshall	B36/28R	1964	LBL, 2005
39818	X	218CLT	AEC Routemaster R2RH	Park Royal/Marshall	B36/28R	1962	LBL, 2005
39827	X	627DYE	AEC Routemaster R2RH	Park Royal/Marshall	B36/28R	1963	LBL, 2005
39835	X	735DYE	AEC Routemaster R2RH	Park Royal/Marshall	B36/28R	1963	LBL, 2005
39840	X	640DYE	AEC Routemaster R2RH	Park Royal/Marshall	B36/28R	1962	LBL, 2005
39853	Ds	ZV6741	AEC Routemaster R2RH	Park Royal	O36/28R	1960	London Coaches, 2002
39862	X	562CLT	AEC Routemaster R2RH	Park Royal/Marshall	B36/28R	1962	LBL, 2005
39876	X	776DYE	AEC Routemaster R2RH	Park Royal/Marshall	B36/28R	1962	LBL, 2005
39880	u	280CLT	AEC Routemaster R2RH	Park Royal/Marshall	B36/28R	1962	LBL, 2005
39901	CEs	YSO231T	Leyland Atlantean AN68A/1R	Alexander AL	O45/29D	1978	
39902	CEs	HRS262V	Leyland Atlantean AN68A/1R	Alexander AL	O45/29D	1980	
39911	CE	A811THW	Leyland Olympian ONLXB/1R	Roe	CO47/29F	1984	
39913	PLs	A813THW	Leyland Olympian ONLXB/1R	Roe	CO47/29F	1984	
39920	WS	L650SEU	Volvo Olympian	Northern Counties Palatine II	O47/29F	1993	
39932	CH	C814BYY	Leyland Olympian ONLXB/1RH	Eastern Coach Works	O42/26D	1986	Arriva, 2008
39933	CH	D183FYM	Leyland Olympian ONLXB/1RH	Eastern Coach Works	PO42/26D	1986	Arriva, 2008
39934	WHs	VDV134S	Bristol VRT/SL3/6LXB	Eastern Coach Works	O43/31F	1978	
39935	CH	D235FYM	Leyland Olympian ONLXB/1RH	Eastern Coach Works	O42/26D	1987	Arriva, 2008
39936	CH	D158FYM	Leyland Olympian ONLXB/1RH	Eastern Coach Works	PO42/26D	1987	Arriva, 2008
39938	CH	D238FYM	Leyland Olympian ONLXB/1RH	Eastern Coach Works	PO42/26D	1987	Arriva, 2008
39939	CH	D251FYM	Leyland Olympian ONLXB/1RH	Eastern Coach Works	O42/26D	1987	Arriva, 2008
39950	Xs	650DYE	AEC Routemaster R2RH	Park Royal/Marshall	B36/28R	1963	Reading Buses, 2000
39971	WH	MOD571P	Bristol VRT/SL3/6LXB	Eastern Coach Works	O43/31F	1976	

The number of Darts and Volvo B6s has reduced since the last edition of this book, as the older buses are replaced by larger single-decks. New to Greater Manchester, although now allocated to Lowestoft where it was pictured is 40185, M610SBA. The bus is a Dennis Dart with Northern Counties Paladin bodywork. *Mark Doggett*

40000	BN	P301LND	Dennis Dart SLF	Plaxton Pointer	N41F	1996	
40001	BN	P309LND	Dennis Dart SLF	Plaxton Pointer	N41F	1996	
40002	PL	S764RNE	Dennis Dart SLF 8.8m	Plaxton Pointer MPD	N28F	1999	Springfield Cs, Wigan, 2001
40003	AG	S766RNE	Dennis Dart SLF 8.8m	Plaxton Pointer MPD	N28F	1999	Springfield Cs, Wigan, 2001

40004-40013   Optare Solo M850   Optare   N27F   1999

40004	YV	T157BBF	40007	AG	T160BBF	40010	NE	T163BBF	40012	YV	T165BBF
40005	YV	T158BBF	40008	AG	T161BBF	40011	NE	T164BBF	40013	AG	T168BBF
40006	YV	T159BBF	40009	AG	T162BBF					

40014-40019   Optare Solo M850   Optare   N27F   2000

40014	AG	W473SVT	40016	NE	W475SVT	40018	NE	W477SVT	40019	NE	W478SVT
40015	NE	W474SVT	40017	NE	W476SVT					

40020-40029   Optare Solo M850   Optare   N27F   2000

40020	AG	X289XFA	40023	AG	X293XFA	40026	AG	X296XFA	40028	AG	X298XFA
40021	AG	X291XFA	40024	AG	X294XFA	40027	AG	X297XFA	40029	AG	X299XFA
40022	AG	X292XFA	40025	AG	X295XFA					

40030	AG	T371NUA	Dennis Dart SLF	Alexander ALX200	N37F	1999	

40033-40039   Dennis Dart SLF 10.7m   Plaxton Pointer 2   N41F   1998-99   New World First Bus, 2001

40033	PL	S343SUX	40035	PL	S375SUX	40037	PL	S377SUX	40039	PL	S389SUX
40034	PL	S374SUX	40036	PL	S376SUX	40038	PL	S378SUX			

40042	BH	S765RNE	Dennis Dart SLF	Plaxton Pointer MPD	N28F	1999	Springfield Cs, Wigan, 2001
40064	WN	P701HMT	Optare Excel L960	Optare	N33F	1996	
40065	WN	P702HMT	Optare Excel L960	Optare	N33F	1996	
40066	WN	P703HMT	Optare Excel L960	Optare	N33F	1996	
40067	WN	P704HMT	Optare Excel L960	Optare	N33F	1996	
40086	HD	K919XRF	Dennis Dart 9m	Plaxton Pointer	BC35F	1992	
40100	CC	L934HFA	Dennis Dart 9m	Plaxton Pointer	BC35F	1993	

    The 2008 First Bus Handbook

40109	BH	M943SRE	Dennis Dart		Marshall C37	BC35F	1994
40110	BH	M945SRE	Dennis Dart		Marshall C37	BC35F	1994
40113	YA	M952SRE	Dennis Dart		Marshall C37	BC35F	1994

40114-40130

Dennis Dart 9.8m				Plaxton Pointer	BC36F	1995

40114	YA	M953XVT	40120	CH	M959XVT	40124	BH	M964XVT	40129 CC M971XVT
40115	AG	M954XVT	40121	CH	M960XVT	40126	AG	M968XVT	40130 CH M972XVT
40116	AG	M955XVT	40123	CC	M962XVT	40128	CH	M970XVT	

40131	BH	P973MBF	Dennis Dart		Plaxton Pointer	B36F	1997
40132	BH	P974MBF	Dennis Dart		Plaxton Pointer	B36F	1997
40133	BH	P975MBF	Dennis Dart		Plaxton Pointer	B36F	1997
40134	CC	P976MBF	Dennis Dart		Plaxton Pointer	B36F	1997

40135-40139

Dennis Dart SLF				Plaxton Pointer 2	N37F	1998

40135	CC	R977NVT	40137	CC	R979NVT	40138	CC	R980NVT	40139 CC R981NVT
40136	CC	R978NVT							

40140-40147

Dennis Dart SLF				Alexander ALX200	N37F	1999

40140	AG	T982LBF	40142	NE	T984LBF	40144	NE	T986LBF	40146 NE V988GBF
40141	AG	T983LBF	40143	NE	T985LBF	40145	NE	T987LBF	40147 NE V989GBF

40148-40155

Dennis Dart SLF				Alexander ALX200	N37F	1999-2000

40148	NE	X991FFA	40150	NE	X993FFA	40152	NE	X995FFA	40154 AG T365NUA
40149	NE	X992FFA	40151	NE	X994FFA	40153	AG	T364NUA	40155 AG T372NUA

40156	CH	V69GEH	Optare Solo M850		Optare	N27F	1999
40157	CH	V470GBF	Optare Solo M850		Optare	N27F	1999

40158-40161

Dennis Dart SLF				Marshall Capital	N31F	1997

40158	AG	P124NLW	40159	AG	P138NLW	40160	RA	P139NLW	40161 RA P117NLW

40163	AG	R431PSH	Dennis Dart SLF		Plaxton Pointer 2	N37F	1998
40164	AG	R335HYG	Dennis Dart SLF		Plaxton Pointer 2	N35F	1998

40165-40173

Dennis Dart SLF				Marshall Capital	N31F	1997

40165	AG	P118NLW	40168	AG	P121NLW	40170	AG	P123NLW	40172 AG P125NLW
40166	AG	P119NLW	40169	AG	P122NLW	40171	AG	P140NLW	40173 AG P126NLW
40167	AG	P120NLW							

40174	AG	S246CSF	Dennis Dart SLF		Plaxton Pointer 2	N38F	1998
40175	AG	S247CSF	Dennis Dart SLF		Plaxton Pointer 2	N38F	1998
40176	AG	P127NLW	Dennis Dart SLF		Marshall Capital	N31F	1997
40177	AG	P128NLW	Dennis Dart SLF		Marshall Capital	N31F	1997
40178	AG	P141NLW	Dennis Dart SLF		Marshall Capital	N31F	1997
40179	AG	R330HYG	Dennis Dart SLF		Plaxton Pointer 2	N35F	1998
40180	AG	V41DTE	Optare Solo M850		Optare	N24F	1999
40181	AG	V42DTE	Optare Solo M850		Optare	N24F	1999
40182	AG	V43DTE	Optare Solo M850		Optare	N24F	1999
40185	LO	M610SBA	Dennis Dart 9.8m		Northern Counties Paladin	B39F	1995
40186	LF	M611SBA	Dennis Dart 9.8m		Northern Counties Paladin	B39F	1995
40187	LO	M612SBA	Dennis Dart 9.8m		Northern Counties Paladin	B39F	1995
40218	QS	N71YNF	Volvo B6LE		Wright Crusader	N37F	1995

40219-40233

Volvo B6LE				Wright Crusader	N38F*	1996	*seating varies

40219	QS	N372CJA	40223	QS	N376CJA	40227	QS	N380CJA	40231 QS N384CJA
40220	QS	N373CJA	40224	QS	N377CJA	40228	QS	N381CJA	40232 QS N385CRJ
40221	QS	N374CJA	40225	QS	N378CJA	40229	QS	N382CJA	40233 QS N386CRJ
40222	QS	N375CJA	40226	QS	N379CJA	40230	QS	N383CJA	

40245	KD	M101RRJ	Dennis Dart 9.8m		Northern Counties Paladin	B39F	1995
40250	SO	M106RRJ	Dennis Dart 9.8m		Northern Counties Paladin	B39F	1995

40251-40270

Dennis Dart 9.8m				Northern Counties Paladin	B39F	1996

40251	YA	N619CDB	40257	YA	N625CDB	40262	HO	N630CDB	40268 BNs N636CDB
40254	LF	N622CDB	40259	YA	N627CDB	40265	HO	N633CDB	40269 KD N637CDB
40256	IP	N624CDB	40261	u	N629CDB	40267	B	N645CDB	40270 LF N638CDB

40273-40285 — Dennis Dart 9.8m — Plaxton Pointer — B40F — 1996

40273	TE	N641CDB	40279	TE	N647CDB	40282	TE	N650CDB	40284	KD	N652CDB
40274	TE	N642CDB	40280	TE	N648CDB	40283	TE	N651CDB	40285	TE	N653CDB
40277	TE	N645CDB									

40288	YA	M944SRE	Dennis Dart 9m	Marshall C37	B39F	1994
40290	u	M947SRE	Dennis Dart 9m	Marshall C37	B39F	1994
40291	YA	M948SRE	Dennis Dart 9m	Marshall C37	B39F	1994

40292-40303 — Dennis Dart 9.8m — Plaxton Pointer — B37F* — 1996 — *40292 is BC36F

40292	SO	N965XVT	40297	SO	N603XJM	40301	B	N608XJM	40303	TE	N610XJM
40295	TE	N601XJM	40298	SO	N604XJM	40302	TE	N609XJM			

40304	AG	V71GEH	Optare Solo M850	Optare	N24F	1999
40305	NE	V472GBF	Optare Solo M850	Optare	N24F	1999

40308-40317 — Optare Solo M850 — Optare — N28F — 2000

40308	TE	X611OBN	40311	QS	X614OBN	40314	TE	X617OBN	40316	TE	X619OBN
40309	TE	X612OBN	40312	TE	X615OBN	40315	TE	X618OBN	40317	TE	X627OBN
40310	TE	X613OBN	40313	TE	X616OBN						

40318-40322 — Optare Solo M920 — Optare — N28F — 2000

40318	OM	Y901KNB	40320	OM	Y903KNB	40321	OM	Y904KNB	40322	OM	Y905KNB
40319	OM	Y902KNB									

40323-40326 — Optare Solo M850 — Optare — N24F — 2001

40323	QS	MA51AET	40324	QS	MA51AEU	40325	QS	MA51AEV	40326	QS	MA51AEW

40327-40336 — Optare Solo M920 — Optare — N28F — 2002

40327	QS	ML02OFW	40330	QS	ML02OFZ	40333	QS	ML02OGC	40335	QS	ML02OGE
40328	QS	ML02OFX	40331	QS	ML02OGA	40334	QS	ML02OGD	40336	u	ML02OGF
40329	QS	ML02OFY	40332	QS	ML02OGB						

40337-40359 — Dennis Dart SLF — Plaxton Pointer — N41F* — 1996-97 — *40341 is N37F

40337	BN	P302LND	40343	BN	P308LND	40349	BN	P315LND	40355	BN	P321LND
40338	BN	P303LND	40344	BN	P310LND	40350	BN	P316LND	40356	BN	P322LND
40339	BN	P304LND	40345	HU	P311LND	40351	BN	P317LND	40357	BN	P323LND
40340	BN	P305LND	40346	HU	P312LND	40352	BN	P318LND	40358	BN	P324LND
40341	BN	P306LND	40347	BN	P313LND	40353	BN	P319LND	40359	BN	P325LND
40342	BN	P307LND	40348	BN	P314LND	40354	BN	P320LND			

40360-40406 — Dennis Dart SLF — Plaxton Pointer 2 — N37F* — 1997 — *40389-99 are N34F

40360	BN	R234SBA	40372	TE	R246SBA	40384	TE	R258SBA	40396	WN	R270SBA
40361	TE	R235SBA	40373	AG	R247SBA	40385	WN	R259SBA	40397	WN	R271SBA
40362	TE	R236SBA	40374	TE	R248SBA	40386	WN	R262SBA	40398	WN	R272SBA
40363	BN	R237SBA	40375	AG	R249SBA	40387	WN	R261SBA	40399	WN	R273SBA
40364	TE	R238SBA	40376	AG	R250SBA	40388	WN	R260SBA	40400	BN	R274SBA
40365	TE	R239SBA	40377	AG	R251SBA	40389	WN	R263SBA	40401	BN	R275SBA
40366	TE	R240SBA	40378	AG	R252SBA	40390	WN	R264SBA	40402	BN	R276SBA
40367	AG	R241SBA	40379	AG	R253SBA	40391	WN	R265SBA	40403	TE	R277SBA
40368	TE	R242SBA	40380	TE	R254SBA	40392	WN	R266SBA	40404	BN	R278SBA
40369	TE	R243SBA	40381	TE	R255SBA	40393	WN	R267SBA	40405	BN	R279SBA
40370	TE	R244SBA	40382	TE	R256SBA	40394	WN	R268SBA	40406	TE	R280SBA
40371	TE	R245SBA	40383	AG	R257SBA	40395	WN	R269SBA			

40407-40436 — Dennis Dart SLF — Wright Crusader — N41F — 1996-97

40407	OM	P501LND	40415	OM	P509LND	40423	OM	P517LND	40430	OM	P524LND
40408	OM	P502LND	40416	OM	P510LND	40424	OM	P518LND	40431	OM	P525LND
40409	OM	P503LND	40417	OM	P511LND	40425	OM	P519LND	40432	OM	P526LND
40410	OM	P504LND	40418	OM	P512LND	40426	OM	P520LND	40433	OM	P527LND
40411	OM	P505LND	40419	OM	P513LND	40427	OM	P521LND	40434	OM	P528LND
40412	OM	P506LND	40420	OM	P514LND	40428	OM	P522LND	40435	OM	P529LND
40413	OM	P507LND	40421	OM	P515LND	40429	OM	P523LND	40436	OM	P530LND
40414	OM	P508LND	40422	OM	P516LND						

The more common body on the low-entry Volvo B6s favoured by First is the Wright Crusader which was introduced in 1995. Seen at Ashton-under-Lyne is 40431, P525LND, from Oldham depot having worked the rural Carrbrook service. *Richard Godfrey*

40437-40444

			Volvo B6BLE			Wright Crusader 2		N36F	1999
40437	QS	T701PND	40439	QS	T703PND	40441	QS	T705PND	40443	QS	T707PND
40438	QS	T702PND	40440	QS	T704PND	40442	QS	T706PND	40444	QS	T708PND

40445	QS	X611NBU	Volvo B6BLE	Wrightbus Crusader 2	N38F	2000
40446	QS	Y394RTD	Volvo B6BLE	Wrightbus Crusader 2	N38F	2001
40447	QS	Y393RTD	Volvo B6BLE	Wrightbus Crusader 2	N38F	2001
40448	DN	M918MRW	Volvo B6LE	Wright Crusader	N36F	1995	Volvo demonstrator, 1996

40450-40479

			Volvo B6-9.9m			Plaxton Pointer		B40F	1995
40450	u	M411VHE	40459	RO	M420VHE	40471	RO	M432VHE	40476	u	M437VHE
40456	RO	M417VHE	40460	u	M421VHE	40472	RO	M433VHE	40477	RO	M438VHE
40457	DN	M418VHE	40468	RO	M429VHE	40475	RO	M436VHE	40479	RO	M440VHE
40458	RO	M419VHE	40470	RO	M431VHE						

40480-40490

			Volvo B6LE			Wright Crusader		N36F*	1995-97	*40489/90 are NC36F
40480	DN	N443BKY	40483	DN	N446BKY	40485	DN	N448BKY	40489	DN	P452LWE
40481	DN	N144BWG	40484	DN	N447BKY	40486	DN	N449BKY	40490	DN	P453LWE
40482	DN	N445BKY									

40493-40502

			Volvo B6BLE			Wright Crusader 2		N36F	1999
40493	DN	T456JDT	40496	DN	T459JDT	40499	DN	T462JDT	40501	DN	T464JDT
40494	DN	T457JDT	40497	DN	T460JDT	40500	DN	T463JDT	40502	DN	T465JDT
40495	DN	T458JDT	40498	DN	T461JDT						

40503	RO	3913WE	Volvo B6-9.9m	Alexander Dash	B40F	1995
40504	RO	KIB6110	Volvo B6-9.9m	Alexander Dash	B40F	1996

40513-40543

			Dennis Dart SLF 11.3m			Plaxton Pointer SPD		N41F	1998
40513	RO	S508UAK	40521	DN	S516UAK	40529	RO	S524UAK	40537	RO	S532UAK
40514	RO	S509UAK	40522	DN	S517UAK	40530	RO	S525UAK	40538	RO	S533UAK
40515	RO	S510UAK	40523	DN	S518UAK	40531	RO	S526UAK	40539	RO	S534UAK
40516	RO	S511UAK	40524	DN	S519UAK	40532	RO	S527UAK	40540	RO	S535UAK
40517	RO	S512UAK	40525	DN	S520UAK	40533	RO	S528UAK	40541	DN	S536UAK
40518	DN	S513UAK	40526	RO	S521UAK	40534	RO	S529UAK	40542	DN	S537UAK
40519	DN	S514UAK	40527	DN	S522UAK	40535	RO	S530UAK	40543	DN	S538UAK
40520	DN	S515UAK	40528	DN	S523UAK	40536	RO	S531UAK			

The Wright Crusader 2 body is fitted to the low-floor B6BLE and this variant is seen on 40558, T307VYG, as it leaves Glasgow for East Kilbride. *Mark Doggett*

40546-40552

		Dennis Dart		Plaxton Pointer		B40F*	1996	*40549-52 are B32F

40546	u	N281JUM	40547	u	N282JUM	40549	DN	N814FLW	40552	DN	N817FLW

40558-40569

		Volvo B6BLE		Wright Crusader 2		N36F	1999

40558	B	T307VYG	40561	B	T310VYG	40564	QS	T313VYG	40567	QS	T316VYG
40559	B	T308VYG	40562	B	T311VYG	40565	QS	T314VYG	40568	QS	T317VYG
40560	B	T309VYG	40563	B	T312VYG	40566	QS	T315VYG	40569	QS	T318VYG

40570-40599

		Volvo B6BLE		Wrightbus Crusader 2		N38F	2001-02

40570	PL	YJ51PZZ	40578	YK	YJ51RHU	40586	PL	YJ51RJX	40593	YK	YG02DHY
40571	YK	YJ51RKO	40579	YK	YJ51RHV	40587	YK	YJ51RFZ	40594	YK	YG02DLK
40572	YK	YJ51RKU	40580	PL	YJ51RHX	40588	YK	YJ51RGO	40595	DN	YG02DLF
40573	YK	YJ51RKV	40581	PL	YJ51RHY	40589	YK	YJ51RGU	40596	DN	YG02DLE
40574	YK	YJ51RSV	40582	PL	YJ51RHZ	40590	YK	YJ51RGV	40597	YK	YG02DKY
40575	YK	YJ51RSX	40583	PL	YJ51RJO	40591	YK	YJ51RGX	40598	YK	YG02DKX
40576	YK	YJ51RSY	40584	PL	YJ51RJU	40592	YK	YG02DHP	40599	YK	YG02DHX
40577	YK	YJ51RHO	40585	PL	YJ51RJV						

40607-40636

		Dennis Dart 9.8m		Plaxton Pointer		B40F	1995

40600	HP	M204VWW	40602	YA	M210VWW	40603	NR	M211VWW	40604	LF	M212VWW

40607-40636

		Dennis Dart 9.8m		Alexander Dash		B40F	1995

40607	u	M234VWW	40614	KT	M242VWW	40624	BM	M255VWW	40630	u	M261VWW
40608	KT	M235VWW	40615	BM	M243VWW	40625	u	M256VWW	40631	u	M262VWW
40609	KT	M236VWW	40616	SO	M244VWW	40626	BM	M257VWW	40632	BM	M263VWW
40610	u	M237VWW	40617	u	M245VWW	40627	SO	M258VWW	40634	HX	M265VWW
40611	u	M238VWW	40618	BM	M246VWW	40628	SO	M259VWW	40635	HX	M266VWW
40612	BM	M240VWW	40620	SO	M248VWW	40629	SO	M260VWW	40636	HX	M267VWW
40613	KT	M241VWW	40623	HO	M254VWW						

Plaxton Pointer bodywork dominates the Dennis Dart midibus chassis. Seen in Leeds, 40650, N285JUM, carries a body built at the Scarborough facility, while later Pointer bodies were built at Falkirk.
Richard Godfrey

40638-40662

			Dennis Dart		Plaxton Pointer		B40F	1996	
40638	HP	N269JUM	**40643**	HP	N274JUM	**40649**	HP	N284JUM	**40655**	CR	N290JUM
40639	HP	N270JUM	**40644**	HP	N275JUM	**40650**	HP	N285JUM	**40657**	CR	N292JUM
40640	HP	N271JUM	**40645**	HP	N276JUM	**40651**	HP	N286JUM	**40658**	HP	N293JUM
40641	HP	N272JUM	**40646**	HP	N277JUM	**40652**	HP	N287JUM	**40659**	HP	N294JUM
40642	HP	N273JUM	**40647**	HP	N278JUM	**40654**	CR	N289JUM	**40662**	HP	N297JUM

40666-40669

			Dennis Dart SLF		Plaxton Pointer 2		N35F	1998	
40666	HX	R326HYG	**40667**	HX	R329HYG	**40668**	HX	R331HYG	**40669**	HU	R332HYG

40670	AG	S341EWU	Dennis Dart SLF	Plaxton Pointer 2	N33F	1998

40671-40680

			Dennis Dart SLF		Alexander ALX200		N37F	1999	
40671	HX	S345EWU	**40674**	HX	T348EUB	**40677**	HX	T351EUB	**40679**	HX	T353EUB
40672	HX	T346EUB	**40675**	HX	T349EUB	**40678**	HX	T352EUB	**40680**	HX	T354EUB
40673	HX	T347EUB	**40676**	HX	T350EUB						

40681	HX	R432PSH	Dennis Dart SLF	Plaxton Pointer 2	N37F	1998	
40682	AG	T166BBF	Optare Solo M850	Optare	N27F	1999	
40683	CH	T167BBF	Optare Solo M850	Optare	N27F	1999	
40687	u	N232KAE	Dennis Dart 9.8m	Plaxton Pointer	B40F	1995	
40688	PL	S337TJX	Dennis Dart SLF	Plaxton Pointer 2	N36F	1998	New World First Bus, 2001
40697	DK	P828YUM	Dennis Dart SLF	Plaxton Pointer	N35F	1997	
40698	DK	P832YUM	Dennis Dart SLF	Plaxton Pointer	N35F	1997	
40701	DK	P835YUM	Dennis Dart SLF	Plaxton Pointer	N35F	1997	
40703	MU	R324HYG	Dennis Dart SLF	Plaxton Pointer 2	N35F	1998	
40706	MU	R342HYG	Dennis Dart SLF	Plaxton Pointer 2	N35F	1998	
40708	MU	R343HYG	Dennis Dart SLF	Plaxton Pointer 2	N35F	1998	
40721	SH	T375NUA	Dennis Dart SLF 10.8m	Alexander ALX200	N37F	1999	
40722	B	R308GHS	Dennis Dart SLF	Plaxton Pointer 2	N37F	1998	
40723	LF	SH51MHO	Optare Solo M920	Optare	N30F	2002	
40724	LF	P2UVG	Dennis Dart SLF	UVG Urbanstar	N39F	1997	UVG demonstrator, 1997

The 2008 First Bus Handbook

40725-40732 — Volvo B6LE — Alexander ALX200 — N35F — 1997

40725	B	P508VOS	40727	B	P511VOS	40729	B	P513VOS	40732	B	P516VOS
40726	B	P510VOS	40728	B	P512VOS	40731	B	P515VOS			

40733-40742 — Dennis Dart SLF — Plaxton Pointer — N40F — 1997

40733	B	P626WSU	40737	B	P630WSU	40739	LF	P632WSU	40741	B	P634WSU
40734	B	P627WSU	40738	B	P631WSU	40740	B	P633WSU	40742	B	P635WSU
40736	B	P629WSU									

40743-40756 — Dennis Dart SLF — UVG Urbanstar — N39F* — 1997 — *40747 is N43F

40743	LF	P748XUS	40747	LF	P752XUS	40751	LF	P757XUS	40754	LF	P760XUS
40744	LF	P749XUS	40748	LF	P753XUS	40752	LF	P758XUS	40755	LF	P761XUS
40745	LF	P750XUS	40749	LF	P754XUS	40753	LF	P759XUS	40756	LF	P762XUS
40746	LF	P751XUS	40750	LF	P756XUS						

40757-40768 — Volvo B6LE — Alexander ALX200 — N35F — 1997

40757	B	P807YUM	40760	B	P810YUM	40764	B	P814YUM	40767	B	P817YUM
40758	B	P808YUM	40762	B	P812YUM	40765	B	P815YUM	40768	B	P818YUM
40759	B	P809YUM	40763	B	P813YUM	40766	B	P816YUM			

40770-40776 — Dennis Dart SLF — Plaxton Pointer — N35F* — 1997 — *40771 is N32F

40770	LF	P822YUM	40773	LF	P825YUM	40775	B	P830YUM	40776	B	P831YUM
40771	HU	P823YUM	40774	B	P829YUM						

40777	HH	P856VUS	Dennis Dart SLF	East Lancs Spryte	N37F	1997
40778	HH	P858VUS	Dennis Dart SLF	East Lancs Spryte	N37F	1997
40779	HH	P859VUS	Dennis Dart SLF	East Lancs Spryte	N37F	1997
40780	LF	P860VUS	Dennis Dart 9.8m	Plaxton Pointer	B40F	1997
40781	LF	P861VUS	Dennis Dart 9.8m	Plaxton Pointer	B40F	1997
40782	LF	P889TCV	Dennis Dart SLF	Plaxton Pointer	N35F	1997
40783	LF	P890TCV	Dennis Dart SLF	Plaxton Pointer	N35F	1997

40784-40813 — Dennis Dart SLF — Plaxton Pointer 2 — N37F — 1997-98

40784	SO	R288GHS	40792	SO	R296GHS	40800	B	R305GHS	40807	B	R314GHS
40785	SO	R289GHS	40793	SO	R297GHS	40801	B	R307GHS	40808	B	R315GHS
40786	SO	R290GHS	40794	SO	R298GHS	40802	B	R309GHS	40809	B	R317GHS
40787	SO	R291GHS	40795	SO	R299GHS	40803	B	R310GHS	40810	B	R319GHS
40788	SO	R292GHS	40796	B	R301GHS	40804	B	R311GHS	40811	B	R321GHS
40789	RO	R293GHS	40797	B	R302GHS	40805	WR	R312GHS	40812	B	R322GHS
40790	SO	R294GHS	40798	B	R303GHS	40806	B	R313GHS	40813	B	R324GHS
40791	SO	R295GHS	40799	B	R304GHS						

40814-40844 — Dennis Dart SLF — Plaxton Pointer 2 — N37F — 1997-98

40814	B	R631DUS	40822	SO	R642DUS	40830	B	R667DUS	40838	WR	R675DUS
40815	B	R632DUS	40823	HO	R643DUS	40831	B	R668DUS	40839	B	R676DUS
40816	B	R633DUS	40824	HO	R644DUS	40832	B	R669DUS	40840	LF	R677DUS
40817	B	R634DUS	40825	SO	R645DUS	40833	WR	R670DUS	40841	RO	R678DUS
40818	B	R636DUS	40826	SO	R646DUS	40834	LF	R671DUS	40842	B	R757DYS
40819	B	R637DUS	40827	SO	R647DUS	40835	BA	R672DUS	40843	RO	R758DYS
40820	B	R638DUS	40828	B	R664DUS	40836	PT	R673DUS	40844	RO	R759DYS
40821	RO	R641DUS	40829	B	R665DUS	40837	WR	R674DUS			

40845-40858 — Optare Solo M920 — Optare — N30F — 2002

40845	LF	SA02BZP	40849	SN	SH51MHM	40853	LF	SH51MHX	40856	SN	SH51MKN
40846	LF	SA02BZR	40850	SN	SH51MHN	40854	LF	SH51MJY	40857	SN	SH51MKO
40847	LF	SA02BZS	40851	LF	SH51MHU	40855	SN	SH51MKM	40858	LF	SH51MKP
40848	SN	SA02BZT	40852	LF	SH51MHV						

40867	HX	R334HYG	Dennis Dart SLF	Plaxton Pointer 2	N35F	1998
40868	HX	R341HYG	Dennis Dart SLF	Plaxton Pointer 2	N35F	1998
40869	HU	N701CPU	Dennis Dart SLF	Plaxton Pointer	N37F	1996
40870	HU	P819YUM	Dennis Dart SLF	Plaxton Pointer	N37F	1997
40871	HU	P702HPU	Dennis Dart SLF	Plaxton Pointer	N37F	1996
40872	HU	P628WSU	Dennis Dart SLF	Plaxton Pointer	N33F	1997
40873	HU	S140AGR	Dennis Dart SLF	Plaxton Pointer 2	N34F	1999
40874	HU	P824YUM	Dennis Dart SLF	Plaxton Pointer	N32F	1997
40875	HU	P827YUM	Dennis Dart SLF	Plaxton Pointer	N32F	1997

The low-floor Pointer 2 was introduced in 1997 and this model now dominates First's midibus fleet. New to Strathclyde as MD116, 40793, R297GHS, is currently based in Southampton where it is seen heading for Moorgreen. *Paul Gainsbury*

40876-40879

			Dennis Dart SLF			Plaxton Pointer		N31F	1996		
40876	HU	P706HPU	**40877**	HU	P707HPU	**40878**	HU	P704HPU	**40879**	HU	P703HPU

40880	HX	R608YCR	Dennis Dart SLF	Plaxton Pointer 2	N37F	1997	
40881	HX	R458BNG	Dennis Dart SLF	Plaxton Pointer 2	N37F	1997	
40882	B	L673RMD	Volvo B6-9.9	Alexander Dash	B31F	1994	
40883	B	L675RMD	Volvo B6-9.9	Alexander Dash	B31F	1994	
40884	B	L676RMD	Volvo B6-9.9	Alexander Dash	B31F	1994	
40885	B	L678RMD	Volvo B6-9.9	Alexander Dash	B31F	1994	
40886	B	L679RMD	Volvo B6-9.9	Alexander Dash	B31F	1994	
40887	MU	P201NSC	Dennis Dart SLF	Plaxton Pointer	N35F	1996	
40888	BK	P202NSC	Dennis Dart SLF	Plaxton Pointer	N35F	1996	
40889	BK	P214NSC	Dennis Dart SLF	Plaxton Pointer	N38F	1997	
40890	MU	P218YSH	Dennis Dart SLF	Plaxton Pointer	N39F	1997	
40891	PT	R224GFS	Dennis Dart SLF	Plaxton Pointer 2	N37F	1997	

40892-40899

			Dennis Dart SLF			Plaxton Pointer 2		N38F*	1998-99	*40892 is N37F	
40892	PT	S241CSF	**40894**	LT	S242CSF	**40896**	LT	S248CSF	**40898**	BK	S250CSF
40893	LW	S240CSF	**40895**	BK	S243CSF	**40897**	BK	S249CSF	**40899**	BK	S251CSF

40900	LT	R327HYG	Dennis Dart SLF	Plaxton Pointer 2	N35F	1998	
40901	BK	R232RBA	Dennis Dart SLF	Plaxton Pointer 2	N37F	1997	

40903-40911

			Dennis Dart			Plaxton Pointer		B37F	1996		
40903	LF	N615XJM	**40909**	GS	N624XJM	**40910**	GS	N626XJM	**40911**	GS	P632CGM
40905	GS	N617XJM									

40912-40923

			Dennis Dart SLF			Plaxton Pointer		N35F	1996-97		
40912	MU	P203NSC	**40915**	GS	P206NSC	**40918**	BK	P209NSC	**40921**	GS	P212NSC
40913	GS	P204NSC	**40916**	MU	P207NSC	**40919**	DK	P210NSC	**40922**	MU	P213NSC
40914	LV	P205NSC	**40917**	GS	P208NSC	**40920**	DK	P211NSC	**40923**	PT	P215NSC

40924	PT	P216YSH	Dennis Dart SLF	Plaxton Pointer	N39F	1997	
40925	PT	P217YSH	Dennis Dart SLF	Plaxton Pointer	N39F	1997	

First was involved in the development of the Marshall Capital body, and for several years that model was sourced for use in London. Several of the early examples have now been dispersed to other depots, with 41204, R204TLM, retaining its dual-door layout and being allocated to Dumbarton depot. *Mark Doggett*

40926-40934 · Dennis Dart SLF · Plaxton Pointer 2 · N37F · 1997

40926	MU	R219GFS	40929	MU	R223GFS	40931	MU	R226GFS	40933	LV	R228GFS
40927	MU	R220GFS	40930	MU	R225GFS	40932	MU	R227GFS	40934	MU	R229GFS
40928	MU	R221GFS

40935	PT	R430PSH	Dennis Dart SLF	Plaxton Pointer 2	N37F	1998
40936	LV	R433PSH	Dennis Dart SLF	Plaxton Pointer 2	N37F	1998
40937	MU	R434PSH	Dennis Dart SLF	Plaxton Pointer 2	N37F	1998
40938	LW	S244CSF	Dennis Dart SLF	Plaxton Pointer 2	N38F	1999
40939	PT	S245CSF	Dennis Dart SLF	Plaxton Pointer 2	N38F	1999

40940-40946 · Dennis Dart SLF · Plaxton Pointer 2 · N37F · 1997

40940	LV	R226SBA	40942	BK	R228SBA	40944	DK	R230SBA	40946	LT	R233SBA
40941	LV	R227SBA	40943	DK	R229SBA	40945	DK	R231SBA

40947	LF	N611XJM	Dennis Dart	Plaxton Pointer	B37F	1996	
40951	LF	N622XJM	Dennis Dart	Plaxton Pointer	B37F	1996	
40956	u	S344SUX	Dennis Dart SLF 10.7m	Plaxton Pointer 2	N41F	1998	New World First Bus, 2001
40957	PL	S372SUX	Dennis Dart SLF 10.7m	Plaxton Pointer 2	N41F	1998	New World First Bus, 2001

40958-40961 · Dennis Dart SLF 10.7m · Plaxton Pointer 2 · N36F · 1998 · New World First Bus, 2001

40958	CE	S334TJX	40959	PL	S335TJX	40960	PL	S338TJX	40961	PL	S474TJX

40963	HU	N213WRD	Dennis Dart SLF	Plaxton Pointer	N37F	1996
40965	LF	SJ03DNY	Optare Solo M920	Optare	N30F	2003
40966	LF	SY03DOA	Optare Solo M920	Optare	N30F	2003

40973-40976 · Transbus Dart SLF · Transbus Pointer · N37F · 2003

40973	RO	YV03UOY	40974	RO	YV03UOX	40975	RO	YV03UOW	40976	RO	YV03UOU

41005-41017 · Dennis Dart SLF 10.3m · East Lancs Spryte · N34F · 1998

41005	HH	R705VLA	41009	HH	R709VLA	41012	HH	R712VLA	41015	HH	R715VLA
41006	HH	R706VLA	41010	HH	R710VLA	41013	HH	R713VLA	41016	HH	R716VLA
41007	HH	R707VLA	41011	HH	R711VLA	41014	HH	R714VLA	41017	HH	R717VLA
41008	HH	R708VLA

41068-41074 — Dennis Dart SLF — Marshall Capital — N37F — 1999 — Chester Bus, 2007

41068	CC	V368KLG	41070	CC	V370KLG	41072	CC	V372KLG	41074	CC	V374KLG
41069	CC	V369KLG	41071	CC	V371KLG	41073	CC	V373KLG			

41129-41157 — Dennis Dart SLF — Marshall Capital — N31F — 1997

41129	TN	P129NLW	41135	TN	P135NLW	41145	RA	P145NLW	41151	RA	P151NLW
41130	BL	P130NLW	41136	HI	P136NLW	41146	RA	P146NLW	41152	RA	P152NLW
41131	TN	P131NLW	41137	HI	P137NLW	41147	RA	P247OEW	41153	RA	P153NLW
41132	TN	P132NLW	41142	RA	P142NLW	41148	RA	P148NLW	41155	RA	P255RFL
41133	BL	P133NLW	41143	RA	P143NLW	41149	HV	P149NLW	41156	TN	P156NLW
41134	TN	P134NLW	41144	RA	P144NLW	41150	RA	P150NLW	41157	RA	P157NLW

41158-41164 — Dennis Dart SLF 9.3m — Marshall Capital — N33F* — 1998 — *41161/2 is N31F

41158	CA	R158TLM	41160	RA	R160TLM	41163	RA	R163TLM	41164	RA	R164TLM
41159	LL	R159TLM	41162	RA	R162TLM						

41165-41190 — Dennis Dart SLF 10.2m — Marshall Capital — N35F* — 1997-98 — *seating varies

41165	SO	R165TLM	41172	SH	R172TLM	41179	RA	R179TLM	41185	RA	R185TLM
41166	SO	R166TLM	41173	RAC	R173TLM	41180	RA	R180TLM	41186	RA	R186TLM
41167	RA	R167TLM	41174	SH	R174TLM	41181	RA	R181TLM	41187	RA	R187TLM
41168	RA	R168TLM	41175	SH	R175TLM	41182	RA	R182TLM	41188	HV	R188TLM
41169	SH	R169TLM	41176	SH	R176TLM	41183	RA	R183TLM	41189	u	R189TLM
41170	SH	R170TLM	41177	RA	R177TLM	41184	RA	R184TLM	41190	RA	R190TLM
41171	RAC	R171TLM	41178	RA	R178TLM						

41191-41200 — Dennis Dart SLF 10.2m — Marshall Capital — N33F — 1998

41191	HV	R191VLD	41194	HV	R194VLD	41197	HV	S197KLM	41199	RAC	S199KLM
41192	HV	R192VLD	41195	RA	R195VLD	41198	HV	S198KLM	41200	RAC	S220KLM
41193	RA	R193VLD	41196	HV	R196VLD						

41201-41234 — Dennis Dart SLF 9.3m — Marshall Capital — N23F* — 1998 — *41211/5/21 are N25F

41201	DU	R201TLM	41210	DU	R210TLM	41218	B	R218TLM	41227	DU	R227TLM
41202	DU	R202TLM	41211	B	R211TLM	41219	DU	R219TLM	41228	DU	R228TLM
41203	DU	R203TLM	41212	DU	R212TLM	41220	LV	R220TLM	41229	L	R229TLM
41204	DU	R204TLM	41213	B	R213TLM	41221	DU	R221TLM	41230	L	R230TLM
41205	DU	R205TLM	41214	B	R214TLM	41222	DU	R322TLM	41232	L	R232TLM
41206	DU	R206TLM	41215	B	R215TLM	41224	B	R224TLM	41233	L	R233TLM
41208	DU	R208TLM	41216	B	R216TLM	41225	B	R225TLM	41234	L	R234TLM
41209	DU	R209TLM	41217	DU	R217TLM	41226	B	R226TLM			

41235-41256 — Dennis Dart SLF 10.2m — Marshall Capital — N29D — 1998

41235	UX	S235KLM	41240	UX	S240KLM	41245	UX	S245KLM	41253	UX	S253JLP
41236	G	S236KLM	41241	UX	S241KLM	41246	UX	S246KLM	41254	UX	S254JLP
41237	G	S237KLM	41242	UX	S242KLM	41247	UX	S247KLM	41255	UX	S255JLP
41238	UX	S238KLM	41243	UX	S243KLM	41248	UX	S248KLM	41256	UX	S256JLP
41239	UX	S239KLM	41244	UX	S244KLM						

41257-41263 — Dennis Dart SLF 8.9m — Marshall Capital — N25F — 1999

41257	DG	T257JLD	41259	X	T259JLD	41261	X	T261JLD	41263	G	T263JLD
41258	u	T258JLD	41260	u	T260JLD	41262	u	T262JLD			

41264-41306 — Dennis Dart SLF 9.3m — Marshall Capital — N22D — 1999

41264	L	T264JLD	41275	L	T275JLD	41286	ON	T286JLD	41297	ON	T297JLD
41265	L	T265JLD	41276	L	T276JLD	41287	DG	T287JLD	41298	ON	T298JLD
41266	L	T266JLD	41277	L	T277JLD	41288	ON	T288JLD	41299	ON	T299JLD
41267	SH	T267JLD	41278	L	T278JLD	41289	ON	T289JLD	41300	ON	T430JLD
41268	L	T268JLD	41279	L	T279JLD	41291	ON	T291JLD	41301	ON	T301JLD
41269	L	T269JLD	41280	L	T280JLD	41292	ON	T292JLD	41302	G	T302JLD
41270	L	T270JLD	41281	L	T281JLD	41293	ON	T293JLD	41303	ON	T303JLD
41271	L	T271JLD	41282	L	T282JLD	41294	ON	T294JLD	41304	ON	T304JLD
41272	L	T272JLD	41283	L	T283JLD	41295	ON	T295JLD	41305	ON	T305JLD
41273	L	T273JLD	41284	L	T284JLD	41296	ON	T296JLD	41306	ON	T306JLD
41274	L	T274JLD	41285	L	T285JLD						

41307-41329 — Dennis Dart SLF 10.2m — Marshall Capital — N28D — 1999

41307	L	V307GBY	41313	L	V313GBY	41319	G	V319GBY	41325	ON	V325GBY
41308	L	V308GBY	41314	L	V314GBY	41320	L	V320GBY	41326	ON	V326GBY
41309	L	V309GBY	41315	L	V315GBY	41321	L	V421HBY	41327	ON	V327GBY
41310	L	V310GBY	41316	L	V316GBY	41322	L	V322GBY	41328	L	V328GBY
41311	L	V311GBY	41317	L	V317GBY	41323	L	V323GBY	41329	L	V329GBY
41312	L	V312GBY	41318	G	V318GBY	41324	L	V324GBY			

41330-41335 — Dennis Dart SLF 8.9m — Marshall Capital — N25F — 1999

41330	WS	V330GBY	41332	WS	V332GBY	41334	WS	V334GBY	41335	WS	V335GBY
41331	WS	V331GBY	41333	WS	V433HBY						

41336 — Dennis Dart SLF 10.2m — Marshall Capital — N33F — 1999

41336	DG	T336ALR

41337-41358 — Dennis Dart SLF 8.9m — Marshall Capital — N25F — 1999

41337	G	T337ALR	41343	G	T343ALR	41348	G	V348DLH	41353	u	V353DLH
41338	G	T338ALR	41344	G	T344ALR	41349	LV	V349DLH	41354	u	V354DLH
41339	G	T339ALR	41345	G	V345DLH	41350	X	V350DLH	41356	DG	V356DLH
41340	G	T340ALR	41346	G	V346DLH	41351	X	V351DLH	41357	LV	V357DLH
41341	G	T341ALR	41347	G	V347DLH	41352	u	V352DLH	41358	LV	V358DLH
41342	G	T342ALR									

41362-41379 — Dennis Dart SLF 10.2m — Marshall Capital — N28D — 2000

41362	G	W362VLN	41367	G	W367VLN	41371	DG	W371VLN	41376	ON	W376VLN
41363	G	W363VLN	41368	G	W368VLN	41372	G	W372VLN	41378	ON	W378VLN
41365	G	W365VLN	41369	G	W369VLN	41377	ON	W377VLN	41379	ON	W379VLN
41366	G	W366VLN	41370	G	W358VLN						

41381-41402 — Dennis Dart SLF 10.2m — Marshall Capital — N28D — 2000

41381	G	X381HLR	41387	G	X387HLR	41393	G	X393HLR	41398	G	X398HLR
41382	G	X382HLR	41388	G	X388HLR	41394	G	X394HLR	41399	G	X399HLR
41383	G	X383HLR	41389	G	X389HLR	41395	G	X395HLR	41400	G	X79HLR
41384	ON	X384HLR	41390	G	X78HLR	41396	G	X396HLR	41401	ON	X401HLR
41385	G	X385HLR	41391	G	X391HLR	41397	G	X397HLR	41402	L	X402HLR
41386	G	X386HLR	41392	G	X392HLR						

41403-41431 — Dennis Dart SLF 10.2m — Marshall Capital — N28D — 2001

41403	WJ	RG51FWZ	41410	UX	RG51FZH	41420	WJ	LK51DXD	41426	WJ	LK51DWK
41404	WJ	RG51FZA	41414	WJ	LK51JYO	41421	WJ	LK51DXE	41427	WJ	LK51DWL
41405	WJ	RG51FZB	41415	WJ	LK51DWY	41422	WJ	LK51DXF	41428	WJ	LK51DWM
41406	WJ	RG51FZC	41416	WJ	LK51DWZ	41423	WJ	LK51DXG	41429	WJ	LK51DWO
41407	WJ	RG51FZD	41417	WJ	LK51DXA	41424	WJ	LK51DXH	41430	WJ	LK51DWP
41408	WJ	RG51FZE	41418	WJ	LK51DXB	41425	WJ	LK51DWJ	41431	WJ	LK51DWU
41409	UX	RG51FZF	41419	WJ	LK51DXC						

41433-41449 — Dennis Dart SLF 9.3m — Marshall Capital — N24D — 2001

41433	L	LN51DWW	41438	WJ	LN51DVZ	41442	WJ	LN51DVT	41446	WJ	LN51DUJ
41434	L	LN51DWX	41439	WJ	LN51DVO	41443	WJ	LN51DVV	41447	WJ	LN51DUU
41435	WJ	LN51DVW	41440	WJ	LN51DVP	41444	WJ	LN51DUA	41448	WJ	LN51DUV
41436	WJ	LN51DVX	41441	WJ	LN51DVR	41445	WJ	LN51DUH	41449	WJ	LN51DUY
41437	WJ	LN51DVY									

41474-41491 — TransBus Dart 8.9m — Marshall Capital — N25F — 2002

41474	NP	LT02NUK	41479	DG	LT02NUV	41484	DG	LT02NVJ	41488	G	LT02ZDZ
41475	DG	LT02NUM	41480	DG	LT02NVE	41485	DG	LT52WUM	41489	G	LT02ZFA
41476	DG	LT02NUO	41481	DG	LT52WUP	41486	DG	LT52WUR	41490	G	LT02ZFB
41477	DG	LT02NUP	41482	DG	LT52WUO	41487	G	LT02ZDY	41491	G	LT02ZFC
41478	DG	LT02NUU	41483	DG	LT02NVH						

The final deliveries of Dart for First's London operation carry the British-built Caetano Nimbus body. Illustrating this styling is 41501, LK03LNX, which is seen in South Street in Romford while working TfL route 165. *Mark Lyons*

41492-41514

TransBus Dart 10.5m   Caetano Nimbus   N29D   2003

41492	DG	LK03LMJ	41498	DG	LK03NLN	41504	UX	LK03NLF	41510	DG	LK03NFY
41493	DG	LK03LLX	41499	DG	LK03LNV	41505	UX	LK03NLG	41511	UX	LK03NFZ
41494	DG	LK03LLZ	41500	DG	LK03LNW	41506	UX	LK03NLJ	41512	UX	LK03NGE
41495	DG	LK03LME	41501	DG	LK03LNX	41507	DG	LK03NLL	41513	UX	LK03NGF
41496	DG	LK03LMF	41502	DG	LK03NLD	41508	DG	LK03NLM	41514	UX	LK03NGG
41497	DG	LK03LNU	41503	UX	LK03NLE	41509	DG	LK03NLT			

41515-41519

Dennis Dart SLF 10.7m   Plaxton Pointer 2   N37F   1998

41515	HO	R415WPX	41517	SO	R417WPX	41518	SO	R418WPX	41519	SO	R419WPX
41516	SO	R416WPX									

41520-41544

TransBus Dart 10.5m   Caetano Nimbus   N29D   2003

41520	DG	LK03UEX	41527	DG	LK53FDD	41533	UX	LK53FDN	41539	UX	LK53FDY
41521	DG	LK03UEY	41528	UX	LK53FDE	41534	UX	LK53FDO	41540	UX	LK53FDZ
41522	UX	LK03UEZ	41529	UX	LK53FDF	41535	UX	LK53FDP	41541	UX	LK53FEF
41523	DG	LK03UFA	41530	UX	LK53FDG	41536	UX	LK53FDU	41542	UX	LK53FEG
41524	UX	LK03UFB	41531	UX	LK53FDJ	41537	UX	LK53FDV	41543	UX	LK53FEH
41525	UX	LK03UFC	41532	UX	LK53FDM	41538	UX	LK53FDX	41544	UX	LK53FEJ
41526	UX	LK53FDC									

41633-41653

Dennis Dart SLF 10.2m   Marshall Capital   N37F*   1997-98   *seating varies

41633	HI	R633VLX	41638	HI	R638VLX	41643	HI	R643TLM	41649	DG	R649TLM
41634	HI	R634VLX	41639	RA	R639VLX	41644	BS	R644TLM	41650	BS	R650TLM
41635	HI	R835VLX	41640	BS	R640VLX	41645	BS	R645TLM	41651	BS	R651TLM
41636	HI	R636VLX	41641	HI	R641VLX	41646	HI	R646TLM	41652	HV	R652TLM
41637	BS	R637VLX	41642	BS	R642TLM	41647	BS	R647TLM	41653	BS	R653TLM

41681-41700

Dennis Dart SLF 9.3m   Marshall Capital   N24D   2000

41681	L	W681ULL	41685	L	W685ULL	41689	L	X689HLF	41698	L	X698HLF
41682	L	W682ULL	41686	L	W686ULL	41690	L	X501JLO	41699	L	X699HLF
41683	L	W683ULL	41687	L	W687ULL	41697	L	X697HLF	41700	L	X502JLO
41684	L	W684ULL	41688	L	X688HLF						

A background of Somerset House enhances this view of Dart 41726, W726ULL, as it crosses Waterloo Bridge in the capital. This vehicle is one of the 10.2 metre examples and is seen on route RV1. *Mark Lyons*

41718-41738
Dennis Dart SLF 10.2m — Marshall Capital — N28D — 2000

41718	L	W718ULL	41724	L	W724ULL	41729	L	X729HLF	41734	L	X734HLF
41719	L	W719ULL	41725	L	W425VLO	41730	L	X503JLO	41735	L	X735HLF
41720	L	W133VLO	41726	L	W726ULL	41731	L	X731HLF	41736	L	X736HLF
41721	L	W721ULL	41727	L	W727ULL	41732	L	X732HLF	41737	L	X737HLF
41722	L	W722ULL	41728	L	W728VLO	41733	L	X733HLF	41738	L	X738HLF
41723	L	W723ULL									

41740-41745
Dennis Dart SLF 10.2m — Marshall Capital — N28D — 2000

41740	L	X504JLO	41742	L	X742HLF	41744	L	X744HLF	41745	L	X745HLF
41741	L	X741HLF	41743	L	X743HLF						

41746	L	X746JLO	Dennis Dart SLF 9.3m	Marshall Capital	N24D	2000
41747	L	X747JLO	Dennis Dart SLF 9.3m	Marshall Capital	N24D	2000
41748	L	X748JLO	Dennis Dart SLF 9.3m	Marshall Capital	N24D	2000

41751-41772
Dennis Dart SLF 10.2m — Marshall Capital — N28D — 2000-01

41751	L	X751HLR	41757	L	X757HLR	41763	L	X763HLR	41768	ON	X768HLR
41752	L	X752HLR	41758	L	X758HLR	41764	L	X764HLR	41769	ON	X769HLR
41753	L	X753HLR	41759	L	X759HLR	41765	L	X508HLR	41770	L	X509HLR
41754	L	X754HLR	41760	L	X507HLR	41766	L	X766HLR	41771	ONt	X771HLR
41755	L	X506HLR	41761	L	X761HLR	41767	ON	X767HLR	41772	DG	X772HLR
41756	L	X756HLR	41762	L	X762HLR						

41773-41788
Dennis Dart SLF 9.3m — Marshall Capital — N28F — 2001

41773	NP	X773HLR	41777	NP	X512HLR	41781	NP	X781HLR	41785	NP	X785HLR
41774	NP	X774HLR	41778	NP	X778HLR	41782	NP	X782HLR	41786	NP	X514HLR
41775	NP	X511HLR	41779	NP	X779HLR	41783	NP	X783HLR	41787	NP	X787HLR
41776	NP	X776HLR	41780	NP	X513HLR	41784	NP	X784HLR	41788	NP	X788HLR

41790-41795
Dennis Dart SLF 9.3m — Marshall Capital — N24D — 2001

41790	WJ	LN51GJV	41792	L	LN51GJY	41794	L	LN51GOP	41795	DG	LN51GOU
41791	L	LN51GJX	41793	L	LN51GJZ						

The 2008 First Bus Handbook

First introduced the *Overground* branding in several towns where a complex route network existed. Each route was allotted a colour code and allocated specific buses. Seen heading for Southsea, 42122, R622YCR, carries the red of route 15. *Mark Lyons*

42109-42123
Dennis Dart SLF — Plaxton Pointer 2* — N37F — 1997-98 — *42110 is a Plaxton Pointer

42109	HO	R609YCR	42113	HO	R613YCR	42117	HO	R617YCR
42110	HU	P710HPU	42114	HO	R614YCR	42118	HO	R618YCR
42111	WH	R611YCR	42115	HO	R615YCR	42119	HO	R619YCR
42112	WH	R612YCR	42116	HO	R616YCR	42120	HO	R620YCR

42121	HO	R621YCR
42122	HO	R622YCR
42123	HO	R623YCR

42124-42134
Dennis Dart SLF — Plaxton Pointer 2 — N37F — 1998-99

42124	HO	S624KTP	42127	HO	S627KTP	42130	HO	S630KTP	42133	HO	S633KTP
42125	HO	S625KTP	42128	HO	S628KTP	42131	HO	S631KTP	42134	HO	S634KTP
42126	HO	S626KTP	42129	HO	S629KTP	42132	HO	S632KTP			

42135-42142
Dennis Dart SLF — Plaxton Pointer 2 — N37F — 1999

42135	HO	S635XCR	42137	HO	S637XCR	42139	HO	S639XCR	42141	HO	S641XCR
42136	HO	S636XCR	42138	HO	S638XCR	42140	HO	S640XCR	42142	HO	S642XCR

42175-42181
Dennis Dart SLF — Plaxton Pointer — N37F — 1996-98

42175	HU	P705HPU	42179	HU	P709HPU	42180	WH	R610YCR	42181	HU	P711HPU
42178	HU	P708HPU									

42207-42222
Dennis Dart SLF — Plaxton Pointer 2 — N37F — 1998

42207	RA	R207MSA	42211	RA	R211MSA	42215	PT	R215MSA	42219	WR	R219MSA
42208	RA	R208MSA	42212	RA	R212MSA	42216	RA	R216MSA	42220	WR	R220MSA
42209	RA	R209MSA	42213	RA	R213MSA	42217	WR	R217MSA	42221	WS	R221MSA
42210	PT	R210MSA	42214	RA	R214MSA	42218	PT	R218MSA	42222	WS	R222MSA

42232	TR	T32JCV	Dennis Dart SLF	Plaxton Pointer 2	NC32F	1999	Truronian, 2008
42234	TR	T34JCV	Dennis Dart SLF	Plaxton Pointer 2	NC32F	1999	Truronian, 2008
42235	TR	T35JCV	Dennis Dart SLF	Plaxton Pointer 2	NC32F	1999	Truronian, 2008
42237	CA	P237NLW	Dennis Dart SLF	Plaxton Pointer	N37F	1997	
42238	CA	P238NLW	Dennis Dart SLF	Plaxton Pointer	N37F	1997	
42239	CA	P239NLW	Dennis Dart SLF	Plaxton Pointer	N37F	1997	
42252	TRt	P452SCV	Dennis Dart SLF	Plaxton Pointer	N34F	1997	Truronian, 2008
42253	TR	P453SCV	Dennis Dart SLF	Plaxton Pointer	N34F	1997	Truronian, 2008
42255	TR	P455SCV	Dennis Dart SLF	Plaxton Pointer	N34F	1997	Truronian, 2008

42302-42305 — Dennis Dart SLF — Plaxton Pointer — N39F — 1997

42302	PT	P302AUM	42303	PT	P303AUM	42304	PT	P304AUM	42305	PT	P305AUM

42322-42337 — Dennis Dart SLF 10.2m — Alexander ALX200 — N37F* — 1999 — *42322-9 are N36F

42322	PT	T622SEJ	42326	RA	T626SEJ	42330	PT	T630SEJ	42334	PT	T634SEJ
42323	PT	T623SEJ	42327	RA	T627SEJ	42331	PT	T631SEJ	42335	PT	T635SEJ
42324	PT	T624SEJ	42328	RA	T628SEJ	42332	PT	T632SEJ	42336	PT	T636SEJ
42325	PT	T625SEJ	42329	RA	T629SEJ	42333	PT	T633SEJ	42337	PT	T637SEJ

42338-42347 — Dennis Dart SLF 10.8m — Alexander ALX200 — N37F — 2000

42338	SH	X238AMO	42341	SH	X241AMO	42343	SH	X243AMO	42346	SH	X246AMO
42339	SH	X239AMO	42342	SH	X242AMO	42344	SH	X244AMO	42347	SH	X247AMO

42350	WH	W809VMA	Dennis Dart SLF		Caetano Nimbus	N37F	2001	Caetano demonstrator, 2002

42351-42356 — Dennis Dart SLF — Caetano Nimbus — N34F — 2001

42351	WR	Y351AUY	42353	WR	Y353AUY	42354	WR	Y354AUY	42356	WR	Y356AUY
42352	WR	Y352AUY									

42376	LF	V676FPO	Dennis Dart SLF		UVG UrbanStar	N38F	1999	Clarkson, South Emsall, 2003

42401-42407 — Dennis Dart SLF 10.1m — Plaxton Pointer — N34F — 1996

42401	UX	P401MLA	42403	UX	P403MLA	42405	UX	P405MLA	42407	WH	P407MLA
42402	UX	P402MLA	42404	KD	P404MLA	42406	UX	P406MLA			

42411-42417 — Dennis Dart SLF 10.1m — Plaxton Pointer — N34F — 1996 — 42411/2 are N32F

42411	BL	N211WRD	42414	BL	N214WRD	42416	BL	N216WRD	42417	BL	N217WRD
42412	BL	N212WRD	42415	BL	N215WRD						

42427-42440 — Dennis Dart SLF — Plaxton Pointer — NC35F — 1996

42427	PT	P427ORL	42431	CE	P431ORL	42435	CE	P435ORL	42438	BB	P438ORL
42428	PT	P428ORL	42432	BB	P432ORL	42436	BB	P436ORL	42439	CE	P439ORL
42429	VN	P429ORL	42433	BB	P433ORL	42437	CE	P437ORL	42440	BB	P440ORL
42430	CE	P430ORL	42434	CE	P434ORL						

42441-42446 — Dennis Dart SLF — Plaxton Pointer — N35F — 1997

42441	YA	P441TCV	42443	YA	P443TCV	42445	YA	P445TCV	42446	YA	P446TCV
42442	YA	P442TCV	42444	YA	P444TCV						

42447-42464 — Dennis Dart SLF — Plaxton Pointer 2 — N35F — 1997-98

42447	YA	R447CCV	42452	BB	R452CCV	42457	CE	R457CCV	42461	BB	R461CCV
42448	YA	R448CCV	42453	u	R453CCV	42458	LO	R458CCV	42462	BB	R462CCV
42449	BB	R449CCV	42454	CE	R454CCV	42459	BB	R459CCV	42463	BB	R463CCV
42450	YA	R450CCV	42455	CE	R445CCV	42460	HU	R460CCV	42464	BB	R464CCV
42451	YA	R451CCV	42456	BB	R456CCV						

42469-42478 — Dennis Dart SLF — Alexander ALX200 — N37F — 1999-2000

42469	CE	T469JCV	42472	CE	T472YTT	42475	CE	X475SCY	42477	CE	X477SCY
42470	CE	T470JCV	42473	CE	T473YTT	42476	CE	X476SCY	42478	CE	X478SCY
42471	CE	T471JCV	42474	CE	X474SCY						

42482-42489 — TransBus Dart — TransBus Pointer — N37F — 2003-04

42482	CM	SN03WLD	42484	CM	SN03WLW	42486	CM	SN03WMX	42488	CM	SN53KJX
42483	CM	SN03WLK	42485	CM	SN03WMM	42487	CM	SN03WME	42489	CM	SN53KJY

42504-42507 — Dennis Dart SLF — Plaxton Pointer — N37F — 1996

42504	SO	P404KOW	42505	SO	P405KOW	42506	SO	P406KOW	42507	SO	P407KOW

42508-42514 — Dennis Dart SLF — Plaxton Pointer 2 — N37F — 1998

42508	SO	R408WPX	42510	SO	R410WPX	42512	SO	R412WPX	42514	SO	R414WPX
42509	SO	R409WPX	42511	SO	R411WPX	42513	SO	R413WPX			

Recently repainted out of Worcester's *Park and Ride* livery is 42356, Y356AUY which is seen on normal service in the city. It is one of five Caetano Nimbus-bodied Darts acquired for the depot. *Mark Lyons*

42515-42519

			TransBus Dart 10.5m		Caetano Nimbus		N29D	2003	
42515	UX	LK03NKH	42517	UX	LK03NKL	42518	DG	LK03NKM	42519	DG	LK03NKN
42516	UX	LK03NKJ								

42520-42527

			Dennis Dart SLF		Plaxton Pointer 2		N37F	1998	
42520	SO	R420WPX	42522	SO	R422WPX	42524	SO	R424WPX	42526	SO	R426WPX
42521	SO	R421WPX	42523	SO	R423WPX	42525	SO	R425WPX	42527	SO	R427WPX

42528	D	99C22528	Dennis Dart SLF	Plaxton Pointer 2	N37D	1999
42529	D	99C22529	Dennis Dart SLF	Plaxton Pointer 2	N37D	1999
42534	D	99C22534	Dennis Dart SLF	Plaxton Pointer 2	N37D	1999
42551	IP	S551WAT	Dennis Dart SLF 8.8m	Plaxton Pointer MPD	N29F	1999

42552-42563

			ADL Dart 9.4m		ADL Pointer		N29F	2005	
42552	BA	WX05UAJ	42555	BA	WX05UAM	42558	CE	SN05DZU	42561	PL	SN05DZX
42553	BA	WX05UAK	42556	BA	WX05UAN	42559	CE	SN05DZV	42562	PL	SN05DZY
42554	BA	WX05UAL	42557	BA	WX05UAO	42560	CE	SN05DZW	42563	PL	SN05DZZ

42569-42580

			Dennis Dart SLF 9m		Plaxton Pointer		N31F	1996	
42569	RA	P569BTH	42572	RA	P572BTH	42575	RA	P575BTH	42578	PT	P578BTH
42570	RA	P570BTH	42573	RA	P573BTH	42576	RA	P576BTH	42579	PT	P579BTH
42571	RA	P571BTH	42574	RA	P574BTH	42577	PT	P577BTH	42580	RA	P580BTH

42581-42599

			Dennis Dart SLF 9m		Plaxton Pointer 2		N29F	1998	
42581	RA	R581SWN	42587	RA	R587SWN	42592	PD	R592SWN	42596	RA	R596SWN
42582	RA	R582SWN	42588	RA	R588SWN	42593	PD	R593SWN	42597	RA	R597SWN
42583	RA	R583SWN	42589	RA	R589SWN	42594	PD	R594SWN	42598	RA	R598SWN
42585	RA	R585SWN	42590	PD	R590SWN	42595	RA	R595SWN	42599	PD	R599SWN
42586	RA	R586SWN	42591	PD	R591SWN					

42600-42614 — ADL Dart 9.4m — ADL Pointer — N31F — 2005

42600	RA	CU54HYK	42604	RA	CU54HYO	42608	u	CU54HYV	42612 RA CU54HYZ
42601	RA	CU54HYL	42605	RA	CU54HYP	42609	RA	CU54HYW	42613 CA CU54HZA
42602	RA	CU54HYM	42606	RA	CU54HYR	42610	RA	CU54HYX	42614 RA CU54HZB
42603	RA	CU54HYN	42607	RA	CU54HYT	42611	RA	CU54HYY	

42620	PD	R120FUP	Dennis Dart SLF	Plaxton Pointer 2	N36F	1997
42621	PD	R121FUP	Dennis Dart SLF	Plaxton Pointer 2	N36F	1997
42622	RA	R122FUP	Dennis Dart SLF	Plaxton Pointer 2	N31F	1997
42626	PT	P826YUM	Dennis Dart SLF	Plaxton Pointer	N35F	1997
42630	YV	R130FUP	Dennis Dart SLF	Plaxton Pointer 2	N33F	1997	York Pullman, 2000
42631	CA	R131FUP	Dennis Dart SLF	Plaxton Pointer 2	N36F	1997	York Pullman, 2000
42632	CA	R132FUP	Dennis Dart SLF	Plaxton Pointer 2	N36F	1997	York Pullman, 2000
42633	PT	P833YUM	Dennis Dart SLF	Plaxton Pointer	N35F	1997
42634	BW	P834YUM	Dennis Dart SLF	Plaxton Pointer	N35F	1997
42636	WH	P836YUM	Dennis Dart SLF	Plaxton Pointer	N39F	1995
42641	WR	N341EUY	Dennis Dart SLF	Plaxton Pointer	NC33F	1996
42642	LL	S342EWU	Dennis Dart SLF	Plaxton Pointer 2	N37F	1998
42643	BL	S343EWU	Dennis Dart SLF	Plaxton Pointer 2	N37F	1998
42644	BL	S344EWU	Dennis Dart SLF	Plaxton Pointer 2	N37F	1998
42654	SH	V154LUA	Dennis Dart SLF	Alexander ALX200	N37F	1999
42656	SH	T356VWU	Dennis Dart SLF 10.8m	Alexander ALX200	N37F	1999
42659	SH	T359VWU	Dennis Dart SLF 10.8m	Alexander ALX200	N37F	1999
42673	SH	T373NUA	Dennis Dart SLF 10.8m	Alexander ALX200	N37F	1999

42674-42692 — TransBus Dart 9.3m — Transbus Pointer — N31F* — 2003 — *seating varies

42674	CA	CU53APO	42679	RAC	CU53ARX	42684	LL	CU53AUP	42689 PT CU53AVW
42675	PD	CU53APV	42680	PD	CU53ARO	42685	PT	CU53AUO	42690 PT CU53AUX
42676	PD	CU53APX	42681	LL	CU53ARF	42686	PT	CU53AUT	42691 PT CU53AUY
42677	PD	CU53ASO	42682	LL	CU53APZ	42687	PT	CU53AUV	42692 PT CU53AVB
42678	PD	CU53ARZ	42683	CA	CU53APY	42688	PT	CU53AUW	

42693	RAC	CU03BHV	TransBus Dart 8.8m	TransBus Pointer	N29F	2003
42694	RAC	CU03BHW	TransBus Dart 8.8m	TransBus Pointer	N29F	2003

42701-42718 — Dennis Dart SLF — Plaxton Pointer 2 — N29F — 1997

42701	HG	R701BAE	42706	HG	R706BAE	42711	HG	R711BAE	42715 PT R715BAE
42702	HG	R702BAE	42707	HG	R707BAE	42712	HG	R712BAE	42716 PD R716BAE
42703	MR	R703BAE	42708	HG	R708BAE	42713	PT	R713BAE	42717 PT R717BAE
42704	HG	R704BAE	42709	HG	R709BAE	42714	PD	R714BAE	42718 HG R718BAE
42705	HG	R705BAE	42710	HG	R710BAE				

42719	HG	R719RAD	Dennis Dart SLF	Plaxton Pointer 2	N29F	1998

42720-42725 — Dennis Dart SLF 10.2m — Plaxton Pointer 2 — N35F — 1998-99

42720	MR	S720AFB	42722	MR	S722AFB	42724	HG	S724AFB	42725 HG S725AFB
42721	MR	S721AFB	42723	MR	S723AFB				

42726	AG	T726REU	Dennis Dart SLF 10.2m	Plaxton Pointer 2	N35F	1999
42727	AG	T727REU	Dennis Dart SLF 10.2m	Plaxton Pointer 2	N35F	1999
42728	HO	T728REU	Dennis Dart SLF 10.2m	Plaxton Pointer 2	N35F	1999
42729	WS	T729REU	Dennis Dart SLF 10.2m	Plaxton Pointer 2	N35F	1999
42730	WS	T730REU	Dennis Dart SLF 10.2m	Alexander ALX200	N37F	1999
42731	WS	T731REU	Dennis Dart SLF 10.2m	Alexander ALX200	N37F	1999

42732-42738 — Dennis Dart SLF — Alexander ALX200 — N36F — 2000

42732	HG	V732FAE	42734	HG	V734FAE	42736	HG	V736FAE	42738 HG V738FAE
42733	HG	V733FAE	42735	HG	V735FAE	42737	HG	V737FAE	

42752-42784 — Dennis Dart SLF — Plaxton Pointer 2 — N36F — 1998-99 — New World First Bus, 2001

42752	CE	S652SNG	42758	PL	S658SNG	42773	PL	S673SNG	42780 PL S680SNG
42753	PL	S753SNG	42759	PL	S659SNG	42777	u	S677SNG	42783 BB S683SNG
42754	PL	S653SNG	42764	PL	S664SNG	42778	u	S678SNG	42784 PL S684SNG
42757	PL	S657SNG	42772	PL	S672SNG	42779	BB	S679SNG	

42801	TR	Y1EDN	Dennis Dart SLF	Plaxton Pointer 2	N37F	2001	Truronian, 2008
42802	TR	Y2EDN	Dennis Dart SLF	Plaxton Pointer 2	N37F	2001	Truronian, 2008

Lettered for the Porthcawl to Cardiff service, Dart 42870, CU53AVT, is in a version of the rail-air base livery. It is seen arriving at the bus station in Cardiff. *Mark Lyons*

42817-42823

			Dennis Dart SLF 10.7m		Plaxton Pointer 2	N39F*	1998	*42822/3 are N37F
42817	BP	S817KPR	42819	WH	S819KPR	42821	WH	S821KPR	42823	WH	S823KPR
42818	WH	S818KPR	42820	WH	S820KPR	42822	WH	S822KPR			

42824	TN	S824WYD	Dennis Dart SLF	East Lancs Spryte	N35F	1999
42825	TN	S825WYD	Dennis Dart SLF	East Lancs Spryte	N35F	1999
42826	WH	T826AFX	Dennis Dart SLF 10.7m	Plaxton Pointer 2	N39F	1999
42827	WH	T827AFX	Dennis Dart SLF 10.7m	Plaxton Pointer 2	N39F	1999
42828	WH	T828AFX	Dennis Dart SLF 10.7m	Plaxton Pointer 2	N39F	1999
42829	WH	T829AFX	Dennis Dart SLF 10.7m	Plaxton Pointer 2	N39F	1999

42830-42835

			Dennis Dart SLF 10.7m		East Lancs Spryte	N37F	1999
42830	BW	T830RYC	42832	BW	V832DYD	42834	BW	V834DYD	42835	TN	V835DYD
42831	BW	T831RYC	42833	BW	V833DYD						

42841-42845

			Dennis Dart SLF 10.7m		Alexander ALX200	N37F	1999
42841	TN	T366NUA	42843	TN	T368NUA	42844	TN	T369NUA	42845	TN	T370NUA
42842	TN	T367NUA									

42852-42857

			Dennis Dart SLF 10.7m		East Lancs Spryte	N37F	1997
42852	HH	P852VUS	42854	HH	P854VUS	42855	HH	P855VUS	42857	HH	P857VUS
42853	HH	P853VUS									

42860	TR	TT03TRU	TransBus Dart 10.2m	TransBus Pointer	N37F	2003	Truronian, 2008

42861-42870

			TransBus Dart 10.7m		TransBus Pointer	N34F	2003
42861	PT	CU53AVJ	42864	PT	CU53AVM	42867	LL	CU53AVR	42869	LL	CU53AVV
42862	PT	CU53AVK	42865	CA	CU53AVN	42868	CA	CU53AVP	42870	LL	CU53AVT
42863	PT	CU53AVL	42866	LL	CU53AVO						

42871-42876

			TransBus Dart 10.7m		TransBus Pointer	N37F	2003
42871	CE	SN53KKA	42873	CE	SN53KKC	42875	CE	SN53KKE	42876	CE	SN53KJZ
42872	CE	SN53KKB	42874	CE	SN53KKD						

42877-42888 ADL Dart 10.7m — ADL Pointer — N37F — 2005

42877	LL	SF05KWY	42880	LL	SF05KXB	42883	LL	SF05KXE	42886	B	SF05KXK
42878	LL	SF05KWZ	42881	LL	SF05KXC	42884	LL	SF05KXH	42887	B	SF05KXL
42879	LL	SF05KXA	42882	LL	SF05KXD	42885	B	SF05KXJ	42888	B	SF05KXM

42889-42894 ADL Dart 10.7m — ADL Pointer — N37F — 2004-05

42889	KD	VX54MUC	42891	KD	VX54MUP	42893	WR	VX54MUV	42894	HD	VX05JWW
42890	KD	VX54MUO	42892	WR	VX54MUU						

42895-42916 ADL Dart 10.7m — ADL Pointer — N32F — 2005

42895	BA	WX05RUW	42901	BA	WX05RVJ	42907	BA	WX05RVP	42912	TN	WX05RVW
42896	BA	WX05RUY	42902	BA	WX05RVK	42908	BA	WX05RVR	42913	TN	WX05RVX
42897	BA	WX05RVA	42903	BA	WX05RVL	42909	BA	WX05RVT	42914	TN	WX05RVZ
42898	BA	WX05RVC	42904	BA	WX05RVM	42910	BA	WX05RVU	42915	TN	WX05RWE
42899	BA	WX05RVE	42905	BA	WX05RVN	42911	BA	WX05RVV	42916	TN	WX05RWF
42900	BA	WX05RVF	42906	BA	WX05RVO						

42918-42939 ADL Dart 10.7m — ADL Pointer — N37F* — 2005 — *42918-23 are N34F

42918	CM	EU05AUK	42924	PL	SN05EAA	42930	CE	SN05EAM	42935	CE	SN05DZR
42919	CM	EU05AUL	42925	PL	SN05EAC	42931	CE	SN05EAO	42936	CE	SN05DZS
42920	CM	EU05AUM	42926	PL	SN05EAE	42932	CE	SN05EAP	42937	CE	SN05DZT
42921	CM	EU05AUN	42927	CE	SN05EAF	42933	CE	SN05DZO	42938	MR	WX05SVD
42922	CM	EU05AUO	42928	CE	SN05EAG	42934	CE	SN05DZP	42939	MR	WX05SVE
42923	CM	EU05AUP	42929	CE	SN05EAJ						

42940-42969 ADL Dart 10.7m — ADL Pointer — N37F — 2006

42940	CE	WA56OAN	42948	PL	WA56FTY	42956	MR	WX06OMO	42963	MR	WX06OMW
42941	CE	WA56OAO	42949	MR	WX06OMF	42957	MR	WX06OMP	42964	MR	WX06OMY
42942	CE	WA56OAP	42950	MR	WX06OMG	42958	MR	WX06OMR	42965	MR	WX06OMZ
42943	CE	WA56OAS	42951	MR	WX06OMH	42959	MR	WX06OMS	42966	MR	WX06ONA
42944	CE	WA56OAU	42952	MR	WX06OMJ	42960	MR	WX06OMT	42967	MR	WX06ONB
42945	CE	WA56OAV	42953	MR	WX06OMK	42961	MR	WX06OMV	42968	MR	WX06ONC
42946	PL	WA56FTV	42954	MR	WX06OML	42962	MR	WX06OMU	42969	PL	WA56FTZ
42947	PL	WA56FTX	42955	MR	WX06OMM						

43356-43360 Dennis Dart SLF 8.8m — Plaxton Pointer MPD — N29F — 1999

43356	IP	V356DVG	43358	KL	V358DVG	43359	IP	V359DVG	43360	IP	V360DVG
43357	KL	V357DVG									

43433-43450 Dennis Dart SLF — Plaxton Pointer — N37F — 1996-97

43433	IP	P433NEX	43438	NR	P438NEX	43442	NR	P442NEX	43447	NR	P447NEX
43434	IP	P434NEX	43439	NR	P439NEX	43444	NR	P844OAH	43448	NR	P448NEX
43435	IP	P435NEX	43440	IP	P440NEX	43445	IP	P445NEX	43449	VN	P449NEX
43436	IP	P436NEX	43441	NR	P441NEX	43446	NR	P446NEX	43450	VN	P450NEX
43437	NR	P437NEX									

43451	VN	P451RPW	Dennis Dart SLF	Plaxton Pointer	N40F	1997
43452	VN	P452RPW	Dennis Dart SLF	Plaxton Pointer	N40F	1997
43453	VN	P453RPW	Dennis Dart SLF	Plaxton Pointer	N40F	1997

43459-43478 Dennis Dart SLF — Plaxton Pointer 2 — N37F — 1997-98

43459	LO	R459BNG	43464	LO	R464CAH	43469	VN	R469CAH	43474	VN	R474CAH
43460	IP	R460BNG	43465	LO	R465CAH	43470	YA	R470CAH	43475	IP	R475CAH
43461	LO	R461BNG	43466	LO	R466CAH	43471	VN	R471CAH	43476	VN	R476CAH
43462	LO	R462BNG	43467	LO	R467CAH	43472	VN	R472CAH	43477	VN	R477CAH
43463	LO	R463CAH	43468	VN	R468CAH	43473	VN	R473CAH	43478	VN	R478CAH

43480-43489 Dennis Dart SLF — Plaxton Pointer 2 — N34F* — 1998 — *47482 is N37F

43480	VN	R680DPW	43483	VN	R683DPW	43486	VN	R686DPW	43488	IP	R688DPW
43481	VN	R681DPW	43484	VN	R684DPW	43487	VN	R687DPW	43489	LO	R689DPW
43482	IP	R682DPW	43485	VN	R685DPW						

43584	RA	P584SWN	Dennis Dart SLF 9m	Plaxton Pointer 2	N29F	1998

Norwich is the location for this view of Dart 43484, R684DPW, with purple *Overground* branding. This bus is seen on route 19 heading for Costessey. Recent changes have seen several of the Norwich-based Darts move to Lowestoft where fifteen are now allocated, leaving forty-two at the two city depots. *Mark Doggett*

43677-43680

| | | Dennis Dart SLF | | Marshall Capital | | NC24D | 1997 | *On loan to Bristol Airport* |

43677	BXs	R677MEW	43678	BXs	R678MEW	43679	BXs	R679MEW	43680	BXs	R680MEW

43712-43721

Dennis Dart SLF — Plaxton Pointer 2 — N37F — 1998

43712	BS	R712DJN	43715	CO	R715DJN	43718	HH	R718DJN	43720	HH	R720DJN
43713	BS	R713DJN	43716	CO	R716DJN	43719	HH	R719DJN	43721	HH	R721DJN
43714	BS	R714DJN	43717	HH	R717DJN						

43729-43738

Dennis Dart SLF — Plaxton Pointer 2 — N37F — 1998

43729	BR	S729TWC	43732	BS	S732TWC	43735	BS	S735TWC	43737	BS	S737TWC
43730	CM	S730TWC	43733	BS	S733TWC	43736	BS	S737TWC	43738	BS	S738TWC
43731	CM	S731TWC	43734	BS	S734TWC						

43739-43744

Dennis Dart SLF — Alexander ALX200 — N37F — 1999

43739	CO	V739GPU	43741	CO	V741GPU	43743	CO	V743GPU	43744	CO	V744GPU
43740	CO	V740GPU	43742	CO	V742GPU						

43800	HA	S979JLM	Dennis Dart SLF 8.8m	Marshall Capital	N27F	1998	
43801	KL	AO02ODM	Dennis Dart SLF 8.8m	Plaxton Pointer MPD	N29F	2002	
43802	KL	AO02ODN	Dennis Dart SLF 8.8m	Plaxton Pointer MPD	N29F	2002	
43803	WR	SN03LGA	Dennis Dart SLF 8.8m	Plaxton Pointer MPD	N29F	2002	*Operated for Worcestershire CC*
43804	AG	DA51XTD	Dennis Dart SLF 8.8m	Plaxton Pointer MPD	N29F	2002	*Operated for Stoke City Council*
43809	TR	S549SCV	Dennis Dart SLF 8.8m	Plaxton Pointer MPD	N29F	1998	Truronian, 2008
43810	TR	KU52RXJ	TransBus Dart SLF 8.8m	TransBus Mini Pointer	N29F	2003	Truronian, 2008
43811	TR	WK52WTV	TransBus Dart SLF 8.8m	TransBus Mini Pointer	N29F	2003	*Operated for Cornwall CC*
43812	TR	T12TRU	Dennis Dart SLF	Plaxton Pointer MPD	N29F	1999	Truronian, 2008
43821	BA	X201HAE	Dennis Dart SLF 8.8m	Plaxton Pointer MPD	N29F	2000	
43822	BA	X202HAE	Dennis Dart SLF 8.8m	Plaxton Pointer MPD	N29F	2000	
43823	BA	X203HAE	Dennis Dart SLF 8.8m	Plaxton Pointer MPD	N29F	2000	
43833	BL	W933JNF	Dennis Dart SLF 8.8m	Plaxton Pointer MPD	N26F	2000	
43834	BL	W934JNF	Dennis Dart SLF 8.8m	Plaxton Pointer MPD	N26F	2000	
43835	SH	W935JNF	Dennis Dart SLF 8.8m	Plaxton Pointer MPD	N26F	2000	

43836-43841				TransBus Dart 8.8m		TransBus Mini Pointer	N26F	2003	
43836	CA	SN53ESV	43838	PD	SN53ESY	43840	PD	SN53ETE	43841	PD	SN53ETF
43837	LL	SN53ESU	43839	PD	SN53ETD					

43843	LW	SN04EFY	TransBus Dart 8.8m	TransBus Mini Pointer	N29F	2004
43844	LT	SN04EFZ	TransBus Dart 8.8m	TransBus Mini Pointer	N29F	2004

43845-43849 ADL Dart 8.8m ADL Mini Pointer N29F 2005

43845	SO	SN55CXH	43847	SO	SN55CXJ	43848	SO	SN55CXE	43849	BB	SN05HEJ
43846	SO	SN55CXF									

43850	TR	WK06AEE	ADL Dart 4 8.9m	ADL Mini Pointer	N29F	2006	Truronian, 2008
43851	TR	WK06AEF	ADL Dart 4 8.9m	ADL Mini Pointer	N29F	2006	Truronian, 2008
43852	TR	WK06AFU	ADL Dart 4 8.9m	ADL Mini Pointer	N29F	2006	Truronian, 2008
43853	TR	WK06AFV	ADL Dart 4 8.9m	ADL Mini Pointer	N29F	2006	Truronian, 2008
43901	PD	SN03LGG	TransBus Dart 11.3m	TransBus Pointer	N41F	2003	
43902	PD	SN03LGJ	TransBus Dart 11.3m	TransBus Pointer	N41F	2003	
43903	PD	SN03LGK	TransBus Dart 11.3m	TransBus Pointer	N41F	2003	

43911-43918 ADL Dart 4 11.4m East Lancs Spryte N39F 2006 *Operated for Surrey CC*

43911	BL	LK55ACY	43913	BL	LK55ADU	43915	BL	LK55ADX	43917	BL	LK55AEA
43912	BL	LK55ACX	43914	BL	LK55ADV	43916	BL	LK55ADZ	43918	BL	LK55ACV

43919-43932 ADL Dart 4 11.6m East Lancs Spryte N39F 2006 *Operated for Surrey CC*

43919	BL	LK06BWB	43923	BL	LK56JKF	43927	BL	LK56JKV	43930	BL	LK07CBU
43920	BL	LK06BWC	43924	BL	LK56JKJ	43928	BL	LK07CBF	43931	BL	LK07CBV
43921	BL	LK06BWD	43925	BL	LK56JKN	43929	BL	LK07CBO	43932	BL	LK07CBX
43922	BL	LK56JKE	43926	BL	LK56JKO						

44001-44006 ADL Dart 4 ADL Enviro 200 N29D 2008

44001	UX	LK57EJD	44003	UX	LK57EJF	44005	UX	LK57EJJ	44006	UX	LK57EJL
44002	UX	LK57EJE	44004	UX	LK57EJG						

44007-44021 ADL Dart 4 ADL Enviro 200 N--D 2008 *On order for London*

44007	UX	LK08	44011	UX	LK08	44015	UX	LK08	44019	UX	LK08
44008	UX	LK08	44012	UX	LK08	44016	UX	LK08	44020	UX	LK08
44009	UX	LK08	44013	UX	LK08	44017	UX	LK08	44021	UX	LK08
44010	UX	LK08	44014	UX	LK08	44018	UX	LK08			

44500	TR	WK56ABZ	ADL Dart 4	ADL Enviro200	N38F	2006	Truronian, 20008

44501-44506 ADL Dart 4 10.8m ADL Enviro 200 N36F 2008

44501	RA	CU08ACY	44503	RA	CU08ADO	44505	RA	CU08ADX	44506	RA	CU08ADY
44502	RA	CU08ACZ	44504	RA	CU08ADV						

44901	TR	MX07NTV	ADL Dart 4 8.9m	ADL Enviro 200	N29F	2007	Truronian, 2008
44902	BA	WX08LNN	ADL Dart 4 8.9m	ADL Enviro 200	N29F	2008	*Operated for Wessex Water*
44903	BA	WX08LNO	ADL Dart 4 8.9m	ADL Enviro 200	N29F	2008	*Operated for Wessex Water*
44904	BA	WX08LNP	ADL Dart 4 8.9m	ADL Enviro 200	N29F	2008	*Operated for Wessex Water*
45307	WH	JDZ2307	Dennis Dart 8.5m	Wright Handybus	B30F	1991	
45315	u	JDZ2315	Dennis Dart 8.5m	Wright Handybus	B30F	1991	
45322	ROs	JDZ2322	Dennis Dart 8.5m	Wright Handybus	B30F	1991	
45389	HO	JDZ2389	Dennis Dart 8.5m	Wright Handybus	B30F	1991	
45408	WH	KDZ5108	Dennis Dart 8.5m	Wright Handybus	B26F	1991	
45424	HO	LDZ9124	Dennis Dart 8.5m	Wright Handybus	B26F	1993	
45471	ROs	K411EWA	Dennis Dart 9.8m	Wright Handybus	B41F	1992	Stagecoach, 2008
46010	HO	H308DRV	Dennis Dart 9m	Reeve Burgess Pointer	B35F	1991	
46062	YA	K62KEX	Dennis Dart 9.8m	East Lancs	BC43F	1993	Blue Bus, 1996
46079	YV	K279XJB	Dennis Dart 9.8m	Plaxton Pointer	B40F	1993	
46081	NR	K281XJB	Dennis Dart 9.8m	Plaxton Pointer	B40F	1993	
46083	NR	K283XJB	Dennis Dart 9.8m	Plaxton Pointer	B40F	1993	

46103-46117 Dennis Dart 9m Plaxton Pointer B35F 1992

46103	u	K903CVW	46109	HH	K909CVW	46113	HH	K913CVW	46117	YV	K917CVW
46108	HH	K908CVW	46110	HH	K910CVW	46116	u	K915CVW			

The 2008 First Bus Handbook

Allocated to TfL route A10 are six Alexander-Dennis Darts with Enviro 200 bodywork are the first of the model for First fleet, although a further batch for London is imminent. Seen in Horton Road in Hayes is 44002, LK57EJE. *Mark Lyons*

46120-46143

		Dennis Dart 9.8m			Plaxton Pointer			B39F	1994

46120	HH	M920TEV	46128	HH	M928TEV	46137	HH	M937TEV	46141	HH	M941TEV
46122	HH	M922TEV	46129	BR	M929TEV	46138	HH	M938TEV	46142	HH	M942TEV
46123	NR	M923TEV	46132	HH	M932TEV	46140	HH	M940TEV	46143	BR	M943TEV
46127	u	M927TEV	46136	HH	M936TEV						

46144-46158

Dennis Dart 9.8m — Plaxton Pointer — B39F — 1995

46144	BR	N944CPU	46148	HH	N948CPU	46152	HH	N952CPU	46156	HH	N956CPU
46145	CN	N945CPU	46149	HH	N949CPU	46153	HH	N953CPU	46157	HH	N957CPU
46146	HH	N946CPU	46150	HH	N950CPU	46154	HH	N954CPU	46158	HH	N958CPU
46147	HH	N947CPU	46151	HH	N951CPU	46155	HH	N955CPU			

46167-46172

Dennis Dart 9.8m — Plaxton Pointer — B37F — 1995

46167	BS	N967CPU	46169	BS	N969CPU	46171	BS	N971CPU	46172	BS	N972CPU
46168	BS	N968CPU	46170	BS	N970CPU						

46173-46187

Dennis Dart 9.8m — Plaxton Pointer — B40F — 1996

46173	CM	N973EHJ	46177	BS	N977EHJ	46182	HH	N982EHJ	46185	BS	N985EHJ
46174	BS	N974EHJ	46179	HH	N979EHJ	46183	BS	N983EHJ	46186	CN	N986EHJ
46175	CN	N975EHJ	46180	HH	N980EHJ	46184	BS	N984EHJ	46187	BS	N987EHJ
46176	CN	N976EHJ	46181	HH	N981EHJ						

46195	BW	L205GMO	Dennis Dart 9.8m			Plaxton Pointer			B37F	1993

46203-46209

Dennis Dart 9.8m — Plaxton Pointer — B40F — 1993

46203	PT	L203SHW	46204	TN	L204SHW	46206	WS	L206SHW	46209	PD	L209SHW

46211-46225

Dennis Dart 9.8m — Plaxton Pointer — B40F — 1994

46211	MS	L211VHU	46216	MR	L216VHU	46218	WS	L218VHU	46220	MR	L220VHU
46215	MR	L215VHU	46217	MR	L217VHU	46223	PT	L223VHU	46225	BA	L225VHU

Much of the fleet has now been repainted into the latest livery, eliminating the Barbie 2 scheme that incorporated the use of vinyls on the lower panels to produce this shade effect. Dart 46239, N239KAE, is seen in Weston-super-Mare. *Richard Godfrey*

46226-46229

Dennis Dart 9.8m — Plaxton Pointer — B40F — 1995

46226	TN	N226KAE	46227	YV	N227KAE	46228	TN	N228KAE	46229	WS	N229KAE

| 46230 | TR | N22BLU | Dennis Dart 9.8m | | Marshall C37 | | B40F | 1995 | Bluebird, Middleton, 1997 |

46231-46242

Dennis Dart 9.8m — Plaxton Pointer — B40F — 1995

46231	WS	N230KAE	46234	BA	N234KAE	46237	BA	N237KAE	46240	BA	N240KAE
46232	MS	N231KAE	46235	BA	N235KAE	46238	WS	N238KAE	46241	WS	N241KAE
46233	TN	N233KAE	46236	TN	N236KAE	46239	WS	N239KAE	46242	MS	N242KAE

46243-46250

Dennis Dart 9.8m — Plaxton Pointer — B40F — 1996

| 46243 | MS | N243LHT | 46245 | BA | N245LHT | 46247 | BA | N247LHT | 46249 | MS | N249LHT |
| 46244 | MS | N244LHT | 46246 | BA | N246LHT | 46248 | MS | N248LHT | 46250 | MS | N250LHT |

46251-46257

Dennis Dart 9.8m — Plaxton Pointer — B40F — 1996

| 46251 | TN | P251PAE | 46253 | WS | P253PAE | 46255 | LV | P256PAE | 46257 | MS | P257PAE |
| 46252 | WS | P252PAE | 46254 | MS | P254PAE | 46256 | MS | P256PAE | | | |

46258-46264

Dennis Dart SLF — Plaxton Pointer — N39F — 1996

| 46258 | WS | P258PAE | 46260 | WS | P260PAE | 46262 | WS | P262PAE | 46264 | WS | P264PAE |
| 46259 | WS | P259PAE | 46261 | WS | P261PAE | 46263 | WS | P263PAE | | | |

46267	TR	N167KAF	Dennis Dart 9.8m	Plaxton Pointer	B37F	1996	Truronian, 2008
46268	TR	N168KAF	Dennis Dart 9.8m	Plaxton Pointer	B37F	1996	Truronian, 2008
46269	TR	N169KAF	Dennis Dart 9.8m	Plaxton Pointer	B37F	1996	Truronian, 2008

46309-46313

Dennis Dart 9m — Plaxton Pointer — B35F — 1993

| 46309 | HO | L309RTP | 46311 | HO | L311RTP | 46312 | HO | L312RTP | 46313 | HO | L313RTP |
| 46310 | HO | L310RTP | | | | | | | | | |

46314-46329   Dennis Dart 9m   Plaxton Pointer   B35F   1994-95

46314	HO	M314YOT	46318	HO	M318YOT	46322	HO	M322YOT	46326	HO	N326ECR
46315	HO	M315YOT	46319	HO	M319YOT	46323	HO	M323YOT	46327	HO	N327ECR
46316	HO	M316YOT	46320	HO	M320YOT	46324	HO	N324ECR	46328	HO	N328ECR
46317	HO	M317YOT	46321	HO	M321YOT	46325	HO	N325ECR	46329	HO	N329ECR

46365	HO	N465ETR	Dennis Dart 9.8m	Plaxton Pointer	B40F	1995
46366	HO	N466ETR	Dennis Dart 9.8m	Plaxton Pointer	B40F	1995
46367	HO	N467ETR	Dennis Dart 9.8m	Plaxton Pointer	B40F	1995
46375	YA	M375YEX	Dennis Dart 9m	Plaxton Pointer	B34F	1994
46379	YA	M379YEX	Dennis Dart 9m	Plaxton Pointer	B34F	1994
46420	CE	M420CCV	Dennis Dart 9.8m	Plaxton Pointer	B38F	1995
46422	CE	M422CCV	Dennis Dart 9.8m	Plaxton Pointer	BC37F	1995
46440	BB	N810VOD	Dennis Dart SLF 9m	Plaxton Pointer	N36F	1996

46501-46522   Dennis Dart 9m   Plaxton Pointer   B31F   1993

46501	PT	L501HCY	46507	RA	L507HCY	46514	PT	L514HCY	46518	LL	L518HCY
46502	PD	L502HCY	46509	PT	L509HCY	46515	PT	L515HCY	46519	PT	L519HCY
46504	PD	L504HCY	46510	PT	L510HCY	46516	RA	L516HCY	46521	LL	L521HCY
46505	PD	L505HCY	46511	PT	L511HCY	46517	PT	L517HCY	46522	PD	L522HCY
46506	PT	L506HCY	46513	PT	L513HCY						

46525-46550   Dennis Dart 9m   Plaxton Pointer   B31F   1994

46525	PT	L525JEP	46531	LL	L531JEP	46537	PT	L537JEP	46545	PD	L545JEP
46526	PD	L526JEP	46532	PT	L532JEP	46538	LL	L538JEP	46546	PD	L546JEP
46527	LL	L527JEP	46533	PT	L533JEP	46539	LL	L539JEP	46547	PD	L547JEP
46528	LL	L528JEP	46534	LL	L534JEP	46540	u	L540JEP	46549	LL	L549JEP
46529	LL	L529JEP	46535	u	L535JEP	46542	PD	L542JEP	46550	PD	L550JEP
46530	LL	L530JEP	46536	LL	L536JEP	46544	RA	L544JEP			

46551-46568   Dennis Dart 9m   Plaxton Pointer   B31F   1995

46551	u	N551UCY	46555	PD	N555UCY	46559	PT	N559UCY	46564	LL	N564UCY
46552	PD	N552UCY	46556	PT	N556UCY	46561	LL	N561UCY	46565	CA	N565UCY
46553	RA	N553UCY	46557	PT	N557UCY	46562	RA	N562UCY	46567	CA	N567UCY
46554	PD	N554UCY	46558	PD	N558UCY	46563	LL	N563UCY	46568	RA	N568UCY

46601-46608   Dennis Dart 9m   Plaxton Pointer   B35F   1994

46601	YA	L501VHU	46603	WS	L503VHU	46605	WS	L505VHU	46607	LH	L507VHU
46602	YA	L502VHU	46604	LH	L504VHU	46606	LH	L506VHU	46608	LH	L508VHU

46609-46648   Dennis Dart 9m   Plaxton Pointer   B35F   1995

46609	LH	M509DHU	46622	LH	M522FFB	46631	HG	M531FFB	46640	MR	N540HAE
46610	LH	M510DHU	46623	LH	M523FFB	46632	HG	M532FFB	46641	MR	N541HAE
46611	LH	M511DHU	46624	LH	M524FFB	46633	HG	M533FFB	46642	MR	N542HAE
46613	MR	M513DHU	46625	MR	M525FFB	46634	HG	M534FFB	46643	MR	N543HAE
46614	HG	M514DHU	46626	LH	M526FFB	46635	HG	M535FFB	46644	HG	N544HAE
46615	LH	M515DHU	46627	HG	M527FFB	46636	HG	M536FFB	46645	HG	N545HAE
46616	LH	M516DHU	46628	LH	M528FFB	46637	LH	M537FFB	46646	MR	N546HAE
46617	LH	M517DHU	46629	LH	M529FFB	46638	LH	M538FFB	46647	MR	N547HAE
46620	LH	M520FFB	46630	LH	M530FFB	46639	MR	N539HAE	46648	MR	N548HAE
46621	LH	M521FFB									

46649-46664   Dennis Dart 9m   Plaxton Pointer   B35F   1996

46649	MR	N549LHU	46653	MR	N553LHU	46657	MR	N557LHU	46662	BB	N562LHU
46650	MR	N550LHU	46654	MR	N554LHU	46658	MR	N558LHU	46663	BB	N563LHU
46651	MR	N551LHU	46656	MR	N556LHU	46659	HG	N559LHU	46664	CE	N564LHU
46652	MR	N552LHU									

46702-46707   Dennis Dart 9.8m   Plaxton Pointer   B40F   1994

46702	LL	L602FKG	46705	PT	L605FKG	46706	PT	L606FKG	46707	PD	L607FKG

46709-46718   Dennis Dart 9.8m   Plaxton Pointer   BC40F   1995   46716 rebodied in 2000

46709	PD	N609MHB	46711	PT	N611MHB	46714	PD	N614MHB	46716	PD	N616MHB
46710	PD	N610MHB	46712	PD	N612MHB	46715	PD	N615MHB	46718	PT	N618MHB

46719	LL	P619VDW	Dennis Dart 9.8m	Plaxton Pointer	B40F	1997
46720	PD	P620VDW	Dennis Dart 9.8m	Plaxton Pointer	B40F	1997

46721	PD	P621VDW	Dennis Dart 9.8m		Plaxton Pointer	B40F	1997
46725	YA	N625GAH	Dennis Dart 9m		Plaxton Pointer	B34F	1995
46726	YA	N626GAH	Dennis Dart 9m		Plaxton Pointer	B34F	1995

46727-46731   Dennis Dart 9.8m   Plaxton Pointer   B37F   1996

| 46727 | BW | P627CGM | 46729 | YV | P629CGM | 46730 | YV | P630CGM | 46731 | TN | P631CGM |
| 46728 | YV | P628CGM | | | | | | | | | |

46733-46737   Dennis Dart 9.8m   Plaxton Pointer   B37F   1996

| 46733 | BP | N633ACF | 46735 | WH | N635ACF | 46736 | WH | N636ACF | 46737 | WH | N637ACF |
| 46734 | WH | N634ACF | | | | | | | | | |

46803-46822   Dennis Dart 9m   Plaxton Pointer   B34F   1993-94

46803	BS	L803OPU	46808	BS	L808OPU	46814	HH	L814OPU	46818	HH	L818OPU
46804	BS	L804OPU	46811	BS	L811OPU	46815	HH	L815OPU	46820	CN	L820OPU
46806	u	L806OPU	46812	BR	L812OPU	46816	BR	L816OPU	46821	BR	L821OPU
46807	YA	L807OPU	46813	BR	L813OPU	46817	BR	L817OPU	46822	BR	L822OPU

46823-46830   Dennis Dart 9.8m   Plaxton Pointer   B39F   1995

| 46823 | BR | N823APU | 46825 | BS | N825APU | 46827 | CM | N827APU | 46829 | CN | N829APU |
| 46824 | BR | N824APU | 46826 | BR | N826APU | 46828 | CN | N828APU | 46830 | CN | N830APU |

46901-46932   Dennis Dart 9m   Plaxton Pointer   B32F   1995

46901	YV	N801FLW	46906	MR	N806FLW	46923	BA	N823FLW	46929	KD	N829FLW
46902	MS	N802FLW	46907	MR	N807FLW	46925	WS	N825FLW	46930	KD	N830FLW
46903	MR	N803FLW	46908	MR	N808FLW	46926	BL	N826FLW	46931	KD	N831FLW
46904	MR	N804FLW	46909	HG	N809FLW	46927	BA	N827FLW	46932	KD	N832FLW
46905	MR	N805FLW	46911	HG	N811FLW						

47001-47009   Dennis Dart 9.8m   Plaxton Pointer   BC35F   1995

47001	HD	N301XAB	47004	HD	N304XAB	47006	HD	N306XAB	47008	HD	N308XAB
47002	HD	N302XAB	47005	HD	N305XAB	47007	HD	N307XAB	47009	PD	N309XAB
47003	HD	N303XAB									

47011-47015   Dennis Dart 9.8m   Plaxton Pointer   BC35F   1995   *47012 is B40F

| 47011 | HD | N311XAB | 47012 | PD | N312XAB | 47013 | HD | N313XAB | 47015 | HO | N615DWY |

| 47070 | PD | N310XAB | Dennis Dart 9.8m | | Plaxton Pointer | B40F | 1995 |

47101-47106   Dennis Dart 9.8m   Alexander Dash   B40F   1995-96

| 47101 | CO | N201VSA | 47103 | CO | N203VSA | 47105 | CN | N205VSA | 47106 | CN | N206VSA |
| 47102 | CO | N202VSA | 47104 | CO | N204VSA | | | | | | |

47111	PL	P411MLA	Dennis Dart 9.8m		Plaxton Pointer	B37F	1996
47201	LO	M201VWW	Dennis Dart 9.8m		Plaxton Pointer	B40F	1995
47202	LO	M202VWW	Dennis Dart 9.8m		Plaxton Pointer	B40F	1995
47203	LO	M203VWW	Dennis Dart 9.8m		Plaxton Pointer	B40F	1995

47206-47218   Dennis Dart 9.8m   Plaxton Pointer   B40F   1995

| 47206 | NR | M206VWW | 47208 | IP | M208VWW | 47215 | YA | M215VWW | 47218 | YA | M218VWW |
| 47207 | NR | M207VWW | 47209 | NR | M209VWW | 47217 | YA | M217VWW | | | |

47219-47252   Dennis Dart 9.8m   Alexander Dash   B40F   1995

47219	CM	M219VWW	47224	CN	M224VWW	47228	CM	M228VWW	47233	YA	M233VWW
47220	CM	M220VWW	47225	CN	M225VWW	47229	CM	M229VWW	47250	NR	M250VWW
47221	CM	M221VWW	47226	CN	M226VWW	47231	NR	M231VWW	47251	NR	M251VWW
47223	CM	M223VWW	47227	CN	M227VWW	47232	YA	M232VWW	47252	CM	M450VWW

47301-47307   Dennis Dart 9.8m   UVG Urban Star   B40F   1995

| 47301 | HO | N601EBP | 47303 | HO | N603EBP | 40705 | HO | N605EBP | 47307 | HO | N607EBP |
| 47302 | HO | N602EBP | 47304 | HO | N604EBP | 40706 | HO | N606EBP | | | |

48013	u	L103WYS	Volvo B6 9.9m		Alexander Dash	B40F	1994
48045	LFs	N345CJA	Volvo B6 9.9m		Alexander Dash	B36F	1996
48046	B	N346CJA	Volvo B6 9.9m		Alexander Dash	B36F	1996
48070	IP	M870DYS	Volvo B6 9.9m		Alexander Dash	B36F	1995
48072	B	L672RMD	Volvo B6 9.9m		Alexander Dash	B36F	1994

Penryn is the location for this view of Wrightbus Crusader 48270, WK02TYD, one of twenty-three Volvo B6BLEs that work from Plymouth depot. Lettering promotes the Train-bus connection, with First being the current franchise holders for Great Western trains which connect the south-west with London. *Mark Lyons*

48084-48090

			Volvo B6 9.9m			Plaxton Pointer			B40F		1994	
48084	IP	M584ANG		48085	IP	M585ANG		48086	IP	M586ANG	48090	IP	M590ANG

48141	DN	N441BKY	Volvo B6LE	Wright Crusader	N36F	1995
48142	DN	N442BKY	Volvo B6LE	Wright Crusader	N36F	1995
48201	PL	T801RHW	Volvo B6BLE	Wright Crusader 2	N36F	1999

48202-48210

Volvo B6BLE · Wright Crusader 2 · N36F · 1999

48202	WH	V802EFB	48205	WH	V805EFB	48207	WH	V807EFB	48209	WH	V809EFB
48203	WH	V803EFB	48206	WH	V806EFB	48208	WH	V808EFB	48210	HG	V810EFB
48204	WH	V804EFB									

48211-48234

Volvo B6BLE · Wright Crusader 2 · N36F · 2000

48211	HG	W811PFB	48217	HG	W817PFB	48224	HG	W824PFB	48229	PL	W829PFB
48212	HG	W812PFB	48218	HG	W818PFB	48225	PL	W825PFB	48231	PL	W831PFB
48213	HG	W813PFB	48219	HG	W819PFB	48226	PL	W826PFB	48232	PL	W832PFB
48214	HG	W814PFB	48221	HG	W821PFB	48227	PL	W827PFB	48233	PL	W833PFB
48215	HG	W815PFB	48222	HG	W822PFB	48228	PL	W828PFB	48234	PL	W834PFB
48216	HG	W816PFB	48223	HG	W823PFB						

48261-48269

Volvo B6BLE · Wright Crusader 2 · N37F · 2000

48261	PL	W601PAF	48264	PL	W604PAF	48266	PL	W606PAF	48268	PL	W608PAF
48262	PL	W602PAF	48265	PL	W605PAF	48267	PL	W607PAF	48269	PL	W609PAF
48263	PL	W603PAF									

48270-48273

Volvo B6BLE · Wrightbus Crusader 2 · N38F · 2002

48270	PL	WK02TYD	48271	PL	WK02TYF	48272	PL	WK02TYH	48273	PL	YG02DLV

49000	WJ	-	MAN 14.240	MCV Evolution	N--D	2008	*On loan from Neopman*

50022-50048 — Mercedes-Benz Vario 0810 — Plaxton Beaver 2 — B27F — 1997

50022	CH	R232ERE	50033	AG	R243ERE	50038	CW	R248ERE	50046	CH	R256ERE
50023	CH	R233ERE	50035	NE	R245ERE	50044	CH	R254ERE	50047	CH	R257ERE
50025	CH	R235ERE	50036	CW	R246ERE	50045	CH	R255ERE	50048	NE	R258ERE

50049-50060 — Mercedes-Benz Vario 0814 — Plaxton Beaver 2 — B27F — 1998

50049	AG	S259AFA	50055	CH	S265AFA	50057	NE	S267AFA	50059	CW	S259AFA
50054	CW	S264AFA	50056	NE	S266AFA	50058	NE	S268AFA	50060	NE	S270AFA

50073	PT	P416NFA	Mercedes-Benz 709D	Plaxton Beaver	B22F	1996
50077	ABM	P420NFA	Mercedes-Benz 709D	Plaxton Beaver	B22F	1996
50088	HO	L556LVT	Mercedes-Benz 709D	Marshall C19	B23F	1994

50095-50105 — Mercedes-Benz 709D — Plaxton Beaver — B22F — 1995

50095	PD	N579CEH	50097	PD	N581CEH	50104	PD	N588CEH	50105	PD	N589CEH
50096	PD	N580CEH									

50122	SO	M159LNC	Mercedes-Benz 811D	Alexander Sprint	B31F	1994	Timeline, 1998
50206	SO	N273JUG	Mercedes-Benz 709D	Plaxton Beaver	B25F	1995	
50210	SO	N279JUG	Mercedes-Benz 709D	Plaxton Beaver	B25F	1995	
50215	SO	N284JUG	Mercedes-Benz 709D	Plaxton Beaver	B25F	1995	

50232-50239 — Optare Solo M850 — Optare — N26F — 2001

50232	RO	Y251HHL	50234	DN	Y253HHL	50236	OG	Y256HHL	50238	RO	YT51EZX
50233	RO	Y252HHL	50235	DN	Y254HHL	50237	DN	YT51EZW	50239	OG	YR02UVU

50252	HX	M243VWU	Mercedes-Benz 709D	Plaxton Beaver	B23F	1995
50255	HX	M253VWU	Mercedes-Benz 709D	Plaxton Beaver	B23F	1995

50261-50269 — Mercedes-Benz 709D — Plaxton Beaver — B23F — 1996

50261	HX	N285JUG	50264	HX	N288JUG	50266	HX	N290JUG	50268	HX	N292JUG
50262	HX	N286JUG	50265	HX	N289JUG	50267	HX	N291JUG	50269	HX	N293JUG
50263	HX	N287JUG									

50270-50275 — Optare Solo M850 — Optare — N27F — 1998

50270	WH	S301EWU	50272	WH	S303EWU	50274	YA	S305EWU	50275	HP	S306EWU
50271	WH	S302EWU	50273	YA	S304EWU						

50276-50296 — Optare Solo M850 — Optare — N27F — 2000

50276	PL	W307DWX	50282	BD	W313DWX	50287	BD	W332DWX	50292	BD	W337DWX
50277	HI	W308DWX	50283	BD	W314DWX	50288	BD	W319DWX	50293	BD	W324DWX
50278	HI	W309DWX	50284	BD	W315DWX	50289	BD	W334DWX	50294	BD	W335DWX
50279	RA	W329DWX	50285	BD	W336DWX	50290	BD	W331DWX	50295	BD	W326DWX
50280	TE	W311DWX	50286	BD	W317DWX	50291	BD	W322DWX	50296	HD	W327DWX
50281	BD	W312DWX									

50297	RA	YG02DJY	Optare Solo M850	Optare	N27F	2002
50298	RA	YG02DJZ	Optare Solo M850	Optare	N27F	2002
50299	HI	R405WWR	Mercedes-Benz Vario 0814	Plaxton Beaver 2	B27F	1998

50300-50307 — Mercedes-Benz Vario 0814 — Plaxton Beaver 2 — B27F — 1998

50300	HI	S406GUB	50303	HI	S409GUB	50306	PL	S412GUB	50307	CE	S413GUB
50301	PL	S407GUB	50304	CE	S410GUB						

50318	HX	YN53ELO	Optare Solo M850	Optare	N27F	2003
50319	HX	YN53ELJ	Optare Solo M850	Optare	N27F	2003
50386	LF	R404HYG	Mercedes-Benz Vario 0814	Plaxton Beaver 2	B27F	1998
50391	LF	S826TCL	Mercedes-Benz Vario 0810	Plaxton Beaver 2	B27F	1998
50395	LF	S830TCL	Mercedes-Benz Vario 0810	Plaxton Beaver 2	B27F	1998
50407	HX	YN03ZVX	Optare Solo M850	Optare	N27F	2003
50408	HX	YN03ZVY	Optare Solo M850	Optare	N27F	2003
50411	AB	K402HRS	Mercedes-Benz 709D	Alexander Sprint	B23F	1993
50416	ABM	N689WLS	Mercedes-Benz 711D	Alexander Sprint	B25F	1995
50417	u	H37USO	Mercedes-Benz 709D	Reeve Burgess Beaver	B23F	1991
50420	u	J778WLS	Mercedes-Benz 709D	Alexander AM	B25F	1991
50421	ABM	M232VWU	Mercedes-Benz 709D	Plaxton Beaver	B25F	1994
50422	ABM	M233VWU	Mercedes-Benz 709D	Plaxton Beaver	B25F	1994

Several of the Optare Solo buses operating in the Glasgow area carry SPTbus livery, the colours of the transport authorty. The scheme is seen on Dumbarton depot's 50462, SJ03DPF. *Mark Doggett*

50460-50468

			Optare Solo M850			Optare			N18F	2003	
50460	DU	SJ03DOH	50463	B	SJ03DPN	50465	B	SJ03DPV	50467	B	SJ03DPY
50461	DU	SJ03DPE	50464	B	SJ03DPU	50466	B	SJ03DPX	50468	DU	SJ03DPZ
50462	DU	SJ03DPF									

50482	PTs	E294VEP	Mercedes-Benz 709D	Plaxton Beaver (1997)	Staff	1988
50951	BP	K751CFJ	Mercedes-Benz 811D	Wright NimBus	B33F	1992

51001-51028

			Mercedes-Benz 709D			Plaxton Beaver	B22F	1993
51001	WS	L801SAE	51025	PT	L825SAE	51028	LL	L828WHY

51079-51107

			Mercedes-Benz 709D			Plaxton Beaver			B23F	1994	
51079	WS	L879VHT	51096	WS	L896VHT	51102	WS	L902VHT	51104	WS	L904VHT
51086	WS	L886VHT	51097	WSu	L897VHT	51103	WS	L903VHT	51107	WS	L907VHT
51091	BA	L891VHT	51101	WS	L901VHT						

51112	u	N212KBJ	Mercedes-Benz 711D	Autobus Classique	BC24F	1995	Truronian, 2008
51120	u	N170KAF	Mercedes-Benz 711D	Plaxton Beaver	BC25F	1996	Truronian, 2008
51125	u	L725WCV	Mercedes-Benz 709D	Plaxton Beaver	B31F	1994	Truronian, 2008
51126	u	L726WCV	Mercedes-Benz 709D	Plaxton Beaver	B31F	1994	Truronian, 2008
51129	WS	L329MYC	Mercedes-Benz 811D	Wright NimBus	B33F	1993	
51130	BP	L330MYC	Mercedes-Benz 811D	Wright NimBus	B33F	1993	
51167	WS	L67EPR	Mercedes-Benz 811D	Wright NimBus	B33F	1994	
51168	WS	L68EPR	Mercedes-Benz 811D	Wright NimBus	B33F	1994	
51211	WS	L651CJT	Mercedes-Benz 811D	Wright NimBus	B33F	1993	
51212	WS	L652CJT	Mercedes-Benz 811D	Wright NimBus	B33F	1993	
51214	BA	M14ABC	Mercedes-Benz 709D	Alexander Sprint	B25F	1995	Stonehouse Coaches, 1997
51228	LL	M228VWW	Mercedes-Benz 709D	Plaxton Beaver	B23F	1995	
51241	WS	M241VYA	Mercedes-Benz 709D	Alexander Sprint	B29F	1996	
51281	HI	M281UYD	Mercedes-Benz 709D	Alexander Sprint	B29F	1994	
51305	YV	M305TSF	Mercedes-Benz 709D	Alexander Sprint	B29F	1994	
51346	BA	M46BEG	Mercedes-Benz 811D	Marshall C16	B31F	1994	Streamline, Bath, 1997
51348	BA	M48BEG	Mercedes-Benz 811D	Marshall C16	B31F	1994	Streamline, Bath, 1997

51380	BA	M882BEU	Mercedes-Benz 709D	Plaxton Beaver	B23F	1994			
51404	BW	M804UYA	Mercedes-Benz 709D	Alexander Sprint	B29F	1994			
51459	HO	M659VJN	Mercedes-Benz 709D	Plaxton Beaver	B23F	1995			
51460	HO	M660VJN	Mercedes-Benz 709D	Plaxton Beaver	B23F	1995			
51537	LLs	M837ATC	Mercedes-Benz 709D	Plaxton Beaver	B22F	1994			
51558	WS	M858ATC	Mercedes-Benz 709D	Plaxton Beaver	B22F	1994			
51569	LL	M869ATC	Mercedes-Benz 709D	Plaxton Beaver	B22F	1994			

51583-51606 Mercedes-Benz 709D Plaxton Beaver B22F 1995

51583	HI	N883HWS	51590	BW	N890HWS	51593	BW	N893HWS	51602	BW	N902HWS
51589	BW	N889HWS	51592	BW	N892HWS	51594	BW	N894HWS	51606	BA	N906HWS

51657	YV	N557EYB	Mercedes-Benz 709D	Alexander Sprint	B29F	1996	
51659	YV	N559EYB	Mercedes-Benz 709D	Alexander Sprint	B29F	1996	
51661	BA	N561EYB	Mercedes-Benz 709D	Alexander Sprint	B29F	1996	
51679	TN	P179LYB	Mercedes-Benz 711D	Plaxton Beaver	B25F	1997	
51682	TN	P182LYB	Mercedes-Benz 711D	Plaxton Beaver	B25F	1997	
51683	TN	P183LYB	Mercedes-Benz 711D	Plaxton Beaver	B25F	1997	
51684	TN	N584WND	Mercedes-Benz 709D	Reeve Burgess Beaver	B27F	1995	Mistral, 1998
51685	BW	N583WND	Mercedes-Benz 709D	Reeve Burgess Beaver	B27F	1995	Mistral, 1998
51686	TN	N586WND	Mercedes-Benz 709D	Reeve Burgess Beaver	B27F	1995	Mistral, 1998
51688	BW	N588WND	Mercedes-Benz 709D	Reeve Burgess Beaver	B27F	1995	Mistral, 1998

51710-51729 Mercedes-Benz 709D Plaxton Beaver B27F 1996

51710	HO	N710GRV	51715	HI	N715GRV	51721	HO	N721GRV	51726	HI	P726KCR
51711	HO	N711GRV	51716	HI	N716GRV	51722	HO	P722KCR	51727	HI	P727KCR
51712	HO	N712GRV	51717	HI	N717GRV	51723	HO	P723KCR	51728	HI	P728KCR
51713	HO	N713GRV	51718	HI	N718GRV	51724	HO	P724KCR	51729	HI	P729KCR
51714	HO	N714GRV	51720	HO	N720GRV	51725	HO	P725KCR			

51742-51748 Mercedes-Benz 711D Alexander Sprint B29F 1996

51742	BW	P442KYC	51745	YV	P445KYC	51747	TN	P447KYC	51748	YV	P448KYC
51743	YV	P443KYC	51746	TN	P446KYC						

51803	BRs	P403HPU	Mercedes-Benz 709D	Plaxton Beaver	B23F	1996	
51880	TN	P181LYB	Mercedes-Benz 711D	Plaxton Beaver	B25F	1997	
52483	LF	R483EDW	Mercedes-Benz Vario 0810	Plaxton Beaver 2	B27F	1998	
52486	LF	R486EDW	Mercedes-Benz Vario 0810	Plaxton Beaver 2	B27F	1998	
52489	u	R489EDW	Mercedes-Benz Vario 0810	Plaxton Beaver 2	B27F	1998	

52501-52564 Mercedes-Benz Vario 0814 Plaxton Beaver 2 B22F 1998

52501	KD	R501CNP	52523	CE	S523RWP	52536	CEt	S536RWP	52555	SO	S955RWP
52502	KD	R502CNP	52526	BB	S526RWP	52540	PL	S540RWP	52556	PL	S556RWP
52503	KD	R503CNP	52528	CE	S528RWP	52547	PL	S547RWP	52557	PLt	S557RWP
52504	HD	R504CNP	52529	PL	S529RWP	52550	BB	S550RWP	52558	HI	S558RWP
52513	HI	S513RWP	52532	BB	S532RWP	52551	CE	S551RWP	52559	HI	S559RWP
52515	PLt	S515RWP	52533	SO	S533RWP	52552	CE	S552RWP	52560	HI	S560RWP
52517	HI	S517RWP	52534	PL	S534RWP	52553	BA	S553RWP	52562	CE	S562RWP
52519	PL	S519RWP	52535	CE	S535RWP	52554	LHC	S554RWP	52564	BA	S564RWP

52566	TR	S866NOD	Mercedes-Benz Vario 0810	Plaxton Beaver 2	B29F	1999	
52567	PLt	S867NOD	Mercedes-Benz Vario 0810	Plaxton Beaver 2	B29F	1999	
52568	CE	S868NOD	Mercedes-Benz Vario 0810	Plaxton Beaver 2	B29F	1999	
52569	CE	S869NOD	Mercedes-Benz Vario 0810	Plaxton Beaver 2	B29F	1999	
52570	CE	S870NOD	Mercedes-Benz Vario 0810	Plaxton Beaver 2	B29F	1999	
52571	BB	S871NOD	Mercedes-Benz Vario 0810	Plaxton Beaver 2	B29F	1999	
52573	TN	S863LRU	Mercedes-Benz Vario 0810	Plaxton Beaver 2	B27F	1998	
52574	TN	S864LRU	Mercedes-Benz Vario 0810	Plaxton Beaver 2	B27F	1998	

52580-52598 Mercedes-Benz Vario 0814 Marshall Master B23F* 1999 *seating varies

52580	HI	V430GTW	52583	HI	V433GTW	52585	BS	V435GTW	52597	PL	R417VPU
52581	HI	V431GTW	52584	BS	V434GTW	52596	PL	R416VPU	52598	PL	R418VPU

52601-52608 Mercedes-Benz Vario 0810 Plaxton Beaver 2 B27F 1998

52601	HI	R501NPR	52603	WH	R503NPR	52605	HI	R505NPR	52607	WH	R507NPR
52602	HI	R502NPR	52604	BP	R504NPR	52606	WH	R506NPR	52608	BP	R508NPR

52640	TN	S340WYB	Mercedes-Benz Vario 0810	Plaxton Beaver 2	B27F	1998	
52653	TRt	R853TFJ	Mercedes-Benz Vario 0810	Plaxton Beaver 2	B27F	1998	

Seen operating the *Falmouth Explorer* is Optare Solo 53006, W806PAF. In the early part of 2008, the Truronian operation which is based in Cornwall was acquired by First and its operations are currently being integrated. *Mark Lyons*

53001-53015

			Optare Solo M850			Optare			N27F	1999-2000	

53001	PL	V801KAF	53005	TR	W805PAF	53009	PL	W809PAF	53013	PL	W813PAF
53002	PL	V802KAF	53006	TR	W806PAF	53011	PL	W811PAF	53014	PL	W814PAF
53003	PL	V803KAF	53007	PL	W807PAF	53012	PL	W812PAF	53015	PL	W815PAF
53004	TR	W804PAF	53008	PL	W808PAF						

53017	D	03D78917	Optare Solo M850	Optare	N26F	2003	
53028	YV	W338DWX	Optare Solo M850	Optare	N27F	2002	
53034	OG	Y546XNW	Optare Solo M850	Optare	N29F	2001	Clarkson, South Emsall, 2003
53035	OG	Y547XNW	Optare Solo M850	Optare	N29F	2001	Clarkson, South Emsall, 2003

53040-53051

			Optare Solo M850			Optare			N22F	2002-03	

53040	HD	VU02PKX	53043	WR	VU03YJV	53046	WR	VU03YJY	53049	WR	VU03YKC
53041	HD	VU02PKY	53044	WR	VU03YJW	53047	WR	VU03YJZ	53050	WR	VU03YKD
53042	KD	VU03YJT	53045	WR	VU03YJX	53048	WR	VU03YKB	53051	WR	VU03YKE

53052-53057

			Optare Solo M850			Optare			N22F	2004	

53052	SH	LK53MBX	53054	SH	LK53MDE	53056	SH	LK53MDJ	53057	SH	LK53PNO
53053	SH	LK53MBY	53055	SH	LK53MDF						

53058-53064

			Optare Solo M850			Optare			N22F	2004	

53058	HD	VX53OEV	53060	HD	VX53OEO	53062	HD	VX53OER	53064	HD	VX53OEU
53059	HD	VX53OEN	53061	HD	VX53OEP	53063	HD	VX53OET			

53071	NN	KX06APV	Optare Solo M850	Optare	N22F	2006	*Operated for Northampton CC*
53072	NN	KX06APY	Optare Solo M850	Optare	N22F	2006	*Operated for Northampton CC*
53073	NN	KX06APZ	Optare Solo M850	Optare	N22F	2006	*Operated for Northampton CC*
53074	TR	MX04VML	Optare Solo M850	Optare	N26F	2004	*Truronian, 2008*
53075	TR	MX06BSY	Optare Solo M850	Optare	N27F	2006	*Truronian, 2008*
53076	SO	YJ05XMR	Optare Solo M850	Optare	N29F	2005	*Operaed for Hampshire CC*

Nineteen slimline Optare Solo buses are used in the Bath area and are lettered with the bubble promotion style of branding. Seen passing through the Grand Parade in the city is 53807, WX05RSV. *Mark Lyons*

53101-53111

Optare Solo M850 | Optare | N26F | 2002

53101	HP	EO02FLA	**53104**	HP	EO02FLD	**53107**	CE	EO02FLG	**53110**	PL	EO02FLK
53102	HP	EO02FLB	**53105**	HP	EO02FLE	**53108**	CE	EO02FLH	**53111**	CE	EO02FKZ
53103	HP	EO02FLC	**53106**	HP	EO02FLF	**53109**	CE	EO02FLJ			

53112-53137

Optare Solo M920 | Optare | N30F | 2002

53112	HA	EO02NDX	**53119**	CM	EO02NEY	**53126**	CM	EO02NFH	**53132**	CM	EO02NFP
53113	CM	EO02NDY	**53120**	CM	EO02NFA	**53127**	CM	EO02NFJ	**53133**	CM	EO02NFR
53114	CM	EO02NDZ	**53121**	CM	EO02NFC	**53128**	CM	EO02NFK	**53134**	CM	EO02NFT
53115	CM	EO02NEF	**53122**	CM	EO02NFD	**53129**	CM	EO02NFL	**53135**	CM	EO02NFU
53116	CM	EO02NEJ	**53123**	CM	EO02NFE	**53130**	CM	EO02NFM	**53136**	CM	EO02NFV
53117	CM	EO02NEN	**53124**	CM	EO02NFF	**53131**	CM	EO02NFN	**53137**	CM	EO02NFX
53118	CM	EO02NEU	**53125**	CM	EO02NFG						

53138	CN	EU54BNK	Optare Solo M920	Optare	N28F	2004
53139	HA	EU54BNJ	Optare Solo M920	Optare	N28F	2004
53140	SO	YJ05XOP	Optare Solo M920	Optare	N24F	2005

53143-53150

Optare Solo M920 | Optare | N30F | 2004

53143	QS	MX54GZA	**53145**	QS	MX54GZC	**53147**	QS	MX54GZE	**53149**	QS	MX54GZG
53144	QS	MX54GZB	**53146**	QS	MX54GZD	**53148**	QS	MX54GZF	**53150**	QS	MX54GZH

53151	HI	YN03ZVW	Optare Solo M850	Optare	N27F	2003	
53154	TR	YJ05XOR	Optare Solo M920	Optare	N29F	2005	Truronian, 2008
53201	LF	YJ54BSV	Optare Solo M950	Optare	N30F	2004	
53202	SN	SF05KUJ	Optare Solo M950	Optare	N28F	2005	
53203	SN	SF05KUK	Optare Solo M950	Optare	N28F	2005	
53204	TR	TU04TRU	Optare Solo M950	Optare	N33F	2004	Truronian, 2008
53205	TR	YJ05XNV	Optare Solo M950	Optare	N33F	2005	Truronian, 2008
53206	TR	T77TRU	Optare Solo M950	Optare	N33F	2004	Truronian, 2008
53301	BD	YV54BVA	Optare Solo M1020	Optare	N29F	2004	*Operated for Metro, WYPTE*
53302	BD	YV54BVB	Optare Solo M1020	Optare	N29F	2004	*Operated for Metro, WYPTE*
53303	BD	YV54BVC	Optare Solo M1020	Optare	N29F	2004	*Operated for Metro, WYPTE*

The 2008 First Bus Handbook

Wanstead is the location for this view of Optare Solo 53702, LK05DXP, one of six 7.8metre slimline buses used on route W12. The local prefix for this type that the London operation applies is OOS. *Mark Lyons*

53401-53404 — Optare Solo M880 — Optare — N29F — 2004 — *53403/4 operated for Cornwall*

53401	TR	TO54TRU	**53402**	TR	T20TVL	**53403**	TR	TL54TVL	**53404** TR TT54TVL

53701-53706 — Optare Solo M780 SL — Optare — N21F — 2005

53701	L	LK05DYO	**53703**	L	LK05DXR	**53705**	L	LK05DXT	**53706** L LK05DXU
53702	L	LK05DXP	**53704**	L	LK05DXS				

53801	BP	YK04KWR	Optare Solo M850 SL	Optare	N21F	2004	

53802-53820 — Optare Solo M850 SL — Optare — N26F — 2005

53802	BA	WX05RRV	**53807**	BA	WX05RSV	**53812**	BA	WX05RTV	**53817**	BA	WX05RUO
53803	BA	WX05RRY	**53808**	BA	WX05RSY	**53813**	BA	WX05RTZ	**53818**	BA	WX05RUR
53804	BA	WX05RRZ	**53809**	BA	WX05RSZ	**53814**	BA	WX05RUA	**53819**	BA	WX05RUU
53805	BA	WX05RSO	**53810**	BA	WX05RTO	**53815**	BA	WX05RUC	**53820**	BA	WX05RUV
53806	BA	WX05RSU	**53811**	BA	WX05RTU	**53816**	BA	WX05RUJ			

53821	HX	YJ54UXF	Optare Solo M780 SL	Optare	N24F	2005	*Operated for Metro, WYPTE*
53822	HX	YJ54UXG	Optare Solo M780 SL	Optare	N24F	2005	*Operated for Metro, WYPTE*
53823	HX	YJ55YJU	Optare Solo M780 SL	Optare	N24F	2005	*Operated for Metro, WYPTE*
53824	HX	YJ06FYS	Optare Solo M780 SL	Optare	N24F	2006	*Operated for Metro, WYPTE*
53825	HX	YJ06FYT	Optare Solo M780 SL	Optare	N24F	2006	*Operated for Metro, WYPTE*
53826	TR	YK05CDN	Optare Solo M780 SL	Optare	N24F	2005	*Truronian, 2008*
53827	TR	YK05CDO	Optare Solo M780 SL	Optare	N26F	2005	*Truronian, 2008*

53904-53909 — Optare Solo M920 SL — Optare — N32F* — 2005 — *Operated for Metro, WYPTE; *53907-9 are N26F*

53904	HP	YJ55ENR	**53906**	HP	YJ55ENN	**53908**	HP	YJ07EHP	**53909** HP YJ07EHR
53905	HP	YJ55ENM	**53907**	HP	YJ07EHO				

A pair of Plaxton Primo buses was placed into service at Harwich in 2006 and the type has been augmented with a similar bus operated by Truronian. The Primo has a Cummins engine and provides up to 28 seats in its 8m long body which is 2.4 metres wide. The model is finished at Scarborough where the 8.9metre Enviro 200 Dart is also built. *Richard Godfrey*

54501	TR	WK02XLT	Mercedes-Benz Vito 110	GM	M8	2002	*Operated for Cornwall CC*
54502	TR	WK52LZA	Mercedes-Benz Vito 110	GM	M8	2002	*Operated for Cornwall CC*
54601	TR	RA04YGX	Ford Transit	Ford	M16	2004	Truronian, 2008
54602	TR	RA04YHS	Ford Transit	Ford	M16	2004	Truronian, 2008
55000	LL	YN53YHH	Optare Alero AL02	Optare	N14C	2003	*Operated for Carmarthenshire CC*
55003	CA	YN04LWV	Optare Alero AL02	Optare	N14C	2004	*Operated for Carmarthenshire CC*
55004	CA	YN04LWW	Optare Alero AL02	Optare	N14C	2004	*Operated for Carmarthenshire CC*
56000	TR	W4TRU	Mercedes-Benz Vario 0814	Plaxton Cheetah	C27F	2000	Truronian, 2008
56001	AB	YN53VBT	Mercedes-Benz Vario 0814	Plaxton Cheetah	C29F	2003	
56002	CM	YN53VBU	Mercedes-Benz Vario 0814	Plaxton Cheetah	C29F	2003	
56003	CM	YN53VBV	Mercedes-Benz Vario 0814	Plaxton Cheetah	C29F	2003	

56004-56009

			Mercedes-Benz Vario 0814	Plaxton Cheetah	C29F	2004	

56004	CM	EY54BPX	56006	CM	EY54BRF	56008	AB	EY54BRX	56009	CM	EY54BRZ
56005	CM	EY54BPZ	56007	AB	EY54BRV						

56501	AB	YX05AVV	Mercedes-Benz Atego 01120L	Optare/Ferqui Solera	C29F	2005	
57000	TR	MX06AEB	Enterprise EB01	Plaxton Primo	N28F	2006	Truronian, 2008
57001	HA	YN56NHE	Enterprise EB01	Plaxton Primo	N28F	2006	
57002	HA	YN56NHF	Enterprise EB01	Plaxton Primo	N28F	2006	

The expansion of services on the Wirral following the acquisition of Chester Bus' routes has seen the use of DAF SB220 buses at Birkenhead. One of these, 60049, H807GRE, is shown. *Steve Rice*

60004-60012

Scania L113CRL — Wright Axcess-ultralow — N40F — 1998

60004	AG	S356MFP	60007	CW	S354MFP	60009	CH	S347MFP	60011	AG	R346SUT
60005	BH	S351MFP	60008	CH	S355MFP	60010	CH	S358MFP	60012	AG	S348MFP
60006	AG	S350MFP									

60013	CW	S103TNB	Scania L94UB	Wright Axcess Floline	N40F	1998
60014	CC	S104TNB	Scania L94UB	Wright Axcess Floline	N40F	1998
60015	CW	S106TNB	Scania L94UB	Wright Axcess Floline	N40F	1998
60021	CH	J422NCP	DAF SB220	Ikarus CitiBus	B48F	1992
60023	BHt	J424NCP	DAF SB220	Ikarus CitiBus	B48F	1992
60024	BH	J425NCP	DAF SB220	Ikarus CitiBus	B48F	1992
60025	CH	J426NCP	DAF SB220	Ikarus CitiBus	B48F	1992
60027	u	K528RJX	DAF SB220	Ikarus CitiBus	B48F	1992
60030	B	R343GHS	Volvo B10M-62	Plaxton Première 320	BC53F	1997
60031	CO	R346GHS	Volvo B10M-62	Plaxton Première 320	BC53F	1997

60032-60042

Blue Bird A3 RE — Blue Bird — B60F — 2002

60032	CH	CX02ECC	60035	CH	CX02EFF	60038	CH	CX02EGD	60041	CH	CX02EGJ
60033	CH	CX02ECN	60036	CH	CX02EFG	60039	CH	CX02EGE	60042	CH	CX02EGK
60034	CH	CX02ECT	60037	CH	CX02EGC	60040	CH	CX02EGF			

60043-60049

DAF SB220 — Optare Delta — BC48F — 1990

60043	NEt	H801GRE	60047	BH	H805GRE	60048	BH	H806GRE	60049	BH	H807GRE
60044	BH	H802GRE								

60052-60063

Scania L113CRL — Wright Axcess-ultralow — N40F — 1998

60052	BH	R810NVT	60055	CH	S813AEH	60058	CW	S816AEH	60061	AG	S819AEH
60053	BH	R811NVT	60056	AG	S814AEH	60059	AG	S817AEH	60062	CW	S820AEH
60054	BH	R812NVT	60057	AG	S815AEH	60060	AG	S818AEH	60063	CW	S821AEH

60064-60074

Scania L94UB — Wright Axcess Floline — N43F — 1999

60064	CW	T822SFS	60067	CW	T825SFS	60070	CW	T828SFS	60073	AG	V831GBF
60065	CW	T823SFS	60068	CW	T826SFS	60071	CW	T829SFS	60074	AG	V832GBF
60066	CW	T824SFS	60069	CW	T827SFS	60072	CW	V830GBF			

Carrying *UniLink* livery for a service to Stirling University is 60197, Y597KNE, a Scania L94UB. The bus was supplied to First Manchester in March 2001 and is now based at Bannockburn depot. *Phillip Stephenson*

60075-60080 Scania L113CRL Wright Axcess-ultralow N40F 1998

| 60075 | AG | R438ALS | 60077 | BH | R440ALS | 60079 | AG | R442ALS | 60080 | BH | S443BSG |
| 60076 | BH | R439ALS | 60078 | AG | R441ALS | | | | | | |

60081	CW	S101TNB	Scania L94UB	Wright Axcess Floline	N40F	1998
60082	AG	S357MFP	Scania L113CRL	Wright Axcess-ultralow	N40F	1998
60083	AG	S353MFP	Scania L113CRL	Wright Axcess-ultralow	N40F	1998
60095	ROt	H861GRE	Leyland Lynx LX2R11C15Z4S	Leyland Lynx	TV	1990
60097	NEt	N863CEH	Dennis Lance 11m	Plaxton Verde	TV	1995
60098	CW	N864CEH	Dennis Lance 11m	Plaxton Verde	BC45F	1995
60100	CWt	N866CEH	Dennis Lance 11m	Plaxton Verde	TV	1995
60102	CO	P868MBF	Dennis Lance 11m	Northern Counties Paladin	B43F	1997
60103	u	P869MBF	Dennis Lance 11m	Northern Counties Paladin	B43F	1997
60104	u	P870MBF	Dennis Lance 11m	Northern Counties Paladin	B43F	1997

60105-60112 Scania L113CRL Wright Axcess-ultralow N51F 1997-98

| 60105 | CH | R871ERE | 60107 | CH | R873ERE | 60109 | BH | R875ERE | 60111 | BH | R877ERE |
| 60106 | BH | R872ERE | 60108 | BH | R874ERE | 60110 | BH | R876ERE | 60112 | BH | R878ERE |

60113	BH	R879HRF	Scania L113CRL	Wright Axcess-ultralow	N40F	1998
60114	BH	R880HRF	Scania L113CRL	Wright Axcess-ultralow	N40F	1998
60115	BH	R881HRF	Scania L113CRL	Wright Axcess-ultralow	N40F	1998
60117	BN	N553WVR	Volvo B10B-58	Wright Endurance	BC50F	1996
60118	BH	S102TNB	Scania L94UB	Wright Axcess Floline	N40F	1998
60119	CW	S107TNB	Scania L94UB	Wright Axcess Floline	N40F	1998
60128	CW	S105TNB	Scania L94UB	Wright Axcess Floline	N40F	1998
60129	B	R345GHS	Volvo B10M-62	Plaxton Interurban	BC53F	1997
60130	CO	R344GHS	Volvo B10M-62	Plaxton Interurban	BC53F	1997
60131	CW	R178GSX	Scania L113CRL	Wright Axcess-ultralow	N40F	1997
60132	CW	N413ENW	Scania L113CRL	Wright Axcess-ultralow	N48F	1996
60133	AG	N414ENW	Scania L113CRL	Wright Axcess-ultralow	N48F	1996
60134	AG	P430GLS	Scania L113CRL	Wright Axcess-ultralow	N48F	1997
60135	CW	R177GSX	Scania L113CRL	Wright Axcess-ultralow	N40F	1998
60136	CW	R179GSX	Scania L113CRL	Wright Axcess-ultralow	N40F	1998
60137	CW	S685BFS	Scania L113CRL	Wright Axcess-ultralow	N40F	1998
60138	LFt	G612NWA	Volvo B10M-55	Alexander PS	B51F	1990
60139	AG	N415ENW	Scania L113CRL	Wright Axcess-ultralow	N48F	1995

Several of the Scania L94 that were new to First Manchester are now allocated to other depots. Illustrating the Wright Axcess Floline body is 60166, S113TNB, seen heading out of Reading on the King's Road towards Bracknell. *Mark Lyons*

60140-60149

Optare Excel L1070 | Optare | | N38F | 1996-97 | Timeline, 1998

60140	WN	P213HRJ	60143	WN	R216SBA	60146	WN	R219SBA	60148	WN	R221SBA
60141	WN	R214SBA	60144	WN	R217SBA	60147	WN	R220SBA	60149	WN	R223SBA
60142	WN	R215SBA	60145	WN	R218SBA						

60151-60160

Optare Excel L1150 | Optare | | N38F | 1997

60151	WN	R882ENF	60155	WN	R5LCB	60157	WN	R7LCB	60159	WN	R9LCB
60152	WN	R2LCB	60156	WN	R6LCB	60158	WN	R8LCB	60160	WN	R10LCB
60154	WN	R4LCB									

60161-60168

Scania L94UB | Wright Axcess Floline | | N40F | 1998

60161	BH	S108TNB	60163	BL	S110TNB	60165	BL	S112TNB	60167	BL	S114TNB
60162	BL	S109TNB	60164	BL	S651RNA	60166	BL	S113TNB	60168	BL	S115TNB

60169-60194

Scania L94UB | Wright Axcess Floline | | N42F* | 1999 | *60169-172 are N40F*

60169	BH	T916SSF	60176	AG	V124DND	60183	AG	V131DND	60189	NE	V137DND
60170	AG	T917SSF	60177	AG	V125DND	60184	AG	V132DND	60190	BH	V138DND
60171	AG	T918SSF	60178	BK	V126DND	60185	AG	V133DND	60191	LT	V139DND
60172	CH	T919SSF	60179	LT	V127DND	60186	BK	V134DND	60192	LT	V140DND
60173	AG	V142DND	60180	BK	V128DND	60187	LT	V135DND	60193	NE	V141DND
60174	AG	V122DND	60181	BK	V129DND	60188	BK	V136DND	60194	NE	W142PSH
60175	AG	V330DBU	60182	LT	V130DND						

60195-60214

Scania L94UB | Wright Axcess Floline | | N43F | 2001

60195	LT	Y343XBN	60200	BH	X271USH	60205	NE	X261USH	60210	QS	X266USH
60196	NE	X253USH	60201	NE	X257USH	60206	QS	Y598KNE	60211	QS	Y962XBU
60197	BK	Y597KNE	60202	NE	Y346XBN	60207	QS	Y961XBU	60212	QS	Y633RTD
60198	LT	Y344XBN	60203	BK	Y632RTD	60208	CC	Y347XBN	60213	QS	X269USH
60199	LT	X256USH	60204	LT	X272USH	60209	QS	X265USH	60214	QS	Y634RTD

60215-60222 — Scania L94UB — Wright Axcess Floline — N40F — 1998-99

60215	CW	S561JSE	60217	QS	T563BSS	60219	BL	T565BSS	60221	BK	T567BSS
60216	AG	T562BSS	60218	QS	T564BSS	60220	LV	T566BSS	60222	BH	S560JSE

60223-60282 — Mercedes-Benz O530 Citaro — Mercedes-Benz — N38F — 2000

60223	BY	W301JND	60238	BY	W334JND	60253	BY	W331RJA	60269	BY	W347RJA
60224	BY	W302JND	60239	BY	W317JND	60254	BY	W332RJA	60270	BY	W348RJA
60225	BY	W303JND	60240	BY	W338JND	60255	BY	W363RJA	60271	BY	W349RJA
60226	BY	W304JND	60241	BY	W319JND	60256	BY	W334RJA	60272	BY	W362RJA
60227	BY	W335JND	60242	BY	W337JND	60257	BY	W335RJA	60273	BY	W351RJA
60228	BY	W336JND	60243	BY	W341JND	60258	BY	W336RJA	60274	BY	W352RJA
60229	BY	W307JND	60244	BY	W322JND	60259	BY	W337RJA	60275	BY	W353RJA
60230	BY	W308JND	60245	BY	W339JND	60260	BY	W338RJA	60276	BY	W354RJA
60231	BY	W309JND	60246	BY	W324JND	60261	BY	W339RJA	60277	BY	W366RJA
60232	BY	W332JND	60247	BY	W378JNE	60262	BY	W361RJA	60278	BY	W356RJA
60233	BY	W311JND	60248	BY	W326JND	60264	LV	W342RJA	60279	BY	W357RJA
60234	BY	W312JND	60249	BY	W327JND	60265	BY	W343RJA	60280	BY	W358RJA
60235	BY	W313JND	60250	BY	W379JNE	60266	BY	W344RJA	60281	BY	W359RJA
60236	BY	W314JND	60251	BY	W329JND	60267	BY	W365RJA	60282	BY	W364RJA
60237	BY	W315JND	60252	BY	W331JND	60268	BY	W346RJA			

60283	BY	W179BVP	Mercedes-Benz O530 Citaro	Mercedes-Benz	N38F	2000	Evobus demonstrator, 2001

60296-60349 — Volvo B10B — Wright Endurance — BC50F — 1994-96

60296	NR	M501PNA	60310	BN	M515PNA	60324	u	N529WVR	60337	SOt	N542WVR
60297	IP	M502PNA	60311	WR	M516PNA	60325	IN	N530WVR	60338	BN	N543WVR
60298	NR	M503PNA	60312	BN	M517PNA	60326	u	N531WVR	60339	QS	N544WVR
60299	SOt	M504PNA	60313	BN	M518PNA	60327	BN	N532WVR	60340	KDt	N545WVR
60300	NR	M505PNA	60314	BN	M519PNA	60328	BN	N533WVR	60341	IN	N546WVR
60301	u	M506PNA	60315	IN	M520PNA	60329	WR	N534WVR	60342	IN	N547WVR
60302	u	M507PNA	60316	AGt	N521WVR	60330	IN	N535WVR	60343	BN	N548WVR
60303	KW	M508PNA	60317	AGt	N522WVR	60331	IN	N536WVR	60344	BN	N549WVR
60304	KW	M509PNA	60318	BN	N523WVR	60332	BN	N537WVR	60345	IN	N550WVR
60305	KW	M510PNA	60319	BN	N524WVR	60333	BN	N538WVR	60346	IN	N551WVR
60306	NR	M511PNA	60320	BN	N525WVR	60334	IN	N539WVR	60347	BN	N552WVR
60307	NR	M512PNA	60321	u	N526WVR	60335	BN	N540WVR	60348	IN	N554WVR
60308	BNt	M513PNA	60322	BN	N527WVR	60336	BN	N541WVR	60349	BN	N556WVR
60309	NR	M514PNA	60323	BN	N528WVR						

60350-60354 — Volvo B10L — Wright Liberator — NC41F — 1996

60350	OG	N557BNF	60352	OG	N559BNF	60353	OG	N561BNF	60354	OG	N562BNF
60351	OG	N558BNF									

60361-60373 — Volvo B10BLE — Wright Renown — N42F — 1997

60361	QS	R571YNC	60365	WN	R575SBA	60368	WN	R578SBA	60371	WN	R581SBA
60362	WN	R572SBA	60366	WN	R576SBA	60369	WN	R579SBA	60372	WN	R582SBA
60363	WN	R573SBA	60367	WN	R577SBA	60370	WN	R580SBA	60373	WN	R583SBA
60364	WN	R574SBA									

60374	LEt	J461OVU	Volvo B10M-50	Northern Counties Paladin	B49F	1991

60376-60400 — Volvo B10BLE — Wright Renown — N41F* — 1998 — *60389-99 are N42F

60376	WN	R621CVR	60383	WN	R654CVR	60389	WN	R645CVR	60395	WN	R651CVR
60377	WN	R622CVR	60384	WN	R629CVR	60390	WN	R646CVR	60396	WN	S652RNA
60378	WN	R623CVR	60385	WN	R630CVR	60391	WN	R647CVR	60397	WN	S653RNA
60379	WN	R624CVR	60386	QS	R631CVR	60392	WN	R648CVR	60398	WN	S654RNA
60380	WN	R625CVR	60387	QS	R632CVR	60393	WN	R649CVR	60399	WN	S655RNA
60381	WN	R626CVR	60388	QS	R633CVR	60394	WN	R650CVR	60400	WN	S656RNA
60382	WN	R627CVR									

60401	WN	S668SVU	Volvo B10BLE	Wright Renown	N40F	1998
60402	WN	S669SVU	Volvo B10BLE	Wright Renown	N40F	1998
60403	WN	S670SVU	Volvo B10BLE	Wright Renown	N40F	1998
60404	WN	S671SVU	Volvo B10BLE	Wright Renown	N40F	1998
60405	WN	X699ADK	Volvo B10BLE	Wright Renown	N41F	2000
60406	OG	Y774TNC	Volvo B7L	Wrightbus Eclipse	N41F	2001

First's original selection of Optare Excel buses that originated with Timeline, Leicester and London have been brought together at Wigan depot from where 60151, R1LCB, was pictured while passing through nearby Ince. Following the sale of the original number, this vehicle has now been re-registered with a Manchester area plate. *Steve Rice*

60407-60420

			Mercedes-Benz 0405			Wright Endurance		B49F	1993		
60407	QS	L501KSA	60411	QS	L505KSA	60415	QS	L509KSA	60418	QS	L512KSA
60408	QS	L502KSA	60412	QS	L506KSA	60416	QS	L510KSA	60419	QS	L513KSA
60409	QS	L503KSA	60413	QS	L507KSA	60417	QS	L511KSA	60420	QS	L514KSA
60410	QS	L504KSA	60414	QS	L508KSA						

60422-60430

			Mercedes-Benz 0405			Optare Prisma		B49F	1995		
60422	OM	M516RSS	60425	QS	M519RSS	60427	OM	M521RSS	60429	OM	M523RSS
60423	OM	M517RSS	60426	QS	M520RSS	60428	OM	M522RSS	60430	OM	M524RSS
60424	QS	M518RSS									

60431-60450

			Mercedes-Benz 0405			Optare Prisma		B47F	1995-97		
60431	OM	N525VSA	60436	QS	N530VSA	60441	OM	P540BSS	60446	OM	P545BSS
60432	OM	N526VSA	60437	QS	N531VSA	60442	OM	P541BSS	60447	OM	P546BSS
60433	QS	N527VSA	60438	QS	N532VSA	60443	OM	P542BSS	60448	OM	P547BSS
60434	QS	N528VSA	60439	OM	N533VSA	60444	OM	P543BSS	60449	OM	P548BSS
60435	QS	N529VSA	60440	OM	N534VSA	60445	OM	P544BSS	60450	OM	P549BSS

60456	CW	R176GSX	Scania L113CRL			Wright Axcess-ultralow		N40F	1998		

60457-60486

			Volvo B10M-55			Alexander PS		B51F*	1990	*60471-81 are B37F	
60457	ROt	G602NWA	60465	RO	G610NWA	60473	OG	G628NWA	60480	OG	G635NWA
60458	ROt	G603NWA	60466	LFt	G613NWA	60474	OG	G629NWA	60481	OG	G636NWA
60459	NNt	G604NWA	60467	BMt	G622NWA	60475	OG	G630NWA	60482	OG	G637NWA
60460	LEt	G605NWA	60468	BMt	G623NWA	60476	OG	G631NWA	60483	RO	G638NWA
60461	HGt	G606NWA	60469	CMt	G624NWA	60477	OG	G632NWA	60484	CMt	G639NWA
60462	HGt	G607NWA	60470	RO	G625NWA	60478	OG	G633NWA	60485	HUt	G640NWA
60463	RO	G608NWA	60471	u	G626NWA	60479	OG	G634NWA	60486	HUt	G641NWA
60464	LFt	G609NWA	60472	OG	G627NWA						

The Alexander PS-bodied Volvo B10M still dominates the South Yorkshire area, although many have now been transferred to elsewhere following the arrival of new vehicles. Doncaster's 60546, J704AWF, is illustrated. *Richard Godfrey*

60487-60494
Volvo B10M-55   Alexander PS   B51F   1990

60487	ROt	H642RKU	60489	DN	H645RKU	60491	OG	H647RKU	60493	DN	H649RKU
60488	DN	H643RKU	60490	OG	H646RKU	60492	DN	H648RKU	60494	DN	H650RKU

60495-60532
Volvo B10M-55   Alexander PS   B51F   1991

60495	DN	H651THL	60506	RO	H662THL	60515	RO	H672THL	60524	RO	H682THL
60496	OG	H652THL	60507	RO	H663THL	60516	RO	H673THL	60525	RO	H683THL
60499	DN	H655THL	60508	ROt	H664THL	60517	RO	H674THL	60526	RO	H684THL
60500	RO	H656THL	60509	u	H691THL	60518	u	H675THL	60527	RO	H685THL
60501	RO	H657THL	60510	RO	H667THL	60519	RO	H676THL	60528	OG	H686THL
60502	RO	H658THL	60511	RO	H668THL	60520	RO	H678THL	60529	OG	H687THL
60503	RO	H659THL	60512	RO	H669THL	60521	RO	H679THL	60530	DN	H688THL
60504	RO	H660THL	60513	RO	H670THL	60522	RO	H680THL	60531	RO	J689XAK
60505	RO	H661THL	60514	RO	H671THL	60523	RO	H681THL	60532	RO	J690XAK

60533-60552
Volvo B10M-55   Alexander PS   B51F   1992

60533	RO	J691AWF	60538	OG	J696AWF	60545	DN	J703AWF	60549	DN	K707EDT
60534	RO	J692AWF	60539	OG	J697AWF	60546	DN	J704AWF	60550	DU	K708EDT
60535	OG	J693AWF	60541	OG	J699AWF	60547	DN	J705AWF	60551	LF	K709EDT
60536	RO	J694AWF	60542	RO	J794AWF	60548	DN	K706EDT	60552	LF	K710EDT
60537	OG	J695AWF	60543	RO	J701AWF						

60553-60577
Volvo B10M-55   Alexander PS   B49F   1995

60553	RO	M716VET	60560	RO	M723VET	60566	OG	M729VET	60572	DN	M735VET
60554	RO	M717VET	60561	OG	M724VET	60567	RO	M730VET	60573	DN	M736VET
60555	RO	M718VET	60562	OG	M725VET	60568	OG	M731VET	60574	DN	M737VET
60556	RO	M719VET	60563	RO	M726VET	60569	RO	M732VET	60575	RO	M738VET
60557	RO	M720VET	60564	OG	M727VET	60570	DN	M733VET	60576	DN	M739VET
60558	RO	M721VET	60565	RO	M728VET	60571	DN	M734VET	60577	DN	M740VET
60559	RO	M722VET									

60578-60617   Volvo B10M-55   Alexander PS   B49F*   1996   *60578-85 are BC49F

60578	LV	N741CKY	60588	LV	N751CKY	60598	BW	N761CKY	60608	OG	N771CKY
60579	LV	N742CKY	60589	LT	N752CKY	60599	TN	N762CKY	60609	OG	N772CKY
60580	LF	N743CKY	60590	LV	N753CKY	60600	TN	N763CKY	60610	OG	N773CKY
60581	LV	N744CKY	60591	LV	N754CKY	60601	LV	N764CKY	60611	OG	N774CKY
60582	LF	N745CKY	60592	LV	N755CKY	60602	OG	N765CKY	60612	OG	N775CKY
60583	LV	N746CKY	60593	LF	N756CKY	60603	OG	N766CKY	60613	OG	N776CKY
60584	LF	N747CKY	60594	LF	N757CKY	60604	OG	N767CKY	60614	OG	N277CKY
60585	LV	N748CKY	60595	LF	N758CKY	60605	OG	N768CKY	60615	OG	N778CKY
60586	LF	N749CKY	60596	LV	N759CKY	60606	OG	N769CKY	60616	OG	N779CKY
60587	LF	N750CKY	60597	TN	N760CKY	60607	OG	N770CKY	60617	OG	N780CKY

60618-60627   Volvo B10BLE   Wright Renown   N44F   1997-98

60618	OG	R781WKW	60621	OG	R784WKW	60624	OG	R787WKW	60626	OG	R789WKW
60619	OG	R782WKW	60622	OG	R785WKW	60625	OG	R788WKW	60627	OG	R790WKW
60620	OG	R783WKW	60623	OG	R86XHL						

60628-60632   Volvo B10BLE   Wright Renown   N41F   1998

60628	HX	S810RWG	60630	OG	S812RWG	60631	OG	S813RWG	60632	OG	S814RWG
60629	OG	S811RWG									

60633-60682   Volvo B10BLE   Wright Renown   N41F   1999

60633	RO	T815MAK	60646	OG	T828MAK	60659	OG	T841MAK	60671	OG	T853MAK
60634	RO	T816MAK	60647	OG	T829MAK	60660	OG	T842MAK	60672	OG	T854MAK
60635	RO	T817MAK	60648	OG	T830MAK	60661	OG	T843MAK	60673	OG	T855MAK
60636	RO	T818MAK	60649	OG	T831MAK	60662	OG	T844MAK	60674	OG	T856MAK
60637	RO	T819MAK	60650	OG	T832MAK	60663	WN	T845MAK	60675	OG	T857MAK
60638	RO	T820MAK	60651	OG	T833MAK	60664	OG	T846MAK	60676	OG	T858MAK
60639	RO	T821MAK	60652	OG	T834MAK	60665	OG	T847MAK	60677	OG	T859MAK
60640	RO	T822MAK	60653	OG	T835MAK	60666	OG	T848MAK	60678	OG	T860MAK
60641	OG	T823MAK	60654	OG	T836MAK	60667	OG	T849MAK	60679	OG	T861MAK
60642	OG	T824MAK	60655	OG	T837MAK	60668	OG	T850MAK	60680	OG	T862MAK
60643	OG	T825MAK	60656	OG	T838MAK	60669	OG	T851MAK	60681	OG	T863MAK
60644	OG	T826MAK	60657	OG	T839MAK	60670	OG	T852MAK	60682	OG	T864MAK
60645	RO	T827MAK	60658	OG	T840MAK						

60683-60702   Volvo B10BLE   Wright Renown   N41F   1999

60683	OG	T865ODT	60688	OG	T870ODT	60693	OG	T875ODT	60698	OG	T880ODT
60684	OG	T866ODT	60689	OG	T871ODT	60694	OG	T876ODT	60699	OG	T881ODT
60685	OG	T867ODT	60690	OG	T872ODT	60695	OG	T877ODT	60700	OG	T882ODT
60686	OG	T868ODT	60691	OG	T873ODT	60696	OG	T878ODT	60701	OG	T883ODT
60687	OG	T869ODT	60692	OG	T874ODT	60697	OG	T879ODT	60702	OG	T884ODT

60703	OG	Y661UKU	Volvo B7L Wrightbus Eclipse N41F 2001

60704-60745   Volvo B7L   Wrightbus Eclipse   N41F   2002

60704	OG	MV02VAA	60715	OG	MV02VBG	60726	OG	MV02VCF	60736	OG	MV02VDK
60705	OG	MV02VAD	60716	OG	MV02VBJ	60727	OG	MV02VCG	60737	OG	MV02VDL
60706	OG	MV02VAE	60717	OG	MV02VBK	60728	OG	MV02VCJ	60738	OG	MV02VDM
60707	OG	MV02VAF	60718	OG	MV02VBL	60729	OG	MV02VCK	60739	OG	MV02VDN
60708	OG	MV02VAH	60719	OG	MV02VBM	60730	OG	MV02VCL	60740	OG	MV02VDO
60709	OG	MV02VAJ	60720	OG	MV02VBN	60731	OG	MV02VDD	60741	OG	MV02VDP
60710	OG	MV02VAK	60721	OG	MV02VBO	60732	OG	MV02VDE	60742	OG	MV02VDR
60711	OG	MV02VAM	60722	OG	MV02VBP	60733	OG	MV02VDF	60743	OG	MV02VDT
60712	OG	MV02VAO	60723	OG	MV02VBT	60734	OG	MV02VDG	60744	OG	MV02VDX
60713	OG	MV02VAU	60724	OG	MV02VCD	60735	OG	MV02VDJ	60745	OG	MV02VDY
60714	OG	MV02VBF	60725	OG	MV02VCE						

60754-60760   Scania L113CRL   Wright Axcess-ultralow   N48F   1995-96

60754	BL	N419ENW	60756	SH	N421MWY	60758	SH	N423MWY	60760	OG	N425MWY
60755	SH	N420MWY	60757	SH	N422MWY						

60761-60765   Scania L113CRL   Wright Axcess-ultralow   N48F   1997

60761	OG	P426GLS	60763	OG	P428GLS	60764	OG	P429GLS	60765	OG	P431GLS
60762	OG	P427GLS									

The Strider was in the early 1990s and was fitted to a variety of chassis . Most of those operating with First originated with West Yorkshire, including 60794, L127PWR, seen here in Huddersfield. *Steve Rice*

| 60766 | IP | R644CVR | Volvo B10BLE | | | Wright Renown | N41F | 1998 | | |
| 60767 | IP | S657RNA | Volvo B10BLE | | | Wright Renown | N41F | 1998 | | |

60768-60797

Volvo B10B · Alexander Strider · B51F · 1993-94

60768	HX	K101HUM	60777	HX	K110HUM	60784	HX	K117HUM	60791	HX	L124PWR
60769	HX	K102HUM	60778	HX	K211HUM	60785	HX	K118HUM	60792	HX	L125PWR
60770	HX	K103HUM	60779	HX	K112HUM	60786	HX	K119HUM	60794	HX	L127PWR
60773	HX	K106HUM	60780	HX	K113HUM	60787	HX	K120HUM	60795	HX	L128PWR
60774	HX	K107HUM	60781	HX	K114HUM	60788	HX	L121PWR	60796	HX	L129PWR
60775	HX	K108HUM	60783	HX	K116HUM	60790	HX	L123PWR	60797	HX	L130PWR
60776	HX	K109HUM									

60798-60806

Volvo B10BLE · Wright Renown · N41F · 1998

60798	OG	R131JYG	60801	OG	R134JYG	60803	OG	R136JYG	60805	OG	R138JYG
60799	OG	R132JYG	60802	OG	R135JYG	60804	OG	R137JYG	60806	OG	R139JYG
60800	OG	R133JYG									

60807-60816

Volvo B10BLE · Wright Renown · N41F · 1998

60807	IP	S658RNA	60810	BD	S661RNA	60813	IP	S664RNA	60815	BD	S667RNA
60808	IP	S659RNA	60811	BD	S662RNA	60814	IP	S665RNA	60816	BD	S668RNA
60809	BD	S660RNA	60812	IP	S663RNA						

60818	HX	S675SVU	Volvo B10BLE			Wright Renown	N41F	1998		
60819	HX	S676SVU	Volvo B10BLE			Wright Renown	N41F	1998		
60820	HX	S677SVU	Volvo B10BLE			Wright Renown	N41F	1998		

60821-60825

Volvo B10BLE · Wright Renown · N44F · 1999

| 60821 | BD | T154OUB | 60823 | BD | T156OUB | 60824 | BD | T157OUB | 60825 | BD | T158OUB |
| 60822 | BD | T255GUG | | | | | | | | | |

Seen in the colours of York's *Park & Ride* is Volvo B7L 60914, YG02DKO. The Volvo B7L features a off-centre engine at the rear of the bus that intrudes into the saloon area at the rear near-side corner. All those operated by First have Wrightbus Eclipse bodies. *Mark Lyons*

60826-60840

			Volvo B10BLE			Wright Renown			N44F	2000		
60826	BD	V759UVY	60830	BD	V763UVY	60834	BD	V767UVY	60838	BD	V771UVY
60827	BD	V760UVY	60831	BD	V764UVY	60835	BD	V768UVY	60839	BD	V772UVY
60828	BD	V721UVY	60832	BD	V765UVY	60836	BD	V769UVY	60840	BD	V773UVY
60829	BD	V762UVY	60833	BD	W766HBT	60837	BD	V770UVY			

60841-60855

			Volvo B10BLE			Wright Renown			N44F	2000		
60841	BD	W801DWX	60845	BD	W805DWX	60849	BD	W809DWX	60853	BD	W814DWX
60842	BD	W802DWX	60846	BD	W806DWX	60850	BD	W811DWX	60854	BD	W815DWX
60843	BD	W803DWX	60847	BD	W807DWX	60851	BD	W812DWX	60855	BD	W816DWX
60844	BD	W804DWX	60848	BD	W808DWX	60852	BD	W813DWX			

60856-60865

			Volvo B10BLE			Wright Renown			N41F	1998		
60856	OG	R634CVR	60859	OG	R637CVR	60862	OG	R640CVR	60864	YA	R642CVR
60857	OG	R635CVR	60860	OG	R638CVR	60863	YA	R641CVR	60865	YA	R643CVR
60858	OG	R636CVR	60861	OG	R639CVR						

60876-60928

			Volvo B7L			Wrightbus Eclipse			N41F	2001-02		
60876	YK	Y445CUB	60890	OG	YJ51RHK	60903	VN	YG02DHM	60916	YK	YG02DKU
60877	YK	Y446CUB	60891	OG	YJ51RGZ	60904	BD	YG02DHL	60917	YK	YG02DKV
60878	YK	Y447CUB	60892	OG	YJ51RHF	60905	VN	YG02DHO	60918	YK	YG02DLJ
60879	u	Y448CUB	60893	OG	YJ51RGY	60906	BD	YG02DHN	60919	YK	YG02DLX
60880	YK	Y449CUB	60894	OG	YJ51REU	60907	BD	YG02DHV	60920	YK	YG02DLU
60881	YK	Y451CUB	60895	YK	YJ51RFE	60908	BD	YG02DHA	60921	YK	YG02DLN
60882	YK	YJ51PZT	60896	YK	YJ51RFF	60909	YK	YG02DGZ	60922	YK	YG02DHJ
60883	YK	YJ51PZU	60897	YK	YJ51RFY	60910	YK	YJ51RFK	60923	BD	YG02DHF
60884	YK	YJ51PZV	60898	YK	YJ51RFX	60911	YK	YG02DLO	60924	VN	YG02DHE
60885	YK	YJ51PZW	60899	YK	YJ51RFL	60912	YK	YG02DLD	60925	BD	YG02DHD
60886	OG	YJ51PZX	60900	YK	YJ51RFN	60913	YK	YG02DLY	60926	YK	YG02DGY
60887	OG	YJ51PZY	60901	YK	YJ51RFO	60914	YK	YG02DKO	60927	YK	YG02DHC
60888	OG	YJ51RDZ	60902	YK	YG02DHK	60915	YK	YG02DLZ	60928	YK	YG02DHU
60889	OG	YJ51RHE									

60929-60938

			Dennis Dart SLF 11.3m			Plaxton Pointer SPD			N41F	1998		
60929	HU	R336HYG	60932	HU	R339HYG	60935	HU	R723HHK	60937	HU	R725HHK
60930	HU	R337HYG	60933	HU	R340HYG	60936	HU	R724HHK	60938	HU	R726HHK
60931	HU	R338HYG	60934	HU	R722HHK						

60939-60982   Dennis Lance 11m   Plaxton Verde   B49F   1995

60939	HU	M401VWW	60951	HU	M413VWW	60964	LH	M426VWW	60975	LH	M437VWW
60941	HGt	M403VWW	60952	LH	M414VWW	60965	LH	M427VWW	60977	LH	M439VWW
60942	u	M404VWW	60953	HUt	M415VWW	60966	HG	M428VWW	60978	u	M440VWW
60943	MS	M405VWW	60954	LE	M416VWW	60967	HU	M429VWW	60979	LH	N441ENW
60944	HUt	M406VWW	60955	HU	M417VWW	60968	TN	M430VWW	60981	LH	N443ENW
60945	LE	M407VWW	60956	u	M418VWW	60969	TN	M431VWW	60982	LH	N544ENW
60946	LE	M408VWW	60957	HU	M419VWW	60971	LH	M433VWW	60983	u	N445ENW
60947	LH	M409VWW	60958	LE	M420VWW	60972	HG	M434VWW	60984	LE	N446ENW
60948	LE	M410VWW	60959	HU	M421VWW	60973	LH	M435VWW	60985	LE	M447VWW
60949	LH	M411VWW	60960	HUs	M422VWW	60974	HU	M436VWW	60986	u	M448VWW
60950	LH	M412VWW	60963	LH	M425VWW						

60987-61016   Dennis Lance 11m   Plaxton Verde   B49F   1996

60987	HGt	N449JUG	60991	LH	N453JUG	61011	LH	N473JUG	61014	MS	N476JUG
60988	HGt	N450JUG	60992	LH	N454JUG	61012	LH	N474JUG	61015	MS	N477JUG
60990	LH	N452JUG	60993	LH	N455JUG	61013	KD	N475JUG	61016	KD	N478JUG

61017-61021   Scania L94UB   Wright Axcess Floline   N40F   1999

61017	LF	S116CSG	61019	LF	S118CSG	61020	LF	S119CSG	61021	LF	S220GKS
61018	LF	S117CSG									

61022-61044   Scania L94UB   Wright Axcess Floline   N43F   1999

61022	LF	T421GUG	61028	LF	T427GUG	61034	IP	V133ESC	61040	BM	V139ESC
61023	LF	T422GUG	61029	CR	T428GUG	61035	CM	V134ESC	61041	BM	V140ESC
61024	LF	T423GUG	61030	CR	T429GUG	61036	CM	V135ESC	61042	CR	V141ESC
61025	LF	T424GUG	61031	CR	T430GUG	61037	CM	V136ESC	61043	LF	V142ESC
61026	LF	T425GUG	61032	HP	T431GUG	61038	CM	V137ESC	61044	LF	V143ESC
61027	LF	T426GUG	61033	HP	T432GUG	61039	CM	V138ESC			

61045-61049   Scania L113CRL   Alexander Strider   N48F   1994

61046	HP	M402UUB	61047	HP	M403UUB	61048	HP	M404UUB	61049	HP	M405UUB

61050-61057   Scania L113CRL   Wright Axcess-ultralow   N40F   1997

61050	CR	N416ENW	61052	BK	P432YSH	61054	BS	R434GSF	61056	CR	P436YSH
61051	HP	N418ENW	61053	BK	P433YSH	61055	CR	P435YSH	61057	BS	R437GSF

61058-61078   Scania L113CRL   Wright Axcess-ultralow   N40F   1998

61058	CR	S644BSG	61064	CR	R450JSG	61069	CR	R455JFS	61074	CR	R460JFS
61059	CR	S445BSG	61065	CR	R451JSG	61070	CR	R456JFS	61075	CR	R461JFS
61060	CR	S446BSG	61066	CR	R452JSG	61071	CR	R457JFS	61076	CR	R462JFS
61061	CR	S447BSG	61067	CR	R453JFS	61072	CR	R458JFS	61077	CR	R463JFS
61062	CR	S448BSG	61068	CR	R454JFS	61073	CR	R459JFS	61078	CR	R464JFS
61063	CR	R449JSG									

61079-61112   Scania N113CRB   Alexander Strider   B50F   1993

61079	HP	K601HUG	61088	HP	K610HUG	61096	BM	K618HUG	61105	BM	K627HUG
61080	HP	K602HUG	61089	HP	K611HUG	61097	BM	K619HUG	61106	BM	K628HUG
61081	HP	K603HUG	61090	BM	K612HUG	61098	BM	K620HUG	61107	BM	K629HUG
61082	HP	K604HUG	61091	BM	K613HUG	61099	BM	K621HUG	61108	BM	K630HUG
61083	HP	K605HUG	61092	HP	K614HUG	61100	BM	K622HUG	61109	BM	K631HUG
61084	HP	K606HUG	61093	HP	K615HUG	61101	BM	K623HUG	61110	BM	K632HUG
61085	HP	K607HUG	61094	BM	K616HUG	61103	BM	K625HUG	61111	BM	K633HUG
61086	HP	K608HUG	61095	BM	K617HUG	61104	BM	K626HUG	61112	BM	K634HUG
61087	HP	K609HUG									

61114-61133   Scania N113CRB   Alexander Strider   B48F   1994

61114	BM	L636PWR	61119	BM	L641PWR	61124	BM	L646PWR	61129	BMt	L651PWR
61115	BM	L637PWR	61120	BM	L642PWR	61125	BM	L647PWR	61130	BMt	L652PWR
61116	BM	L638PWR	61121	BM	L643PWR	61126	BM	L648PWR	61131	BMt	L653PWR
61117	BM	L639PWR	61122	BM	L644PWR	61127	BM	L649PWR	61132	BMt	L654PWR
61118	BM	L640PWR	61123	BM	L645PWR	61128	BM	L650PWR	61133	BMt	L655PWR

61134	CR	8995WY	Scania N113CRL	East Lancs MaxCi	N46F	1995	Scania demonstrator, 1997
61135	BL	YS51JVA	Bluebird A3 RE	Bluebird	B60F	2002	

Eastgate in Leeds is the location for this view of Alexander Strider-bodied Scania 61081, K603HUG, which is based in the new Hunslet Park depot. *Richard Godfrey*

61136	BL	YS51JVK	Bluebird A3 RE		Bluebird			B60F	2002

61137-61140

			Scania L94UB			Wright Axcess Floline		N40F	1998
61137	BH	S101CSG	61138	BH	S103CSG	61139	BH	S104CSG	61140	BH	S105CSG

61141	AG	S359MFP	Scania L94UB	Wright Axcess Floline	N40F	1998
61142	BH	S360MFP	Scania L94UB	Wright Axcess Floline	N40F	1998
61143	AG	S361MFP	Scania L94UB	Wright Axcess Floline	N40F	1998
61144	CH	S688BFS	Scania L113CRL	Wright Axcess-ultralow	N40F	1998
61145	AG	S690BFS	Scania L113CRL	Wright Axcess-ultralow	N40F	1998
61148	NN	MV02VBU	Volvo B7L	Wrightbus Eclipse	N41F	2002
61149	QS	M501GRY	Mercedes-Benz O405	Optare Prisma	B49F	1995
61150	QS	M502GRY	Mercedes-Benz O405	Optare Prisma	B49F	1995
61151	QS	M504GRY	Mercedes-Benz O405	Optare Prisma	B49F	1995
61157	BH	S682BFS	Scania L113CRL	Wright Axcess-ultralow	N40F	1998
61158	BH	R175GSX	Scania L113CRL	Wright Axcess-ultralow	N40F	1998
61159	CW	R173GSX	Scania L113CRL	Wright Axcess-ultralow	N40F	1998
61160	CW	S684BFS	Scania L113CRL	Wright Axcess-ultralow	N40F	1998

61192-61211

			Volvo B7L			Wrightbus Eclipse		N41F	2002
61192	OG	YU52VXH	61197	OG	YU52VXN	61202	OG	YU52VXT	61207	OG	YU52VXZ
61193	OG	YU52VXJ	61198	OG	YU52VXO	61203	OG	YU52VXV	61208	OG	YU52VYA
61194	OG	YU52VXK	61199	OG	YU52VXP	61204	OG	YU52VXW	61209	OG	YU52VYB
61195	OG	YU52VXL	61200	OG	YU52VXR	61205	OG	YU52VXX	61210	OG	YU52VYC
61196	OG	YU52VXM	61201	OG	YU52VXS	61206	OG	YU52VXY	61211	OG	YU52VYD

61212	WSt	L64UOU	Volvo B10M-60		Plaxton Expressliner 2			TV	1993

61214-61233

			Scania L94UB			Wrightbus Solar		N43F	2003
61214	DK	YM52UVK	61219	MU	YM52UVR	61224	MU	YM52UVZ	61229	MU	YM52UWG
61215	MU	YM52UVL	61220	DK	YM52UVS	61225	GS	YM52UWA	61230	DK	YM52UWH
61216	LT	YM52UVN	61221	DK	YM52UVT	61226	DK	YM52UWB	61231	DK	YM52UWJ
61217	MU	YM52UVO	61222	BK	YM52UVU	61227	MU	YM52UWD	61232	MU	YM52UWK
61218	DK	YM52UVP	61223	LT	YM52UVW	61228	GS	YM52UWF	61233	LT	YM52UWN

61234	BH	R174GSX	Scania L113CRL	Wright Axcess-ultralow	N40F	1997	
61235	AG	S680BFS	Scania L113CRL	Wright Axcess-ultralow	N40F	1998	
61237	AG	S681BFS	Scania L113CRL	Wright Axcess-ultralow	N40F	1998	
61238	AG	S683BFS	Scania L113CRL	Wright Axcess-ultralow	N40F	1998	
61239	AG	S689BFS	Scania L113CRL	Wright Axcess-ultralow	N40F	1998	
61240	WN	R340GHS	Volvo B10BLE	Wright Renown	N43F	1998	
61241	WN	R339GHS	Volvo B10BLE	Wright Renown	N43F	1998	
61243	AG	R126GSF	Scania L113CRL	Wright Axcess-ultralow	N40F	1997	
61244	CH	R124GSF	Scania L113CRL	Wright Axcess-ultralow	N40F	1997	
61245	CH	R127GSF	Scania L113CRL	Wright Axcess-ultralow	N40F	1997	
61246	AG	S686BFS	Scania L113CRL	Wright Axcess-ultralow	N40F	1998	
61247	OM	M503GRY	Mercedes-Benz O405	Optare Prisma	B49F	1995	
61248	OM	M506GRY	Mercedes-Benz O405	Optare Prisma	B49F	1995	
61249	QS	M507GRY	Mercedes-Benz O405	Optare Prisma	B49F	1995	
61250	QS	M509GRY	Mercedes-Benz O405	Optare Prisma	B49F	1995	
61251	QS	M510GRY	Mercedes-Benz O405	Optare Prisma	B49F	1995	
61254	HGt	L229AAB	Dennis Lance 11m	Plaxton Verde	B49F	1994	
61255	DU	G620NWA	Volvo B10M-55	Alexander PS	B51F	1990	
61256	LFt	G601NWA	Volvo B10M-55	Alexander PS	B51F	1990	
61258	BL	N417ENW	Scania L113CRL	Wright Axcess-ultralow	N48F	1995	

61259-61266   Volvo B10M-55   Alexander PS   B51F   1990

61259	LFt	G611NWA	61261	LFt	G615NWA	61263	LF	G617NWA	61265	DU	G619NWA
61260	LFt	G614NWA	61262	LFt	G616NWA	61264	LF	G618NWA	61266	LFt	G621NWA

61268-61271   Volvo B10M-55   Alexander PS   B51F   1991

61268	LF	K712EDT	61269	DU	K713EDT	61270	DU	K714EDT	61271	DU	K715EDT

61288	BD	S808RWG	Volvo B10BLE	Wright Renown	N41F	1998	
61289	BD	S809RWG	Volvo B10BLE	Wright Renown	N41F	1998	

61291-61300   Scania L94UB   Wright Axcess Floline   N40F   1998

61291	LF	S106CSG	61294	LF	S109CSG	61296	LF	S211CSG	61299	LF	S114CSG
61292	LF	S107CSG	61295	LF	S110CSG	61298	LF	S113CSG	61300	LF	S115CSG
61293	LF	S108CSG									

61306	PH	SJ51DJZ	Volvo B10BLE	Wrightbus Renown	N42F	2001	
61347	LF	K711EDT	Volvo B10M-55	Alexander PS	B51F	1991	

61348-61359   Volvo B10B   Alexander Strider   B51F   1993

61348	NR	L201KFS	61351	WNt	L204KSX	61356	OMt	L209KSX	61358	NR	L211KSX
61349	NR	L202KFS	61353	OMt	L206KSX	61357	NR	L210KSX	61359	QSt	L212KSX
61350	WNt	L203KSX	61354	OMt	L207KSX						

61360-61369   Volvo B10B   Alexander Strider   B51F   1993

61360	QSt	L301VSU	61363	YKt	L304VSU	61366	OMt	L307VSU	61368	NR	L309VSU
61361	BYt	L302VSU	61364	YKt	L305VSU	61367	NR	L308VSU	61369	BNt	L310VSU
61362	BYt	L303VSU	61365	QSt	L306VSU						

61370-61387   Volvo B10M-55   Alexander PS   BC48F   1994   Stagecoach, 1995

61370	DU	M428RRN	61375	SN	M769PRS	61380	SN	M774PRS	61384	SN	M779PRS
61371	SN	M765PRS	61376	SN	M770PRS	61381	SN	M775PRS	61385	SN	M780PRS
61372	CD	M766PRS	61377	SN	M771PRS	61382	SN	M776PRS	61386	SN	M781PRS
61373	SN	M767PRS	61378	SN	M772PRS	61383	SN	M778PRS	61387	B	M877PRS
61374	SN	M768PRS	61379	SN	M773PRS						

61388-61408   Volvo B10M-55   Alexander PS   B49F   1996

61388	PH	N120OGG	61394	DU	N126OGG	61399	DU	N131OGG	61404	DU	N136OGG
61389	DU	N121OGG	61395	DU	N127OGG	61400	DU	N132OGG	61405	LF	N137OGG
61390	DU	N122OGG	61396	DU	N128OGG	61401	LF	N133OGG	61406	B	N138OGG
61391	DU	N123OGG	61397	DU	N129OGG	61402	B	N134OGG	61407	DU	N190OGG
61392	DU	N124OGG	61398	LF	N130OGG	61403	B	N135OGG	61408	B	N199OGG
61393	DU	N125OGG									

New to Strathclyde, 61513, P543TYS, is an Alexander PS-bodied Volvo B10M. Currently based at the new depot in Blantyre, it is seen heading for Hamilton. *Mark Doggett*

61409-61477

			Volvo B10M-55			Alexander PS			B49F	1996		
61409	DU	N89OGG	61427	CD	N943LSU	61445	CD	N95OGG	61462	DU	N975LSU
61410	DU	N91OGG	61428	CD	N944LSU	61446	PH	N960LSU	61463	B	N976LSU
61412	LF	N92OGG	61430	CD	N946LSU	61447	PH	N961LSU	61464	DU	N977LSU
61413	CD	N930LSU	61431	PH	N947LSU	61448	PH	N962LSU	61465	DU	N978LSU
61414	LF	N931LSU	61432	PH	N948LSU	61449	PH	N963LSU	61466	SN	N979LSU
61415	LF	N932LSU	61433	LF	N949LSU	61450	PH	N964LSU	61467	B	N97OGG
61416	B	N933LSU	61434	CD	N94OGG	61451	PH	N965LSU	61468	DU	N980LSU
61417	B	N934LSU	61435	PH	N950LSU	61452	PH	N966LSU	61469	LF	N981LSU
61418	CD	N935LSU	61436	PH	N951LSU	61453	PH	N967LSU	61470	DU	N982LSU
61419	DU	N936LSU	61437	PH	N952LSU	61454	PH	N968LSU	61471	LF	N983LSU
61420	DU	N937LSU	61438	PH	N953LSU	61455	PH	N969LSU	61472	LF	N984LSU
61421	CD	N938LSU	61439	CD	N954LSU	61456	B	N96OGG	61473	LF	N985LSU
61422	CD	N939LSU	61440	PH	N955LSU	61457	LF	N970LSU	61474	LF	N986LSU
61423	LF	N93OGG	61441	DU	N956LSU	61458	PH	N971LSU	61475	LF	N987LSU
61424	DU	N940LSU	61442	PH	N957LSU	61459	PH	N972LSU	61476	LF	N988LSU
61425	DU	N941LSU	61443	LF	N958LSU	61460	B	N973LSU	61477	B	N98OGG
61426	DU	N942LSU	61444	DU	N959LSU	61461	DU	N974LSU			

61478-61482

			Scania L113CRL			Wright Axcess-ultralow			N47F	1996		
61478	LF	P106MFS	61480	LF	P108MFS	61481	LF	P109MFS	61482	CH	P113YSH
61479	LF	P107MFS									

61483-61488

			Volvo B10L			Wright Liberator			B43F	1996		
61483	OG	P188UNS	61485	u	P190UNS	61487	OG	P192UNS	61488	OG	P193UNS
61484	OG	P189UNS	61486	OG	P191UNS						

61489-61519

			Volvo B10M-55			Alexander PS			B49F	1996-97		
61489	DU	P519TYS	61497	B	P527TYS	61505	CD	P535TYS	61513	B	P543TYS
61490	B	P520TYS	61498	PH	P528TYS	61506	CD	P536TYS	61514	B	P544TYS
61491	DU	P521TYS	61499	DU	P529TYS	61507	CD	P537TYS	61515	B	P545TYS
61492	B	P522TYS	61500	DU	P530TYS	61508	CD	P538TYS	61516	B	P546TYS
61493	B	P523TYS	61501	DU	P531TYS	61509	CD	P539TYS	61517	B	P547TYS
61494	B	P524TYS	61502	PH	P532TYS	61510	CD	P540TYS	61518	B	P548TYS
61495	SN	P525TYS	61503	CD	P533TYS	61511	B	P541TYS	61519	B	P549TYS
61496	SN	P526TYS	61504	CD	P534TYS	61512	B	P542TYS			

Illustrating the nearside of the Volvo B7L-Wrightbus Eclipse combination is Glasgow's 61632, SH51MKG, seen here heading for Clydebank. The Eclipse was the first model from Wrightbus that featured the low windscreen.
Mark Doggett

61520-61523

			Volvo B10L			Wright Liberator		N43F	1997	
61520	u	P761XHS	61521	OG	P762XHS	61522	OG	P763XHS	61523	u	P764XHS

61524-61541

Scania L113CRL · Wright Axcess-ultralow · N40F · 1997

61524	LF	R110GSF	61529	BH	R117GSF	61534	LF	R122GSF	61538	CC	R129GSF
61525	LF	R112GSF	61530	CH	R118GSF	61535	LF	R123GSF	61539	LF	R130GSF
61526	LF	R114GSF	61531	BH	R119GSF	61536	BH	R125GSF	61540	LF	R131GSF
61527	CC	R115GSF	61532	LF	R120GSF	61537	LF	R128GSF	61541	CC	R132GSF
61528	CC	R116GSF	61533	CH	R121GSF						

61542-61557

Scania L113CRL · Wright Access-ultralow · N40F · 1997

61542	CC	R153GSF	61546	LF	R161GSF	61550	LF	R165GSF	61554	CC	R169GSF
61543	LF	R158GSF	61547	LF	R162GSF	61551	CC	R166GSF	61555	CC	R170GSF
61544	LF	R159GSF	61548	LF	R163GSF	61552	LF	R167GSF	61556	CC	R171GSF
61545	LF	R160GSF	61549	LF	R164GSF	61553	CC	R168GSF	61557	CC	R172GSX

61558	LF	R195GSX	Scania L94UB	Wright Axcess Floline	N43F	1998
61559	LF	R211GSF	Scania L113CRL	Wright Access-ultralow	N40F	1997
61560	WN	R338GHS	Volvo B10BLE	Wright Renown	N43F	1998

61561-61565

Scania L113CRL · Wright Axcess-ultralow · N40F · 1999

61561	LF	R341SUT	61563	BH	R343SUT	61564	LF	R344SUT	61565	LF	R345SUT
61562	LF	R342SUT									

61567-61576

Scania L94UB · Wright Axcess Floline · N40F · 1999

61567	LF	S550JSE	61570	LF	S553JSE	61573	LF	S556JSE	61575	LF	S558JSE
61568	LF	S551JSE	61571	LF	S554JSE	61574	LF	S557JSE	61576	LF	S559JSE
61569	LF	S552JSE	61572	LF	S555JSE						

61577	LF	S687BFS	Scania L113CRL	Wright Axcess-ultralow	N40F	1998
61578	CC	S691BFS	Scania L113CRL	Wright Axcess-ultralow	N40F	1998

The 2008 First Bus Handbook

Concurrent with Wrightbus Eclipse deliveries, buses with the more conventional engine position were also being supplied. Seen on the North Motherwell service is Volvo B10BLE 61604, SF51YAO, which carries a Wrightbus Renown body. *Mark Doggett*

61579-61586

Scania L94UB — Wright Axcess Floline — N40F — 1998

61579	LF	S692BFS	61581	LF	S694BFS	61583	LF	S697BFS	61585	LF	S699BFS
61580	LF	S693BFS	61582	LF	S696BFS	61584	LF	S698BFS	61586	LF	S701BFS

61587-61596

Volvo B7L — Wrightbus Eclipse — N40F — 2002

61587	SN	SA02BZD	61590	SN	SA02BZG	61593	SN	SA02BZK	61595	SN	SA02BZM
61588	SN	SA02BZE	61591	SN	SA02BZH	61594	SN	SA02BZL	61596	SN	SA02BZN
61589	SN	SA02BZF	61592	SN	SA02BZJ						

61597-61614

Volvo B10BLE — Wrightbus Renown — N42F — 2001

61597	B	SF51YAA	61602	B	SF51YAJ	61607	B	SF51YAW	61611	B	SF51YBB
61598	B	SF51YAD	61603	B	SF51YAK	61608	B	SF51YAX	61612	B	SF51YBC
61599	B	SF51YAE	61604	B	SF51YAO	61609	B	SF51YAY	61613	B	SF51YBD
61600	B	SF51YAG	61605	B	SF51YAU	61610	B	SF51YBA	61614	B	SF51YBE
61601	B	SF51YAH	61606	B	SF51YAV						

61615	PH	SF51YBG	Volvo B7L	Wrightbus Eclipse	N42F	2001

61616-61626

Volvo B10BLE — Wrightbus Renown — N42F — 2001

61616	B	SF51YBH	61619	B	SF51YBL	61622	B	SF51YBO	61625	B	SF51YBS
61617	B	SF51YBJ	61620	B	SF51YBM	61623	B	SF51YBP	61626	B	SF51YBT
61618	B	SF51YBK	61621	B	SF51YBN	61624	B	SF51YBR			

61627-61635

Volvo B7L — Wrightbus Eclipse — N42F — 2001

61627	PH	SH51MHY	61630	SN	SH51MJF	61632	PH	SH51MKG	61634	PH	SH51MKK
61628	PH	SH51MHZ	61631	PH	SH51MKF	61633	PH	SH51MKJ	61635	PH	SH51MKL
61629	SN	SH51MJE									

61636-61651

Volvo B7L — Wrightbus Eclipse — N40F — 2001

61636	SN	SJ51DHD	61640	PH	SJ51DHK	61644	PH	SJ51DHO	61648	PH	SJ51DHZ
61637	PH	SJ51DHE	61641	PH	SJ51DHL	61645	PH	SJ51DHP	61649	PH	SJ51DJD
61638	PH	SJ51DHF	61642	PH	SJ51DHM	61646	PH	SJ51DHV	61650	PH	SJ51DJE
61639	PH	SJ51DHG	61643	PH	SJ51DHN	61647	PH	SJ51DHX	61651	PH	SJ51DJF

61652	B	SJ51DJK	Volvo B10BLE	Wrightbus Renown	N42F	2001	
61653	B	SJ51DJO	Volvo B10BLE	Wrightbus Renown	N42F	2001	
61654	B	SJ51DJU	Volvo B10BLE	Wrightbus Renown	N42F	2001	

61656-61664   Volvo B7L   Wrightbus Eclipse   N40F   2001

61656	PH	SJ51DJX	61659	PH	SJ51DKD	61661	PH	SJ51DKF	61663	PH	SJ51DKL
61657	PH	SJ51DJY	61660	PH	SJ51DKE	61662	SN	SJ51DKK	61664	PH	SJ51DKN
61658	PH	SJ51DKA									

61667-61673   Scania L94UB   Wright Axcess Floline   N40F   1999

61667	LF	V116FSF	61669	LF	V118FSF	61671	LF	V120FSF	61673	LF	V221GLS
61668	LF	V117FSF	61670	LF	V119FSF	61672	LF	V122FSF			

61674	LV	W723PSF	Scania L94UB	Wright Solar	N47F	2000	

61675-61704   Scania L94UB   Wright Axcess Floline   N43F   2000

61675	LF	X424UMS	61683	LF	X434UMS	61691	LF	X443UMS	61698	LF	X452UMS
61676	LF	X425UMS	61684	LF	X435UMS	61692	LF	X445UMS	61699	LF	X453UMS
61677	LF	X426UMS	61685	LF	X436UMS	61693	LF	X446UMS	61700	LF	X454UMS
61678	LF	X427UMS	61686	LF	X437UMS	61694	LF	X447UMS	61701	LF	X457UMS
61679	LF	X429UMS	61687	LF	X438UMS	61695	LF	X448UMS	61702	LF	X458UMS
61680	LF	X431UMS	61688	LF	X439UMS	61696	LF	X449UMS	61703	LF	X459UMS
61681	LF	X432UMS	61689	LF	X441UMS	61697	LF	X451UMS	61704	LF	X461UMS
61682	LF	X433UMS	61690	LF	X442UMS						

61705-61710   Volvo B10BLE   Wrightbus Renown   N42F   2001

61705	B	Y301RTD	61707	B	Y303RTD	61709	B	Y307RTD	61710	B	Y949RTD
61706	B	Y302RTD	61708	B	Y304RTD						

61738	LFs	A38VDS	Leyland Tiger TRBLXB/2RH	Alexander TS	B53F	1984	
62116	HP	N424MWY	Scania L113CRL	Wright Axcess-ultralow	N48F	1996	
62117	HP	N412ENW	Scania L113CRL	Wright Axcess-ultralow	N48F	1996	
62118	HX	S672SVU	Volvo B10BLE	Wright Renown	N40F	1998	
62119	ABp	SRS56K	AEC Swift 2MP2R	Alexander W	B41F	1972	new to Aberdeen
62120	ABp	HSO61N	Leyland Leopard PSU4C/4R	Alexander AY	BC45F	1975	new to Aberdeen
62121	ABp	RG1173	Albion PMA28	Walker	B31R	1930	new to Aberdeen

62122-62141   Volvo B10BLE   Wright Renown   N43F   2000

62122	AB	X601NSS	62127	AB	X606NSS	62132	AB	X611NSS	62137	AB	X616NSS
62123	AB	X602NSS	62128	AB	X607NSS	62133	AB	X612NSS	62138	AB	X617NSS
62124	AB	X603NSS	62129	AB	X608NSS	62134	AB	X613NSS	62139	AB	X618NSS
62125	AB	X604NSS	62130	AB	X609NSS	62135	AB	X614NSS	62140	AB	X619NSS
62126	AB	X605NSS	62131	AB	X69NSS	62136	AB	X615NSS	62141	AB	X944NSO

62142-62148   Volvo B10BLE   Wright Renown   N40F   1998-99

62142	QS	R588SBA	62145	QS	R591SBA	62147	QS	R327GHS	62148	QS	R329GHS
62143	QS	R589SBA	62146	QS	R326GHS						

62149-62169   Volvo B10BLE   Wright Renown   N43F   1998-2001

62149	AB	X621NSS	62155	AB	Y627RSA	62160	AB	R335GHS	62165	AB	Y701RSA
62150	AB	X622NSS	62156	AB	R330GHS	62161	AB	R336GHS	62166	AB	Y631RSA
62151	AB	X623NSS	62157	AB	R331GHS	62162	AB	R337GHS	62167	AB	Y632RSA
62152	AB	X624NSS	62158	AB	R332GHS	62163	AB	Y628RSA	62168	AB	Y633RSA
62153	AB	X477NSS	62159	AB	R334GHS	62164	AB	Y629RSA	62169	AB	Y634RSA
62154	AB	Y626RSA									

62170-62176   Volvo B10BLE   Alexander ALX300   N40F   2000

62170	AB	W577RFS	62172	AB	W579RFS	62174	AB	W582RFS	62176	AB	W584RFS
62171	AB	W578RFS	62173	AB	W581RFS	62175	AB	W583RFS			

62177-62183   Volvo B10BLE   Wright Renown   N43F   2000-01

62177	AB	Y635RSA	62179	AB	Y637RSA	62181	AB	Y639RSA	62183	AB	X684ADK
62178	AB	Y636RSA	62180	AB	Y638RSA	62182	AB	X683ADK			

Pictured heading for the Falkirk Wheel is Larbert depot's 62296, N408ENW, a Scania L113CRL with Wright Axcess-ultralow bodywork. This vehicle first entered service at York depot. *Mark Doggett*

62184-62190
Volvo B10BLE | Alexander ALX300 | N40F | 2000

62184	AB	W585RFS	62186	AB	W587RFS	62188	AB	W589RFS
62185	AB	W586RFS	62187	AB	W588RFS	62189	AB	W591RFS

62190 AB W592RFS

62191-62204
Volvo B10BLE | Wright Renown | N43F | 2000

62191	AB	X685ADK	62195	AB	X689ADK	62199	AB	X694ADK
62192	AB	X686ADK	62196	AB	X691ADK	62200	AB	X695ADK
62193	BA	X687ADK	62197	AB	X692ADK	62201	AB	X696ADK
62194	BA	X688ADK	62198	AB	X693ADK			

62202 AB X697ADK
62203 AB X698ADK
62204 AB W681RNA

62205-62211
Volvo B10BLE | Alexander ALX300 | N40F | 2000

62205	AB	W593RFS	62207	AB	W595RFS	62209	AB	W597RFS
62206	AB	W594RFS	62208	AB	W596RFS	62210	AB	W598RFS

62211 AB W599RFS

62212-62218
Volvo B10BLE | Wright Renown | N43F | 1998-2000

62212	AB	W682RNA	62214	AB	S673SVU	62216	QS	R585SBA
62213	AB	W683RNA	62215	QS	R584SBA	62217	QS	R586SBA

62218 QS R587SBA

62219-62227
Volvo B10BLE | Alexander ALX300 | N40F | 2000

62219	AB	W601RFS	62222	AB	W604RFS	62224	AB	W606RFS
62220	AB	W602RFS	62223	AB	W605RFS	62225	AB	W607RFS
62221	AB	W603RFS						

62226 AB W608RFS
62227 AB W609RFS

62228 ABM YS51JVD Blue Bird AARE | Blue Bird | B60F | 2002

62231-62245
Volvo B10BLE | Wrightbus Renown | N44F | 2001

62231	WN	Y941CSF	62235	OG	Y946CSF	62239	OG	Y948CSF
62232	OG	Y937CSF	62236	WN	Y944CSF	62240	OG	Y949CSF
62233	WN	Y942CSF	62237	OG	Y945CSF	62241	QS	Y951CSF
62234	OG	Y943CSF	62238	MS	Y947CSF	62242	MS	Y939CSF

62243 OG Y953CSF
62244 OG Y952CSF
62245 MS Y938CSF

62266	B	P20GRT	Scania L94IB			Irizar InterCentury 12.32		C51FT	1997		
62268	GS	N500TCC	Volvo B10M-62			Plaxton Première 350		C48F	1994	Travellers, Hounslow, 2001	
62272	GS	J302ASH	Leyland Tiger TR2R56V16Z4			Alexander Q		BC49F	1991		
62273	LW	J303ASH	Leyland Tiger TR2R56V16Z4			Alexander Q		BC49F	1991		
62281	DK	N535VSA	Mercedes-Benz O405			Optare Prisma		B47F	1996		
62283	DK	N536VSA	Mercedes-Benz O405			Optare Prisma		B47F	1996		
62286	DK	N538VSA	Mercedes-Benz O405			Optare Prisma		B47F	1996		
62291	LT	P503XSH	Scania L113CRL			Wright Axcess-ultralow		NC47F	1996		
62292	LT	P504XSH	Scania L113CRL			Wright Axcess-ultralow		NC47F	1996		
62293	LT	P505XSH	Scania L113CRL			Wright Axcess-ultralow		NC47F	1996		
62294	LW	P506XSH	Scania L113CRL			Wright Axcess-ultralow		NC47F	1996		
62295	LT	N407ENW	Scania L113CRL			Wright Axcess-ultralow		N48F	1995		
62296	LT	N408ENW	Scania L113CRL			Wright Axcess-ultralow		N48F	1995		
62298	BF	N411ENW	Scania L113CRL			Wright Axcess-ultralow		N48F	1995		
62299	BF	N406ENW	Scania L113CRL			Wright Axcess-ultralow		N48F	1995		

62300-62312   Scania L113CRL   Wright Axcess-ultralow   N40F   1998

62300	LT	R443ALS	62303	BF	R446ALS	62306	LT	R519BMS	62310	BK	R524BMS
62301	BF	R544ALS	62304	BF	R447ALS	62308	LT	R521BMS	62311	BK	S525UMS
62302	BF	R445ALS	62305	BK	R448ALS	62309	BK	S523UMS	62312	BK	S526UMS

62317-62332   Scania N113CRB   Wright Endurance   BC49F   1994

62317	LT	L552HMS	62323	LF	L558JLS	62326	LT	L60HMS	62331	LT	L565JLS
62322	LT	L557JLS	62324	LV	L559JLS	62328	LT	L562JLS	62332	LT	L566JLS

62334	LF	M568RMS	Scania N113CRB			Wright Endurance		BC49F	1995
62335	LF	M569RMS	Scania N113CRB			Wright Endurance		BC49F	1995
62339	LF	N572VMS	Scania N113CRB			Wright Endurance		BC49F	1995
62340	LF	N573VMS	Scania N113CRB			Wright Endurance		BC49F	1995
62341	LF	M574VMS	Scania N113CRB			Wright Endurance		BC49F	1995

62342-62349   Scania L113CRL   Wright Axcess-ultralow   N47F   1996

62342	LT	P575DMS	62344	LT	P577DMS	62346	LW	P579RSG	62349	LT	P581RSG
62343	LT	P576DMS	62345	LT	P578DMS	62348	LT	P580RSG			

62350-62354   Scania L113CRL   Wright Axcess-ultralow   N40F   1998

62350	LT	R587BMS	62352	LT	R589BMS	62353	LT	R590BMS	62354	LT	R591BMS
62351	LT	R588BMS									

62355-62358   Scania L94UB   Wrightbus Solar   NC43F   2001

62355	GS	SN51MSV	62356	GS	SN51MSU	62357	GS	SN51MSY	62358	GS	SN51MSX

62359	BK	R154GSF	Scania L113CRL			Wright Axcess-ultralow		NC40F	1998
62360	BK	R156GSF	Scania L113CRL			Wright Axcess-ultralow		NC40F	1998
62361	BK	R157GSF	Scania L113CRL			Wright Axcess-ultralow		NC40F	1998
62369	GS	P171DMS	Mercedes-Benz O405			Optare Prisma		BC49F	1997
62370	DK	P172DMS	Mercedes-Benz O405			Optare Prisma		BC49F	1997
62371	DK	P173DMS	Mercedes-Benz O405			Optare Prisma		BC49F	1997
62373	BF	P879YKS	Mercedes-Benz O405			Optare Prisma		B49F	1997
62381	LT	N409ENW	Scania L113CRL			Wright Axcess-ultralow		N47F	1995
62382	MU	N410ENW	Scania L113CRL			Wright Axcess-ultralow		N47F	1995
62383	MU	S520UMS	Scania L113CRL			Wright Axcess-ultralow		N41F	1998
62384	LV	R522BMS	Scania L113CRL			Wright Axcess-ultralow		N41F	1998

62385-62392   Scania L94UB   Wright Axcess Floline   N43F   1999

62385	LV	V527ESH	62387	LV	V529ESH	62389	LV	V531ESH	62391	LV	V34ESC
62386	LV	V528ESH	62388	LV	V530ESH	62390	LV	V532ESH	62392	LV	V35ESC

62393-62398   Scania L113CRL   Wright Axcess-ultralow   N40F   1998

62393	MU	R582YMS	62395	MU	R584YMS	62396	BF	R585YMS	62398	MU	R155GSF
62394	MU	R583YMS									

62400-62405   Mercedes-Benz O405   Optare Prisma   B49F   1995-97

62400	DK	N68CSC	62402	DK	P875YKS	62404	MU	P877YKS	62405	MU	P878YKS
62401	BF	N69CSC	62403	MU	P876YKS						

Mercedes-Benz have made several attempts to supply large buses to the British market and until the O530 Citaro model these mostly comprised a chassis/cowl version of the O405 model with British-built bodywork. 62403, P876YKS, carries Optare Prisma bodywork. *Mark Lyons*

62406-62410   Scania L94UB   Wrightbus Solar   N44F   2003

62406	CO	YS03ZKA	62408	CO	YS03ZKE	62409	CO	YS03ZKD	62410	CO	YS03ZKF
62407	CO	YS03ZKB									

62411	LT	SN03WMJ	TransBus E300	TransBus Enviro 300	N44F	2003
62412	LT	SN03WMU	TransBus E300	TransBus Enviro 300	N44F	2003

62602-62643   Leyland Lynx LX2R11C15Z4R   Leyland Lynx   B49F   1989-90

62602	LE	F602RTC	62612	u	F612RTC	62630	HO	F630RTC	62643	HO	H643YHT
62609	u	F609RTC	62626	ROu	F626RTC	62641	HO	H641YHT			

62706-62749   Leyland Lynx LX2R11C15Z4R   Leyland Lynx   B49F   1990

62706	ROt	G106HNP	62717	u	G117HNP	62733	LE	G133HNP	62744	u	G144HNP
62713	LE	G113HNP	62726	ROt	G126HNP	62735	u	G135HNP	62749	LE	G149HNP
62714	RHt	G114HNP	62729	ROt	G129HNP	62740	u	G140HNP			

62801-62808   BMC Falcon 777   BMC   N40F   2003   Chester Bus, 2007

62801	CC	BU53PNE	62803	CC	BU53PNJ	62805	CC	BU53PNL	62807	CC	BU53PNO
62802	CC	BU53PNF	62804	CC	BU53PNK	62806	CC	BU53PNN	62808	CC	BU53PNV

62901	D	99D95548	DAF SB220	East Lancs Myllennium	N33D	1999	
62902	D	99D88621	DAF SB220	East Lancs Myllennium	N33D	1999	
62903	D	99D88702	DAF SB220	East Lancs Myllennium	N33D	1999	
62935	B	T735JGB	Optare Excel L1070	Optare	N38F	1999	Hutchinson, Overtown, 2007
62936	B	T736JGB	Optare Excel L1070	Optare	N38F	1999	Hutchinson, Overtown, 2007
62949	B	W49WDS	Optare Excel L1070	Optare	N38F	2000	Hutchinson, Overtown, 2007
62952	B	W52WDS	Optare Excel L1070	Optare	N38F	2000	Hutchinson, Overtown, 2007
64000	D	02D78371	Mercedes-Benz O530	Mercedes-Benz Citaro	N38D	2002	TfL, 2005

64001-64011   Mercedes-Benz Citaro O530   Mercedes-Benz   N36D   2002

64001	L	LT02NTV	64004	L	LT02NUA	64007	L	LT02NUE	64010	L	LT02NUJ
64002	L	LT02NTX	64005	L	LT02NUB	64008	L	LT02NUF	64011	L	LT02NVY
64003	L	LT02NTY	64006	L	LT02NUC	64009	L	LT02NUH			

There are several versions of the Citaro, a fully integral Mercedes-Benz bus, with a limited number in right-hand drive format. The O530 K model, supplied to First for the Heathrow Airport series of services, is shown here by 64042, LK08FNL, a supplementary vehicle delivered in 2008 for Slough depot. *Mark Lyons*

64012-64019

Mercedes-Benz Citaro O530   Mercedes-Benz   N40F   2003

| 64012 | SH | LT52WXA | 64014 | SH | LT52WXL | 64016 | SH | LT52WXO | 64018 | SH | LK03LNE |
| 64013 | SH | LT52WXB | 64015 | SH | LT52WXN | 64017 | SH | LT52WXP | 64019 | SH | LK03LNF |

| 64020 | SH | BU04EZF | Mercedes-Benz Citaro O530 | Mercedes-Benz | N40F | 2004 |
| 64021 | SH | BU04EZG | Mercedes-Benz Citaro O530 | Mercedes-Benz | N40F | 2004 |

64022-64028

Mercedes-Benz Citaro O530   Mercedes-Benz   N31D   2003

| 64022 | D | 03D36145 | 64024 | D | 03D36152 | 64026 | D | 03D36160 | 64028 | D | 03D36164 |
| 64023 | D | 03D36149 | 64025 | D | 03D36156 | 64027 | D | 03D36162 | | | |

| 64029 | BY | BX02CMK | Mercedes-Benz Citaro O530 | Mercedes-Benz | N38F | 2002 | Evobus demonstrator, 2004 |

64030-64042

Mercedes-Benz Citaro O530 K   Mercedes-Benz   N40F   2007-08

64030	SH	LK07CCA	64033	SH	LK07CCF	64036	SH	LK07CCO	64039	SH	LK07CCX
64031	SH	LK07CCD	64034	SH	LK07CCJ	64037	SH	LK07CCU	64042	SH	LK08FNL
64032	SH	LK07CCE	64035	SH	LK07CCN	64038	SH	LK07CCV			

64043-64048

Mercedes-Benz Citaro O530 K   Mercedes-Benz   N40F   2008

| 64043 | SH | LK08 | 64045 | SH | LK08 | 64047 | SH | LK08 | 64048 | SH | LK08 |
| 64044 | SH | LK08 | 64046 | SH | LK08 | | | | | | |

64501	CA	YJ55BJE	Optare Tempo X1200	Optare	N41F	2005	*operated for Ceredigion CC*
64502	CA	YJ55BJF	Optare Tempo X1200	Optare	N41F	2005	*operated for Ceredigion CC*
64503	CA	YJ55BJK	Optare Tempo X1200	Optare	N41F	2005	*operated for Ceredigion CC*

64791-64798

Scania K113CRB   Berkhof Excellence 1000LD   C53F   1995

| 64791 | BLt | M791TCF | 64793 | BLt | M793TCF | 64795 | BLt | N795WAN | 64797 | BLt | N797WAN |
| 64792 | BLt | M792TCF | 64794 | BLt | M794TCF | 64796 | BLt | N796WAN | 64798 | BLt | N798WAN |

| 64808 | HP | P818AWT | Scania L113CRL | East Lancs Flyte | B49F | 1996 | Black Prince, Morley, 2005 |

The 2008 First Bus Handbook

Another integral bus selected by First is the Scania OmniCity with examples operating in Southampton, Chelmsford and the Potteries. Allocated to the depot in Stoke is 65036, YN06WMJ, which is lettered for route 101 that serves Stafford. *Steve Rice*

64810-64817

Scania L113CRL*   Northern Counties Paladin   B51F   1995   *64810 is type L113CLL

64810	u	M810PGM	64811	LFt	M811PGM	64812	LFt	M812PGM	64817	BL	M817PGM

65001-65005

Scania OmniCity CN94UB   Scania   N42F   2004

65001	AG	YN04YJC	65003	AG	YN04YJE	65004	AG	YN04YJF	65005	AG	YN04YJG
65002	AG	YN04YJD									

65006-65025

Scania OmniCity CN94UB   Scania   N44F   2004

65006	HI	YN54NZA	65011	HI	YN54NZG	65016	HI	YN54NZO	65021	HI	YN54NZV
65007	HI	YN54NZC	65012	HI	YN54NZH	65017	HI	YN54NZP	65022	HI	YN54NZW
65008	HI	YN54NZD	65013	HI	YN54NZJ	65018	HI	YN54NZR	65023	HI	YN54NZX
65009	HI	YN54NZE	65014	HI	YN54NZK	65019	HI	YN54NZT	65024	HI	YN54NZY
65010	HI	YN54NZF	65015	HI	YN54NZM	65020	HI	YN54NZU	65025	HI	YN54NZZ

65026-65042

Scania OmniCity CN94UB   Scania   N44F*   2005-06   *65028-32 are NC41F

65026	AG	YN54OCK	65031	CM	YN06TDX	65035	AG	YN06WMG	65039	AG	YN06WMM
65027	AG	YN05HCL	65032	CM	YN06TDZ	65036	AG	YN06WMJ	65040	AG	YN06WMO
65028	CM	YN06TDO	65033	AG	YN06WME	65037	AG	YN06WMK	65041	AG	YN06WMP
65029	CM	YN06TDU	65034	AG	YN06WMF	65038	AG	YN06WML	65042	AG	YN06WMT
65030	CM	YN06TDV									

65521-65540

Scania L113CRL   Wright Axcess-ultralow   N40F   1997

65521	VN	R141GSF	65526	KL	R146GSF	65531	KL	R151GSF	65536	LF	R136GSF
65522	VN	R142GSF	65527	KL	R147GSF	65532	KL	R152GSF	65537	VN	R137GSF
65523	VN	R143GSF	65528	KL	R148GSF	65533	LF	R133GSF	65538	VN	R138GSF
65524	VN	R144GSF	65529	KL	R149GSF	65534	VN	R134GSF	65539	VN	R139GSF
65525	KL	R145GSF	65530	LF	R150GSF	65535	LF	R135GSF	65540	VN	R140GSF

65541-65550

Scania L113CRL   Wright Axcess-ultralow   N47F   1997

65541	IP	P541RNG	65544	IP	P544RNG	65547	IP	P547RNG	65549	IP	P549RNG
65542	IP	P542RNG	65545	IP	P545RNG	65548	IP	P548RNG	65550	IP	P550RNG
65543	IP	P543RNG	65546	IP	P546RNG						

65551-65564 — Scania L113CRL — Wright Axcess-ultralow — N40F — 1998

65551	VN	R551CNG	65556	VN	R556CNG	65559	u	R259DVF	65562	u	R262DVF
65552	VN	R552CNG	65557	VN	R257DVF	65560	u	R260DVF	65563	u	R263DVF
65553	VN	R553CNG	65558	VN	R258DVF	65561	u	R261DVF	65564	VN	R264DVF
65554	VN	R554CNG									

65565-65574 — Scania L94UB — Wright Axcess Floline — N40F — 1999

65565	u	S565TPW	65568	YA	S568TPW	65571	u	S571TPW	65573	u	S573TPW
65566	u	S566TPW	65569	VN	S569TPW	65572	u	S572TPW	65574	u	S574TPW
65567	u	S567TPW	65570	IP	S570TPW						

65575-65580 — Scania L94UB — Wright Axcess Floline — N40F — 1999

65575	VN	T575JNG	65577	VN	T577JNG	65579	VN	T579JNG	65580	VN	T580JNG
65576	VN	T576JNG	65578	VN	T578JNG						

65586-65601 — Scania L94UB — Wright Axcess Floline — N40F — 1999-2000

65586	VN	V586DVF	65590	IP	V590DVF	65594	LT	W594SNG	65598	BK	W598SNG
65587	VN	V587DVF	65591	LF	W591SNG	65595	LT	W595SNG	65599	LT	W599SNG
65588	IP	V588DVF	65592	LF	W592SNG	65596	LF	W596SNG	65601	LT	W601SNG
65589	IP	V589DVF	65593	LF	W593SNG	65597	LT	W597SNG			

| 65602 | BL | S102CSG | Scania L94UB | | | Wright Axcess Floline | | N40F | 1998 |

65620-65625 — Scania L94UB — Wright Axcess Floline — N40F — 1999

65620	BL	T820JBL	65622	BL	T822JBL	65624	BL	T824JBL	65625	BL	T825JBL
65621	BL	T821JBL	65623	BL	T823JBL						

65626-65632 — Scania L94UB — Wright Axcess Floline — N43F — 2000

65626	BS	V826FSC	65628	BS	V828FSC	65630	BS	V830FSC	65632	BS	V832FSC
65627	BS	V827FSC	65629	BS	V829FSC	65631	BS	V831FSC			

65650-65654 — Scania L94UB — Wright Axcess Floline — N43F — 1999

65650	CO	T650SSF	65652	CO	T652SSF	65653	CO	T653SSF	65654	CO	T654SSF
65651	CO	T651SSF									

65662	LT	V362CNH	Scania L94UB			Wright Axcess Floline		N43F	1999
65663	LT	V363CNH	Scania L94UB			Wright Axcess Floline		N43F	1999
65664	LT	V364CNH	Scania L94UB			Wright Axcess Floline		N43F	1999

65665-65677 — Scania L94UB — Wrightbus Solar — N43F — 2001

65665	BS	SN51UXX	65669	BS	SN51UYB	65672	BS	SN51UYE	65675	BS	SN51UYJ
65666	BS	SN51UXY	65670	BS	SN51UYC	65673	BS	SN51UYG	65676	BS	SN51UYK
65667	BS	SN51UXZ	65671	BS	SN51UYD	65674	BS	SN51UYH	65677	BS	SN51UYL
65668	BS	SN51UYA									

65678-65692 — Scania L94UB — Wrightbus Solar — N44F — 2002-03

65678	CO	YP02ABN	65682	CM	YR52VEP	65686	CO	YS03ZKC	65690	CO	YS03ZKK
65679	CO	YR52VEH	65683	CM	YR52VEU	65687	CO	YS03ZKG	65691	CO	YS03ZKL
65680	CM	YR52VEK	65684	CM	YR52VEY	65688	CO	YS03ZKH	65692	CO	YS03ZKM
65681	CM	YR52VEL	65685	CO	YR52VFO	65689	CO	YS03ZKJ			

65693-65699 — Scania L94UB — Wrightbus Solar — N43F — 2003

65693	GS	SN53KHH	65695	BK	SN53KHK	65697	GS	SN53KHM	65699	LT	SN53KHP
65694	BK	SN53KHJ	65696	GS	SN53KHL	65698	LT	SN53KHO			

65700-65707 — Scania L94UB — Wrightbus Solar — N43F — 2004

65700	LT	SN04CKY	65702	LT	SN04CLF	65704	BP	YN04GNU	65706	NE	YN04GMF
65701	LT	SN04CKX	65703	LV	SN04CNK	65705	NE	YN04GME	65707	CH	YN04GMG

65708-65723 — Scania L94UB — Wrightbus Solar — N43F — 2004-05

65708	BK	SN54KDF	65712	BK	SN54KDU	65716	BK	SN54KEJ	65720	BK	SN54KFC
65709	BK	SN54KDJ	65713	BK	SN54KDV	65717	BK	SN54KEK	65721	BK	SN54KFD
65710	BK	SN54KDK	65714	BK	SN54KDX	65718	BK	SN54KEU	65722	BK	SN54KFE
65711	BK	SN54KDO	65715	BK	SN54KDZ	65719	BK	SN54KFA	65723	BK	SN54KFF

Seen heading for Livingston Centre is Larbert's 65701, SN04CKX, a Scania L94UB with Wrightbus Solar bodywork. *Mark Doggett*

65724-65733

		Scania L94UB				Wrightbus Solar			N43F	2005	
65724	BL	LK55ABZ	65727	NE	YN05HCO	65730	NE	YN05HCV	65732	NE	YN05HCY
65725	BL	LK55ACF	65728	NE	YN05HCP	65731	NE	YN05HCX	65733	NE	YN05HCZ
65726	BL	LK55ACJ	65729	NE	YN05HCU						

65734-65754

		Scania L94UB				Wrightbus Solar			N43F	2005-06	
65734	CH	YN05WKC	65740	CH	YN05WKJ	65745	GS	SN55JVK	65750	GS	SN55JVA
65735	CH	YN05WKD	65741	CH	YN05WKK	65746	GS	SN55JVL	65751	GS	SN55JVC
65736	CH	YN05WKE	65742	GS	SN55JVG	65747	GS	SN55JVM	65752	LT	SN55JVD
65737	CH	YN05WKF	65743	GS	SN55JVH	65748	GS	SN55JVO	65753	LT	SN55JVE
65738	CH	YN05WKG	65744	GS	SN55JVJ	65749	GS	SN55JVP	65754	DK	SN06AHK
65739	CH	YN05WKH									

65755	LF	SK02ZYG	Scania L94UB	Wrightbus Solar	N43F	2002	Hutchinson, Overtown, 2007
65756	LF	SK02ZYH	Scania L94UB	Wrightbus Solar	N43F	2002	Hutchinson, Overtown, 2007
65757	LF	SN03CLX	Scania L94UB	Wrightbus Solar	N43F	2003	Hutchinson, Overtown, 2007
65758	LF	SN03CLY	Scania L94UB	Wrightbus Solar	N43F	2003	Hutchinson, Overtown, 2007
66100	WS	R460VOP	Volvo B10BLE	Wright Renown	N44F	1997	Volvo demonstrator, 1999

66101-66120

		Volvo B10BLE				Wright Renown			N47F	1998	
66101	OG	R901BOU	66106	WS	R906BOU	66112	OG	R912BOU	66117	MS	R917BOU
66102	WS	R902BOU	66107	WS	R907BOU	66113	OG	R913BOU	66118	MS	R918BOU
66103	WS	R903BOU	66108	WS	R908BOU	66114	OG	R914BOU	66119	OG	R919BOU
66104	WS	R904BOU	66109	MS	R909BOU	66115	MS	R915BOU	66120	MS	R920COU
66105	WS	R905BOU	66110	MS	R910BOU	66116	MS	R916BOU			

66121-66130

		Volvo B10BLE				Wright Renown			N41F	1998-99	
66121	HI	S121JTP	66126	NR	S116JTP	66128	SO	S118JTP	66130	SO	S120JTP
66122	SO	S122UOT	66127	SO	S117JTP	66129	SO	S119JTP			

66151-66163 — Volvo B10BLE — Wright Renown — N44F — 1998-99

66151	HO	S351NPO	66155	HO	S355XCR	66158	HO	S358XCR
66152	HO	S352NPO	66156	HO	S356XCR	66159	HI	S359XCR
66153	HO	S353NPO	66157	HO	S357XCR	66160	HI	S360XCR
66154	HO	S354NPO						

66161	HO	S361XCR
66162	HO	S362XCR
66163	HO	S363XCR

66164-66181 — Volvo B10BLE — Wright Renown — N44F — 2000

66164	HO	W364EOW	66168	BP	W368EOW	66173	TN	W373EOW
66165	BP	W365EOW	66169	WH	W369EOW	66174	TN	W374EOW
66166	TN	W366EOW	66171	TN	W371EOW	66176	HO	W376EOW
66167	TN	W367EOW	66172	TN	W372EOW	66177	WH	W377EOW

66178	TN	W378EOW
66179	WH	W379EOW
66181	HO	W381EOW

66191-66207 — Volvo B10BLE — Wright Renown — N41F — 1998

66191	QS	S791RWG	66195	QS	S795RWG	66199	HO	S799RWG
66192	QS	S792RWG	66196	HO	S796RWG	66201	HO	S801RWG
66193	QS	S793RWG	66197	HO	S797RWG	66202	HO	S802RWG
66194	QS	S794RWG	66198	HO	S798RWG	66203	HO	S803RWG

66204	HO	S804RWG
66205	HO	S805RWG
66206	WS	S806RWG
66207	WS	S807RWG

66233	B	X303JGE	Volvo B10BLE	Alexander ALX300	N44F	2000	Hutchinson, Overtown, 2007
66234	B	X304JGE	Volvo B10BLE	Alexander ALX300	N44F	2000	Hutchinson, Overtown, 2007
66281	B	Y181BGB	Volvo B10BLE	Wrightbus Renown	N44F	2001	Hutchinson, Overtown, 2007
66282	B	Y182BGB	Volvo B10BLE	Wrightbus Renown	N44F	2001	Hutchinson, Overtown, 2007

66301-66323 — Volvo B7L — Wrightbus Eclipse — N41F — 2002

66301	u	KV02VVC	66307	LE	KV02VVJ	66313	LE	KV02VVP
66302	LE	KV02VVD	66308	LE	KV02VVK	66314	LE	KV02VVR
66303	LE	KV02VVE	66309	LE	KV02VVL	66315	LE	KV02VVS
66304	LE	KV02VVF	66310	LE	KV02VVM	66316	LE	KV02VVT
66305	LE	KV02VVG	66311	LE	KV02VVN	66317	LE	KV02VVU
66306	LE	KV02VVH	66312	LE	KV02VVO	66318	LE	KV02VVW

66319	LE	KV02VVX
66320	LE	KV02VVY
66321	LE	KV02VVZ
66322	u	KV02VWA
66323	LE	KV02VWB

66324-66348 — Volvo B7L — Wrightbus Eclipse — N41F — 2002

66324	NN	MV02VAX	66330	NN	MV02VBE	66337	NN	MV02VCM
66325	u	MV02VAY	66332	NN	MV02VBX	66338	NN	MV02VCN
66326	NN	MV02VBA	66333	NN	MV02VBY	66339	NN	MV02VCO
66327	NN	MV02VBB	66334	NN	MV02VBZ	66340	NN	MV02VCP
66328	NN	MV02VBC	66335	NN	MV02VCA	66341	NN	MV02VCT
66329	NN	MV02VBD	66336	NN	MV02VCC	66342	NN	MV02VCU

66343	NN	MV02VCW
66344	NN	MV02VCX
66345	NN	MV02VCY
66346	NN	MV02VCZ
66347	NN	MV02VDA
66348	NN	MV02VDC

During 2007 the Scottish operator Hutchinson of Overtown was acquired. Several vehicles were taken into stock, including Y182BGB which has been numbered 66282 with First. *Mark Doggett*

66349-66356   Volvo B7L   Wrightbus Eclipse   N41F   2002

66349	SN	MV02VDZ	66351	BA	MV02VEB	66353	BA	MV02VEH	66355	BA	MV02VEL
66350	BA	MV02VEA	66352	BA	MV02VEF	66354	BA	MV02VEK	66356	BA	MV02VEM

66357	LA	Y185HNH	Volvo B7L	Wrightbus Eclipse	N26D	2002	Dawson Rentals, 2007
66358	LA	Y186HNH	Volvo B7L	Wrightbus Eclipse	N26D	2002	Dawson Rentals, 2007
66503	YV	620HOD	Volvo B10M-56	Alexander P	BC53F	1987	
66511	YV	RIL1069	Volvo B10M-56	Alexander P	BC53F	1987	
66651	BDt	K114PRV	Volvo B10B	Northern Counties Paladin	BC47F	1993	
66652	BDt	M967GDU	Volvo B10B	Plaxton Verde	B51F	1994	Plaxton demonstrator, 1995

66700-66715   Volvo B7RLE   Wrightbus Eclipse Urban   N43F*   2003-04   *seating varies

66700	HP	YJ53HVC	66704	HP	YJ53GXN	66708	HP	YJ53GXT	66712	BM	YK04EZL
66701	HP	YJ53GXJ	66705	HP	YJ53GXO	66709	BM	YJ53GXU	66713	BM	YK04EZG
66702	HP	YJ53GXL	66706	HP	YJ53GXP	66710	BM	YJ53GXV	66714	BM	YK04EZM
66703	HP	YJ53GXM	66707	HP	YJ53GXR	66711	BM	YK04EZJ	66715	BM	YK04EZH

66716-66737   Volvo B7RLE   Wrightbus Eclipse Urban   NC43F   2004

66716	WS	WX54XDA	66722	WS	WX54XDL	66728	BA	WX54XCN	66733	BA	WX54XCU
66717	WS	WX54XDD	66723	WS	WX54XDH	66729	BA	WX54XCO	66734	BA	WX54XCV
66718	WS	WX54XDB	66724	WS	WX54XDG	66730	BA	WX54XCP	66735	BA	WX54XCW
66719	WS	WX54XDC	66725	WS	WX54XDJ	66731	BA	WX54XCR	66736	BA	WX54XCY
66720	WS	WX54XDF	66726	WS	WX54XDK	66732	BA	WX54XCT	66737	BA	WX54XCZ
66721	WS	WX54XDE	66727	BA	WX54XCM						

66738-66758   Volvo B7RLE   Wrightbus Eclipse Urban   N43F   2005

66738	HX	YJ54XVM	66744	HU	YJ54XVU	66749	HU	YJ54XWA	66754	HX	YJ05KNV
66739	HX	YJ54XVN	66745	HU	YJ54XVW	66750	HU	YJ05KOB	66755	HX	YJ05KNW
66740	HU	YJ54XVO	66746	HU	YJ54XVX	66751	HU	YJ05KOD	66756	HX	YJ05KNX
66741	HU	YJ54XVP	66747	HU	YJ54XVY	66752	HU	YJ05KOE	66757	HU	YJ05KNY
66742	HU	YJ54XVR	66748	HU	YJ54XVZ	66753	HU	YJ05KOH	66758	HU	YJ05KNZ
66743	HU	YJ54XVT									

66759-66792   Volvo B7RLE   Wrightbus Eclipse Urban   N43F   2005

66759	HX	YJ05VVA	66768	HU	YJ05VVL	66777	HX	YJ05VVW	66785	HU	YK05FPA
66760	HX	YJ05VVB	66769	HU	YJ05VVM	66778	HX	YJ05VVX	66786	HU	YK05FLC
66761	HX	YJ05VVC	66770	HU	YJ05VVN	66779	HX	YJ05VVY	66787	HU	YK05FOV
66762	HX	YJ05VVD	66771	HU	YJ05VVO	66780	HX	YJ05VVZ	66788	HU	YK05FOU
66763	HX	YJ05VVE	66772	HU	YJ05VVP	66781	HX	YK05FJJ	66789	HX	YK05FOT
66764	HU	YJ05VVF	66773	HU	YJ05VVR	66782	HX	YK05FLB	66790	HX	YK05SOU
66765	HU	YJ05VVG	66774	HU	YJ05VVS	66783	HX	YK05FJF	66791	HU	YK05FOP
66766	HU	YJ05VVH	66775	HU	YJ05VVT	66784	HU	YK05FJE	66792	HU	YK05SOJ
66767	HU	YJ05VVK	66776	HX	YJ05VVU						

Seen in Devizes is Volvo B7L 66356, MV02VEM, one of a batch allocated to Bath depot. *Richard Godfrey*

The First Manchester depots of Oldham, Bury and Bolton now employ a large number of Volvo B7RLE buses, although several are expected to be reallocated once new double-deck buses arrive later in 2008. Seen near Bromley Cross rail station is 69156, MX06VNM, operating route 533 to Bolton. *Bill Potter*

66794-66933 Volvo B7RLE   Wrightbus Eclipse Urban   N43F   2005

66794	OM	MX05CBF	66829	OM	MX05CFG	66864	OM	MX05CJJ	66899	BN	MX55FFK
66795	OM	MX05CBU	66830	OM	MX05CFJ	66865	OM	MX05CJO	66900	BN	MX55FFL
66796	OM	MX05CBV	66831	OM	MX05CFK	66866	OM	MX05CJU	66901	BN	MX55FFM
66797	OM	MX05CBY	66832	OM	MX05CFL	66867	OM	MX05CJV	66902	BN	MX55FFO
66798	OM	MX05CCA	66833	OM	MX05CFM	66868	OM	MX05CJY	66903	BN	MX55FFP
66799	OM	MX05CCD	66834	OM	MX05CFN	66869	OM	MX05CJZ	66904	BN	MX55FFR
66800	OM	MX05CCF	66835	OM	MX05CFO	66870	OM	MX05CKA	66905	BN	MX55FFS
66801	OM	MX05CCJ	66836	OM	MX05CFP	66871	OM	MX05CKC	66906	OM	MX55FFT
66802	OM	MX05CCK	66837	OM	MX05CFU	66872	OM	MX05CKD	66907	OM	MX55FFU
66803	OM	MX05CCN	66838	OM	MX05CFV	66873	OM	MX05CKE	66908	OM	MX55FFV
66804	OM	MX05CCO	66839	OM	MX05CFY	66874	OM	MX05CKF	66909	OM	MX55FFW
66805	OM	MX05CCU	66840	OM	MX05CGE	66875	OM	MX55NWE	66910	OM	MX55FFY
66806	OM	MX05CCV	66841	OM	MX05CGF	66876	OM	MX05CKJ	66911	OM	MX55FFZ
66807	OM	MX05CCY	66842	OM	MX05CGG	66877	OM	MX05CKK	66912	OM	MX55FGA
66808	OM	MX05CCZ	66843	OM	MX05CGK	66878	OM	MX05CKL	66913	OM	MX55FGC
66809	OM	MX05CDE	66844	OM	MX05CGO	66879	OM	MX05CKN	66914	BY	MX55FGE
66810	OM	MX05CDF	66845	OM	MX05CGU	66880	OM	MX05CKO	66915	BY	MX55FGF
66811	OM	MX05CDK	66846	OM	MX05CGV	66881	OM	MX05CKP	66916	BY	MX55FGG
66812	OM	MX05CDN	66847	OM	MX05CGY	66882	OM	MX55HHR	66917	BY	MX55FGJ
66813	OM	MX05CDO	66848	OM	MX05CGZ	66883	OM	MX55HHP	66918	BY	MX55FGK
66814	OM	MX05CDU	66849	OM	MX05CHC	66884	OM	MX55HHO	66919	BY	MX55FGM
66815	OM	MX05CDV	66850	OM	MX05CHD	66885	OM	MX05CLF	66920	BY	MX55FGN
66816	OM	MX05CDY	66851	OM	MX05CHF	66886	OM	MX55LHL	66921	BY	MX55FGO
66817	OM	MX05CDZ	66852	OM	MX05CHG	66887	OM	MX55HHN	66922	BY	MX55FGP
66818	OM	MX05CEA	66853	OM	MX05CHH	66888	OM	MX55NWF	66923	BY	MX55FGU
66819	OM	MX05CEF	66854	OM	MX05CHJ	66889	OM	MX55HHM	66924	BY	MX55FGV
66820	OM	MX05CEJ	66855	OM	MX05CHK	66890	OM	MX55NWH	66925	BY	MX55FGZ
66821	OM	MX05CEK	66856	OM	MX05CHL	66891	OM	MX55UAA	66926	BY	MX55FHA
66822	OM	MX05CEO	66857	OM	MX05CHN	66892	OM	MX55LDJ	66927	BY	MX55FHB
66823	OM	MX05CEU	66858	OM	MX05CHO	66893	OM	MX55LDK	66928	BY	MX55FHC
66824	OM	MX05CEV	66859	OM	MX05CHV	66894	OM	MX55FFD	66929	BY	MX55FHD
66825	OM	MX05CEY	66860	OM	MX05CHY	66895	OM	MX55FFE	66930	BY	MX55FHE
66826	OM	MX05CFA	66861	OM	MX05CHZ	66896	OM	MX55FFG	66931	BY	MX55FHF
66827	OM	MX05CFD	66862	OM	MX05CJE	66897	BN	MX55FFH	66932	VN	MX55FHG
66828	OM	MX05CFE	66863	OM	MX05CJF	66898	BN	MX55FFJ	66933	QS	MX55FHH

The 2008 First Bus Handbook

During 2008, First increased its order with Volvo and Wrightbus for further standard products. One from the current single-deck choice, the Volvo B7RLE, is 66996, YJ07LWD, seen leaving Leeds for Wetherby.
Richard Godfrey

66934-66961   Volvo B7RLE   Wrightbus Eclipse Urban   N43F   2005

66934	WS	WX55UAA	66941	BA	WX55TZC	66948	BA	WX55TZK	66955	BA	WX55TZS
66935	WS	WX55UAB	66942	BA	WX55TZD	66949	BA	WX55TZL	66956	YV	WX55TZT
66936	WS	WX55UAC	66943	BA	WX55TZE	66950	YA	WX55TZM	66957	VN	WX55TZU
66937	BA	WX55UAD	66944	BA	WX55TZF	66951	BA	WX55TZN	66958	YV	WX55TZV
66938	BA	WX55TYZ	66945	BA	WX55TZG	66952	BA	WX55TZO	66959	YA	WX55TZW
66939	BA	WX55TZA	66946	BA	WX55TZH	66953	BA	WX55TZP	66960	YV	WX55TZY
66940	BA	WX55TZB	66947	BA	WX55TZJ	66954	BA	WX55TZR	66961	TN	WX55TZZ

66962-66987   Volvo B7RLE   Wrightbus Eclipse Urban   N43F   2005

66962	LE	KX05MHY	66969	LE	KX05MJU	66976	LE	KX05MGZ	66982	LE	KX05MHL
66963	LE	KX05MHZ	66970	LE	KX05MJV	66977	LE	KX05MHA	66983	LE	KX05MHM
66964	LE	KX05MJE	66971	LE	KX05MJY	66978	LE	KX05MHE	66984	LE	KX05MHN
66965	LE	KX05MJF	66972	LE	KX05AOC	66979	LE	KX05MHF	66985	LE	KX05MHO
66966	LE	KX05MJJ	66973	LE	KX05AOD	66980	LE	KX05MHJ	66986	LE	KX05MHU
66967	LE	KX05MJK	66974	LE	KX05AOE	66981	LE	KX05MHK	66987	LE	KX05MHV
66968	LE	KX05MJO	66975	LE	KX05MGY						

66988-66999   Volvo B7RLE   Wrightbus Eclipse Urban   N43F   2006-07   *66992-4 N34D

66988	PH	SF56GYP	66991	PH	SF56GYT	66994	D	06D85192	66997	CR	YJ07LWE
66989	PH	SF56GYR	66992	BT	RKZ4761	66995	CR	YJ07LWC	66998	CR	YJ07LWF
66990	PH	SF56GYS	66993	BT	RKZ4760	66996	CR	YJ07LWD	66999	BD	YK57FCL

67001-67013   Dennis Lance 11m   Northern Counties Paladin   B49F   1997

67001	BS	P501MNO	67005	CO	P505MNO	67008	CO	P508MNO	67011	CN	P511MNO
67002	CO	P502MNO	67006	CO	P506MNO	67009	CN	P509MNO	67012	CN	P512MNO
67003	CO	P503MNO	67007	CO	P507MNO	67010	CN	P510MNO	67013	CN	P513MNO
67004	CO	P504MNO									

67036-67040   Dennis Lance 11m   Northern Counties Paladin   B49F   1993

67036	BS	K736JAH	67038	CMt	K738JAH	67039	BDt	K739JAH	67040	CMt	K740JAH
67037	CMt	K737JAH									

67112	NN	L822HCY	Dennis Lance 11m	Plaxton Verde	BC45F	1993
67117	NN	L817HCY	Dennis Lance 11m	Plaxton Verde	BC45F	1993

Firstgroup was formed with the merger of the Badgerline Group and the GRT Bus Group in June 1995. The two companies had previously chosen differing vehicle suppliers with Badgerline selecting the Dennis Lance, mostly bodied by Plaxton with their Verde model. One that was new to Midland Red West is 67207, L207AAB, which is currently based at Redditch. *Mark Doggett*

67122-67136

		Dennis Lance 11m			Plaxton Verde			B49F	1993-94		
67122	MS	L122TFB	67126	MS	L126TFB	67130	MS	L130TFB	67134	MS	L134TFB
67123	TN	L123TFB	67127	MS	L127TFB	67132	MS	L132TFB	67135	TN	L135TFB
67124	MS	L124TFB	67128	MS	L128TFB	67133	TN	L133TFB	67136	MS	L136TFB
67125	MS	L125TFB	67129	BAt	L129TFB						

67201-67220

		Dennis Lance 11m			Plaxton Verde			B49F	1994		
67201	KD	L201AAB	67206	KD	L206AAB	67211	RH	L211AAB	67216	u	L216AAB
67202	KD	L202AAB	67207	RH	L207AAB	67212	KD	L212AAB	67217	RH	L217AAB
67203	NN	L203AAB	67208	RH	L208AAB	67213	KD	L213AAB	67218	NN	L218AAB
67204	NN	L204AAB	67209	RH	L209AAB	67214	KD	L214AAB	67219	RH	L219AAB
67205	KD	L205AAB	67210	NN	L210AAB	67215	KD	L215AAB	67220	RH	L220AAB

67222-67237

		Dennis Lance 11m			Plaxton Verde			B49F	1994		
67222	HGt	L322AAB	67227	MS	L227AAB	67232	RH	L232AAB	67235	RH	L235AAB
67223	MS	L223AAB	67228	MS	L228AAB	67233	NN	L233AAB	67236	u	L236AAB
67224	MS	L224AAB	67231	RH	L231AAB	67234	WR	L234AAB	67237	RH	L237AAB
67225	BAt	L225AAB									

67238-67256

		Dennis Lance 11m			Plaxton Verde			B49F	1995		
67238	KD	M238MRW	67243	RH	M243MRW	67248	RH	M248MRW	67253	WR	M253MRW
67239	KD	M239MRW	67244	KD	M244MRW	67249	RH	M249MRW	67254	WR	M254MRW
67240	RH	M240MRW	67245	RH	M245MRW	67250	RH	M250MRW	67255	WR	M255MRW
67241	RH	M241MRW	67246	RH	M246MRW	67251	u	M251MRW	67256	RH	M256MRW
67242	RH	M242MRW	67247	u	M247MRW	67252	NN	M252MRW			

67296	DG	M796MPM	Dennis Lance 11m		Alexander PS	B46F	1995	Dennis demonstrator, 1998
67301	WR	M221EAF	Dennis Lance SLF		Wright Pathfinder 320	N40F	1995	

67311-67324

		Dennis Lance SLF			Wright Pathfinder 320			N34D*	1993	*67311-7 are N39F	
67311	RH	ODZ8911	67315	WR	ODZ8915	67318	WR	ODZ8918	67322	WR	ODZ8922
67312	RH	ODZ8912	67316	BA	ODZ8916	67319	WR	ODZ8919	67323	WR	ODZ8923
67313	RH	ODZ8913	67317	BA	ODZ8917	67321	WR	ODZ8921	67324	WR	ODZ8924
67314	WR	ODZ8914									

The replacement for the Lance on the Alexander-Dennis chassis line is the Enviro 300, which was initially sold as a single product from ADL. First's examples are also allocated to the former Midland Red West depots and 67633, VX54MPF, is also allocated to Redditch where it is seen on Church Green. *Mark Lyons*

67337-67342			Dennis Lance SLF			Wright Pathfinder 320		N37F	1995	
67337	BA	M137FAE	67340	BA	M140FAE	67341	BA	M141FAE	67342	BA	M142FAE
67338	BA	M138FAE								

67501	LL	M626XWS	Dennis Javelin 12m		Wadham Stringer Vanguard 3	BC70F	1995	Munden, Bristol, 2005
67600	RH	SN53KKY	TransBus Enviro 300		TransBus Enviro 300	N43F	2003	

67601-67604			TransBus Enviro 300			TransBus Enviro 300		N43F	2004	
67601	WR	VX53VJV	67602	WR	VX53VJZ	67603	HD	VX53VKA	67604	HD	VX53VKB

67623	LEt	L623XFP	Dennis Falcon HC SDA422		Northern Counties Paladin	B48F	1993

67631-67651			ADL Enviro 300			ADL Enviro 300		N44F	2005	
67631	WR	VX54MOV	67637	RH	VX54MPY	67642	RH	VX54MRY	67647	WR	VX54MTF
67632	u	VX54MPE	67638	RH	VX54MPZ	67643	RH	VX54MSO	67648	WR	VX54MTJ
67633	RH	VX54MPF	67639	RH	VX54MRO	67644	RH	VX54MSU	67649	WR	VX54MTK
67634	RH	VX54MPO	67640	RH	VX54MRU	67645	WR	VX54MSY	67650	RH	VX54MTO
67635	RH	VX54MPU	67641	RH	VX54MRV	67646	WR	VX54MTE	67651	WR	VX54MTU
67636	RH	VX54MPV								

67652-67664			ADL Enviro 300			ADL Enviro 300		N44F	2005	
67652	WR	VX05LVS	67656	WR	VX05LVW	67659	WR	VX05LWC	67662	WR	VX05LWF
67653	WR	VX05LVT	67657	WR	VX05LVY	67660	WR	VX05LWD	67663	WR	VX05LWG
67654	WR	VX05LVU	67658	WR	VX05LVZ	67661	WR	VX05LWE	67664	WR	VX05LWH
67655	WR	VX05LVV								

68000	LFs	Q275LBA	Blue Bird		Blue Bird		B60F	1999

68001-68006			Blue Bird AARE			Blue Bird		B60F	2002	
68001	BL	RD51FKV	68003	BL	RD51FKZ	68005	BL	YS51JVE	68006	BL	YS51JVH
68002	BL	RD51FKW	68004	BL	RD51FLA					

68204-68218 Irisbus Scolabus 24 Vehixel B67F* 2002-05 *Operated for GMPTE*
68211-7 are B63F; 68218 ex Belle Vue, 2008

68204	IN	FE52HFH	68208	IN	MH04HCN	68212	IN	FJ55XLK	68216	IN	NX07DAU
68205	IN	FE52HFJ	68209	IN	MH04HCP	68213	IN	FJ55XLL	68217	IN	FX57LKM
68206	IN	FE52HFK	68210	IN	MH04HCU	68214	IN	FX56AHU	68218	TE	FJ55KNA
68207	TE	MH04HCL	68211	IN	FJ55XLH	68215	IN	NX07DAO			

68301	TR	BX55NZV	Autosan Eagle A1012T	Autosan	B67D	2006	Truronian, 2008
68302	TR	BX06NZT	Autosan Eagle A1012T	Autosan	B67D	2006	Truronian, 2008

68501-68552 BMC 1100FE Student BMC B60F 2004-05 *68549-52 are B55F*
68515/6/25-30/45-8 are operated for Metro, WYPTE

68501	KW	BU04CAA	68512	SO	RX54AOY	68527	HX	YA54WBL	68537	SO	LK54FNH
68503	CA	BX54VUN	68513	CA	CU54DCE	68528	HX	YA54WBK	68545	HX	YJ05VWA
68504	CA	CU54CYX	68514	CA	CU54DCF	68529	HX	YA54WBO	68546	HX	YJ55CAO
68505	LL	CU54CYY	68515	HX	YJ54YCO	68530	HX	YA54WBN	68547	HX	YJ55CAV
68506	CA	CU54CYZ	68516	HX	YJ54YCP	68531	BL	LK54FNC	68548	HX	YJ55CAU
68507	NN	KX54AHP	68518	AB	SV54CFY	68532	CM	LK54FNE	68549	HX	VX05LWA
68508	NN	KX54AHU	68519	AB	SV54CFZ	68533	SO	LK54FNJ	68550	SO	HX05BUO
68509	NN	KX54AHY	68520	WR	KP54AZU	68534	CM	LK54FNL	68551	CM	EU05DXS
68510	NN	KX54ANR	68521	CM	KP54AZV	68535	CM	EU05DXR	68552	CM	EU05DXT
68511	SO	RX54AOV	68522	BL	RX54OGZ	68536	SO	LK54FNF			

68553-68566 BMC 1100FE Student BMC B55F 2005-06

68553	HO	HX05BUJ	68557	KW	MX55NWD	68561	SO	HX55AOJ	68564	DU	SF55TXA
68554	SO	LK05FCE	68558	Lon	LK55ABU	68562	SO	HX55AOH	68565	DU	SF55TXB
68555	CM	MX55NWS	68559	Lon	LK55ABV	68563	SO	HX55AOK	68566	DU	SF55TXC
68556	KW	MX55NWC	68560	Lon	LK55ABX						

68567-68571 BMC 1100FE Student BMC B55F 2007-08

68567	RAC	BV57MSO	68569	RAC	BV57MSX	68570	RAC	BV57MSY	68571	SO	BG57ZGJ
68568	RAC	BV57MSU									

68600	TR	BX55NYD	BMC 1100FE Student	BMC	B55F	2006	Truronian, 2008

68601-68648 BMC Condor 220 BMC NC57F 2005-06 *Operated for Metro WYPTE*

68601	HX	YJ55ZZY	68613	HU	YK55AUC	68625	BM	YK55AVM	68637	HX	YK06EHL
68602	HX	YK55AAE	68614	HU	YK55AUE	68626	BM	YJ06WTV	68638	HX	YK06DNN
68603	HX	YK55AAJ	68615	HU	YK55AUF	68627	BM	YJ06WTW	68639	BD	YK06DTZ
68604	HX	YK55AUN	68616	BM	YK55AUH	68628	BM	YJ06WYV	68640	BD	YJ06XEK
68605	HX	YK55AUO	68617	BM	YK55AVB	68629	BD	YJ06WTY	68641	BD	YJ06XEL
68606	HX	YK55AUP	68618	BM	YK55AVC	68630	BD	YJ06WTZ	68642	HX	YK06ATO
68607	HX	YJ06XFS	68619	BM	YK55AVD	68631	HU	YJ06WUA	68643	BD	YK06CZZ
68608	HX	YJ06XFR	68620	BM	YK55AVE	68632	HU	YK06DNU	68644	HX	YK06CZY
68609	HX	YK55AUU	68621	BM	YK55AVF	68633	HU	YK06DNO	68645	BD	YK06FHC
68610	HX	YK55AAN	68622	BM	YK55AVG	68634	HX	YK06EHM	68646	BD	YK06DAA
68611	HX	YK55AAF	68623	BM	YK55AVJ	68635	HX	YK06DYJ	68647	BD	YK06DAO
68612	HX	YK55AUA	68624	BM	YK55AVL	68636	HU	YK06DYH	68648	BD	YK06EHE

68649-68676 BMC Condor 220 BMC NC57F 2006-07 *Operated for Metro WYPTE*

68649	BD	YJ56LJA	68656	BD	YJ56LLG	68663	HX	YJ56LKE	68670	HX	YJ56LRU
68650	BD	YJ56LJC	68657	HX	YJ56LLK	68664	HX	YJ56LJY	68671	HX	YJ56LRN
68651	BD	YJ56LJE	68658	BD	YJ56LLM	68665	HX	YJ56LJZ	68672	HX	YJ56LRL
68652	BD	YJ56LJF	68659	BD	YJ56LLN	68666	HX	YJ56LKA	68673	HX	YJ56WGC
68653	BD	YJ56LJK	68660	BD	YJ56LLO	68667	HX	YJ56LKC	68674	HX	YJ56WGA
68654	BD	YJ56LJN	68661	BD	YJ56LNC	68668	HX	YJ56LKD	68675	HX	YJ56ZMU
68655	BD	YJ56LJL	68662	HX	YJ56LNA	68669	HX	YJ56LMX	68676	HX	YK07FTU

68677-68693 BMC Condor 220 BMC NC57F 2007-08 *Operated for Metro WYPTE*

68677	HX	YK07FUD	68682	HX	YK07FTP	68686	HU	YJ57VVA	68690	HU	YJ08XCO
68678	HX	YK07FTY	68683	HX	YK07FTT	68687	HU	YJ57VYY	68691	HU	YJ08XCP
68679	HX	YK07FTZ	68684	HU	YJ57VYX	68688	HX	YK57FOM	68692	HU	YJ08XCN
68680	HX	YK07FUA	68685	HU	YJ57VTV	68689	HU	YJ08XCR	68693	HU	YJ08XCS
68681	HX	YK07FUB									

A further example of First's standard single-deck is 69006, AU05DMF, which is seen in Norwich *Park & Ride* livery. Recent transfers have seen this vehicle move to Great Yarmouth. *Mark Lyons*

69000-69011

Volvo B7RLE   Wrightbus Eclipse Urban   N43F   2005

69000	YK	YK54ENP	69003	YK	YK54ENN	69006	YA	AU05DMF
69001	YK	YK54ENL	69004	YK	YK54ENO	69007	YA	AU05DMO
69002	YK	YK54ENM	69005	YA	AU05DME	69008	YA	AU05DMV

69009	YA	AU05DMX
69010	YA	AU05DMY
69011	YA	AU05DMZ

69012-69134

Volvo B7RLE   Wrightbus Eclipse Urban   N43F   2006-07

69012	PH	SF55UAD	69043	PH	SF55UBC	69074	SN	SF06GXX	69105	SN	SF06GZP
69013	PH	SF55UAE	69044	PH	SF55UBD	69075	SN	SF06GXY	69106	SN	SF06GZR
69014	PH	SF55UAG	69045	PH	SF55UBE	69076	SN	SF06GXZ	69107	SN	SF06GZS
69015	PH	SF55UAH	69046	PH	SF55UBG	69077	SN	SF06GYA	69108	SN	SF06GZT
69016	PH	SF55UAJ	69047	PH	SF55UBH	69078	SN	SF06GYJ	69109	SN	SF06GZV
69017	PH	SF55UAK	69048	PH	SF55UBJ	69079	PH	SF06GYK	69110	AB	SV06GRF
69018	PH	SF55UAL	69049	PH	SF55UBK	69080	PH	SF06GYN	69111	PH	SF06GZX
69019	PH	SF55UAM	69050	PH	SF55UBL	69081	PH	SF06GYO	69112	PH	SF06GZY
69020	PH	SF55UAN	69051	PH	SF55UBM	69082	PH	SF06GYP	69113	PH	SF06GZZ
69021	PH	SF55UAO	69052	PH	SF55UBN	69083	PH	SF06GYR	69114	PH	SF06HAA
69022	PH	SF55UAP	69053	SN	SF55UBO	69084	PH	SF06GYS	69115	PH	SF06HAE
69023	PH	SF55UAR	69054	SN	SF55UBP	69085	PH	SF06GYT	69116	PH	SF06HAO
69024	PH	SF55UAS	69055	SN	SF55UBR	69086	PH	SF06GYU	69117	PH	SF06HAU
69025	PH	SF55UAT	69056	SN	SF55UBS	69087	PH	SF06GYV	69118	PH	SF06HAX
69026	PH	SF55UAU	69057	SN	SF06GXM	69088	PH	SF06GYW	69119	PH	SF06HBA
69027	SN	SF55UAV	69058	SN	SF06GXN	69089	PH	SF06GYX	69120	PH	SF06HBB
69028	SN	SF55UAW	69059	SN	SF06GXH	69090	PH	SF06GYY	69121	PH	SF06HBC
69029	SN	SF55UAX	69060	SN	SF06GXO	69091	PH	SF06GYZ	69122	AB	SV06GRK
69030	SN	SF55UAY	69061	SN	SF06GXP	69092	PH	SF06GZA	69123	AB	SV06GRU
69031	SN	SF55UAZ	69062	SN	SF06GXR	69093	PH	SF06GZB	69124	AB	SV06GRX
69032	SN	SF55UBA	69063	SN	SF06GXS	69094	PH	SF06GZC	69125	AB	SV07EHB
69033	SN	SF55UBT	69064	SN	SF06GXT	69095	PH	SF06GZD	69126	AB	SV07EHC
69034	SN	SF55UBU	69065	SN	SF06GXU	69096	PH	SF06GZE	69127	AB	SV07EHD
69035	SN	SF55UBV	69066	SN	SF06GYB	69097	PH	SF06GZG	69128	AB	SV07EHE
69036	SN	SF55UBW	69067	SN	SF06GYC	69098	PH	SF06GZH	69129	AB	SV07EHF
69037	SN	SF55UBX	69068	SN	SF06GYD	69099	PH	SF06GZJ	69130	AB	SV07EHG
69038	SN	SF06GXJ	69069	SN	SF06GYE	69100	PH	SF06GZK	69131	AB	SV07EHH
69039	SN	SF06GXG	69070	SN	SF06GYG	69101	PH	SF06GZL	69132	AB	SV07EHJ
69040	SN	SF06GXK	69071	SN	SF06GYH	69102	PH	SF06GZM	69133	AB	SV07EHK
69041	SN	SF06GXL	69072	SN	SF06GXV	69103	SN	SF06GZN	69134	AB	SV07EHL
69042	SN	SF55UBB	69073	SN	SF06GXW	69104	SN	SF06GZO			

First has been advocating the use of dedicated buses for school transport in Britain and has invested in two main types, the Turkish-built BMC, many of which are operated for Metro - West Yorkshire PTE and the Irisbus Scolabus. A BMC Condor, 68562, HX55AOH is illustrated. *Mark Lyons*

69135-69244			Volvo B7RLE			Wrightbus Eclipse Urban			N43F	2006	
69135	BN	MV06CZS	69163	BN	MX06VNU	69191	BN	MX56ADZ	69218	QS	MX56AEG
69136	BN	MV06CZG	69164	BN	MX06VNV	69192	BN	MX56AEA	69219	BY	MX56AEJ
69137	BN	MV06CZT	69165	BN	MX06VMW	69193	BN	MX56AEB	69220	BY	MX56AEK
69138	BN	MV06CXB	69166	BN	MX06VMZ	69194	BN	MX56AEC	69221	BY	MX56AEL
69139	BN	MX06VOP	69167	BN	MX06VNB	69195	BN	MX06VPR	69222	BY	MX56AEM
69140	BN	MX06VOT	69168	BN	MX06VNC	69196	BN	MX06VPT	69223	BY	MX56AEN
69141	BN	MX06VOU	69169	BN	MX06VND	69197	BN	MX06VPU	69224	BY	MX56AEO
69142	BN	MX06VOV	69170	BN	MX06VNE	69198	BN	MX06VPV	69225	BY	MX56AEP
69143	BN	MX06VOY	69171	BN	MX06VNF	69199	BN	MX06VPW	69226	BY	MX56AET
69144	BN	MX06VPA	69172	BN	MV06CZJ	69200	BN	MX06VPY	69227	BY	MX56AEU
69145	BN	MX06VNW	69173	BN	MV06DWZ	69201	BN	MX06VPZ	69228	BY	MX56AEV
69146	BN	MX06VNY	69174	BN	MX06VNK	69202	BN	MX06VRC	69229	BY	MX56AEW
69147	BN	MX06VNZ	69175	BN	MX06VPO	69203	BN	MX06VPC	69230	BY	MX56AEY
69148	BN	MX06VOA	69176	BN	MX06VPP	69204	BN	MX06VPD	69231	BY	MX56AEZ
69149	BN	MX06VOB	69177	BN	MX06YXJ	69205	QS	MX06VPE	69232	BY	MX56AFA
69150	BN	MX06VOC	69178	BN	MX06YXK	69206	QS	MV06DYU	69233	BY	MX56AFE
69151	BN	MX06VOD	69179	BN	MX06YXL	69207	QS	MX06VPG	69234	BY	MX56AFF
69152	BN	MX06VOF	69180	BN	MX06YXM	69208	QS	MX06VPJ	69235	BY	MX56AFJ
69153	BN	MX06VOG	69181	BN	MX06YXN	69209	QS	MX06VPK	69236	BY	MX56AFK
69154	BN	MX06VOH	69182	BN	MX06YXO	69210	QS	MX06VPL	69237	BY	MX56AFN
69155	BN	MX06VNL	69183	BN	MX06YXP	69211	QS	MX06VPM	69238	BY	MX56AFO
69156	BN	MX06VNM	69184	BN	MX06YXR	69212	QS	MX06VPN	69239	BN	MX56AFU
69157	BN	MX06VNN	69185	BN	MX56ACV	69213	QS	MX06YXS	69240	BN	MX56AFV
69158	BN	MX06VNO	69186	BN	MX56ACY	69214	QS	MX06YXT	69241	BN	MX56AFY
69159	BN	MX06VNP	69187	BN	MX56ACZ	69215	QS	MX56AED	69242	BN	MX56AFZ
69160	BN	MX06VNR	69188	BN	MX56ADO	69216	QS	MX56AEE	69243	BN	MX56AGO
69161	BN	MX06VNS	69189	BN	MX56ADU	69217	QS	MX56AEF	69244	BN	MX56AGU
69162	BN	MX06VNT	69190	BN	MX56ADV						

The 2008 First Bus Handbook

69245-69294 Volvo B7RLE Wrightbus Eclipse Urban N43F 2007

69245	BD	YS07WFM	69258	GS	SK57ADU	69271	BD	YS07WFX	69283	LW	SN57JCO
69246	BD	YS07WFN	69259	GS	SK57ADV	69272	BD	YS07WFY	69284	LW	SN57JCU
69247	BD	YS07WFO	69260	GS	SK57ADX	69273	BD	YS07WFZ	69285	LW	SN57JCV
69248	BD	YS07WFP	69261	GS	SK57ADZ	69274	BD	YS07WGA	69286	LW	SN57JCX
69249	BD	YS07WFR	69262	GS	SK57AEA	69275	YK	YJ57YSN	69287	LW	SN57JCY
69250	BD	YS07WFS	69263	GS	SK57AEB	69276	YK	YJ57YSM	69288	LW	SN57JCZ
69251	BD	YS07WFT	69264	GS	SK57AEC	69277	YK	YJ57YSO	69289	LW	SN57JDF
69252	BD	YS07WFU	69265	AB	SV57EYH	69278	YK	YJ57YSP	69290	LW	SN57JDJ
69253	BD	YS07WFV	69266	AB	SV57EYJ	69279	YK	YJ57YSR	69291	LW	SN57JDK
69254	LW	SK07JVN	69267	AB	SV57EYK	69280	LW	SN57JBY	69292	LW	SN57HZX
69255	LW	SK07JVO	69268	YK	YJ57YSK	69281	LW	SN57JBZ	69293	LW	SN57HZY
69256	LW	SK07JVP	69269	YK	YJ57YSL	69282	LW	SN57JCJ	69294	LW	SN57HZZ
69257	GS	SK57ADO	69270	BD	YJ07WFW						

69295-69298 Volvo B7RLE Wrightbus Eclipse Urban N38F 2004 Hutchinson, Overtown, 2007

69295	B	SF04HXW	69296	B	SF04HXX	69297	B	SF04ZPE	69298	B	SF04ZPG

69299-69305 Volvo B7RLE Wrightbus Eclipse Urban N40F 2008

69299	BD	YJ08GWX	69301	RA	CU08AHN	69303	RA	CU08AHP	69305	RA	CU08AHX
69300	BD	YJ08GWY	69302	RA	CU08AHO	69304	RA	CU08AHV			

69329-69350 Volvo B7RLE Wrightbus Eclipse Urban N43F 2008

69329	VN	YJ08CDE	69335	CR	YJ08CDV	69341	CR	YJ08CEK	69346	CR	YJ08CEX
69330	VN	YJ08CDF	69336	CR	YJ08CDX	69342	CR	YJ08CEN	69347	CR	YJ08CEY
69331	VN	YJ08CDK	69337	CR	YJ08CDY	69343	CR	YJ08CEO	69348	BA	YJ08CFA
69332	CR	YJ08CDN	69338	CR	YJ08CDZ	69344	CR	YJ08CEU	69349	BA	YJ08CFD
69333	CR	YJ08CDO	69339	BA	YJ08CEA	69345	CR	YJ08CEV	69350	BA	YJ08CFE
69334	CR	YJ08CDU	69340	BA	YJ08CEF						

69351-69379 Volvo B7RLE Wrightbus Eclipse Urban N43F 2008

69351	AB	SV08FHA	69359	YK	YJ08ZGM	69366	YK	YJ08XYE	69373	YK	-
69352	AB	SV08FHB	69360	YK	YJ08ZGN	69367	YK	YJ08XYF	69374	YK	-
69353	AB	SV08FHC	69361	YK	YJ08ZGO	69368	YK	YJ08XYG	69375	YK	-
69354	AB	SV08FHD	69362	YK	YJ08ZGP	69369	YK	YJ08XYJ	69376	YK	-
69355	AB	SV08FHE	69363	YK	YJ08XYB	69370	YK	YJ08XYK	69377	YK	-
69356	AB	SV08FHF	69364	YK	YJ08XYC	69371	YK	-	69378	YK	-
69357	AB	SV08FHG	69365	YK	YJ08XYD	69372	YK	-	69379	YK	-
69358	YK	YJ08ZGL									

90087	u	J612UTW	Mercedes-Benz 709	Plaxton Beaver	TV	1992
90091	u	DUG167C	Leyland Titan PD3	Roe	RV	1965
90092	u	OWJ782A	Leyland Titan PD3	Roe	RV	1963
90103	ROp	3904WE	Leyland Titan PD3/1	Roe	B39/30R	1959
90141	BKs	XMS244R	Leyland Leopard PSU3C/3R	Alexander AY	RV	1977
90146	LTs	PSU317	Scania K113CRB	Plaxton Paramount 3500 III	classroom	1990
90147	LTs	PSU315	Scania K113CRB	Plaxton Paramount 3500 III	classroom	1990
90176	DGt	H135FLX	Leyland Olympian ON2R50C13Z4	Northern Counties	TV	1990
90178	Lon	F601XMS	Mercedes-Benz 811D	Alexander Sprint	ferry	1988
90179	PLp	OTA290G	Bristol VRT/SL/6LX	Eastern Coach Works	B39/31F	1969
90180	PLp	VOD125K	Bristol LHS6L	Marshall	B33F	1972
90230	HAp	WNO479	Bristol KSW5G	Eastern Coach Works	O33/28R	1953
90236	CNs	H397OHK	Mercedes-Benz 709D	Reeve Burgess Beaver	Staff	1991
90243	HHs	S935RBE	Mercedes-Benz 410D	Autobus Classique	ferry	1998
90252	LEp	FJF193	Leyland Titan PD2/1	Leyland	B33/29R	1950
90256	LEt	C930GYD	Ford Transit 190	Dormobile	TV	1986
90258	LEs	E419KUY	Mercedes-Benz 609D	Reeve Burgess	Marketing	1987
90269	WRt	D350ESC	Leyland Tiger TRBTL11/2RP	Alexander TE	TV	1987
90274	WRs	NOE614R	Leyland Leopard PSU3D/4R	Plaxton Supreme III	RV	1976	Midland Red Coaches, 1986
90277	CMs	S936RBE	Mercedes-Benz 410D	Autobus Classique	ferry	1998

Allocations - June 2008

First Aberdeen

First Aberdeen Ltd; Kirkpatrick of Deeside Ltd; G E Mair Hire Services Ltd
395 King Street, Aberdeen, AB24 5RP

Aberdeen (King Street) - AB

Mercedes-Benz O405	10046							
Volvo B7LA	10047	10048	10049	10050	10051	10052	10154	10155
	10156	10157	10158	10159	10160	10161	10162	10163
	10164	10165	10166	10167	10168	10169	10170	10171
	10172	10173						
Dennis Javelin	20027	21153						
Volvo B10M coach	20011	20012	20013	20014	20015	20019	20020	20029
Scania coach	20008	20009	20016	20017	20018	23401	23402	
Volvo B12 coach	20021	20204	20205	20206	20207			
Olympian	31547	31548	31549	31550	31551			
	31552	31553	31554	31555	31556	31557		
Volvo B7TL	31558	31559	31560	31561	31562	31563		
Mercedes-Benz Mini	50071	50411	50416	50421	50422			
Mercedes-Benz Vario	56001	56007	56008					
Mercedes-Benz Atego	56501							
Volvo B10BLE	62122	62123	62124	62125	62126	62127	62128	62129
	62130	62131	62132	62133	62134	62135	62136	62137
	62138	62139	62140	62141	62149	62150	62151	62152
	62153	62154	62155	62156	62157	62158	62159	62160
	62161	62162	62163	62164	62165	62166	62167	62168
	62169	62170	62171	62172	62173	62174	62175	62176
	62177	62178	62179	62180	62181	62182	62183	62184
	62185	62186	62187	62188	62189	62190	62191	62192
	62193	62194	62195	62196	62197	62198	62199	62200
	62201	62202	62203	62204	62205	62206	62207	62208
	62209	62210	62211	62212	62213	62219	62220	62221
	62222	62223	62224	62225	62226	62227		
Bluebird	62228							
BMC Schoolbus	68518	68519						
Volvo B7RLE	69110	69122	69123	69124	69125	69126	69127	69128
	69129	69130	69131	69132	69133	69134	69265	69266
	69267	69351	69352	69353	69354	69355	69356	69357

Ancillary / Reserve / For disposal / Specials:

AEC Swift	62119	
Leopard	62120	
Albion	62121	
Atlantean	31528	31577
Daimler CVG6	31529	

First Edinburgh

First Edinburgh Ltd; Midland Bluebird Ltd, Carmuirs House, Stirling Road, Larbert, Falkirk, FK5 3NJ

Balfron (Dunmore Street) - BF

Olympian	31727	31728	31729	31730	31731	31732	31733	31734
	31735							
Mercedes-Benz O405	62373	62401						
Scania	62298	62299	62301	62302	62303	62304	62396	

Bannockburn (Cowie Road, Stirling) - BK

Volvo B10M	20405							
Olympian	30740	30741	30743	30750	30751	34015	34066	34067
	34073	34075	34076	34083				
Dart	40888	40889	40895	40897	40898	40899	40901	40918
	40942							
Scania L	60178	60180	60181	60186	60188	60197	60203	60221
	61052	61053	61222	62305	62309	62310	62311	62312
	62329	62359	62360	62361	65598	65694	65695	65708
	65709	65710	65711	65712	65713	65714	65715	65716
	65717	65718	65719	65720	65721	65722	65723	

Dalkeith (Eskbank Road) - DK

Volvo B7R	20356	20364						
Volvo Citybus	30351	38089	38132					
Olympian	30742	30744	30745	30746	30747	30748	30749	31634
	31636	31638	31639	31640	31641	31643	31644	31646
	31650	31651	31652	31653				
Volvo B7TL	32669	32670	32671	32672	32673	32674	32675	32676
	32677	32678	32679	32680	32681	32682	32683	
Dart	40697	40698	40701	40919	40920	40943	40944	40945
Mercedes-Benz O405	62281	62283	62286	62370	62371	62400	62402	
Scania	61214	61218	61220	61221	61226	61230	61231	65754

Galashiels (Duke Street) - GS

Volvo B7R	20370	20371						
Volvo Citybus	30358	38091	38092	38096				
Olympian	31572	31655	31660	31684	31687	31688		
Volvo B9TL	37133	37134						
Dart	40905	40909	40910	40911	40913	40915	40917	40921
Volvo B10M	62268							
Tiger	62272							
Mercedes-Benz O405	62369							
Scania	61225	61228	62355	62356	62357	62358	32369	65693
	65696	65697	65742	65743	65744	65745	65746	65747
	65748	65749	65750	65751				
Volvo B7RLE	69257	69258	69259	69260	69261	69262	69263	69264

Larbert (Stirling Road) - LT

Volvo B10M	20116							
Olympian	30826	30828	30833	31569	31570	31571	31642	31647
	31649	31654	31679	31680	31681	31682		
Dart	40894	40896	40900	40946	43844			
Leyland Tiger	62250							
Leyland Lynx	62644	62711	62748					
Volvo B10B	60302							
Scania	60179	60182	60187	60191	60192	60195	60198	60199
	60204	61216	61223	61233	62291	62292	52293	62295
	62296	62300	62306	62308	62317	62322	62328	62331
	62334	62342	62343	62344	62345	62348	62349	62350
	62351	62352	62353	62354	62381	65594	65595	65597
	65599	65601	65662	65663	65664	65698	65699	65700
	65701	65702	65752	65753				
Enviro 300	62411	62412						

Linlithgow (High Street) - LW

Volvo B9TL	37135	37266	37267	37268	37269	37270	37271	37272
	37273							
Dart	40893	40938	43843					
Tiger	62273							
Scania bus	62294	62346						
Volvo B7RLE	69254	69255	69256	69280	69281	69282	69283	69284
	69285	69286	69287	69288	69289	69290	69291	69292
	69293	69249						

Livingston (Deans) - LV

Volvo B10M	20404	20438						
Volvo B7R	20354	20355	20357					
Olympian	31635	31645	31648	31656	31657	31659	31675	31678
Scania OmniDekka	36007	36008	36009	36010	36011	36012	36013	36014
	36015	36016	36017	36018	36019	36020	36021	36022
	36023	36024	36025	36026	36027	36028	36029	36030
Volvo B9TL	37136	37137	37138	37139	37140	37141	37142	37143
	37144	37145						
Dart	40914	40933	40936	40940	40941	41220	41349	41357
	41359							
Volvo B10M	60578	60579	60581	60583	60585	60588	60590	60591
	60592	60596	60601					
Scania	60220	61674	62384	62385	62386			
	62387	62388	62389	62390	62391	62392	65703	

Musselburgh (The Mall) - MU

Olympian	30827	30829	30830	30831	30832	31637	31661	31662
	31663	31664	31665	31666	31667	31668	31669	31670
	31671	31672						
Dart	40703	40706	40708	40887	40890	40912	40916	40922
	40926	40927	40928	40929	40930	40931	40932	40934
	40937							
Mercedes-Benz O405	62403	62404	62405					
Scania	61215	61217	61219	61224	61227	61229	61232	62382
	62383	62393	62394	62395	62398			

First in Glasgow

First Glasgow (No1) Ltd, 197 Victoria Road, Larkfield, Glasgow, G42 7AD
First Glasgow (No2) Ltd, 197 Victoria Road, Larkfield, Glasgow, G42 7AD

Blantyre - B

Scania coach	23126							
Olympian	31200	31421	31472	31483	31491	31492	31493	31494
	31495	31516	31520	31521				
Dart	40267	40301	40722	40733	40734	40736	40737	40738
	40740	40741	40742	40774	40775	40776	40796	40797
	40798	40799	40800	40801	40802	40803	40804	40805
	40806	40807	40808	40809	40810	40811	40812	40813
	40814	40815	40816	40817	40818	40819	40820	40828
	40830	40831	40832	40839	40842	41211	41213	41214
	41215	41216	41218	41224	41225	41226	42885	42886
	42887	42888						
Volvo B6	40882	40883	40884	40885	40886	48046	48072	
Optare Solo	50463	50464	50465	50466	50467			
Volvo B10M	60030	60129	61387	61402	61403	61406	61408	61416
	61417	61456	61460	61463	61467	61477	61490	61492
	61493	61494	61495	61496	61497	61511	61512	61513
	61514	61515	61516	61517	61518	61519		
Volvo B10BLE	61597	61598	61599	61600	61601	61602	61603	61604
	61605	61606	61607	61608	61609	61610	61611	61612
	61613	61614	61616	61617	61618	61619	61620	61621
	61622	61623	61624	61625	61626	61652	61653	61654
	61705	61706	61707	61708	61709	61710	66233	66234
	66281	66282	69295	69296	69297	69298		
Scania	62266							

Cumbernauld (Glencryan Road) - CD

Olympian	31414	31415	31416	31417	31418	31419	31420	31422
	31423	31425	31426	31427	31428	31433	31434	31435
	31436	31437	31468	31470	31471	31487	31496	31497
	31517	31523						
Trident	32805	32811	32820	32821	32823	32824	32825	32826
	32827	32828	32829	32830	32831	32832	32833	32834
	32835	32836	32837	32848				
Volvo B7TL	32611	32612	32613	32614	32615	32616	32617	32618
	32619	32620	32621	32622	32623	32624	32625	32626
Volvo B10M	61372	61413	61418	61421	61422	61427	61428	61430
	61434	61439	61445	61503	61504	61505	61506	61507
	61508	61509	61510					

Dumbarton (Broadmeadow Industrial Estate) - DU

Dart	41201	41202	41203	41204	41205	41206	41208	41209
	41210	41212	41217	41219	41221	41222	41227	41228
Optare Solo	50460	50461	50462	50468				
Volvo B10M	60550	61255	61265	61269	61270	61271	61370	61389
	61390	61391	61392	61393	61395	61396	61397	61399
	61400	61404	61407	61409	61410	61419	61420	61424
	61425	61426	61441	61444	61461	61462	61464	61465
	61468	61470	61470	61489	61491	61499	61500	61501
BMC Student	68564	68565	68566					

Glasgow (Victoria Road, Larkfield) - LF

Volvo Citybus	38129	38132						
Olympian	31381	31382	31383	31384	31385	31386	31392	31393
	31394	31395	31396	31397	31398	31399	31400	31401
	31402	31403	31404	31405	31406	31407	31408	31409
	31410	31411	31412	31413				
Volvo B7TL	32547	32566	32567	32568	32580	32581	32582	32583
	32584	32585	32586	32587	32588	32589	32603	32604
	32605	32606	32607	32608	32609	32610	37166	37167
	37168	37169	37170	37171	37172	37173	37174	37175
	37176	37177	37178	37179	37180	37181	37182	37183
	37184	37185	37186					
Volvo B9TL	37187	37188	37189	37190	37191	37192	37193	37194
	37195	37196	37197	37198	37199	37200	37201	37202
	37203	37204	37205	37206	37207	37208	37209	37210
	37211	37212	37213	37214	37215	37216	37217	37218
	37219	37220	37221	37222	37223	37224	37225	37226
	37227							
Solo	40723	40845	40846	40847	40851	40852	40853	40854
	40858	40965	40966	53201				
Dart	40186	40254	40270	40604	40724	40739	40743	40744
	40745	40746	40747	40748	40749	40750	40751	40752
	40753	40754	40755	40756	40770	40773	40780	40781
	40782	40783	40834	40840	40903	40947	40951	42376
Mercedes-Benz	50386	50391	50395	52483	52486	52489		
Volvo B10M	60138	60464	60466	60551	60552	60580	60582	60584
	60586	60587	60589	60593	60594	60595	61256	61259
	61260	61261	61262	61263	61264	61266	61268	61347
	61398	61401	61405	61412	61414	61415	61423	61457
	61469	61471	61472	61473	61474	61475	61476	
Scania	61017	61018	61019	61020	61021	61022	61023	61024
	61025	61026	61027	61028	61043	61044	61291	61292
	61293	61294	61295	61296	61298	61299	61300	61478
	61479	61480	61481	61524	61525	61526	61532	61534
	61535	61537	61539	61540	61543	61544	61545	61546
	61547	61548	61549	61550	61552	61558	61559	61561
	61562	61564	61565	61567	61568	61569	61570	61571
	61572	61573	61574	61575	61576	61577	61579	61580
	61581	61582	61583	61584	61585	61586	61667	61668
	61669	61670	61671	61672	61673	61675	61676	61677
	61678	61679	61680	61681	61682	61683	61684	61685
	61686	61687	61688	61689	61690	61691	61692	61693
	61694	61695	61696	61697	61698	61699	61700	61701
	61702	61703	61704	62324	62334	62335	62341	64811
	64812	65530	65533	65535	65536	65591	65592	65593
	65596	65755	65756	65757	65758			

Glasgow (Tollcross Road, Parkhead) - PH

Volvo Citybus	30340	30341	30342	30343	30344	30345	30346	30347
	30348	30349	31285	31300	31310	31314	31317	31318
	31320	38130						
Olympian	30107	31429	31430	31473	31474	31475	31476	31477
	31478	31479	31480	31481	31482	31484	31485	31486
Dennis Trident	32931	32934	32935	32936	32937	32939	32940	32941
	32942	32946	32947	32948	32949	32950	32951	32952
Volvo B7TL	31506	31507	31508	31509	31510	31511	31512	31513
	31514	31515						
Volvo B10M	61388	61431	61431	61432	61433	61435	61436	61437
	61438	61439	61440	61442	61443	61446	61447	61448
	61449	61450	61451	61452	61453	61454	61455	61458
	61459	61498	61502					

Volvo B7L	61306	61615	61627	61628	61631	61632	61633	61634
	61635	61637	61638	61639	61640	61641	61642	61643
	61644	61645	61646	61647	61648	61649	61650	61651
	61656	61657	61658	61659	61660	61661	61663	61664
Volvo B7RLE	66988	66989	66990	66991	69012	69013	69014	69015
	69016	69017	69018	69019	69020	69021	69023	69024
	69025	69026	69043	69044	69045	69046	69047	69048
	69049	69050	69051	69052	69079	69080	69081	69082
	69083	69084	69085	69086	69087	69088	69089	69090
	69091	69092	69093	69094	69095	69096	69097	69098
	69099	69100	69101	69102	69111	69112	69113	69114
	69115	69116	69117	69118	69119	69120	69121	

Glasgow (Scotstoun) - SN

Volvo B7LA	10015	10016	10033	10034	10131	10132	10133	10134
	10136	10137	10138	10139	10141	10142	10143	10144
	10146	10147	10148	10149	10183			
Volvo B10BLA	10044	10045	10103	10104	10105	10106	10107	10108
	10109	10110						
Olympian	31431	31432	31438	31439	31440	31441	31442	31443
	31444	31445	31446	31447	31448	31449	31450	31469
	31488	31489	31490	31498	31499	31500	31501	31503
	31504	31505						
Volvo B7TL	32543	32544	32545	32546	32548	32549	32550	32551
	32552	32553	32554	32555	32556	32557	32558	32559
	32560	32561	32562	32563	32564	32569	32571	32572
	32573	32574	32575	32576	32577	32578	32579	32590
	32591	32592	32593	32594	32595	32596	32597	32598
	32599	32600	32601	32602				
Solo	40848	40849	40850	40855	40856	53202	53203	
Volvo B10M	61371	61373	61374	61375	61376	61377	61378	61379
	61380	61381	61382	61383	61384	61385	61386	61466
Volvo B7L	61587	61588	61589	61590	61591	61592	61593	61594
	61595	61596	61629	61630	61636	61662	66349	
Volvo B7RLE	69027	69028	69029	69030	69031	69032	69033	69034
	69035	69036	69037	69038	69039	69040	69041	69042
	69053	69054	69055	69056	69057	69058	69059	69060
	69061	69062	69063	69064	69065	69066	69067	69068
	69069	69070	69071	69072	69073	69075	69076	69077
	69078	69103	69104	69105	69106	69107	69108	69109

First Manchester

First Manchester Ltd; First Pioneer Bus Ltd, Wallshaw Street, Oldham, OL1 3T

Bolton (Weston Street) - BN

Volvo B10LA	10000	10001	10002	10003	10004	10005	10006	10007
	10008	10009	10010	10011	10012	10013	10014	
Scania L94UA	10017							
Olympian	34251	34252	34253	34254	34255			
Volvo B9TL	37302	37303	37304	37305				
Dart	40000	40001	40337	40338	40339	40340	40341	40342
	40343	40344	40347	40348	40349	40350	40351	40352
	40353	40354	40355	40356	40357	40358	40359	40360
	40363	40400	40401	40402	40404	40405		
Volvo B10B	60117	60308	60310	60312	60313	60314	60318	60319
	60320	60322	60328	60332	60333	60335	60336	60338
	60343	60344	60347	60349	61369			
Volvo B7RLE	66897	66898	66899	66900	66901	66902	66903	66904
	66905	69135	69136	69137	69138	69139	69140	69141
	69142	69143	69144	69145	69146	69147	69148	69149
	69150	69151	69152	69153	69154	69155	69156	69157
	69158	69159	69160	69161	69162	69163	69164	69165
	69166	69167	69168	69169	69170	69171	69172	69173
	69174	69175	69176	69177	69178	69179	69180	69181
	69182	69183	69184	69185	69186	69187	69188	69189
	69190	69191	69192	69193	69194	69195	69196	69197
	69198	69199	69200	69201	69202	69203	69204	69239
	69240	69241	69242	69243	69244			

Bury (Rochdale Road) - BY

Scania OmniCity G	12001	12002	12003	12004	12005	12006	12007	12008
	12009	12010	12011	12012	12013	12014	12015	12016
	12017	12018						
Olympian	34255	34256	34257	34260	34262	34263		
Volvo B9TL	37299	37300	37301					
Mercedes-Benz Citaro	60223	60224	60225	60226	60227	60228	60229	60230
	60231	60232	60233	60234	60235	60236	60237	60238
	60239	60240	60241	60242	60243	60244	60245	60246
	60247	60248	60249	60250	60251	60252	60253	60254
	60255	60256	60257	60258	60259	60260	60261	60262
	60264	60265	60266	60267	60268	60269	60270	60271
	60272	60273	60274	60275	60276	60277	60278	60279
	60280	60281	60282	60283	64029			
Volvo B10B	61361	61362						
Volvo B7RLE	66914	66915	66916	66917	66918	66919	66920	66921
	66922	66923	66924	66925	66926	66927	66928	66929
	66930	66931	69219	69220	69221	69222	69223	69224
	69225	69226	69227	69228	69229	69230	69231	69232
	69233	69234	69235	69236	69237	69238		

Ince (Seaman Way, Ince, Wigan) - IN

Dennis Arrow	30579	30580	30581	30582	30583	30584	30585	30586
	30587	30588	31902	31903	31904	31905	31906	31915
	31917	31919	31926	31928	31941	31942	31943	31944
	31945	31946	31947	31948	31953	31954		
Volvo B10B	60315	60325	60330	60331	60334	60341	60342	60345
	60346	60348						
Irisbus Scolarbus	68204	68205	68206	68208	68209	68210	68211	68212
	68213	68214	68215	68216	68217			

Knowsley - KW

Olympian	34019	34023	34028	34029	34031	34035	34036	34037
	34038	34039	34040	34057	34058	34061	34069	34070
	34080	34082	34291	34292	34293	34294	34295	34296
Volvo B10B	60303	60304	60305					
BMC Schoolbus	68555	68556	68557					

Manchester (Queen's Road) - QS

Volvo B9TL	37279	37280	37281	37282	37283	37284	37285	37286
	37287	37288	37289	37290	37291	37292	37293	37294
	37295	37296	37297	37298				
Volvo B6	40218	40219	40220	40221	40222	40223	40224	40225
	40226	40227	40228	40229	40230	40231	40232	40233
	40437	40438	40439	40440	40441	40442	40443	40444
	40445	40446	40447	40564	40565	40566	40567	40568
	40569							
Solo	40311	40323	40324	40325	40326	40327	40328	40329
	40330	40331	40332	40333	40334	40335	53143	53144
	53145	53146	53147	53148	53149	53150		
Volvo B10B	60339	61359	61360	61365				
Volvo B10BLE	60361	60386	60387	60388	62142	62143	62145	62146
	62147	62148	62214	62215	62216	62217	62218	62241
	66191	66192	66193	66194	66195			
Mercedes-Benz O405	60407	60408	60409	60410	60411	60412	60413	60414
	60415	60416	60417	60418	60419	60420	60424	60425
	60426	60433	60434	60436	60437	60438	61149
	61150	61151	61249	61250	61251			
Volvo B7BLE	66933	69205	69206	69207	69208	69209	69210	69211
	69212	69213	69214	69215	69216	69217	69218	

Oldham (Wallshaw Street) - OM

Volvo Citybus	38127	38128						
Olympian	30216	30217	30218	30219	30220	30221	30222	30223
	30224	30225	30226	30227	30228	30234	30236	31121
Solo	40318	40319	40320	40321	40322			
Dart	40407	40408	40409	40410	40411	40412	40413	40414
	40415	40416	40417	40418	40419	40420	40421	40422
	40423	40424	40425	40426	40427	40428	40429	40430
	40431	40432	40433	40434	40435	40436		
Mercedes-Benz O405	60422	60423	60427	60428	60429	60430	60431	60432
	60439	60440	60441	60442	60443	60444	60445	60446
	60447	60448	60449	60450	61247	61248		
Volvo B10B	61353	61354	61356	61366				
Volvo B7RLE	66794	66795	66796	66797	66798	66799	66800	66801
	66802	66803	66804	66805	66806	66807	66808	66809
	66810	66811	66812	66813	66814	66815	66816	66817
	66818	66819	66820	66821	66822	66823	66824	66825
	66826	66827	66828	66829	66830	66831	66832	66833
	66834	66835	66836	66837	66838	66839	66840	66841
	66842	66843	66844	66845	66846	66847	66848	66849
	66850	66851	66852	66853	66854	66855	66856	66857
	66858	66859	66860	66861	66862	66863	66864	66865
	66866	66867	66868	66869	66870	66871	66872	66873
	66874	66875	66876	66877	66878	66879	66880	66881
	66882	66883	66884	66885	66886	66887	66888	66889
	66890	66891	66892	66893	66894	66895	66896	66906
	66907	66908	66909	66910	66911	66912	66913	

Tameside (Broadway, Dukinfield) - TE

Dennis Arrow	31925	31927	31929	31930	31935	31936	31937	31938
	31939	31940	31949	31950				
Dart	40273	40274	40277	40279	40280	40282	40283	40285
	40295	40302	40303	40361	40362	40364	40365	40366
	40368	40369	40370	40371	40372	40374	40380	40381
	40382	40384	40403	40406				
Solo	40308	40309	40310	40312	40313	40314	40315	40316
	40317	50280						
Irisbus Scollabus	68207	68218						

Wigan (Melverley Street) - WN

Dennis Arrow	31918	31920	31921	31922	31923	31924	31932	31933
	31934	31951	31952					
Volvo B9TL	37306	37307	37308	37309	37310	37311	37312	37313
	37314							
Dart	40385	40386	40387	40388	40389	40390	40391	40392
	40393	40394	40395	40396	40397	40398	40399	
Excel	40064	40065	40066	40067	60140	60141	60142	60143
	60144	60145	60146	60147	60148	60149	60151	60152
	60154	60155	60156	60157	60158	60159	60160	
Volvo B10B	60350	60351						
Volvo B10BLE	60362	60363	60364	60365	60366	60367	60368	60369
	60370	60371	60372	60373	60376	60377	60378	60379
	60380	60384	60385	60389	60390	60391	60392	60393
	60394	60395	60396	60397	60398	60399	60400	60401
	60402	60403	60404	60405	60663	61240	61241	61560
	62231	62233	62236					

First Potteries

First PMT Ltd, Hobson Street, Burslem, Stoke-on-Trent ST6 2AQ

Birkenhead (New Chester Road) - BH

Olympian	30802	30803	30804	30805	30806	30807	34223	34224
	34225	34226	34227	34228	34229	34230	34231	34232
	34233	34236	34237					
Dart	40042	40109	40110	40124	40131	40132	40133	
DAF SB220	60044	60047	60048	60049				
Scania L113	60005	60052	60053	60054	60076	60077	60080	60106
	60108	60109	60110	60111	60112	60113	60114	60115
	60116	60161	60169	60190	60200	60222	61137	61138
	61139	61140	61142	61157	61158	61234	61529	61531
	61536	61563						

Ancillary / Reserve / For disposal / Specials

DAF SB220	60023	60024

Chester (Liverpool Road) - CH and CC

Outstation - Wrexham

Leyland Olympian	30037	30060	30072	30074	30077	30078	39932	39933
	39935	39936	39938	39939				
Scania dd	31080	31084	31088	31089	31110	31113		
Solo	40100	40156	40157	40683				

Dart	40100	40120	40121	40123	40128	40129	40130	40134
	40135	40136	40137	40138	40139	41068	41069	41070
	41071	41072	41073	41074				
Mercedes-Benz	50022	50023	50025	50044	50045	50046	50047	50055
DAF SB220	60021	60025						
Scania L113	60008	60009	60010	60014	60055	60105	60107	60172
	60208	61144	61244	61245	61482	61527	61528	61530
	61533	61538	61541	61542	61551	61553	61554	61555
	61556	61557	61578	65707	65734	65735	65736	65737
	65738	65739	65740	65741				
Blue Bird	60032	60033	60034	60035	60036	60037	60038	60039
	60040	60041	60042					
BMC	62801	62802	62803	62804	62805	62806	62807	62808

Crewe (Second Avenue, Crewe Gates Farm Ind Est) - CW

Olympian	30029	30030	30031	30033	30034	30035	30038	30069
	31518	31519	31522					
Mercedes-Benz	50036	50038	50054	50059				
Scania L113	60007	60013	60015	60058	60062	60063	60064	60065
	60066	60067	60068	60069	60070	60071	60072	60081
	60098	60100	60119	60128	60131	60132	60135	60136
	60137	60215	60456	61159	61160			

Ancillary / Reserve / For disposal / Specials:
Dennis Lance	60098	60100

Newcastle-under-Lyme (Liverpool Road) - NE

Solo	40010	40011	40015	40016	40017	40018	40019	40305
Dart	40142	40143	40144	40145	40146	40147	40148	40149
	40150	40151	40152					
Mercedes-Benz	50035	50048	50056	50057	50058	50060		
Scania L94	60189	60190	60193	60194	60196	60201	60202	60205
	65705	65706	65727	65728	65729	65730	65731	65732
	65733							

Ancillary / Reserve / For disposal / Specials
DAF SB220	60043	60120
Lance	60097	

Stoke-on-Trent (Dividy Road, Adderley Green) - AG

Solo	40007	40008	40009	40013	40014	40020	40021	40022
	40023	40024	40025	40026	40027	40028	40029	40180
	40181	40182	40304	40682				
Dart	40003	40030	40115	40116	40126	40140	40141	40153
	40154	40155	40158	40159	40163	40164	40165	40166
	40167	40168	40169	40170	40171	40172	40173	40174
	40175	40176	40177	40178	40179	40367	40373	40375
	40376	40377	40378	40379	40383	40670	42726	42727
	43804							
Mercedes-Benz	50033	50049						
Volvo B10B	60316	60317						
Scania SD	60004	60006	60011	60012	60056	60057	60059	60060
	60061	60073	60074	60075	60078	60079	60082	60083
	60133	60134	60139	60170	60171	60172	60173	60174
	60175	60176	60177	60183	60184	60185	60216	61141
	61143	61145	61235	61237	61238	61239	61243	61246
Scania OmniCity	65001	65002	65003	65004	65005	65026	65027	65033
	65034	65035	65036	65037	65038	65039	65040	65041
	65042							

First in West Yorkshire

First West Yorkshire Ltd, Kirkstall Garage, Kirkstall Road, Leeds, LS3 1LH
First in York Ltd, James Street, York, YO10 3WW

Bradford (Bowling Back Lane) - BD

Olympian	30627	30640	30643	30646	30651	30652	30654	30672
	30673	30674	30675	30676	30677	30678	30685	30686
	30687	30688	30689	30690	30691	30692	30693	30694
	30695	30696	30697	30698	30699	30700	30701	30703
	30704	30705	30706	30707	30754	30755	30756	30757
	30758	30761	30762	30781	30782	30783	30784	30785
	34606	34607	34608	34609	34610	34611	34612	34613
	34614	34615	34616	34617	34618	34619	34620	34621
Volvo B7TL	30881	30882	30883	30884	30885	30890	30891	30892
	30893	30894	30895	30896	30897	30898	30899	30903
	30905	30906	30907	30908	30909	30910	30911	30912
	30913	30914	30915	30939	30940	37043	37044	37045
	37046	37047	37048	37049	37050	37051	37052	37053
	37054	37055	37056	37057	37058	37059	37060	37061
	37062							
Volvo B9TL	37063	37064	37065	37066	37067	37068	37069	37070
	37071	37072	37073	37074	37075	37076	37077	37078
	37079	37080	37081	37082	37083	37084	37085	37086
	37087	37088	37089	37090	37091	37092	37093	37094
	37095	37096	37097	37098	37099	37100	37101	37102
Optare Solo	50281	50282	50283	50284	50285	50286	50287	50288
	50289	50290	50291	50292	50293	50294	50295	53301
	53302	53303						
Dennis Lance	67039							
Volvo B10B	66651	66652						
Volvo B10BLE	60798	60800	60801	60802	60803	60804	60806	60807
	60808	60809	60810	60811	60815	60816	60821	60822
	60823	60824	60825	60826	60827	60828	60829	60830
	60831	60832	60833	60834	60835	60836	60837	60838
	60839	60840	60841	60842	60843	60844	60845	60846
	60847	60848	60849	60850	60851	60852	60853	60854
	60855	60858	60859	60860	60861	60862	60863	60864
	60865	61288	61289					
Volvo B7L	60904	60906	60907	60908	60923			
Volvo B7RLE	66999	69245	69246	69247	69248	69249	69250	69251
	69252	69253	69270	69271	69272	69273	69274	
BMC Condor	68629	68630	68639	68640	68641	68643	68645	68646
	68647	68648	68649	68650	68651	68652	68653	68654
	68655	68656	68657	68658	68659	68660	68661	

Bramley (Henconner Lane, Bramley, Leeds) - BM

Volvo B7LA	19012	19013	19014	19015	19016	19017	19018	19019
	19020	19021	19022	19023	19024	19025	19026	19027
	19028							
Olympian	30238	30239	30240	30241	30242	30243	30244	30245
	30246	30247	30709	30710	30712	30713	30714	30715
	30716	30717	30718	30719	30720	30808	30809	
Scania N113	31095	31096	31097	36922	36930	36932		
Volvo B7TL	30941	30942	30943	30944	30945	30946	30947	30948
	30949	30950	30951	30952	30953	32431	32432	32433
	32434	32435	32436	32437	32438	32439	32440	32441
	32442	32443	32444	32445	32446	32447	32448	32449
	32450	32451	32452	32453	32454	32455	32456	32457
	32458	32459	32460	32461	32462	32463	32464	32465
	32466	32467	32468	32469	32470	32471	32472	32473

The 2008 First Bus Handbook

Dart	40612	40615	40618	40624	40626	40632		
Volvo B10M	60467	60468						
Scania SD	61035	61036	61037	61038	61039	61040	61041	61079
	61090	61091	61094	61095	61096	61097	61098	61099
	61100	61101	61103	61104	61105	61106	61107	61108
	61109	61110	61111	61112	61114	61115	61116	61117
	61118	61119	61120	61121	61122	61123	61124	61125
	61126	61127	61128	61129	61130	61131	61132	61133
Volvo B7RLE	66709	66710	66711	66712	66713	66714	66715	
BMC Condor	68616	68617	68618	68619	68620	68621	68622	68623
	68624	68625	68626	68627	68628			

Halifax (Skircoat Lane) - HX

Olympian	30655	30657	30658	30659	30660	30661	30662	30663
	30664	30665	30666	30667	30668	30669	30670	30671
	30722	30737	30738	30739	30844	31737	31738	31740
Volvo B7TL	32509	32510	32511	32512	32513	32514	32515	32516
	32517	32518	32519	32520	32521	32522	32523	32524
	32525	32526	32527	32528	32529	32530	32531	32532
	32533	32534	32535	32536	32537	32538	32539	32540
	32541	32542						
Dart	40634	40635	40636	40666	40667	40668	40671	40672
	40673	40674	40675	40676	40677	40678	40679	40680
	40681	40867	40868	40880	40881			
Mercedes-Benz	50252	50255	50261	50262	50263	50264	50265	50266
	50267	50268	50269					
Solo	50318	50319	50407	50408	53821	53822	53823	53824
	53825							
Volvo B10B	60768	60769	60770	60773	60774	60775	60776	60777
	60778	60779	60780	60781	60783	60784	60785	60786
	60787	60788	60790	60791	60792	60794	60795	60796
	60797							
Volvo B10BLE	60628	60818	60819	60820	62118			
Volvo B7RLE	66738	66739	66754	66755	66759	66760	66761	66762
	66763	66776	66777	66778	66779	66780	66781	66782
	66783	66789	66790					
BMC Schoolbus	68515	68516	68527	68528	68529	68530	68545	68546
	68547	68548	68549	68601	68602	68603	68604	68605
	68606	68607	68608	68610	68634	68637	68638	68642
	68657	68662	68663	68664	68665	68666	68667	68668
	68669	68670	68671	68673	68674	68675	68676	68677
	68678	68679	68680	68681	68682	68683		

Huddersfield (Old Fieldhouse Lane) - HU

Volvo B10M	20407	20409						
Volvo Citybus	30350	30359	30362	30365	30377	30379	31127	31269
	31270	31284	31297					
Olympian	30229	30231	30730	30731	30734	30735	30736	30752
	30753	30816	30817	30818	30819	30820	30821	30822
	30823	30824	30825	30840	30841	30842	30843	30845
	31150	31151	31152	31739				
Volvo B7TL	32503	32504	32505	32506	32507	32508		
Dart	40345	40346	40669	40771	40869	40870	40871	40872
	40873	40874	40875	40876	40877	40878	40879	40963
	42110	42175	42178	42179	42181	42460	60929	60930
	60931	60932	60933	60934	60935	60936	60937	60938
Lance	60939	60944	60951	60953	60955	60957	60959	60967
	60974							
Volvo B7RLE	66740	66741	66742	66743	66744	66745	66746	66747
	66748	66749	66750	66751	66752	66753	66757	66758
	66764	66765	66766	66767	66768	66769	66770	66771
	66772	66773	66774	66775	66784	66785	66786	66787
	66788	66791	66792					
BMC Schoolbus	68543	68544	68612	68613	68614	68615	68631	68632
	68633	68635	68636	68672	68684	68685	68686	68687
	68688							

Leeds (Cherry Row) - CR

Scania dd	31081	31090	31091	31092	31093	31094	31095	31096
	31097	31098	31099	31102	31103	31104	31105	31106
	31107	31108	31109	31111	31114	31115	31116	31117
	31118	31119						
Volvo B7TL	30855	30856	30857	30858	30859	30860	30861	30862
	30863	30864	30865	30866	30867	30868	30869	30870
	30921	30922	30923	30924	30925	30926	30927	30928
	30929	30930	30931	30932	30933	30934	30935	30936
	30937	30938	31146	31147	32692	32693	32694	32695
	32696	32697	37021	37022	37023	37024	37025	37026
	37027	37028	37029	37030	37031	37032	37033	37034
	37035	37036	37037	37038	37039	37040	37041	37042
Dart	40653	40654	40655	40656	40657	40658		
Scania L113	61029	61030	61031	61042	61050	61055		
	61056	61058	61059	61060	61061	61062	61063	61064
	61065	61066	61067	61068	61069	61070	61071	61072
	61073	61074	61075	61076	61077	61078	61134	
Volvo B7RLE	66995	66996	66997	66998				

Leeds (Hunslet Park) - HP

Volvo B10BLA	10018	10019	10020	10021	10022	10023	10024	10025
	10026	10027	10028	10029	10030	10031	10032	
Olympian	30786	30787	30788	30789	30790	30791	30792	30793
	30794	30795	30796	30797	30798	30799	30800	30801
	30810	30811	30812	30813	30814	30815	30834	30835
	30836	30837	30838	30839	31673	31674	31676	31677
	31683	31685	31686	31760	31761	31762	31763	31764
	31765	31766	31767	31768	31769	31770	31771	31772
	31773	31774	31775	31805	31806	31807	31808	31811
	31812	31813	31814	31815	31816	31818	34234	34238
Volvo B7TL	30846	30847	30848	30849	30850	30851	30852	30853
	30854	30916	30917	30918	30919	30920	31142	31143
	31144	31145	37103	37104	37105	37106	37107	37108
	37109	37110	37111	37112	37113	37114	37115	37116
	37117	37118	37119	37120	37121	37122	37123	37124
	37125	37126	37127	37128	37129	37130	37131	37132
Dart	40600	40608	40609	40613	40614	40638	40639	40640
	40641	40642	40643	40644	40645	40646	40647	40649
	40650	40651	40652	40658	40659	40662		
Solo	50275	53101	53102	53103	53104	53105	53106	53904
	53905	53906	53907	53908	53909			
Scania SD	61032	61033	61034	61046	61047	61048	61049	61051
	61079	61080	61081	61082	61083	61084	61085	61086
	61087	61088	61089	62116	62117	64808		
Volvo B7RLE	66700	66701	66702	66703	66704	66705	66706	66707
	66708							

York (James Street) - YK

Volvo B7LA	10035	10036	10037	10038	10039	10040	10041	10042
	10043	19001	19002	19003	19004	19005	19006	19007
	19008	19009	19010	19011	19029			
Volvo B10M coach	20461	20462						
Volvo B7TL	30954	30955	30956	30957	30958	30959	30960	30961
	30962	30963	30964	30965				
Volvo B6BLE	40571	40572	40573	40574	40575	40576	40577	40578
	40579	40581	40582	40583	40584	40585	40586	40587
	40588	40589	40590	40591	40592	40593	40594	40595
	40596	40597	40598	40599				
Volvo B10B	61363	61364						
Volvo B7L	60876	60877	60878	60880	60881	60882	60883	60884
	60895	60896	60897	60898	60899	60900	60901	60902
	60909	60910	60911	60912	60913	60914	60915	60916
	60917	60918	60919	60920	60921	60922	60926	60927
	60928							

Volvo B7RLE	69000	69001	69002	69003	69004	69268	69269	69275
	69276	69277	69278	69279	69358	69359	69360	69361
	69362	69363	69364	69365	69366	69367	69368	69369
	69370							

First in South Yorkshire

First South Yorkshire Ltd, Midland Road, Rotherham, S61 1TF

Doncaster (Leger Way) - DN

Volvo Olympian	34088	34089	34090	34091	34092	34093	34094	34095
	34096	34097	34098	34099	34100	34101	34102	34103
	34104	34105	34106	34107	34214			
Volvo B7TL	30871	30872	30873	30874	30875	30882	30883	30904
	31776	31776	31777	31778	31779	31780		
Volvo B9TL	37228	37229	37230	37231	37232	37233	37234	37235
	37236	37237	37238	37239	37240	37241	37242	37243
	37244	37245	37278					
Volvo B6	40448	40457	40480	40481	40482	40483	40484	40485
	40486	40489	40490	40493	40494	40495	40496	40497
	40498	40499	40500	40501	40502	40595	40596	48141
	48142							
Dart	40507	40512	40518	40519	40520	40521	40522	40523
	40524	40525	40526	40527	40528	40541	40542	40543
	40546	40549	40552					
Solo	50234	50235	50237					
Volvo B10M	60488	60489	60492	60493	60494	60495	60530	60545
	60546	60547	60548	60549	60570	60571	60572	60573
	60574	60576	60577					

Rotherham (Midland Road) - RO

Olympian	34206	34207	34208	34209	34210	34211	34212	34213
	34217	34219	34220	34221	34222	34239	34240	34242
	34247							
Volvo B7TL	30876	30877	30878	30879	30880			
Volvo B9TL	37233	37246	37247	37248	37249	37250	37251	37252
	37253	37254	37255	37256	37257	37258	37259	37260
	37261	37262	37263	37264	37265			
Volvo B6	40449	40456	40458	40459	40461	40465	40467	40468
	40470	40471	40472	40475	40476	40477	40479	40503
	40504							
Dart	40513	40514	40515	40516	40517	40526	40529	40530
	40531	40532	40533	40534	40535	40536	40537	40538
	40539	40540	40789	40821	40841	40843	40844	40973
	40974	40975	40976					
Solo	50232	50233	50238					
Volvo B10M	60457	60458	60463	60465	60470	60483	60487	60500
	60501	60502	60503	60504	60505	60506	60507	60508
	60509	60510	60511	60512	60513	60514	60515	60516
	60517	60518	60519	60520	60521	60522	60523	60524
	60525	60526	60527	60531	60532	60533	60534	60536
	60542	60553	60554	60555	60556	60557	60558	60559
	60560	60563	60565	50567	60569	60757		
Volvo B10BLE	60633	60634	60635	60636	60637	60638	60639	60640
	60645							

Ancillary / Reserve / For disposal / Specials

Lynx	60095	62626	62706	62717	62729	62740

Sheffield (Olive Grove) - OG

Olympian	30546	30547	30548	30549	30550	30551	30552	30553
	30554	30555	30556	30557	34053	34054	34055	34241
	34246							
Volvo B7TL	30561	30562	30563	30564	30565	30566	30567	30568
	30569	30570	30571	30572	30573	30574	30575	30576
	30577	30578	31129	31130	31131	31132	31133	31134
	31135	31137	31138	31139	31141	31148	31781	31782
	31783	31784	31785	31786	31787	31788	31789	31790
	31791	31792	31793	31794	31795	31796	31797	31797
	31798	31799	31800	31801	31802	31803	31804	37147
	37148	37149	37150	37151	37152	37153	37154	37155
Volvo B6	40464							
Volvo B10M	60472	60473	60474	60475	60476	60477	60478	60479
	60480	60481	60482	60490	60491	60496	60499	60528
	60529	60535	60537	60538	60539	60541	60543	60561
	60562	60564	60566	60568	60602	60603	60604	60605
	60606	60607	60608	60609	60610	60611	60612	60613
	60614	60615	60616	60617	60799	60805	60856	60857
Volvo B10L	61483	61484	61486	61487	61488	61520	61521	61522
	61523							
Volvo B10BLE	60618	60619	60620	60621	60622	60623	60624	60625
	60626	60627	60630	60631	60632	60641	60642	60643
	60644	60646	60647	60648	60649	60650	60651	60652
	60653	60654	60655	60657	60658	60659	60660	60661
	60662	60664	60665	60666	60667	60668	60669	60670
	60671	60672	60673	60674	60675	60676	60677	60678
	60679	60680	60681	60682	60683	60684	60685	60686
	60687	60688	60689	60690	60691	60692	60693	60694
	60695	60696	60697	60698	60699	60700	60701	60702
	60703	60861	60862	62232	62234	62235	62237	62239
	62240	62243	62244	66101	66112	66113	66114	66119
Scania L113	60760	60761	60762	60763	60764	60765		
Volvo B7L	60406	60703	60704	60705	60706	60707	60708	60709
	60710	60711	60712	60713	60714	60715	60716	60717
	60718	60719	60720	60721	60722	60723	60724	60725
	60726	60727	60728	60729	60730	60731	60732	60733
	60734	60735	60736	60737	60738	60739	60740	60741
	60742	60743	60744	60745	60885	60886	60887	60888
	60889	60890	60891	60892	60893	60894	61192	61193
	61194	61195	61196	61197	61198	61199	61200	61201
	61202	61203	61204	61205	61206	61207	61208	61209
	61210	61211						

First in Wyvern

First Midland Red Buses Ltd, Heron Lodge, London Road, Worcester, WR5 2EU

Hereford (Friar Street) - HD

Dart	40086	42894	47001	47002	47003	47004	47005	47006
	47007	47008	47011	47013				
Mercedes-Benz	52504							
Solo	50296	53040	53041	53058	53059	53060	53061	53062
	53063	53064						
Enviro 300	67603	67604						

Kidderminster (Island Drive) - KD

Volvo Citybus	38123	38125						
Dart	40245	40269	40284	42889	42890	42891	46929	46930
	46931	46932						
Mercedes-Benz	52501	52502	52503					
Solo	53042							
Lance	61013	61016	67201	67202	67205	67206	67212	67213
	67214	67215	67238	67239	67244			

Redditch (Plymouth Road) - RH

Olympian	31380							
Volvo Citybus	38124	38126						
Trident	33401	33402	33403	33404	33405			
Lance	67207	67208	67209	67211	67217	67219	67231	67232
	67235	67237	67240	67241	67242	67243	67245	67246
	67248	67249	67250	67251	67256	67311	67312	67313
Enviro 300	67600	67633	67634	67635	67636	67637	67638	67639
	67640	67641	67642	67643	67644	67650		

Ancillary / Reserve / For disposal / Specials
Lynx   62714

Worcester (Padmore Street) - WR

Olympian	31452	34289						
Volvo Citybus	38085	38097						
Dart	40805	40833	40837	40838	42217	42219	42220	42352
	42353	42354	42356	42641	42892	42893		
Solo	53043	53044	53045	53046	53047	53048	53049	53050
	53051							
Lance	67234	67253	67254	67255	67301	67314	67315	67318
	67319	67321	67322	67323	67324			
Enviro 300	67601	67602	67631	67645	67646	67647	67648	67648
	67651	67652	67653	67654	67655	67656	67657	67658
	67659	67660	67661	67662	67663	67664		
BMC Condor	68520							

Ancillary / Reserve / For disposal / Specials
Tiger   90269

First in Leicester

Leicester CityBus Ltd, Abbey Park Road, Leicester, LE4 5AH

Leicester (Abbey Park Road) - LE

Dominator	39167							
Volvo B7TL	32053	32054	32055	32056	32057	32058	32059	32061
	32062	32063	32064	32065	32066	32067	32068	32069
	32070	32071	32072	32073	32074	32075	32076	32077
	32078	32079	32080	32081	32082	32083	32084	32085
	32086	32087	32088	32089	32090	32091	32092	32093
	32094	32095	32096	32097	32098	32099	32277	32627
	32628	32631	32632	32633	32634	32635	32639	32640
	32641	32642	32643	32644	32645	32646	32647	32648
	32649	32650						
Lance	60945	60946	60948	60954	60958	60984	60985	
Falcon	67623							
Lynx	62602	62603	62713	62733	62749			
Volvo B7L	66302	66303	66304	66305	66306	66307	66308	66309
	66310	66311	66312	66313	66314	66315	66316	66317
	66318	66319	66320	66321	66322	66323		
Volvo B7RLE	66962	66963	66964	66965	66966	66968	66969	66970
	66971	66972	66973	66974	66975	66976	66977	66978
	66979	66980	66981	66982	66984	66986	66987	

First in Northampton

Northampton Transport Ltd, The Bus Depot, St James Road, Northampton, NN5 5JD

Northampton (St James Road) - NN

Olympian	31454	34287						
Volvo B7TL	32629	32630						
Volvo Citybus	38082	38083	38098	38099	38121	38122		
Solo	53071	53072	53073					
Volvo B10M	60459							
Volvo B7L	61148	66324	66325	66326	66327	66328	66329	66330
	66332	66333	66334	66335	66336	66337	66338	66339
	66340	66342	66343	66344	66345	66346	66347	66348
Lance	67112	67117	67203	67204	67210	67218	67233	67252
BMC Schoolbus	68507	68508	68509	68510				

The 2002 First Bus Handbook

First in the Eastern Counties

First Eastern Counties Buses Ltd, Rouen House, Rouen Road, Norwich, NR1 1RB

Great Yarmouth (Caister Road) - YA

Volvo B10M	20126	20129						
Routemaster	39480	39623	39717					
Olympian	30097	30098	30099	30100	30101	30102	30103	30104
	30105	30106	34337					
Volvo B7TL	32480	32481	32482	32483	32484	32485		
Dart	40113	40114	40251	40257	40259	40288	40290	40291
	42441	42442	42443	42444	42445	42446	42447	42448
	42450	42451	46062	46375	46379	46601	46602	46725
	46726	46807	47215	47217	47218	47232	47233	
Volvo B6	48013							
Volvo B7RLE	66950	66957	66959	69005	69006	69007	69008	69009
	69010	69011						

Ipswich (Foundation Street) - IP

Volvo B10M	20122							
Olympian	34872	34873	34925	34928	34933			
Volvo B7TL	32487	32488	32489	32490	32491	32492	32493	32494
Dart	40256	42551	43356	43359	43360	43433	43434	43435
	43436	43440	43445	43460	43482	43488	47208	
Volvo B6	48070	48084	48085	48086	48090			
Optare Solo	50273	50274						
Volvo B10B	60297							
Volvo B10BLE	60766	60767	60808	60812	60813			
Scania	65541	65542	65543	65544	65545	65546	65547	65548
	65549	65550	65570	65588	65589	65590		

King's Lynn (Vancouver Avenue) - KL

Volvo B10M	20105	20106	20109	20112	20118	20141	20142	
Volvo B12M	20500	20501	20502	20503	20504	20505	20506	20507
	20508	20509						
Olympian	30235	34822	34901	34904	34923	34946	30951	34955
Dart	43357	43358	43801	43802				
Scania L	65525	65526	65527	65528	65529	65521	65532	

Lowestoft (Gas Works Road) - LO

Volvo B10M	20103	20104	20107	20111	20114	20119	20120	20121
	20123	20124	20127	20131				
Olympian	34825	34876	34921	34922	34926	34948	34950	34952
	34972	34973						
Dart	40185	40187	42458	43459	43461	43462	43463	43464
	43465	43466	43467	43489	47201	47202	47203	

Norwich (Roundtree Way) - NR

Volvo B10M	20125	20128						
Olympian	34333	34902	34903					
Volvo B7TL	30887	30900	30901					
Dart	40603	42437	43438	43439	43441	43442	43444	43446
	43447	43448	46081	46083	46123	47206	47207	47209
	47231	47250	47251					
Volvo B10B	60296	60298	60300	60306	60307	60309	61348	61349
	61357	61358	61367	61368				
Volvo B10BLE	60807	60814	66126					

Norwich (Vulcan Road) - VN

Volvo B7TL	30886	30888	30889	30902	32475	32476	32477	32478
	32479	32486	32651	32652	32653	32654	32655	32656
	37146	37156	37157	37158	37159	37160		
Dart	42429	43449	43450	43451	43452	43453	43468	43469
	34370	34371	43472	43473	43474	43476	43477	43478
	43480	43481	43483	43484	43485	43486	43487	
Volvo B7L	60903	60905	60924					
Volvo B7RLE	66932							
Scania	65521	65522	65523	65524	65534	65537	65538	65539
	65540	65551	65552	65553	65554	65556	65557	65558
	65569	65576	65577	65578	65580	65587		

First Essex

First Essex Buses Ltd, Stapleford Close, New Writtle Street, Chelmsford, CM2 0SD

Basildon (Cherrydown) - BS

Olympian	31373	31374	31375	34011	34012			
Dart	41637	41640	41642	41644	41645	41647	41650	41651
	41653	43712	43713	43714	43732	43733	43734	43735
	43736	43737	43738	46167	46168	46169	46170	46171
	46172	46174	46177	46183	46184	46185	46187	46803
	46804	46808	46811	46825				
Mercedes-Benz	52584	52585						
Lance	67036							
Scania sd	61054	61057	65626	65627	65628	65629	65630	65631
	65632	65665	65666	65667	65668	65669	65670	65671
	65672	65673	65674	65675	65676	65677		
Volvo B7RLE	67001							

Braintree (Fairfield Road) - BR

| Dart | 43729 | 46129 | 46143 | 46144 | 46812 | 46813 | 46816 | 46817 |
| | 46821 | 46822 | 46823 | 46824 | 46826 | | | |

Chelmsford (Duke Street) - CM

Outstations: Great Dunmow and Maldon.

Volvo B12	20201	20202	20203					
Volvo B10M	20463							
Olympian	31198	34807	34815	34818				
Dart	42482	42483	42484	42485	24286	24287	42488	42489
	42918	42919	42920	42921	42922	42923	43730	43731
	46827	47219	47220	47221	47223	47228	47229	47252
Mercedes-Benz	56002	56003	56004	56005	56006	56009		
Solo	53112	53113	53114	53115	53116	53117	53118	53119
	53120	53121	53122	53123	53124	53125	53126	53127
	53128	53129	53130	53131	53132	53133	53134	53135
	53136	53137						
Lance	67037	67038	67040	67103	67104			
Volvo B10M bus	60469	60484						
Scania OmniCity	65028	65029	65030	65031	65032			
Scania L94	65680	65681	65682	65683	65684			
BMC Schoolbus	68521	68532	68534	68535	68551	68552	68555	

Clacton-on-Sea (Telford Road) - CN

Dart	46145	46175	46176	46186	46820	46828	46829	46830
	47105	47106	47224	47225	47226	47227		
Lance	67009	67010	67011	67012	67013			

Colchester (Queen Street) - CO

Outstation: Hythe

Volvo B10M	20102	20110	60031	60130				
Olympian	30558	30560	34013	34014	34018	34056	34290	34301
	34302	34303	34304	34305	34307	34308	34309	34310
	34311	34314	34315					
Dart	43715	43716	43739	43740	43741	43742	43743	43744
	47101	47102	47103	47104				
Scania	62406	62407	62408	62409	62410	65650	65651	65652
	65653	65654	65678	65679	65685	65686	65687	65688
	65689	65690	65691	65692				
Lance	60102	67002	67003	67004	67005	67006	67007	67008

Hadleigh (London Road) - HH

Olympian	31376	31456	31462					
Dart	40777	40778	40779	41005	41006	41007	41008	41009
	41010	41011	41012	41013	41014	41015	41016	41017
	42852	42853	42854	42855	42857	43717	43718	43719
	43720	43721	46108	46109	46110	46113	46120	46122
	46128	46132	46136	46137	46138	46140	46141	46142
	46146	46147	46148	46149	46150	46151	46152	46153
	46154	46155	46156	46157	46158	46179	46180	46181
	46182	46814	46815	46818				

Harwich (Station Road) - HA

Olympian	31377	34280	34282	34284	34285	34286	34288	34290
Dart	43800							
Optare Solo	53138	53139						
Primo	57001	57002						

Mini Pointer Dart 42559, SN05DZV, displays its Alexander Dennis badge as it heads for Longford.
Richard Godfrey

First in London

First Capital East Ltd, First Capital North Ltd,
Centrewest London Buses Ltd,
Macmillan House, Paddington Station, London, W2 1TY

Alperton (Ealing Road) - ON

Volvo B7TL	32052	32200	32201	32202	32203	32204	32205	32206
	32207	32208	32209	32210	32211	32212	32213	32214
	32215	32216	32217	32218	32219	32220	32328	32329
	32330	32331	32332	32333	32334	32335	32336	32337
	32338	32339	32340	32341	32342	32343	32344	32345
	32346	32347	32348	32349	32350	32351	32352	32353
	32354	32355	32356	32357	32358	32359	32360	32495
	32496	32497	32498	32499	32500	32501	32502	
Trident	32807							
Dart	41286	41287	41289	41291	41292	41293	41294	41295
	41296	41297	41298	41299	41300	41301	41303	41304
	41305	41306	41325	41326	41327	41376	41377	41378
	41379	41384	41401	41767	41768	41769	41771	

Dagenham (Chequers Lane) - DG

Javelin coach	21090	21121	21122					
Olympian	30559	34215	34216	34329	34330	34331	34339	34341
	34345	90176						
Volvo B7TL	32657	32658	32659	32660	32661	32662	32663	32664
	32665	32666	32667	32668				
Trident	32806	32822	33029	33030	33031	33032	33036	33039
	33041	33042	33043	33044	33045	33047	33048	33049
	33051	33052	33053	33054	33055	33056	33057	33058
	33060	33061	33062	33063	33064	33065	33066	33067
	33069	33070	33071	33072	33073	33074	33075	33076
	33077	33078	33079	33080	33081	33082	33083	33084
	33085	33086	33087	33088	33091	33092	33094	33099
Trident 2/Enviro 400	33501	33502	33504	33505	33506	33507	33508	
Dart	41336	41356	41371	41475	41476	41477	41478	41479
	41480	41481	41482	41483	41484	41485	41486	41492
	41493	41494	41495	41496	41497	41498	41499	41500
	41501	41502	41507	41508	41509	41510	41511	41520
	41521	41523	41527	41649	41772	42518	42519	
Lance	67296							

Greenford (Greenford Road) - G

Trident	32809	32897	32898	32899	32954	32955	32956	32984
	32985	32986	32987	32988	32989	32990	32991	32992
	32993	32994	32995	32996	32997	32998	32999	33000
	33046	33141	33142	33143	33144	33145	33146	33147
	33148	33149	33150	33152	33153	33154	33155	33156
	33157	33158	33159	33160	33161	33162	33163	33164
	33165	33166	33167	33168	33169	33170	33171	33172
	33173	33174	33175	33176	33177	33277	33278	33279
	33280	33282	33283	33284	33285	33286	33287	
	33288	33289	33290	33291	33292	33293		
Dart	41236	41237	41263	41288	41302	41318	41319	41337
	41338	41339	41340	41341	41342	41343	41344	41345
	41346	41347	41348	41362	41363	41365	41366	41367
	41368	41369	41370	41372	41381	41382	41383	41385
	41386	41387	41388	41389	41390	41391	41392	41393
	41394	41395	41396	41397	41398	41399	41400	41487
	41488	41489	41490	41491				

Isleworth - IS

Citaro G	11039	11040	11041	11042	11043	11044	11045	11046
	11047	11048	11049	11050	11051	11052	11053	11054
	11055	11056	11057	11058	11059	11060	11061	11062
	11063	11064	11065					
Trident	32906	32908	32909	32910	32911	32912	32913	32914
	32915	32916	32917	32918	32919	32920	32921	32922
	32923	32924	32925	32926	32927	32928	32929	

Leyton (Temple Mills) - L

Trident	32818	33006	33007	33008	33009	33010	33011	33012
	33013	33014	33015	33016	33017	33018	33019	33020
	33021	33022	33023	33024	33025	33026	33027	33028
	33033	33034	33035	33090	33096	33097		
Dart	41229	41230	41232	41233	41234	41264	41265	41266
	41268	41269	41270	41271	41272	41273	41274	41275
	41276	41277	41278	41279	41280	41281	41282	41283
	41284	41285	41307	41308	41309	41310	41311	41312
	41313	41314	41315	41316	41317	41320	41321	41322
	41323	41324	41328	41329	41402	41433	41434	41681
	41682	41683	41684	41685	41686	41687	41688	41689
	41690	41697	41698	41699	41700	41718	41719	41720
	41721	41722	41723	41724	41725	41726	41727	41728
	41729	41730	41731	41732	41733	41734	41735	41736
	41737	41738	41740	41741	41742	41743	41744	41745
	41746	41747	41748	41751	41752	41753	41754	41755
	41756	41757	41758	41759	41760	41761	41762	41763
	41764	41765	41766	41770	41791	41792	41793	41794
Solo	53701	53702	53703	53704	53705	53706		
MB Citaro O530	64001	64002	64003	64004	64005	64006	64007	64008
	64009	64010	64011					

Tottenham (Marsh Lane, Northumberland Park) - NP

Volvo B7TL	32221	32222	32223	32224	32225	32226	32227	32228
	32294	32295	32296	32297	32298	32299	32300	32301
	32302	32303	32304	32305	32306	32307	32308	32309
	32310	32311	32312	32313	32314	32315	32316	32317
	32318	32319	32320	32321	32322	32323	32324	32325
	32326	32327						
Trident	32804	32810	32813	32814	32815	32816	32838	32839
	32840	32841	32842	32843	32844	32845	32847	32849
	32850	32851	32852	32853	32854	32855	32856	32857
	32858	32859	32860	32861	32862	32863	32864	32865
	32866	32867	32868	32869	32870	32871	32872	32873
	32874	32875	32876	32877	32878	32879	32880	32881
	32882	32883	32884	32885	32886	32887	32894	32957
	32967	32968	32969	32970	32971	32972	32973	32974
	32975	32976	32977	32978	32979	32980	32981	32982
	32983	33001	33002	33003	33004	33068	33093	33098
	33113	33114	33115	33116	33117	33118	33119	33120
	33121	33122	33123	33124	33125	33126	33127	33128
	33129							
Olympian	34218							
Dart	41474	41773	41774	41775	41776	41777	41778	41779
	41780	41781	41782	41783	41784	41785	41786	41787
	41788							

Uxbridge (Bakers Road) - UX

Trident	32888	32889	32890	32891	32892	32893	32895	32896
	32907	32930	33037	33050	33059	33131	33132	33133
	33134	33135	33136	33137	33138	33139	33140	33328
	33329	33330	33331	33332	33333	33334	33335	33336
	33337	33338	33339	33340	33341	33342		
Dart	41235	41238	41239	41240	41241	41242	41243	41244
	41245	41246	41247	41248	41253	41254	41255	41256
	41409	41410	41503	41504	41505	41506	41512	41513
	41514	41522	41524	41525	41526	41528	41529	41530
	41531	41532	41533	41534	41535	41536	41537	41538
	41539	41540	41541	41542	41543	41544	42401	42402
	42403	42404	42405	42406	42515	42516	42517	

Westbourne Park (Great Western Road) - X

Outstation: - Ariel Way, White City.

Volvo B7TL	32100	32101	32102	32103	32104	32105	32106	32107
	32108	32109	32110	32111	32112	32249	32250	32251
	32252	32253	32254	32255	32256	32257	32258	32259
	32260	32261	32262	32263	32264	32265	32266	32267
	32268	32269	32270	32271	32272	32273	32274	32275
	32276	32361	32362	32363	32364	32365	32366	32367
	32368	32369	32370	32371	32372	32373	32374	32375
	32376	32377	32378	32379	32380	32381	32382	32383
	32384	32385	32386	32387	32388	32389	32390	32391
	32392	32393	32394	32395	32396	32397	32398	32399
	32400	32401	32402	32403	32404	32405	32406	32407
	32408	32409	32410	32411	32412	32413	32414	32415
	32416	32417	32418	32419	32420	32421	32422	32423
	32424	32425	32426	32427	32428	32429	32430	
Trident	32801	32900	32901	32902	32903	32904	32905	32958
	32959	32960	32961	32962	32963	32964	32965	32966
	33040	33089	33095	33178	33179	33180	33181	33182
	33183	33184	33185	33186	33187	33188	33189	33190
	33191	33192	33193	33194	33195	33196	33197	33198
	33199	33229	33230	33231	33232	33233	33234	33235
	33236	33237	33238	33239	33240	33242	33244	33245
	33246	33247	33248	33343	33344	33345	33346	33347
	33348	33349	33350	33351	33352	33353	33354	33355
	33356	33357	33358	33359	33360	33361	33362	33363
	33364	33365	33366	33367	33368	33369	33370	33371
	33372	33373	33374	33375	33376	33377	33378	33379
	33380	33381	33382	33383	33384	33385	33386	
Trident 2/Enviro 400	33503	33509	33510	33511	33512	33513	33514	33515
	33516	33517	33518	33519				
Routemaster	39735	39804	39813	39818	39827	39835	39840	39862
	39876							
Dart	41259	41261	41350	41351				

Willesden Junction (Station Road) - WJ

Citaro G	11000	11001	11002	11003	11004	11005	11006	11007
	11008	11009	11010	11011	11012	11013	11014	11015
	11016	11017	11018	11019	11020	11021	11022	11023
	11024	11025	11026	11027	11028	11029	11030	11031
	11032	11066	11067	11068	11069			
Dart	41403	41404	41405	41406	41407	41408	41414	41415
	41416	41417	41418	41419	41420	41421	41422	41423
	41424	41425	41426	41427	41428	41429	41430	41431
	41435	41436	41437	41438	41439	41440	41441	41442
	41443	41444	41445	41446	41447	41448	41449	41790
	41795							

London Ancillary / Reserve / For disposal / Specials:

Coach	23016	23017	23018
Olympian	34346		
BMC Student	68558	68559	68560

First in Berkshire

First Beeline Buses Ltd, First Student Ltd
Macmillan House, Paddington Station, London, W2 1TY

Bracknell (Market Street) - BL

Outstations: - Chertsey and Reading

Volvo B7R	20366	20367	20369	20372	20373	20374		
Volvo B12B	20611	20612	20613					
Scania K114	23008	23009	23010	23011	23012	23013	23014	23015
Olympian	34276	34277	34278					
Dart	41130	41133	42411	42412	42414	42415	42416	42417
	42643	42644	43833	43834	43911	43912	43913	43914
	43915	43916	43917	43918	43919	43920	43921	43922
	43923	43924	43925	43926	43927	43928	43929	43930
	43931	43932	46926					
Scania bus	60162	60163	60164	60165	60166	60167	60168	60219
	60754	61135	61136	61258	64791	64792	64793	64794
	64795	64796	64797	64798	64817	65602	65620	65621
	65622	65623	65624	65625	65626	65724	65725	65726
Blue Bird	68001	68002	68003	68004	68005	68006		
BMC Schoolbus	68522	68531	68571					

Slough (Stanley Cottages) - SH

Olympian	34274	34275	43279					
Dart	40721	41169	41170	41172	41174	41175	41176	41267
	42338	42339	42341	42342	42343	42344	42346	42347
	42654	42656	42659	42673	43835			
Optare Solo	53052	53053	53054	53055	53056	53057		
Scania bus	60755	60756	60757	60758				
Citaro	64012	64013	64014	64015	64016	64017	64018	64019
	64020	64021	64030	64031	64032	64033	64034	64035
	64036	64037	64038	64039	64042			

First Cymru

First Cymru Buses Ltd, Heol Gwyrosydd, Penlan, Swansea, SA5 7BN

Carmarthen (Dolgwili Road) - CA

Javelin	21098	21099	21112	21123	21152			
Dart	41158	42237	52238	42239	42613	42631	42632	42674
	42683	42865	42868	43836	46565	46567		
Alero	55003	55004						
Tempo	64501	64502	54503					
BMC Schoolbus	68503	68504	68506	68513	68514			

Haverfordwest (Withybush Industrial Estate) - HV

Outstation: Pembroke Dock

Dart	41149	41188	41191	41192	41194	41196	41197	41198
	41652							

Llanelli (Inkerman Street) - LL

Javelin	21113	21151	67501					
Dart	41159	42642	42681	42682	42684	42866	42867	42869
	42870	42877	42878	42879	42880	42881	42883	42883
	42884	43837	46518	46521	46527	46528	46529	46530
	46531	46534	46536	46538	46539	46549	46561	46563
	46564	46702	46719					
Mercedes-Benz	51028	51228	51569					
Alero	55000							
BMC Schoolbus	68505							

Pontardawe (Tawe Terrace) - PD

Olympian	34349	34350	34351					
Dart	42590	42591	42592	42593	42594	42599	42620	42621
	42675	42676	42677	42678	42680	42714	42716	43839
	43840	43841	43901	43902	43903	46209	46502	46504
	46505	46522	46526	46542	46545	46546	46547	46552
	46554	46555	46558	46707	46709	46710	46712	46714
	46715	46716	46720	46721	47009	47012	47070	
Mercedes-Benz	50095	50096	50097	50104	50105			

Port Talbot (Acacia Avenue, Sandfields Estate) - PT

Dart	40836	40891	40892	40923	40924	40925	40935	40939
	42210	42215	42218	42302	42303	42304	42305	42322
	42323	42324	42325	42330	42331	42332	42333	42334
	42335	42336	42337	42427	42428	42577	42578	42579
	42626	42633	42685	42686	42687	42688	42689	42690
	42691	42692	42713	42715	42717	42861	42862	42863
	42864	46203	46223	46501	46506	46509	46510	46511
	46513	46514	46515	46517	46519	46525	46532	46533
	46535	46537	46556	46557	46559	46705	46706	46711
	46718							
Mercedes-Benz	50073	51025						

Ravenhill (Pentregethin Road, Swansea) - RA

Volvo B7LA	19033	19035	19036	19037	19038	19039		
Dart	40160	40161	41142	41143	41144	41145	41146	41147
	41148	41150	41151	41152	41153	41155	41157	41160
	41162	41163	41164	41167	41168	41177	41178	41179
	41180	41181	41182	41183	41184	41185	41186	41187
	41190	41193	41195	41639	42207	42208	42209	42211
	42212	42213	42214	42216	42326	42327	42328	42329
	42569	42570	42571	42572	42573	42574	42575	42576
	42580	42581	42582	42583	42585	42586	42587	42588
	42589	42595	42596	42597	42598	42600	42601	42602
	42603	42604	42605	42606	42607	42608	42609	42610
	42611	42612	42614	42622	43584	46507	46516	46550
	46544	46553	46562	46568				
Dart 4 / Enviro 200	44501	44502	44503	44504	44505	44506		
Optare Solo	50279	50297	50298					
Volvo B7RLE	69301	69302	69303	69304	69305			

The 2008 First Bus Handbook

Coaching Unit (Pentregethin Road, Swansea) - RAC

Volvo B7R	20321	20322	20323	20324	20325	20326	20327	20358
	20359	20360	20361	20362	20363	20365	20368	
Volvo B10M	20411	20424	20428					
Volvo B12M	20512	20513	20521	20534	20538	20539	20542	20543
	20544	20549						
Volvo B12B	20550	20551	23205	23206	23207			
Javelin	21014	21097	21109	21110	21111	21114	21115	21119
	21127	21132	21133	21135	21136	21145	21146	21147
	21148	21150						
Scania	23501	23502	23503	23504				
Dart	41171	41173	41199	41200	42679	42693	42694	
BMC Schoolbus	68567	68568	68569	68570				

First in Hampshire & Dorset

First Hampshire & Dorset Ltd, 226 Portswood Road, Southampton, SO17 2BE

Bridport (Tannery Road) - BP

Volvo B10M	20055	20439		
Olympian	34509			
Dart	42817	46733		
Mercedes-Benz	50951	51130	52604	52608
Solo	53801			
Scania L94	65704			
Volvo B10BLE	66165	66168		

Hilsea (London Road) - HI

Dart	41136	41137	41633	41634	41635	41636	41638	41641
	41643	41646						
Mercedes-Benz	50277	50278	50299	50300	50303	51281	51583	51715
	51716	51717	51718	51726	51727	51728	51729	52513
	52517	52558	52559	52560	52580	52581	52583	52601
	52602	52605						
Solo	53151							
Scania L94	65006	65007	65008	65009	65010	65011	65012	65013
	65014	65015	65016	65017	65018	65019	65020	65021
	65022	65023	65024	65025				
Volvo B10BLE	66121	66159	66160					

Hoeford (Gosport Road) - HO

Volvo B10M	20418							
Olympian	34016	34017	34021	34022	34060	34071	34072	
Dart	40262	40265	40623	40823	40824	41515	42109	42113
	42114	42115	42116	42117	42118	42119	42120	42121
	42122	42123	42124	42125	42126	42127	42128	42129
	42130	42131	42132	42133	42134	42135	42136	42137
	42138	42139	42140	42141	42142	42728	45389	45424
	46010	46309	46310	46311	46312	46313	46314	46315
	46316	46317	46318	46319	46320	46321	46322	46323
	46324	46325	46326	46327	46328	46329	46365	46366
	46367	47015	47301	47302	47303	47304	47305	47306
	47307							

Mercedes-Benz	50088	51459	51460	51710	51711	51712	51713	51714
	51720	51721	51722	51723	51724	51725		
Lynx	62630	62641	62643					
Volvo B10BLE	66151	66152	66153	66154	66155	66156	66157	66158
	66161	66162	66163	66164	66176	66181	66196	66197
	66198	66199	66201	66202	66203	66204	66205	
BMC Schoolbus	68553							

Southampton (Portswood Road) - SO

Volvo B10M	20417	20457						
Olympian	31820	31821	31825	31826	31828	31830	31836	31877
	31878	34033	34059	34068	34078	34079	34128	34129
	34130	34249	34259	34261	34989	34990		
Volvo B7TL	32031	32032	32033	32034	32035	32036	32037	32038
	32039	32041	32042	32043	32044	32045	32046	37161
	37162	37163	37164	37165				
Dart	40250	40292	40297	40298	40616	40619	40620	40627
	40628	40629	40784	40785	40786	40787	40788	40790
	40791	40792	40793	40794	40795	40822	40825	40826
	40827	41165	41166	41516	41517	41518	41519	42504
	42505	42506	42507	42508	42509	42510	42511	42512
	42513	42514	42520	42521	42522	42523	42524	42525
	42526	42527	43845	43846	43847	43848		
Mercedes-Benz	50122	50206	50210	50215	52533	52555		
Optare Solo	53076	53140						
Volvo B10B	60299	60337						
Volvo B10BLE	66122	66127	66128	66129	66130			
BMC Schoolbus	68511	68512	68533	68536	68537	68550	68554	68561
	68562	68563						

Weymouth (Edward Street) - WH

Volvo B10M	20437	20440	20454	20464				
Javelin coach	21120							
Bristol VRT	39971							
Olympian	34020	34062	34258	34335	34336	34342	34344	34502
	34540	34541	34810	34814				
Scania OmniDekka	36001	36002	36003	36004	36005	36006		
Dart	42111	42112	42180	42350	42407	42636	42818	42819
	42820	42821	42822	42823	42826	42827	42828	42829
	45307	45408	46734	46735	46736	46737		
Volvo B6	48202	48203	48204	48205	48206	48207	48208	48209
Mercedes-Benz	52603	52606	52607					
Optare Solo	50270	50271	50272					
Volvo B10BLE	66169	66177	66179					

First Somerset & Avon

First Somerset & Avon Ltd, Badger House, Oldmixon, Weston-super-Mare, BS24 9AY.

Bridgwater (East Quay) - BW

Outstation: Minehead

Volvo B10M	21032							
Olympian	34149	34172	34178	34179	34180			
Dart	42634	42830	42831	42832	42833	42834	46195	46727
Mercedes-Benz	51404	51589	51590	51592	51593	51594	51602	51685
	51688	51742						
Volvo B10M	60598							

Bath (Western Island, Lower Bristol Road) - BA

Outstations: Chippenham; Colerne; Devizes; Frome; Melksham; Radstock and Trowbridge

Volvo B7LA	10151	10152	10153	10174	10175	10176	10177	10178
	10179	10180	10181	10182				
Volvo B12M	20514	20515	20516	20517	20525	20526	20527	
Volvo B7TL	32684	32685	32686	32687	32688	32689	32690	32691
Olympian	34108	34109	34110	34111	34112	34113	34114	34151
	34152	34202	34203	34205				
Dart	40835	42552	42553	42554	42555	42556	42557	42895
	42896	42897	42898	42899	42900	42901	42902	42903
	42904	42905	42906	42907	42908	42909	42910	42911
	43821	43822	43823	46225	46234	46235	46237	46240
	46245	46246	46247	46923	46927			
Mercedes-Benz	51091	51214	51346	51348	51380	51606	51661	52553
	52564							
Optare Solo	53802	53803	53804	53805	53806	53807	53808	53809
	53810	53811	53812	53813	53814	53815	53816	53817
	53818	53819	53820					
Volvo B10BLE	62193	62194						
Volvo B7L	66350	66351	66352	66353	66354	66355	66356	
Volvo B7RLE	66727	66728	66729	66730	66731	66732	66733	66734
	66735	66736	66737	66937	66938	66939	66940	66941
	66942	66943	66944	66945	66946	66947	66948	66949
	66951	66952	66953	66954	66955			
Lance	67129	67225	67316	67317	67337	67338	67340	67341
	67342							

Bristol (Marlborough Street) - MS

Olympian	34153	34155	34156	34157	34158	34159	34160	
Dart	46211	46232	46242	46243	46244	46248	46249	46250
	46254	46356	46357	46902				
Lance	60943	61014	61015	67122	67124	67125	67126	67127
	67128	67130	67132	67134	67136	67223	67224	67227
	67228							
Volvo B10BLE	62238	62242	62245	66109	66110	66115	66116	66117
	66118	66120						

Taunton (Hamilton Road) -TN

Outstations: Burnham-on-Sea; Chard; Honiton; Minehead; Martock; Wells; Willand and Wiveliscombe

Volvo B10M	20455	20456						
Olympian	34063	34064	34173	34174	34175	34176	34177	
Dart	41129	41131	41132	41134	41135	41156	42824	42825
	42835	42841	42842	42843	42844	42845	42912	42913
	42914	42915	42916	46115	46204	46226	46228	
	46233	46236	46251	46731				
Mercedes-Benz	51382	51679	51682	51683	51684	51686	51746	51747
	51880	52573	52574	52640				
Lance	60968	60969	67123	67133	67135			
Volvo B10M	60597	60599	60600					
Volvo B10BLE	66166	66167	66171	66172	66173	66174	66178	
Volvo B7RLE	66961							

Weston-super-Mare (Searle Crescent) - WS

Javelin	21053							
Tiger	22045							
Olympian	31841	31846	34154	34165	34167	34168	34169	34170
	34171	34188	34189	34190	34191	39920		
Volvo B7TL	32636	32637	32638					
Volvo B9TL	37315	37316	37317					
Dart	41330	41331	41332	41333	41334	41335	42221	42222
	42729	42730	42731	46206	46218	46229	46231	46238
	46239	46241	46252	46253	46258	46259	46260	46261
	46262	46263	46264	46603	46605	46925		
Mercedes-Benz	51001	51079	51086	51096	51097	51101	51102	51103
	51104	51107	51129	51167	51168	51211	51212	51241
	51558							
Volvo B10M	61212							
Volvo B10BLE	66100	66102	66103	66104	66105	66106	66107	66108
	66206	66207						
Volvo B7RLE	66716	66717	66718	66719	66720	66721	66722	66723
	66724	66725	66726	66934	66935	66936		

Yeovil (Reckleford) - YV

Outstations: Chard; Gillingham; Martock; Rampisham; Sturminster Newton and Wincanton.

Javelin	21064							
Olympian	34966	34967						
Solo	40004	40005	40006	40012	53028			
Dart	41200	42630	46079	46117	46227	46728	46729	46730
	46901							
Mercedes-Benz	51305	51657	51659	51743	51745	51748		
Volvo B10M	66503	66511						
Volvo B7RLE	66956	66958	66960					

First Bristol

First Bristol Ltd, Enterprise House, Easton Road, Bristol, BS5 0DZ

Bristol (Hengrove) - HG

Volvo Citybus	38010							
Volvo B7TL	32003	32004	32005	32278	32279	32280	32281	32282
	32283	32284	32285	32286	32287	32288	32289	32290
	32291	32292	37001	37002	37003	37004	37005	37006
	37007	37008	37009	37010	37011	37012	37013	37014
	37015	37016	37017	37018	37019	37020		
Trident	32701	32702	32703	32704	32705	32706	32707	32708
Dart	42701	42702	42704	42705	42706	42707	42708	42709
	42710	42711	42712	42718	42719	42724	42725	42732
	42733	42734	42735	42736	42737	42738	46614	46627
	46631	46632	46633	46634	46635	46636	46644	46645
	46659	46909	46911					
Volvo B6	48210	48211	48212	48213	48214	48215	48216	48217
	48218	48219	48221	48222	48223	48224		
Lance	60941	60972	60987	60988	61254	67222		
Volvo B10M	60461	60462						

Bristol (Easton Road, Lawrence Hill) - LH

Olympian	34134	34135	34136	34137	34138	34139	34140	34141
	34142	34143	34144	34145	34146	34147	34148	34161
	34162	34163	34164	34186	34187			
Volvo B7TL	32001	32002	32006	32007	32008	32009	32011	32012
	32013	32014	32015	32016	32017	32018	32019	32021
	32022	32023	32024					
Volvo B9TL	37318	37319	37320	37321	37322	37323	37324	37325
	37326	37327	37328	37329	37330	37331	37332	37333
	37334	37335	37336	37337	37338	37339	37340	37341
	37342	37343	37344	37345	37346	37347	37348	37349
	37350	37351	37352	37353	37354	37355	37356	37357
	37358	37359						
Dart	46604	46606	46607	46608	46609	46610	46611	46616
	46617	46620	46621	46622	46623	46624	46626	46628
	46629	46630	46637	46638				
Lance	60947	60949	60950	60952	60963	60964	60965	60966
	60971	60973	60975	60977	60979	60981	60982	60990
	60991	60992	60993	61011	61012			

Bristol (Muller Road, Horfield) - MR

Olympian	34006	34007	34008	34009	34010	34041	34042	34043
	34044	34045	34046	34047	34048	34049	34050	34051
	34052	34131	34132	34133	34181	34182	34183	34184
	34185	34622	34623	34624	34625	34626	34627	34628
	34629	34630						
Dart	42703	42720	42721	42722	42723	42938	42939	42949
	42950	42951	42952	42953	42954	42955	42956	42957
	42958	42959	42960	42961	42962	42963	42964	42965
	42966	42967	42968	46215	46216	46217	46220	46613
	46615	46625	46639	46640	46641	46642	46643	46646
	46647	46648	48849	46650	46651	46652	46653	46654
	46656	46657	46658	46903	46904	46905	46906	46907
	46908							

First Coaches

First Southern National Ltd, Enterprise House, Easton Road, Bristol, BS5 0DZ

Bristol (Easton Road, Lawrence Hill) - LHC

Volvo B7R	20300	20301	20302	20303	20307			
Volvo B10M	20458	20459	20460					
Volvo B12M	20510	20511	20533					
Scania K114	23019	23020	23021	23201	23202	23203	23204	23301
	23302	23303	23304	23305	23306	23307	23308	23309
	23310	23311	23312	23313	23314	23315	23316	23317
	23318	23319	23320	23321	23322	23323	23324	23325
Olympian	30230							
Routemaster	39442							
Mercedes-Benz	52554							

First Devon & Cornwall

First Devon & Cornwall Ltd, The Ride, Chelson Meadow, Plymouth, PL4 6ZB

Barnstaple (Coney Avenue) - BB

Outstations - Bideford; Bow; Bude; Ilfracombe; Morchard Bishop; Tiverton and Torrington

Volvo B7R	20351	20352	20353					
Olympian	34001	34003	34004	34115	34116	34117		
Trident	32751	32752	32753	32754	32755	32764	32765	32766
	32767	32768						
Dart	42432	42433	42436	42438	42440	42449	42452	42456
	42459	42461	42462	42463	42464	42779	42783	43849
	46440	46662	46663					
Mercedes-Benz	52526	52532	52550	52571				

Camborne (Union Street) - CE

Outstations: Flambards, Helston; Trecerus Ind Est, Padstow; Long Rock Ind Est, Penzance; Bodmin; Camworthy Water; Delabole; Tregonnigie Industrial Estate, Falmouth; Tolcarne Street, Newquay;North Petherwin and Pelynt.

Volvo B10M	20044	20050	20053	20144	20145	20412	20413	20443
	20421							
Volvo B7R	20304							
Volvo B12M	20518	20519	20520	20522	20523	20524	20528	20529
	20530	20531	20532	20535	20536	20537	20540	20541
	20545	20546	20547	20548				
Volvo B12B	23208							
Volvo Citybus	38000	38001	38002	38004	38005	38005	38006	
Olympian	31458	31460	31461	31531	31534	31536	31539	31542
	34192	34193	34194	34195	34196	34197	34199	34200
	34709	34710	34713	34714	34751	34752	34753	34754
	34755	34858	34961	34962	34964	34965	34968	34969
	34970	39911						
Dart	40958	42430	42431	42434	42435	42437	42439	42454
	42455	42457	42469	42470	42471	42472	42473	42474
	42475	42476	42477	42478	42558	42559	42560	42752
	42871	42872	42873	42874	42875	42876	42927	42928
	42929	42930	42931	42932	42933	42934	42935	42936
	42937	42940	42941	42942	42943	42944	42945	46420
	46422	46664						
Mercedes-Benz	50304	50307	52523	52528	52535	52536	52551	52552
	52562	52568	52569	52570				
Solo	53107	53108	53109	53111				

Plymouth (Laira Bridge Road) - PL

Outstations: New Road, Callington; Little Cotton Farm, Dartmouth; Okehampton; Crowndale Road, Tavistock; Wills Road Ind Est, Totnes and Trevol Road, Torpoint.

Volvo B10M	20052	20408	20410	20416	20436	20441	20442	
Volvo B7R	20305	20306						
Citybus	38015	38016						
Olympian	31457	31459	34002	34198	34809	34812	34813	34817
Trident	32709	32711	32712	32713	32714	32715	32716	32717
	32756	32757	32758	32759	32760	32761	32762	32763
	32802	32803	32808	32812	32817	32819	32846	
Trident 2	33411	33412	33413	33414	33415	33416	33417	33418
	33419							

Dart	40002	40033	40034	40035	40036	40037	40038	40039
	40570	40580	40581	49582	40583	40584	40585	40586
	40688	40957	40959	40960	40961	42561	42562	42563
	42753	42754	42757	42759	42764	42772	42773	42777
	42780	42784	42924	42925	42926	42946	42947	42948
	42969	47111						
Volvo B6	48201	48225	48226	48227	48228	48229	48231	48232
	48233	48234	48261	48262	48263	48264	48265	48266
	48267	48268	48269	48270	48271	48272	48273	
Mercedes-Benz	50301	50306	52515	52519	52529	52534	52540	52547
	52596	52597	52598	52653				
Solo	53001	53002	53003	53007	53009	53011	53012	53013
	53014	53015	53107	53108	53109	53110	53111	

Truro (Newham Industrial Estate) - TR

Mercedes-Benz Cirato	11070	11071	11072					
Mercedes-Benz Touro	25401							
Tiger	22062							
Volvo B10M	20085	20089	20094	20426	20471	20472	20473	20475
	20498	20499						
Volvo B12B	20556	20557	20558	20559	20560	20701	20702	
MAN - Noge	25654							
Volvo Citybus	38007	38008	38009					
Olympian	30065	34719	34724	34779	34787			
Dart	42232	42234	42235	42252	42253	42255	42801	24802
	42860	43809	43810	43811	43812	43850	43851	43852
	43853	46230	46267	46268	46269			
Dart 4/Enviro 200	44500	44901						
Ford Transit	54801	54802						
Mercedes-Benz	51112	51120	51125	51126	52566	54501	54502	56000
Primo	57000							
Optare Solo	53004	53005	53006	53074	53075	53204	53205	53206
	53401	53402	53403	53404	53826	53827		
Autosan	68301	68302						
BMC Schoolbus	68600							

Aircoach

First Aircoach Ltd, Airport Business Park, Dublin Airport, Dublin

Dublin (Dublin Airport) - Aircoach - D

Mercedes Citaro G	11033	11034	11035	11036	11037	11038		
Setra S415HD	24000	24017	24018	24019	24020	24021	24022	24023
	24024	24025	24026	24027	24028	24029	24030	24031
	24032	24033	24034	24035	24036	24037	24038	24039
	24040	24041	24042	24043	24044	24045	24046	24047
	24048							
Mercedes Citaro	64000	64022	64023	64024	64025	64026	64027	64028
Volvo B7RLE	66357	66358						

Belfast (Belfast Airport) - BT

Volvo B7RLE	66992	66993	66994

FirstGroup Rhein-Necker GmbH

FirstGroup Rhein-Necker GmbH, Heinkelstrasse, 67346 Speyer

3	SP	SP-XY3	Mercedes-Benz O405N	Mercedes-Benz	N45F	1993
4	SP	SP-XY4	Mercedes-Benz O405N	Mercedes-Benz	N45F	1993
10	SP	SP-AM10	Mercedes-Benz O408	Mercedes-Benz	BC50D	1992
13	SP	SP-AM13	Mercedes-Benz Citaro O530	Mercedes-Benz	N35D	1999
14	SP	SP-AM14	Mercedes-Benz O405G	Mercedes-Benz	AB60D	1987
15	SP	SP-AE15	Truronianutura FHD12	Bova	C51F	2003
17	SP	SP-AY17	Mercedes-Benz O405	Mercedes-Benz	B45D	1993
18	SP	SP-AJ18	Mercedes-Benz O405N	Mercedes-Benz	N43F	1992
20	SP	SP-AE20	Volkswagen	Volkswagen	M9	1994
23	SP	SP-AM23	Mercedes-Benz O405GN	Mercedes-Benz	AN53T	1995
25	SP	SP-XY25	Mercedes-Benz Citaro O530G	Mercedes-Benz	AN51T	1999
26	SP	SP-AY26	Mercedes-Benz O405	Mercedes-Benz	B45D	1995
28	SP	SP-AY28	Mercedes-Benz O405	Mercedes-Benz	B45D	1994
31	SP	SP-AE31	Mercedes-Benz O405N	Mercedes-Benz	N41F	1994
33	SP	SP-AM33	Mercedes-Benz O405	Mercedes-Benz	B45D	1989
40	SP	SP-AE40	Mercedes-Benz O407	Mercedes-Benz	B50F	1994
41	SP	SP-AM41	Van Hool A308	Van Hool	N19D	1997
43	SP	SP-AF43	Mercedes-Benz O405	Mercedes-Benz	B45D	1992
44	SP	SP-AO44	Bova Futura FHD12	Bova	C51F	1997
45	SP	SP-AJ45	Mercedes-Benz O405N	Mercedes-Benz	N43F	1992
46	SP	SP-AM46	Mercedes-Benz Citaro O530	Mercedes-Benz	N34D	2002
48	SP	SP-AM48	Van Hool A308	Van Hool	N19C	1997
49	SP	SP-AM49	Mercedes-Benz O305	Mercedes-Benz	B45D	1982
51	SP	SP-LX51	Setra S317 HDH	Setra	C61F	1998
58	SP	SP-AM58	Mercedes-Benz O407	Mercedes-Benz	B49F	1993
63	SP	SP-XY63	Mercedes-Benz O405	Mercedes-Benz	B45D	1997
66	SP	SP-AM66	Mercedes-Benz O405N	Mercedes-Benz	N34D	1997
69	SP	SP-JH69	Mercedes-Benz O405	Mercedes-Benz	B45D	1992
70	SP	SP-AD70	Bova Futura FHD12	Bova	C51F	2000
73	SP	SP-AY73	Mercedes-Benz O405	Mercedes-Benz	B45D	1998
76	SP	SP-AY76	Mercedes-Benz O407	Mercedes-Benz	B50F	1995
82	SP	SP-AM82	Van Hool A308	Van Hool	N19D	1997
84	SP	SP-AM84	Mercedes-Benz O407	Mercedes-Benz	B54F	1990
85	SP	SP-AM85	Mercedes-Benz O405	Mercedes-Benz	B45D	1992
89	SP	SP-AM89	Mercedes-Benz O405N	Mercedes-Benz	N37D	1991
91	SP	SP-AM91	Bova Futura FHD13	Bova	C55F	2004
92	SP	SP-XY92	Mercedes-Benz O405N	Mercedes-Benz	N--D	1991
94	SP	SP-AM94	Mercedes-Benz Citaro O530	Mercedes-Benz	N39F	2001
95	SP	SP-XM95	Van Hool A308	Van Hool	N19C	1997
97	SP	SP-AM97	Mercedes-Benz O407	Mercedes-Benz	B50F	1993
98	SP	SP-XY98	Mercedes-Benz O405N	Mercedes-Benz	N--D	1991
99	SP	SP-AM99	Bova Futura FHD12	Bova	C51F	2002
113	HB	HP-FR113	Mercedes-Benz Vario O814	Ernst Auwarter	BC18F	1994
114	HB	HP-FR114	Mercedes-Benz 212D	Mercedes-Benz	M8	1996
132	HB	HP-FR132	Mercedes-Benz Vario O814	Ernst Auwarter	BC21F	199
134	SP	HP-FR134	Bova Futura FHD12	Bova	C51F	2000
135	SP	HP-FR135	Bova Futura FHD12	Bova	C51F	2001
137	HB	HP-FR137	MAN 18.360	Marcopolo	C53F	1997
147	HB	HP-FR147	Neoplan Starliner N316 SHD	Neoplan	C54F	1995
148	HB	HP-FR148	Setra S215 HR	Setra	C51F	1991
149	HB	HP-FR149	Irisbus TurboDaily 50C	Irisbus	BC20F	2004
151	HB	HP-FR151	Irisbus TurboDaily 50C	Irisbus	BC20F	2004
152	SP	HP-FR152	Volvo B12B	Volvo	C48D	1997
153	HB	HP-FR153	Mercedes-Benz O305	Mercedes-Benz	B45D	1987
154	HB	HP-FR154	Mercedes-Benz O303	Mercedes-Benz	C33F	1990
157	HB	HP-FR157	Mercedes-Benz O303	Mercedes-Benz	C56F	1990
158	HB	HP-FR158	Mercedes-Benz O407	Mercedes-Benz	B50F	1991
159	HB	HP-FR159	Mercedes-Benz O303	Mercedes-Benz	C56F	1992
165	HB	HP-FR165	Droegmoeller EuroComet E330	Dreoegmoeller	C38F	1987
167	HB	HP-FR167	Setra S215 UL	Setra	B52D	1988
168	SP	HP-FR168	Neoplan Skyliner N122/3	Neoplan	C(80)D	1993
169	HB	HP-FR169	Setra S215 SL	Setra	B45D	1993
172	HB	HP-FR172	Mercedes-Benz O305	Mercedes-Benz	B45D	1985
183	SP	HP-FR183	Bova Futura FHD10	Bova	C40F	1998
185	HB	HP-FR185	Mercedes-Benz 208D	Mercedes-Benz	M8	1990

192	HB	HP-FR192	Mercedes-Benz 614	Kusters	B21F	1990
198	HB	HP-FR198	Setra S215 RL	Setra	BC56F	1987
208	HB	HP-FR208	Droegmoeller E280	Dreoegmoeller	C40F	1985
209	HB	HP-FR209	MAN SR202	MAN	B59F	1988
213	HB	HP-FR213	Droegmoeller Super Pullman E310	Dreoegmoeller	C55F	1985
218	HB	HP-FR218	Mercedes-Benz Vario O814	Ernst Auwarter	B21F	1991
219	HB	HP-FR219	Mercedes-Benz O305	Mercedes-Benz	B45D	1984
225	HB	HP-FR225	Mercedes-Benz O307	Mercedes-Benz	B54D	1982
226	HB	HP-FR226	Mercedes-Benz 309D	Mercedes-Benz	B27F	1986
238	HB	HP-FR238	Mercedes-Benz 309D	Mercedes-Benz	B26F	1986
249	HB	HP-FR249	Mercedes-Benz 100D	Mercedes-Benz	M8	1991
254	HB	HP-FR254	Mercedes-Benz O407	Mercedes-Benz	B50F	1989
259	HB	HP-FR259	Mercedes-Benz O307	Mercedes-Benz	B54D	1988
262	HB	HP-FR262	Volkswagen	Volkswagen	BC18F	2002
263	HB	HP-FR263	Renault JL	Renault	M9	2004
268	HB	HP-FR268	MAN 18.360	Marcopolo	C52F	1998
269	HB	HP-FR269	Mercedes-Benz 410	Mercedes-Benz	B15F	1993
270	HB	HP-FR270	Renault JL	Renault	M8	2004
271	HB	HP-FR271	Setra S215 HU	Setra	BC55F	1981
272	HB	HP-FR272	Renault JL	Renault	M9	2004
274	SP	HP-FR274	Neoplan Skyliner N122/3	Neoplan	C(79)D	1998
277	SP	HP-FR277	Neoplan Cityliner N116	Neoplan	C50F	2000
287	SP	HP-FR287	Bova Futura FHD15	Bova	C67F	1996
292	HB	HP-FR292	Neoplan Transliner N316K	Neoplan	BC57D	1993
293	HB	HP-FR293	Neoplan Transliner N316L	Neoplan	BC57D	1995

295-309

			Mercedes-Benz O405	Mercedes-Benz	B45D*	1979-92	*302 is B44D

295	HB	HP-FR295	302	HB	HP-FR302	306	HB	HP-FR306	308	HB	HP-FR308
296	HB	HP-FR296	305	HB	HP-FR305	307	HB	HP-FR307	309	HB	HP-FR309
301	HB	HP-FR301									

310	SP	HP-FR310	Bova Futura FHD12	Bova	C51F	2002
311	HB	HP-FR311	Mercedes-Benz O405	Mercedes-Benz	B45D	1985
312	HB	HP-FR312	Mercedes-Benz O405	Mercedes-Benz	B45D	1985
314	HB	HP-FR314	Mercedes-Benz O408	Mercedes-Benz	B45D	1993
315	HB	HP-FR315	Mercedes-Benz 308D	Mercedes-Benz	M8	1995
316	HB	HP-FR316	Mercedes-Benz 308D	Mercedes-Benz	M8	1995
317	HB	HP-FR317	Mercedes-Benz O303	Mercedes-Benz	C60F	1989
318	HB	HP-FR318	Mercedes-Benz O405	Mercedes-Benz	B45D	1991

322-325

			VDL Bova Futura FHD12	VDL Bova	C51F	2007D

322	SP	HP-FR322	323	SP	HP-FR323	324	SP	HP-FR324	325	SP	HP-FR325

410-417

			Volvo 7000	Volvo	N39T	2001

410	LN	SP-RN10	413	LN	SP-RN13	416	LN	SP-RN16	417	LN	SP-RN17

418	LN	SP-RN18	Solaris Urbino 10	Solaris	N24D	2008

419-429

			Solaris Urbino 12	Solaris	N31T	2008

419	LN	SP-RN19	427	LN	SP-RN27	428	LN	SP-RN28	429	LN	SP-RN29

430	LN	SP-RN30	Solaris Urbino 10	Solaris	N24D	2008
432	LN	SP-RN32	Solaris Urbino 10	Solaris	N24D	2008
437	LN	SP-RN37	Mercedes-Benz O405N	Mercedes-Benz	B35T	1995
438	LN	SP-RN38	Mercedes-Benz O405N	Mercedes-Benz	B35T	1995
443	LN	SP-RN43	Mercedes-Benz O405N	Mercedes-Benz	B35T	1995
800	SP	SUW-U800	Mercedes-Benz 208D	Mercedes-Benz	M9	1998
803	SP	SUW-U803	Mercedes-Benz Sprinter 308D	Mercedes-Benz	N14F	2005
804	SP	SUW-U804	Mercedes-Benz Sprinter 308D	Mercedes-Benz	N14F	2005
806	SP	SUW-U806	Mercedes-Benz Vario O814	Ernst Auwarter	B24F	1992
807	SP	SUW-U807	Mercedes-Benz Sprinter 416 cdi	Mercedes-Benz	N23F	2002
808	SP	SUW-U803	Mercedes-Benz 308D	Mercedes-Benz	B14F	1999
812	SP	SUW-U812	Mercedes-Benz 208D	Mercedes-Benz	M8	1998
814	SP	SUW-U814	Mercedes-Benz 208D	Mercedes-Benz	M8	1998
816	SP	SUW-U816	Mercedes-Benz 208D	Mercedes-Benz	M8	1998
829	SP	SUW-U829	Mercedes-Benz 308D	Mercedes-Benz	B14F	1999
840	SP	SUW-U840	Mercedes-Benz O305G	Mercedes-Benz	AB60D	1985
848	SP	SUW-U848	Mercedes-Benz 308D	Mercedes-Benz	B14F	2003
868	SP	SUW-U868	Mercedes-Benz 308D	Mercedes-Benz	B14F	1998
870	SP	SUW-U870	Mercedes-Benz 308D	Mercedes-Benz	B14F	1998
894	SP	SUW-U894	Mercedes-Benz 208D	Mercedes-Benz	M9	1998

Vehicle index

Reg	No	Operator	Reg	No	Operator	Reg	No	Operator
2GRT	20011	Aberdeen	AU53HJN	32477	Eastern C	C413HJN	34813	Devon & C
204CLT	39804	London	AU53HJO	32478	Eastern C	C414HJN	34814	Hampshire
218CLT	39818	London	AU53HJV	32479	Eastern C	C415HJN	34815	Essex
260ERY	20426	Devon & C	AU53HJX	32480	Eastern C	C417HJN	34817	Devon & C
3913WE	40503	S Yorkshire	AU53HJY	32481	Eastern C	C418HJN	34818	Essex
481FPO	34194	Devon & C	AU53HJZ	32482	Eastern C	C79CHM	34779	Devon & C
530OHU	34192	Devon & C	AU53HKA	32483	Eastern C	C814BYY	39932	Potteries
542GRT	20008	Aberdeen	AU53HKB	32484	Eastern C	C819 BYY	34719	Devon & C
562CLT	39862	London	AU53HKC	32485	Eastern C	C87CHM	34787	Devon & C
620HOD	66503	Somerset &A	AU53HKD	32486	Eastern C	C930GYD	90256	Leicester
627DYE	39827	London	AU53HKE	32487	Eastern C	CN02EDN	11072	Devon & C
640DYE	39840	London	AU53HKF	32488	Eastern C	CU03AVC	20538	Wales
735DYE	39835	London	AU53HKG	32489	Eastern C	CU03AVD	20539	Wales
776DYE	39876	London	AU53HKH	32490	Eastern C	CU03BHV	42693	Wales
8995WY	61134	W Yorkshire	AU53HKJ	32491	Eastern C	CU03BHW	42694	Wales
A102FSA	31531	Devon & C	AU53HKK	32492	Eastern C	CU04AYP	20550	Wales
A105FSA	31534	Devon & C	AU53HKL	32493	Eastern C	CU04AYS	20551	Wales
A107FSA	31536	Devon & C	AU53HKM	32494	Eastern C	CU05LGJ	20354	Edinburgh
A120KUM	30627	W Yorkshire	B112MSO	31539	Devon & C	CU05LGK	20355	Edinburgh
A162VDM	30060	Potteries	B115MSO	31542	Devon & C	CU08AHN	69301	Wales
A167VDM	30065	Devon & C	B121MSO	31547	Aberdeen	CU08AHO	69302	Wales
A751VAF	34751	Devon & C	B134RWY	30640	W Yorkshire	CU08AHP	69303	Wales
A752VAF	34752	Devon & C	B137RWY	30643	W Yorkshire	CU08AHV	69304	Wales
A753VAF	34753	Devon & C	B143RWY	30761	W Yorkshire	CU08AHX	69305	Wales
A754VAF	34754	Devon & C	B144RWY	30762	W Yorkshire	CU08ACY	44501	Wales
A755VAF	34755	Devon & C	B181BLG	30072	Potteries	CU08ACZ	44502	Wales
A809THW	34709	Devon & C	B188BLG	30074	Potteries	CU08ADO	44503	Wales
A810THW	34710	Devon & C	B200DTU	30077	Potteries	CU08ADV	44504	Wales
A811THW	39911	Devon & C	B201DTU	30078	Potteries	CU08ADX	44505	Wales
ALD913B	39813	London	B501RWY	30646	W Yorkshire	CU08ADZ	44506	Wales
AN02EDN	11070	Devon & C	B7FTR	19004	W Yorkshire	CU53AEG	20548	Devon & C
AO02ODM	43801	Eastern C	BG57ZGJ	68571	Berkshire	CU53AFZ	20549	Wales
AO02ODN	43802	Eastern C	BN02CDN	11071	Devon & C	CU53APO	42674	Wales
AO02RBX	20500	Eastern C	BU04FAJ	25401	Devon & C	CU53APV	42675	Wales
AO02RBY	20501	Eastern C	BU04CAA	68501	Manchester	CU53APX	42676	Wales
AO02RBZ	20502	Eastern C	BU04EZF	64020	Berkshire	CU53APY	42683	Wales
AO02RCF	20503	Eastern C	BU04EZG	64021	Berkshire	CU53APZ	42682	Wales
AO02RCU	20504	Eastern C	BU53PNE	62801	Potteries	CU53ARF	42681	Wales
AO02RCV	20505	Eastern C	BU53PNF	62802	Potteries	CU53ARO	42680	Wales
AO02RCX	20506	Eastern C	BU53PNJ	62803	Potteries	CU53ARX	42679	Wales
AO02RCY	20507	Eastern C	BU53PNK	62804	Potteries	CU53ARZ	42678	Wales
AO02RCZ	20508	Eastern C	BU53PNL	62805	Potteries	CU53ASO	42677	Wales
AO02RDU	20509	Eastern C	BU53PNN	62806	Potteries	CU53AUO	42685	Wales
AU05DME	69005	Eastern C	BU53PNO	62807	Potteries	CU53AUP	42684	Wales
AU05DMF	69006	Eastern C	BU53PNV	62808	Potteries	CU53AUT	42686	Wales
AU05DMO	69007	Eastern C	BV57MSO	68567	Wales	CU53AUV	42687	Wales
AU05DMV	69008	Eastern C	BV57MSU	68568	Wales	CU53AUW	42688	Wales
AU05DMX	69009	Eastern C	BV57MSX	68569	Wales	CU53AUX	42690	Wales
AU05DMY	69010	Eastern C	BV57MSY	68570	Wales	CU53AUY	42691	Wales
AU05DMZ	69011	Eastern C	BX02CMK	64029	Manchester	CU53AVB	42692	Wales
AU05MUO	32651	Eastern C	BX06NZT	68302	Devon & C	CU53AVJ	42861	Wales
AU05MUP	32652	Eastern C	BX54EBC	11000	London	CU53AVK	42862	Wales
AU05MUV	32653	Eastern C	BX54VUN	68503	Wales	CU53AVL	42863	Wales
AU05MUW	32654	Eastern C	BX55NYD	68600	Devon & C	CU53AVM	42864	Wales
AU05MUY	32655	Eastern C	BX55NZV	68301	Devon & C	CU53AVN	42865	Wales
AU05MVA	32656	Eastern C	C146KBT	30651	W Yorkshire	CU53AVO	42866	Wales
AU07DXS	37156	Eastern C	C148KBT	30652	W Yorkshire	CU53AVP	42868	Wales
AU07DXT	37157	Eastern C	C150KBT	30654	W Yorkshire	CU53AVR	42867	Wales
AU07DXV	37158	Eastern C	C24CHM	34724	Devon & C	CU53AVT	42870	Wales
AU07DXW	37159	Eastern C	C407HJN	34807	Essex	CU53AVV	42869	Wales
AU07DXX	37160	Eastern C	C409HJN	34809	Devon & C	CU53AVW	42689	Wales
AU53HJJ	32475	Eastern C	C410HJN	34810	Hampshire	CU54CYX	68504	Wales
AU53HJK	32476	Eastern C	C412HJN	34812	Devon & C	CU54CYY	68505	Wales

The 2008 First Bus Handbook

Reg	No	Location	Reg	No	Location	Reg	No	Location
CU54CYZ	68506	Wales	E122DRS	31548	Aberdeen	F102AVG	34822	Eastern C
CU54DCE	68513	Wales	E123DRS	31549	Aberdeen	F105AVG	34825	Eastern C
CU54DCF	68514	Wales	E124DRS	31550	Aberdeen	F157XYG	30655	W Yorkshire
CU54HYK	42600	Wales	E125DRS	31551	Aberdeen	F158XYG	34858	Devon & C
CU54HYL	42601	Wales	E126DRS	31552	Aberdeen	F160XYG	30069	Potteries
CU54HYM	42602	Wales	E127DRS	31553	Aberdeen	F161XYG	30657	W Yorkshire
CU54HYN	42603	Wales	E128DRS	31554	Aberdeen	F162XYG	30658	W Yorkshire
CU54HYO	42604	Wales	E130DRS	31556	Aberdeen	F163XYG	30659	W Yorkshire
CU54HYP	42605	Wales	E131DRS	31557	Aberdeen	F164XYG	30660	W Yorkshire
CU54HYR	42606	Wales	E215BTA	38015	Devon & C	F165XYG	30661	W Yorkshire
CU54HYT	42607	Wales	E216BTA	38016	Devon & C	F166XYG	30662	W Yorkshire
CU54HYV	42608	Wales	E289HRV	34989	Hampshire	F167XYG	30663	W Yorkshire
CU54HYW	42609	Wales	E290HRV	34990	Hampshire	F168XYG	30664	W Yorkshire
CU54HYX	42610	Wales	EO02FKZ	53111	Devon & C	F169XYG	30665	W Yorkshire
CU54HYY	42611	Wales	EO02FLA	53101	W Yorkshire	F170XYG	30666	W Yorkshire
CU54HYZ	42612	Wales	EO02FLB	53102	W Yorkshire	F171XYG	30667	W Yorkshire
CU54HZA	42613	Wales	EO02FLC	53103	W Yorkshire	F172LBL	34872	Eastern C
CU54HZB	42614	Wales	EO02FLD	53104	W Yorkshire	F172XYG	30668	W Yorkshire
CU57AJV	19030	Luton Airport	EO02FLE	53105	W Yorkshire	F173LBL	34873	Eastern C
CU57AJX	19032	Luton Airport	EO02FLF	53106	W Yorkshire	F173XYG	30669	W Yorkshire
CU57AJY	19034	Luton Airport	EO02FLG	53107	Devon & C	F174XYG	30670	W Yorkshire
CU57AKG	19035	Wales	EO02FLH	53108	Devon & C	F175XYG	30671	W Yorkshire
CU57AKJ	19036	Wales	EO02FLJ	53109	Devon & C	F176LBL	34876	Eastern C
CU57AKK	19038	Wales	EO02FLK	53110	Devon & C	F422GWG	36922	W Yorkshire
CU57AKN	19037	Wales	EO02NDX	53112	Essex	F602RTC	62602	Leicester
CV55ABK	20357	Edinburgh	EO02NDY	53113	Essex	F603RTC	62603	Leicester
CV55ABN	20356	Edinburgh	EO02NDZ	53114	Essex	F626RTC	62626	S Yorkshire
CV55ACO	20358	Wales	EO02NEF	53115	Essex	F630RTC	62630	Hampshire
CV55ACU	20359	Wales	EO02NEJ	53116	Essex	F792LSU	30350	W Yorkshire
CV55ACX	20360	Wales	EO02NEN	53117	Essex	F793LSU	30351	Edinburgh
CV55ACY	20361	Wales	EO02NEU	53118	Essex	F83XBD	38083	Leicester
CV55ACZ	20363	Wales	EO02NEY	53119	Essex	F85XBD	38085	Midland Red
CV55AFA	20362	Wales	EO02NFA	53120	Essex	F88DVV	38088	Edinburgh
CV55AFE	20364	Edinburgh	EO02NFC	53121	Essex	F91JYS	31269	W Yorkshire
CV55AFF	20366	Berkshire	EO02NFD	53122	Essex	F92JYS	31270	W Yorkshire
CV55AGX	20367	Berkshire	EO02NFE	53123	Essex	FC52AFC	20021	Aberdeen
CV55AGY	20370	Edinburgh	EO02NFF	53124	Essex	FE52HFH	68204	Manchester
CV55AGZ	20368	Wales	EO02NFG	53125	Essex	FE52HFJ	68205	Manchester
CV55AHA	20365	Berkshire	EO02NFH	53126	Essex	FE52HFK	68206	Manchester
CV55AMU	20369	Berkshire	EO02NFJ	53127	Essex	FJ55KNA	68218	Manchester
CV55AMX	20371	Edinburgh	EO02NFK	53128	Essex	FJ55XLH	68211	Manchester
CV55ANF	20372	Berkshire	EO02NFL	53129	Essex	FJ55XLK	68212	Manchester
CV55ANP	20373	Berkshire	EO02NFM	53130	Essex	FJ55XLL	68213	Manchester
CV55AOO	20374	Berkshire	EO02NFN	53131	Essex	FJ56OBO	23501	Wales
CX02ECC	60032	Potteries	EO02NFP	53132	Essex	FJ56PFG	23502	Wales
CX02ECN	60033	Potteries	EO02NFR	53133	Essex	FJ56PFK	23503	Wales
CX02ECT	60034	Potteries	EO02NFT	53134	Essex	FJ56PFN	23504	Wales
CX02EFF	60035	Potteries	EO02NFU	53135	Essex	FN06FLC	20701	Devon & C
CX02EFG	60036	Potteries	EO02NFV	53136	Essex	FN06FLD	20702	Devon & C
CX02EGC	60037	Potteries	EO02NFX	53137	Essex	FX56AHU	68214	Manchester
CX02EGD	60038	Potteries	EU05AUK	42918	Essex	FX57LKM	68217	Manchester
CX02EGE	60039	Potteries	EU05AUL	42919	Essex	G106HNP	62706	S Yorkshire
CX02EGF	60040	Potteries	EU05AUM	42920	Essex	G111HNP	62711	Edinburgh
CX02EGJ	60041	Potteries	EU05AUN	42921	Essex	G113HNP	62713	Leicester
CX02EGK	60042	Potteries	EU05AUO	42922	Essex	G114HNP	62714	Midland Red
D158FYM	39936	Potteries	EU05AUP	42923	Essex	G115JBO	22045	Somerset &A
D183FYM	39933	Potteries	EU05DXR	68535	Essex	G117HNP	62717	S Yorkshire
D235FYM	39935	Potteries	EU05DXS	68551	Essex	G121YEV	34921	Eastern C
D238FYM	39938	Potteries	EU05DXT	68552	Essex	G122YEV	34922	Eastern C
D251FYM	39939	Potteries	EU54BNJ	53139	Essex	G123YEV	34923	Eastern C
D350ESC	90269	Midland Red	EU54BNK	53138	Essex	G125YEV	34925	Eastern C
D513HUB	34713	Devon & C	EY54BPX	56004	Essex	G126HNP	62726	S Yorkshire
D514HUB	34714	Devon & C	EY54BPZ	56005	Essex	G126YEV	34926	Eastern C
D700GHY	38000	Devon & C	EY54BRF	56006	Essex	G128YEV	34928	Eastern C
D707GHY	38007	Devon & C	EY54BRV	56007	Aberdeen	G129HNP	62729	S Yorkshire
D709GHY	38009	Devon & C	EY54BRX	56008	Aberdeen	G133ATW	34933	Eastern C
DA51XTD	43804	Potteries	EY54BRZ	56009	Essex	G133HNP	62733	Leicester

Reg	No	Location	Reg	No	Location	Reg	No	Location
G140HNP	62740	S Yorkshire	G619OWR	30704	W Yorkshire	H138FLX	31739	W Yorkshire
G148HNP	62748	Edinburgh	G620NWA	61255	Glasgow	H139FLX	34339	London
G149HNP	62749	Leicester	G620OWR	30705	W Yorkshire	H140FLX	34340	London
G176JYG	30229	W Yorkshire	G621NWA	61266	Glasgow	H141FLX	34341	London
G177JYG	30230	Bristol	G621OWR	30706	W Yorkshire	H142FLX	34342	Hampshire
G178JYG	30231	W Yorkshire	G622NWA	60467	W Yorkshire	H143FLX	31740	W Yorkshire
G179JYG	30672	W Yorkshire	G622OWR	30707	W Yorkshire	H144FLX	34344	Hampshire
G180JYG	30673	W Yorkshire	G623NWA	60468	W Yorkshire	H145FLX	34345	London
G181JYG	30674	W Yorkshire	G623OWR	30685	W Yorkshire	H232LOM	36932	W Yorkshire
G182JYG	30675	W Yorkshire	G624NWA	60469	Essex	H289VRP	38089	Edinburgh
G183JYG	30676	W Yorkshire	G625NWA	60470	S Yorkshire	H290VRP	38090	Edinburgh
G184JYG	30677	W Yorkshire	G626NWA	60471	S Yorkshire	H291VRP	38091	Edinburgh
G185JYG	30678	W Yorkshire	G627NWA	60472	S Yorkshire	H292VRP	38092	Edinburgh
G251JYG	60120	Potteries	G628NWA	60473	S Yorkshire	H294VRP	38094	Edinburgh
G281OGE	30358	Edinburgh	G629NWA	60474	S Yorkshire	H308ERV	46010	Hampshire
G282OGE	30359	W Yorkshire	G630NWA	60475	S Yorkshire	H611VNW	31088	Potteries
G286OGE	30362	W Yorkshire	G631NWA	60476	S Yorkshire	H612VNW	31089	Potteries
G293OGE	30365	W Yorkshire	G632NWA	60477	S Yorkshire	H613VNW	31090	W Yorkshire
G298OGE	31127	W Yorkshire	G633NWA	60478	S Yorkshire	H615VNW	31092	W Yorkshire
G303OGE	31284	W Yorkshire	G634NWA	60479	S Yorkshire	H616VNW	31093	W Yorkshire
G304OGE	31285	Glasgow	G635NWA	60480	S Yorkshire	H619VNW	31096	W Yorkshire
G379NRC	36930	W Yorkshire	G636NWA	60481	S Yorkshire	H620VNW	31097	W Yorkshire
G46XLO	34946	Eastern C	G637NWA	60482	S Yorkshire	H633VNW	31110	Potteries
G48XLO	34948	Eastern C	G638NWA	60483	S Yorkshire	H636VNW	31113	Potteries
G50XLO	34950	Eastern C	G639NWA	60484	Essex	H641YHT	62641	Hampshire
G51XLO	34951	Eastern C	G640NWA	60485	W Yorkshire	H642RKU	60487	S Yorkshire
G523RDS	30379	W Yorkshire	G641NWA	60486	W Yorkshire	H643RKU	60488	S Yorkshire
G527RDS	31297	W Yorkshire	G667FKA	39167	Leicester	H643YHT	62643	Hampshire
G52XLO	34952	Eastern C	G686PNS	31313	Devon & C	H644YHT	62644	Edinburgh
G531RDS	31300	Glasgow	G692PNS	31314	Glasgow	H645RKU	60489	S Yorkshire
G544RDS	31310	Glasgow	G693PNS	31315	W Yorkshire	H646RKU	60490	S Yorkshire
G55XLO	34955	Eastern C	G695PNS	31317	Glasgow	H647RKU	60491	S Yorkshire
G601NWA	61256	Glasgow	G696PNS	31318	Glasgow	H648RKU	60492	S Yorkshire
G601OWR	30686	W Yorkshire	G698PNS	30377	W Yorkshire	H649RKU	60493	S Yorkshire
G602NWA	60457	S Yorkshire	G702PNS	31320	Glasgow	H650RKU	60494	S Yorkshire
G602OWR	30687	W Yorkshire	G753XRE	30029	Potteries	H651THL	60495	S Yorkshire
G603NWA	60458	S Yorkshire	G754XRE	30030	Potteries	H652THL	60496	S Yorkshire
G603OWR	30688	W Yorkshire	G755XRE	30031	Potteries	H655THL	60499	S Yorkshire
G604NWA	60459	Leicester	G757XRE	30033	Potteries	H656THL	60500	S Yorkshire
G604OWR	30689	W Yorkshire	G758XRE	30034	Potteries	H657THL	60501	S Yorkshire
G605OWR	30690	W Yorkshire	G759XRE	30035	Potteries	H658THL	60502	S Yorkshire
G606NWA	60461	Bristol	G761XRE	30037	Potteries	H659THL	60503	S Yorkshire
G606OWR	30691	W Yorkshire	G762XRE	30038	Potteries	H660THL	60504	S Yorkshire
G607NWA	60462	Bristol	G803JYG	31080	Potteries	H661THL	60505	S Yorkshire
G607OWR	30692	W Yorkshire	G901TWS	34961	Devon & C	H662THL	60506	S Yorkshire
G608NWA	60463	S Yorkshire	G902TWS	34962	Devon & C	H663THL	60507	S Yorkshire
G608OWR	30693	W Yorkshire	G904TWS	34964	Devon & C	H664THL	60508	S Yorkshire
G609NWA	60464	Glasgow	G905TWS	34965	Devon & C	H667THL	60510	S Yorkshire
G609OWR	30694	W Yorkshire	G906TWS	34966	Somerset &A	H668THL	60511	S Yorkshire
G610NWA	60465	S Yorkshire	G907TWS	34967	Somerset &A	H669THL	60512	S Yorkshire
G610OWR	30695	W Yorkshire	G908TWS	34968	Devon & C	H670THL	60513	S Yorkshire
G611NWA	61259	Glasgow	G909TWS	34969	Devon & C	H671THL	60514	S Yorkshire
G611OWR	30696	W Yorkshire	G910TWS	34970	Devon & C	H672THL	60515	S Yorkshire
G612NWA	60138	Glasgow	GIL2967	20044	Devon & C	H673THL	60516	S Yorkshire
G612OWR	30697	W Yorkshire	H101KVX	34901	Eastern C	H674THL	60517	S Yorkshire
G613NWA	60466	Glasgow	H102KVX	34902	Eastern C	H676THL	60519	S Yorkshire
G613OWR	30698	W Yorkshire	H103KVX	34903	Eastern C	H678THL	60520	S Yorkshire
G614NWA	61260	Glasgow	H104KVX	34904	Eastern C	H679THL	60521	S Yorkshire
G614OWR	30699	W Yorkshire	H129FLX	34429	London	H680THL	60522	S Yorkshire
G615NWA	61261	Glasgow	H130FLX	34330	London	H681THL	60523	S Yorkshire
G615OWR	30700	W Yorkshire	H131FLX	30734	W Yorkshire	H682THL	60524	S Yorkshire
G616NWA	61262	Glasgow	H132FLX	34333	Eastern C	H683THL	60525	S Yorkshire
G616OWR	30701	W Yorkshire	H133FLX	31737	W Yorkshire	H684THL	60526	S Yorkshire
G617NWA	61263	Glasgow	H134FLX	31738	W Yorkshire	H685THL	60527	S Yorkshire
G618NWA	61264	Glasgow	H135FLX	90176	London	H686THL	60528	S Yorkshire
G618OWR	30703	W Yorkshire	H136FLX	34336	Hampshire	H687THL	60529	S Yorkshire
G619NWA	61265	Glasgow	H137FLX	34337	Eastern C	H688THL	60530	S Yorkshire

Reg	No	Region	Reg	No	Region	Reg	No	Region
H691THL	60509	S Yorkshire	J693AWF	60535	S Yorkshire	K601HUG	61079	W Yorkshire
H701GVM	30340	Glasgow	J694AWF	60536	S Yorkshire	K601LAE	30216	Manchester
H702GVM	30341	Glasgow	J695AWF	60537	S Yorkshire	K602HUG	61080	W Yorkshire
H703GVM	30342	Glasgow	J696AWF	60538	S Yorkshire	K602LAE	30217	Manchester
H704GVM	30343	Glasgow	J697AWF	60539	S Yorkshire	K603HUG	61081	W Yorkshire
H705GVM	30344	Glasgow	J699AWF	60541	S Yorkshire	K603LAE	30218	Manchester
H706GVM	30345	Glasgow	J701AWF	60543	S Yorkshire	K604HUG	61082	W Yorkshire
H707GVM	30346	Glasgow	J703AWF	60545	S Yorkshire	K604LAE	30219	Manchester
H708GVM	30347	Glasgow	J704AWF	60546	S Yorkshire	K605HUG	61083	W Yorkshire
H801GRE	60043	Potteries	J705AWF	60547	S Yorkshire	K605LAE	30220	Manchester
H802GRE	60044	Potteries	J709ONF	30348	Glasgow	K606HUG	61084	W Yorkshire
H805GRE	60047	Potteries	J710ONF	30349	Glasgow	K606LAE	34606	W Yorkshire
H806GRE	60048	Potteries	J732KBC	21032	Somerset &A	K607HUG	61085	W Yorkshire
H807GRE	60049	Potteries	J794AWF	60542	S Yorkshire	K607LAE	34607	W Yorkshire
H807TWX	31084	Potteries	J864WSC	21064	Somerset &A	K608HUG	61086	W Yorkshire
H861GRE	60095	S Yorkshire	JDZ2307	45307	Hampshire	K608LAE	34608	W Yorkshire
HVJ716	34197	Devon & C	JDZ2389	45389	Hampshire	K609HUG	61087	W Yorkshire
HWU885Y	20085	Devon & C	JHU902X	34502	Hampshire	K609LAE	34609	W Yorkshire
HX05BUJ	68553	Hampshire	JHU909X	34509	Hampshire	K610HUG	61088	W Yorkshire
HX05BUO	68550	Hampshire	JIL7904	20094	Devon & C	K610LAE	34610	W Yorkshire
HX55AOH	68562	Hampshire	JJD442D	39442	Bristol	K611HUG	61089	W Yorkshire
HX55AOJ	68561	Hampshire	JJD480D	39480	Eastern C	K611LAE	34611	W Yorkshire
HX55AOK	68563	Hampshire	K101HUM	60768	W Yorkshire	K612HUG	61090	W Yorkshire
HY07FSU	37164	Hampshire	K102HUM	60769	W Yorkshire	K612LAE	34612	W Yorkshire
HY07FSV	37162	Hampshire	K103HUM	60770	W Yorkshire	K613HUG	61091	W Yorkshire
HY07FSX	37165	Hampshire	K106HUM	60773	W Yorkshire	K613LAE	34613	W Yorkshire
HY07FSZ	37163	Hampshire	K107HUM	60774	W Yorkshire	K614HUG	61092	W Yorkshire
HY07FTA	37161	Hampshire	K108HUM	60775	W Yorkshire	K614LAE	34614	W Yorkshire
J11GRT	20013	Aberdeen	K109HUM	60776	W Yorkshire	K615HUG	61093	W Yorkshire
J129YRM	30730	W Yorkshire	K110HUM	60777	W Yorkshire	K615LAE	34615	W Yorkshire
J130YRM	30731	W Yorkshire	K112HUM	60779	W Yorkshire	K616HUG	61094	W Yorkshire
J131YRM	34331	London	K113HUM	60780	W Yorkshire	K616LAE	34616	W Yorkshire
J135PVC	34346	London	K114HUM	60781	W Yorkshire	K617HUG	61095	W Yorkshire
J135YRM	34335	Hampshire	K114PRV	66651	W Yorkshire	K617LAE	34617	W Yorkshire
J136YRM	30714	W Yorkshire	K116HUM	60783	W Yorkshire	K618HUG	61096	W Yorkshire
J138YRM	30716	W Yorkshire	K117HUM	60784	W Yorkshire	K618LAE	34618	W Yorkshire
J139YRM	30717	W Yorkshire	K118HUM	60785	W Yorkshire	K619HUG	61097	W Yorkshire
J140YRM	30718	W Yorkshire	K119HUM	60786	W Yorkshire	K619LAE	34619	W Yorkshire
J141YRM	30709	W Yorkshire	K120HUM	60787	W Yorkshire	K620HUG	61098	W Yorkshire
J142YRM	30710	W Yorkshire	K121URP	38121	Leicester	K620LAE	34620	W Yorkshire
J144YRM	30712	W Yorkshire	K123URP	38123	Midland Red	K621HUG	61099	W Yorkshire
J145YRM	30713	W Yorkshire	K124URP	38124	Midland Red	K621LAE	34621	W Yorkshire
J146YRM	30719	W Yorkshire	K125URP	38125	Midland Red	K622HUG	61100	W Yorkshire
J148YRM	30720	W Yorkshire	K126URP	38126	Midland Red	K622LAE	34622	Bristol
J149YRM	34349	Wales	K129GNH	38129	Glasgow	K623HUG	61101	W Yorkshire
J150YRM	34350	Wales	K130GNH	38130	Glasgow	K623LAE	34623	Bristol
J151YRM	34351	Wales	K132GNH	38132	Glasgow	K624LAE	34624	Bristol
J155YRM	30235	Eastern C	K174EUX	30107	Glasgow	K625HUG	61103	W Yorkshire
J247YRM	30715	W Yorkshire	K1GRT	10046	Aberdeen	K625LAE	34625	Bristol
J295GNV	38095	Edinburgh	K1YRL	32431	W Yorkshire	K626HUG	61104	W Yorkshire
J296GNV	38096	Edinburgh	K211HUM	60778	W Yorkshire	K626LAE	34626	Bristol
J297GNV	38097	Midland Red	K279XJB	46079	Somerset &A	K627HUG	61105	W Yorkshire
J298GNV	38098	Leicester	K281XJB	46081	Eastern C	K627LAE	34627	Bristol
J299GNV	38099	Leicester	K283XJB	46083	Eastern C	K628HUG	61106	W Yorkshire
J302ASH	62272	Edinburgh	K350SDS	31727	Edinburgh	K628LAE	34628	Bristol
J303ASH	62273	Edinburgh	K401EDT	40449	S Yorkshire	K629HUG	61107	W Yorkshire
J304ASH	62274	Edinburgh	K402HRS	50411	Aberdeen	K629LAE	34629	Bristol
J422NCP	60021	Potteries	K480EUX	30106	Eastern C	K62KEX	46062	Eastern C
J424NCP	60023	Potteries	K481EUX	30097	Eastern C	K630HUG	61108	W Yorkshire
J425NCP	60024	Potteries	K482EUX	30098	Eastern C	K630LAE	34630	Bristol
J426NCP	60025	Potteries	K483EUX	30099	Eastern C	K631HUG	61109	W Yorkshire
J622BVG	34972	Eastern C	K484EUX	30100	Eastern C	K632HUG	61110	W Yorkshire
J623BVG	34973	Eastern C	K485EUX	30101	Eastern C	K633HUG	61111	W Yorkshire
J689XAK	60531	S Yorkshire	K486EUX	30102	Eastern C	K634HUG	61112	W Yorkshire
J690XAK	60532	S Yorkshire	K487EUX	30103	Eastern C	K706EDT	60548	S Yorkshire
J691AWF	60533	S Yorkshire	K488EUX	30104	Eastern C	K707EDT	60549	S Yorkshire
J692AWF	60534	S Yorkshire	K489EUX	30105	Eastern C	K708EDT	60550	Glasgow

Reg	Fleet	Location	Reg	Fleet	Location	Reg	Fleet	Location
K709EDT	60551	Glasgow	KP51WDD	32098	Leicester	KX05MJF	66965	Leicester
K710EDT	60552	Glasgow	KP51WDE	32099	Leicester	KX05MJJ	66966	Leicester
K711EDT	61347	Glasgow	KP51WDF	32277	Leicester	KX05MJK	66967	Leicester
K712EDT	61268	Glasgow	KP54AZA	32639	Leicester	KX05MJO	66968	Leicester
K713EDT	61269	Glasgow	KP54AZB	32640	Leicester	KX05MJU	66969	Leicester
K714EDT	61270	Glasgow	KP54AZC	32641	Leicester	KX05MJV	66970	Leicester
K715EDT	61271	Glasgow	KP54AZD	32642	Leicester	KX05MJY	66971	Leicester
K736JAH	67036	Essex	KP54AZF	32643	Leicester	KX06APV	53071	Leicester
K737JAH	67037	Essex	KP54AZG	32644	Leicester	KX06APY	53072	Leicester
K738JAH	67038	Essex	KP54AZJ	32645	Leicester	KX06APZ	53073	Leicester
K739JAH	67039	W Yorkshire	KP54AZL	32646	Leicester	KX54AHP	68507	Leicester
K740JAH	67040	Essex	KP54AZN	32647	Leicester	KX54AHU	68508	Leicester
K751VFJ	50951	Hampshire	KP54AZU	68520	Midland Red	KX54AHY	68509	Leicester
K801ORL	34001	Devon & C	KP54AZV	68521	Essex	KX54ANR	68510	Leicester
K802ORL	34002	Devon & C	KP54KAO	32627	Leicester	L103WYS	48013	Eastern C
K803ORL	34003	Devon & C	KP54KAU	32628	Leicester	L121PWR	60788	W Yorkshire
K804ORL	34004	Devon & C	KP54KAX	32629	Leicester	L122TFB	67122	Somerset &A
K888BFG	30226	Manchester	KP54KBE	32630	Leicester	L123PWR	60790	W Yorkshire
K888BWU	30227	Manchester	KP54KBF	32631	Leicester	L123TFB	67123	Somerset &A
K888ELR	30222	Manchester	KP54KBJ	32632	Leicester	L124PWR	60791	W Yorkshire
K888LAD	30224	Manchester	KP54KBK	32648	Leicester	L124TFB	67124	Somerset &A
K888PFD	30225	Manchester	KP54KBN	32649	Leicester	L125PWR	60792	W Yorkshire
K888TKS	30228	Manchester	KP54KBO	32650	Leicester	L125TFB	67125	Somerset &A
K888TTT	30221	Manchester	KP54LAE	32633	Leicester	L126TFB	67126	Somerset &A
K888TWY	30223	Manchester	KP54LAO	32634	Leicester	L127PWR	60794	W Yorkshire
K908CVW	46108	Essex	KU52 RXJ	43810	Devon & C	L127TFB	67127	Somerset &A
K909CVW	46109	Essex	KV02VVD	66302	Leicester	L128PWR	60795	W Yorkshire
K910CVW	46110	Essex	KV02VVE	66303	Leicester	L128TFB	67128	Somerset &A
K913CVW	46113	Essex	KV02VVF	66304	Leicester	L129PWR	60796	W Yorkshire
K915CVW	46115	Somerset &A	KV02VVG	66305	Leicester	L129TFB	67129	Somerset &A
K917CVW	46117	Somerset &A	KV02VVH	66306	Leicester	L130PWR	60797	W Yorkshire
K919XRF	40086	Midland Red	KV02VVJ	66307	Leicester	L130TFB	67130	Somerset &A
K947JWE	40507	S Yorkshire	KV02VVK	66308	Leicester	L132TFB	67132	Somerset &A
KDZ5108	45408	Hampshire	KV02VVL	66309	Leicester	L133TFB	67133	Somerset &A
KIB6110	40504	S Yorkshire	KV02VVM	66310	Leicester	L134TFB	67134	Somerset &A
KP51VZO	32066	Leicester	KV02VVN	66311	Leicester	L135TFB	67135	Somerset &A
KP51VZR	32067	Leicester	KV02VVO	66312	Leicester	L136TFB	67136	Somerset &A
KP51VZS	32068	Leicester	KV02VVP	66313	Leicester	L14BMS	21014	Wales
KP51VZT	32069	Leicester	KV02VVR	66314	Leicester	L156UNS	31732	Edinburgh
KP51VZW	32070	Leicester	KV02VVS	66315	Leicester	L157UNS	31733	Edinburgh
KP51VZX	32071	Leicester	KV02VVT	66316	Leicester	L158UNS	31734	Edinburgh
KP51VZY	32072	Leicester	KV02VVU	66317	Leicester	L159UNS	31735	Edinburgh
KP51VZZ	32073	Leicester	KV02VVW	66318	Leicester	L160UNS	31373	Essex
KP51WAJ	32074	Leicester	KV02VVX	66319	Leicester	L161UNS	31374	Essex
KP51WAO	32075	Leicester	KV02VVY	66320	Leicester	L162UNS	31375	Essex
KP51WAU	32076	Leicester	KV02VVZ	66321	Leicester	L163UNS	31198	Essex
KP51WBD	32077	Leicester	KV02VWB	66323	Leicester	L164UNS	31376	Essex
KP51WBG	32078	Leicester	KX05AOC	66972	Leicester	L165UNS	31377	Essex
KP51WBJ	32079	Leicester	KX05AOD	66973	Leicester	L168UNS	31380	Midland Red
KP51WBK	32080	Leicester	KX05AOE	66974	Leicester	L169UNS	31381	Glasgow
KP51WBL	32081	Leicester	KX05MGV	32635	Leicester	L170UNS	31382	Glasgow
KP51WBO	32082	Leicester	KX05MGY	66975	Leicester	L171UNS	31383	Glasgow
KP51WBT	32083	Leicester	KX05MGZ	66976	Leicester	L172UNS	31384	Glasgow
KP51WBU	32084	Leicester	KX05MHA	66977	Leicester	L173UNS	31385	Glasgow
KP51WBV	32085	Leicester	KX05MHE	66978	Leicester	L174UNS	31386	Glasgow
KP51WBY	32086	Leicester	KX05MHF	66979	Leicester	L180UNS	31392	Glasgow
KP51WBZ	32087	Leicester	KX05MHJ	66980	Leicester	L181UNS	31393	Glasgow
KP51WCA	32088	Leicester	KX05MHK	66981	Leicester	L182UNS	31394	Glasgow
KP51WCF	32089	Leicester	KX05MHL	66982	Leicester	L183UNS	31395	Glasgow
KP51WCG	32090	Leicester	KX05MHM	66983	Leicester	L184UNS	31396	Glasgow
KP51WCJ	32091	Leicester	KX05MHN	66984	Leicester	L185UNS	31397	Glasgow
KP51WCN	32092	Leicester	KX05MHO	66985	Leicester	L186UNS	31398	Glasgow
KP51WCO	32093	Leicester	KX05MHU	66986	Leicester	L187UNS	31399	Glasgow
KP51WCR	32094	Leicester	KX05MHV	66987	Leicester	L188UNS	31400	Glasgow
KP51WCW	32095	Leicester	KX05MHY	66962	Leicester	L189UNS	31401	Glasgow
KP51WCX	32096	Leicester	KX05MHZ	66963	Leicester	L190UNS	31402	Glasgow
KP51WCY	32097	Leicester	KX05MJE	66964	Leicester	L191UNS	31403	Glasgow

Reg	No	Location	Reg	No	Location	Reg	No	Location
L192UNS	31404	Glasgow	L28GAN	31152	W Yorkshire	L512KSA	60418	Manchester
L193UNS	31405	Glasgow	L301PWR	34301	Essex	L513HCY	46513	Wales
L194UNS	31406	Glasgow	L301VSU	61360	Manchester	L513KSA	60419	Manchester
L195UNS	31407	Glasgow	L302PWR	34302	Essex	L514HCY	46514	Wales
L196UNS	31408	Glasgow	L302VSU	61361	Manchester	L514KSA	60420	Manchester
L198UNS	31410	Glasgow	L303PWR	34303	Essex	L515HCY	46515	Wales
L199UNS	31411	Glasgow	L303VSU	61362	Manchester	L517HCY	46517	Wales
L201AAB	67201	Midland Red	L304PWR	34304	Essex	L518HCY	46518	Wales
L201KFS	61348	Eastern C	L304VSU	61363	W Yorkshire	L519HCY	46519	Wales
L201UNS	31412	Glasgow	L305PWR	34305	Essex	L521HCY	46521	Wales
L202AAB	67202	Midland Red	L305VSU	61364	W Yorkshire	L522HCY	46522	Wales
L202KFS	61349	Eastern C	L306PWR	30737	W Yorkshire	L525JEP	46525	Wales
L202UNS	31413	Glasgow	L306VSU	61365	Manchester	L526JEP	46526	Wales
L203AAB	67203	Leicester	L307PWR	34307	Essex	L527JEP	46527	Wales
L203KSX	61350	Manchester	L307VSU	61366	Manchester	L528JEP	46528	Wales
L203SHW	46203	Wales	L308PWR	34308	Essex	L529JEP	46529	Wales
L204AAB	67204	Leicester	L308VSU	61367	Eastern C	L530JEP	46530	Wales
L204KSX	61351	Manchester	L309PWR	34309	Essex	L531JEP	46531	Wales
L204SHW	46204	Somerset &A	L309RTP	46309	Hampshire	L532JEP	46532	Wales
L205AAB	67205	Midland Red	L309VSU	61368	Eastern C	L533JEP	46533	Wales
L205GMO	46195	Somerset &A	L310PWR	34310	Essex	L534JEP	46534	Wales
L206AAB	67206	Midland Red	L310RTP	46310	Hampshire	L535JEP	46535	Wales
L206KSX	61353	Manchester	L310VSU	61369	Manchester	L536JEP	46536	Wales
L206SHW	46206	Somerset &A	L311PWR	34311	Essex	L537JEP	46537	Wales
L207AAB	67207	Midland Red	L311RTP	46311	Hampshire	L538JEP	46538	Wales
L207KSX	61354	Manchester	L312PWR	30738	W Yorkshire	L539JEP	46539	Wales
L208AAB	67208	Midland Red	L312RTP	46312	Hampshire	L542JEP	46542	Wales
L209AAB	67209	Midland Red	L313PWR	30739	W Yorkshire	L545JEP	46545	Wales
L209KSX	61356	Manchester	L313RTP	46313	Hampshire	L546JEP	46546	Wales
L209SHW	46209	Wales	L314PWR	34314	Essex	L547JEP	46547	Wales
L210AAB	67210	Leicester	L315PWR	34315	Essex	L549JEP	46549	Wales
L210KSX	61357	Eastern C	L322AAB	67222	Bristol	L550JEP	46550	Wales
L211AAB	67211	Midland Red	L329MYC	51129	Somerset &A	L551USU	31728	Edinburgh
L211KSX	61358	Eastern C	L330MYC	51130	Hampshire	L552HMS	62317	Edinburgh
L211VHU	46211	Somerset &A	L401PWR	30754	W Yorkshire	L552USU	31729	Edinburgh
L212AAB	67212	Midland Red	L402PWR	30755	W Yorkshire	L553USU	31730	Edinburgh
L212KSX	61359	Manchester	L403PWR	30756	W Yorkshire	L554USU	31731	Edinburgh
L213AAB	67213	Midland Red	L404PWR	30757	W Yorkshire	L556LVT	50088	Hampshire
L214AAB	67214	Midland Red	L405PWR	30758	W Yorkshire	L557JLS	62322	Edinburgh
L215AAB	67215	Midland Red	L501HCY	46501	Wales	L559JLS	62324	Edinburgh
L215VHU	46215	Bristol	L501KSA	60407	Manchester	L562JLS	62328	Edinburgh
L216VHU	46216	Bristol	L501VHU	46601	Eastern C	L563JLS	62329	Edinburgh
L217AAB	67217	Midland Red	L502HCY	46502	Wales	L565JLS	62331	Edinburgh
L217VHU	46217	Bristol	L502KSA	60408	Manchester	L566JLS	62332	Edinburgh
L218AAB	67218	Leicester	L502VHU	46602	Eastern C	L601PWR	30781	W Yorkshire
L218VHU	46218	Somerset &A	L503KSA	60409	Manchester	L602FKG	46702	Wales
L219AAB	67219	Midland Red	L503VHU	46603	Somerset &A	L602PWR	30782	W Yorkshire
L219VHU	46219	Somerset &A	L504HCY	46504	Wales	L603PWR	30783	W Yorkshire
L220VHU	46220	Bristol	L504KSA	60410	Manchester	L604PWR	30784	W Yorkshire
L223AAB	67223	Somerset &A	L504VHU	46604	Bristol	L605FKG	46705	Wales
L223VHU	46223	Wales	L505HCY	46505	Wales	L605PWR	30785	W Yorkshire
L224AAB	67224	Somerset &A	L505KSA	60411	Manchester	L606FKG	46706	Wales
L225AAB	67225	Somerset &A	L505VHU	46605	Somerset &A	L607FKG	46707	Wales
L225VHU	46225	Somerset &A	L506HCY	46506	Wales	L60HMS	62326	Edinburgh
L227AAB	67227	Somerset &A	L506KSA	60412	Manchester	L623XFP	67623	Leicester
L228AAB	67228	Somerset &A	L506VHU	46606	Bristol	L631SEU	34131	Bristol
L229AAB	61254	Bristol	L507HCY	46507	Wales	L632SEU	34132	Bristol
L231AAB	67231	Midland Red	L507KSA	60413	Manchester	L633SEU	34133	Bristol
L232AAB	67232	Midland Red	L507VHU	46607	Bristol	L634SEU	34134	Bristol
L233AAB	67233	Leicester	L508KSA	60414	Manchester	L635SEU	34135	Bristol
L234AAB	67234	Midland Red	L508VHU	46608	Bristol	L636PWR	61114	W Yorkshire
L235AAB	67235	Midland Red	L509HCY	46509	Wales	L636SEU	34136	Bristol
L237AAB	67237	Midland Red	L509KSA	60415	Manchester	L637PWR	61115	W Yorkshire
L24GAN	31150	W Yorkshire	L510HCY	46510	Wales	L637SEU	34137	Bristol
L25GAN	30735	W Yorkshire	L510KSA	60416	Manchester	L638PWR	61116	W Yorkshire
L26GAN	30736	W Yorkshire	L511HCY	46511	Wales	L638SEU	34138	Bristol
L27GAN	31151	W Yorkshire	L511KSA	60417	Manchester	L639PWR	61117	W Yorkshire

The 2008 First Bus Handbook

Reg	No.	Location	Reg	No.	Location	Reg	No.	Location
L639SEU	34139	Bristol	L831YGA	31418	Glasgow	LK03NJY	32325	London
L640PWR	61118	W Yorkshire	L832YGA	31419	Glasgow	LK03NJZ	32326	London
L640SEU	34140	Bristol	L833YGA	31420	Glasgow	LK03NKA	32327	London
L641PWR	61119	W Yorkshire	L879VHT	51079	Somerset &A	LK03NKC	33277	London
L641SEU	34141	Bristol	L883VHT	51083	Somerset &A	LK03NKD	33278	London
L642PWR	61120	W Yorkshire	L886VHT	51086	Somerset &A	LK03NKE	33279	London
L642SEU	34142	Bristol	L888TTT	30752	W Yorkshire	LK03NKF	33280	London
L643PWR	61121	W Yorkshire	L888YTT	30753	W Yorkshire	LK03NKG	33281	London
L643SEU	34143	Bristol	L891VHT	51091	Somerset &A	LK03NKH	42515	London
L644PWR	61122	W Yorkshire	L896VHT	51096	Somerset &A	LK03NKJ	42516	London
L644SEU	34144	Bristol	L897VHT	51097	Somerset &A	LK03NKL	42517	London
L645PWR	61123	W Yorkshire	L8BMS	21008	Wales	LK03NKM	42518	London
L645SEU	34145	Bristol	L901VHT	51101	Somerset &A	LK03NKN	42519	London
L646PWR	61124	W Yorkshire	L902VHT	51102	Somerset &A	LK03NKP	33282	London
L646SEU	34146	Bristol	L903VHT	51103	Somerset &A	LK03NKR	33283	London
L647PWR	61125	W Yorkshire	L904VHT	51104	Somerset &A	LK03NKS	33284	London
L647SEU	34147	Bristol	L907VHT	51107	Somerset &A	LK03NKT	33285	London
L648PWR	61126	W Yorkshire	L934HFA	40100	Potteries	LK03NKU	33286	London
L648SEU	34148	Bristol	L971NET	40512	S Yorkshire	LK03NKW	33287	London
L649PWR	61127	W Yorkshire	LDZ9124	45424	Hampshire	LK03NKX	33288	London
L649SEU	34149	Somerset &A	LK03LLX	41493	London	LK03NKZ	33289	London
L64UOU	61212	Somerset &A	LK03LLZ	41494	London	LK03NLA	33290	London
L650PWR	61128	W Yorkshire	LK03LME	41495	London	LK03NLC	33291	London
L650SEU	39920	Somerset &A	LK03LMF	41496	London	LK03NLD	41502	London
L651CJT	51211	Somerset &A	LK03LMJ	41492	London	LK03NLE	41503	London
L651PWR	61129	W Yorkshire	LK03LNE	64018	Berkshire	LK03NLF	41504	London
L651SEU	34151	Somerset &A	LK03LNF	64019	Berkshire	LK03NLG	41505	London
L652CJT	51212	Somerset &A	LK03LNU	41497	London	LK03NLJ	41506	London
L652PWR	61130	W Yorkshire	LK03LNV	41499	London	LK03NLL	41507	London
L652SEU	34152	Somerset &A	LK03LNW	41500	London	LK03NLM	41508	London
L653PWR	61131	W Yorkshire	LK03LNX	41501	London	LK03NLN	41498	London
L653SEU	34153	Somerset &A	LK03NFY	41510	London	LK03NLP	33292	London
L654PWR	61132	W Yorkshire	LK03NFZ	41511	London	LK03NLR	33293	London
L654SEU	34154	Somerset &A	LK03NGE	41512	London	LK03NLT	41509	London
L655PWR	61133	W Yorkshire	LK03NGF	41513	London	LK03UEX	41520	London
L67EPR	51167	Somerset &A	LK03NGG	41514	London	LK03UEY	41521	London
L68EPR	51168	Somerset &A	LK03NGJ	32294	London	LK03UEZ	41522	London
L6BMS	21006	Wales	LK03NGN	32295	London	LK03UFA	41523	London
L725 WCV	51125	Devon & C	LK03NGU	32296	London	LK03UFB	41524	London
L726 WCV	51126	Devon & C	LK03NGV	32297	London	LK03UFC	41525	London
L801SAE	51001	Somerset &A	LK03NGX	32298	London	LK03UFD	33328	London
L803OPU	46803	Essex	LK03NGY	32299	London	LK03UFE	33329	London
L804OPU	46804	Essex	LK03NGZ	32300	London	LK03UFG	33330	London
L807OPU	46807	Eastern C	LK03NHA	32301	London	LK03UFJ	33331	London
L808OPU	46808	Essex	LK03NHB	32302	London	LK03UFL	33332	London
L811OPU	46811	Essex	LK03NHC	32303	London	LK03UFM	33333	London
L812OPU	46812	Essex	LK03NHD	32304	London	LK03UFN	33334	London
L813OPU	46813	Essex	LK03NHE	32305	London	LK03UFP	33335	London
L814OPU	46814	Essex	LK03NHF	32306	London	LK03UFR	33336	London
L815CFJ	34115	Devon & C	LK03NHG	32307	London	LK03UFS	33337	London
L815OPU	46815	Essex	LK03NHH	32308	London	LK03UFT	33338	London
L816CFJ	34116	Devon & C	LK03NHJ	32309	London	LK03UFU	33339	London
L816OPU	46816	Essex	LK03NHL	32310	London	LK03UFV	33340	London
L817CFJ	34117	Devon & C	LK03NHM	32311	London	LK03UFW	33341	London
L817HCY	67117	Leicester	LK03NHN	32312	London	LK03UFX	33342	London
L817OPU	46817	Essex	LK03NHP	32313	London	LK04HXA	32392	London
L818OPU	46818	Essex	LK03NHT	32314	London	LK04HXB	32393	London
L820OPU	46820	Essex	LK03NHV	32315	London	LK04HXC	32394	London
L821OPU	46821	Essex	LK03NHX	32316	London	LK04HXD	32395	London
L822HCY	67112	Leicester	LK03NHY	32317	London	LK04HXE	32396	London
L822OPU	46822	Essex	LK03NHZ	32318	London	LK04HXH	32399	London
L825SAE	51025	Wales	LK03NJE	32319	London	LK04HXJ	32400	London
L827YGA	31414	Glasgow	LK03NJF	32320	London	LK04HXL	32401	London
L828WHY	51028	Wales	LK03NJJ	32321	London	LK04HXM	32402	London
L828YGA	31415	Glasgow	LK03NJN	32322	London	LK04HXN	32403	London
L829YGA	31416	Glasgow	LK03NJV	32323	London	LK04HXP	32404	London
L830YGA	31417	Glasgow	LK03NJX	32324	London	LK04HXR	32405	London

Reg	No	Area	Reg	No	Area	Reg	No	Area
LK04HXS	32406	London	LK05FBY	11057	London	LK51UYN	33031	London
LK04HXT	32407	London	LK05FBZ	11062	London	LK51UYO	33032	London
LK04HXU	32408	London	LK05FCA	11063	London	LK51UYP	33033	London
LK04HXV	32409	London	LK05FCC	11065	London	LK51UYR	33034	London
LK04HXW	32410	London	LK05FCD	11064	London	LK51UYS	33015	London
LK04HXX	32411	London	LK05FCE	68554	Hampshire	LK51UYT	33016	London
LK04HYA	32367	London	LK05FCM	11051	London	LK51UYU	33017	London
LK04HYB	32424	London	LK05FCN	11052	London	LK51UYV	33018	London
LK04HYC	32425	London	LK05FCO	11053	London	LK51UYW	33019	London
LK04HYF	32426	London	LK05FCP	11054	London	LK51UYX	33020	London
LK04HYG	32427	London	LK05FCU	11055	London	LK51UYY	33021	London
LK04HYH	32428	London	LK05FCV	11056	London	LK51UYZ	33022	London
LK04HYJ	32429	London	LK05FCX	11058	London	LK51UZA	33023	London
LK04HYL	32430	London	LK05FCY	11059	London	LK51UZB	33024	London
LK04HYM	32362	London	LK05FCZ	11060	London	LK51UZD	33006	London
LK04HYN	32361	London	LK05FDA	11061	London	LK51UZE	33007	London
LK04HYP	32360	London	LK05FDC	11041	London	LK51UZF	33008	London
LK04HYS	32368	London	LK05FDD	11042	London	LK51UZG	33009	London
LK04HYT	32364	London	LK05FDE	11043	London	LK51UZH	33010	London
LK04HYU	32369	London	LK05FDF	11044	London	LK51UZJ	33011	London
LK04HYV	32370	London	LK05FDG	11046	London	LK51UZL	33012	London
LK04HYW	32363	London	LK05FDJ	11045	London	LK51UZM	33013	London
LK04HYX	32365	London	LK05FDL	11047	London	LK51UZN	33014	London
LK04HYY	32366	London	LK06BWB	43919	Berkshire	LK51UZO	33001	London
LK04HYZ	32422	London	LK06BWC	43920	Berkshire	LK51UZP	33002	London
LK04HZA	32371	London	LK06BWD	43921	Berkshire	LK51UZS	33003	London
LK04HZB	32372	London	LK07CBF	43928	Berkshire	LK51UZT	33004	London
LK04HZC	32373	London	LK07CBO	43929	Berkshire	LK53EXT	33355	London
LK04HZD	32374	London	LK07CBU	43930	Berkshire	LK53EXU	33356	London
LK04HZE	32375	London	LK07CBV	43931	Berkshire	LK53EXV	33357	London
LK04HZF	32376	London	LK07CBX	43932	Berkshire	LK53EXW	33358	London
LK04HZG	32377	London	LK07CCA	64030	Berkshire	LK53EXX	33359	London
LK04HZH	32378	London	LK07CCD	64031	Berkshire	LK53EXZ	33360	London
LK04HZJ	32379	London	LK07CCE	64032	Berkshire	LK53EYA	33361	London
LK04HZL	32380	London	LK07CCF	64033	Berkshire	LK53EYB	33362	London
LK04HZM	32381	London	LK07CCJ	64034	Berkshire	LK53EYC	33363	London
LK04HZN	32382	London	LK07CCN	64035	Berkshire	LK53EYD	33364	London
LK04HZP	32413	London	LK07CCO	64036	Berkshire	LK53EYF	33365	London
LK04HZS	32384	London	LK07CCU	64037	Berkshire	LK53EYG	33366	London
LK04HZT	32385	London	LK07CCV	64038	Berkshire	LK53EYH	33367	London
LK04HZU	32386	London	LK07CCX	64039	Berkshire	LK53EYJ	33368	London
LK04HZV	32387	London	LK07CDE	20611	Berkshire	LK53EYL	33369	London
LK04HZW	32388	London	LK07CDF	20612	Berkshire	LK53EYM	33370	London
LK04HZX	32389	London	LK07CDN	20613	Berkshire	LK53EYO	33371	London
LK04HZY	32390	London	LK08FNL	64042	Berkshire	LK53EYP	33372	London
LK04HZZ	32391	London	LK08FNE	33503	London	LK53EYR	33373	London
LK04JBE	32412	London	LK08LMA	33509	London	LK53EYT	33374	London
LK04JBU	32383	London	LK08LMO	33510	London	LK53EYU	33375	London
LK04JBV	32414	London	LK08LMP	33511	London	LK53EYV	33376	London
LK04JBX	32415	London	LK08LMU	33512	London	LK53EYW	33377	London
LK04JBY	32416	London	LK08LMV	33513	London	LK53EYX	33378	London
LK04JBZ	32417	London	LK08LMX	33514	London	LK53EYY	33379	London
LK04JCJ	32418	London	LK08LMY	33515	London	LK53EYZ	33380	London
LK04JCU	32419	London	LK08LMZ	33516	London	LK53EZA	33381	London
LK04JCV	32420	London	LK08LNA	33517	London	LK53EZB	33382	London
LK04JCX	32421	London	LK08LNC	33518	London	LK53EZC	33383	London
LK04JCZ	32423	London	LK08LND	33519	London	LK53EZD	33384	London
LK05DXP	53702	London	LK51JYO	41414	London	LK53EZE	33385	London
LK05DXR	53703	London	LK51UYD	33035	London	LK53EZF	33386	London
LK05DXS	53704	London	LK51UYE	33036	London	LK53EZV	33343	London
LK05DXT	53705	London	LK51UYF	33025	London	LK53EZW	33344	London
LK05DXU	53706	London	LK51UYG	33026	London	LK53EZX	33345	London
LK05DYO	53701	London	LK51UYH	33027	London	LK53EZZ	33346	London
LK05EZW	11048	London	LK51UYJ	33028	London	LK53FAA	11001	London
LK05EZX	11049	London	LK51UYL	33029	London	LK53FAF	11002	London
LK05EZZ	11050	London	LK51UYM	33030	London	LK53FAJ	11003	London

LK53FAM	11004	London	LK53LYZ	32339	London	LK55ADV	43914	Berkshire
LK53FAO	11005	London	LK53LZA	32340	London	LK55ADX	43915	Berkshire
LK53FAU	11006	London	LK53LZB	32341	London	LK55ADZ	43916	Berkshire
LK53FBA	11007	London	LK53LZC	32342	London	LK55AEA	43917	Berkshire
LK53FBB	11008	London	LK53LZD	32343	London	LK56JKE	43922	Berkshire
LK53FBC	11009	London	LK53LZE	32344	London	LK56JKF	43923	Berkshire
LK53FBD	11010	London	LK53LZF	32345	London	LK56JKJ	43924	Berkshire
LK53FBE	11011	London	LK53LZG	32346	London	LK56JKN	43925	Berkshire
LK53FBF	11012	London	LK53LZH	32347	London	LK56JKO	43926	Berkshire
LK53FBG	11013	London	LK53LZL	32348	London	LK56JKV	43927	Berkshire
LK53FBJ	11014	London	LK53LZM	32349	London	LK57EJD	44001	London
LK53FBL	11015	London	LK53LZN	32350	London	LK57EJE	44002	London
LK53FBN	11016	London	LK53LZO	32351	London	LK57EJF	44003	London
LK53FBO	11017	London	LK53LZP	32352	London	LK57EJG	44004	London
LK53FBU	11018	London	LK53LZR	32353	London	LK57EJJ	44005	London
LK53FBV	11019	London	LK53LZT	32354	London	LK57EJL	44006	London
LK53FBX	11020	London	LK53LZU	32355	London	LK57EJN	33501	London
LK53FBY	11021	London	LK53LZV	32356	London	LK57EJO	33502	London
LK53FBZ	11022	London	LK53LZW	32357	London	LN51DUA	41444	London
LK53FCA	11023	London	LK53LZX	32358	London	LN51DUH	41445	London
LK53FCC	11024	London	LK53MBF	32359	London	LN51DUJ	41446	London
LK53FCD	11025	London	LK53MBX	53052	Berkshire	LN51DUU	41447	London
LK53FCE	11026	London	LK53MBY	53053	Berkshire	LN51DUV	41448	London
LK53FCF	33347	London	LK53MDE	53054	Berkshire	LN51DUY	41449	London
LK53FCG	33348	London	LK53MDF	53055	Berkshire	LN51DVG	33043	London
LK53FCJ	33349	London	LK53MDJ	53056	Berkshire	LN51DVH	33044	London
LK53FCL	33350	London	LK53PNO	53057	Berkshire	LN51DVK	33045	London
LK53FCM	11027	London	LK54FKW	11039	London	LN51DVL	33046	London
LK53FCN	11028	London	LK54FKX	11040	London	LN51DVM	33047	London
LK53FCO	11029	London	LK54FLA	32495	London	LN51DVO	41439	London
LK53FCP	11030	London	LK54FLB	32496	London	LN51DVP	41440	London
LK53FCU	11031	London	LK54FLC	32497	London	LN51DVR	41441	London
LK53FCV	11032	London	LK54FLD	32498	London	LN51DVT	41442	London
LK53FCX	33351	London	LK54FLE	32499	London	LN51DVV	41443	London
LK53FCY	33352	London	LK54FLF	32500	London	LN51DVW	41435	London
LK53FCZ	33353	London	LK54FLG	32501	London	LN51DVX	41436	London
LK53FDA	33354	London	LK54FLH	32502	London	LN51DVY	41437	London
LK53FDC	41526	London	LK54FNC	68531	Berkshire	LN51DVZ	41438	London
LK53FDD	41527	London	LK54FNE	68532	Essex	LN51DWA	33037	London
LK53FDE	41528	London	LK54FNF	68536	Hampshire	LN51DWD	33039	London
LK53FDF	41529	London	LK54FNH	68537	Hampshire	LN51DWE	33040	London
LK53FDG	41530	London	LK54FNJ	68533	Hampshire	LN51DWF	33041	London
LK53FDJ	41531	London	LK54FNL	68534	Essex	LN51DWG	33042	London
LK53FDM	41532	London	LK54FNO	32397	London	LN51DWJ	41425	London
LK53FDN	41533	London	LK54FNP	32398	London	LN51DWK	41426	London
LK53FDO	41534	London	LK55AAE	32659	London	LN51DWL	41427	London
LK53FDP	41535	London	LK55AAF	32660	London	LN51DWM	41428	London
LK53FDU	41536	London	LK55AAJ	32661	London	LN51DWO	41429	London
LK53FDV	41537	London	LK55AAN	32662	London	LN51DWP	41430	London
LK53FDX	41538	London	LK55AAU	32663	London	LN51DWU	41431	London
LK53FDY	41539	London	LK55AAV	32664	London	LN51DWW	41433	London
LK53FDZ	41540	London	LK55AAX	32665	London	LN51DWX	41434	London
LK53FEF	41541	London	LK55AAY	32666	London	LN51DWY	41415	London
LK53FEG	41542	London	LK55AAZ	32667	London	LN51DWZ	41416	London
LK53FEH	41543	London	LK55ABF	32668	London	LN51DXA	41417	London
LK53FEJ	41544	London	LK55ABU	68558	London	LN51DXB	41418	London
LK53LYH	32328	London	LK55ABV	68559	London	LN51DXC	41419	London
LK53LYJ	32329	London	LK55ABX	68560	London	LN51DXD	41420	London
LK53LYO	32330	London	LK55ABZ	65724	Berkshire	LN51DXE	41421	London
LK53LYP	32331	London	LK55ACF	65725	Berkshire	LN51DXF	41422	London
LK53LYR	32332	London	LK55ACJ	65726	Berkshire	LN51DXG	41423	London
LK53LYT	32333	London	LK55ACO	32657	London	LN51DXH	41424	London
LK53LYU	32334	London	LK55ACU	32658	London	LN51GJJ	33057	London
LK53LYV	32335	London	LK55ACV	43918	Berkshire	LN51GJK	33058	London
LK53LYW	32336	London	LK55ACX	43912	Berkshire	LN51GJO	33059	London
LK53LYX	32337	London	LK55ACY	43911	Berkshire	LN51GJU	33060	London
LK53LYY	32338	London	LK55ADU	43913	Berkshire	LN51GJV	41790	London

The 2008 First Bus Handbook

LN51GJX	41791	London	LR02LXO	33155	London	LT02NVZ	33117	London
LN51GJY	41792	London	LR02LXP	33156	London	LT02NWA	33118	London
LN51GJZ	41793	London	LR02LXS	33157	London	LT02NWB	33119	London
LN51GKA	33071	London	LR02LXT	33158	London	LT02NWC	33120	London
LN51GKD	33048	London	LR02LXU	33159	London	LT02NWD	33121	London
LN51GKE	33049	London	LR02LXV	33160	London	LT02ZBX	33131	London
LN51GKF	33050	London	LR02LXW	33161	London	LT02ZBY	33132	London
LN51GKG	33051	London	LR02LXX	33162	London	LT02ZBZ	33133	London
LN51GKJ	33052	London	LR02LXZ	33163	London	LT02ZCA	33134	London
LN51GKK	33053	London	LR02LYA	33164	London	LT02ZCE	33135	London
LN51GKL	33054	London	LR02LYC	33165	London	LT02ZCF	33136	London
LN51GKO	33055	London	LR02LYD	33166	London	LT02ZCJ	32100	London
LN51GKP	33056	London	LR02LYF	33167	London	LT02ZCK	32101	London
LN51GKU	33061	London	LR02LYG	33168	London	LT02ZCL	32102	London
LN51GKV	33062	London	LR02LYJ	33169	London	LT02ZCN	32103	London
LN51GKX	33063	London	LR02LYK	33170	London	LT02ZCO	32104	London
LN51GKY	33064	London	LR02LYO	33171	London	LT02ZCU	32105	London
LN51GKZ	33065	London	LR02LYP	33172	London	LT02ZCV	32106	London
LN51GLF	33066	London	LR02LYS	33173	London	LT02ZCX	32107	London
LN51GLJ	33067	London	LR02LYT	33174	London	LT02ZCY	32108	London
LN51GLK	33068	London	LR02LYU	33175	London	LT02ZDH	32109	London
LN51GLV	33069	London	LR02LYV	33176	London	LT02ZDJ	32110	London
LN51GLY	33070	London	LR02LYW	33177	London	LT02ZDK	32111	London
LN51GLZ	33099	London	LR02LYX	33178	London	LT02ZDL	32112	London
LN51GME	33084	London	LR02LYY	33179	London	LT02ZDY	41487	London
LN51GMF	33085	London	LR02LYZ	33180	London	LT02ZDZ	41488	London
LN51GMG	33086	London	LR02LZA	33181	London	LT02ZFA	41489	London
LN51GMO	33087	London	LR02LZB	33182	London	LT02ZFB	41490	London
LN51GMU	33088	London	LR02LZC	33183	London	LT02ZFC	41491	London
LN51GMV	33089	London	LR02LZD	33184	London	LT02ZFJ	33137	London
LN51GMX	33090	London	LR02LZE	33185	London	LT02ZFK	33138	London
LN51GMY	33091	London	LSK530	20027	Aberdeen	LT02ZFL	33139	London
LN51GMZ	33092	London	LSK570	20014	Aberdeen	LT02ZFM	33140	London
LN51GNF	33077	London	LSK571	20015	Aberdeen	LT52WTE	32200	London
LN51GNJ	33078	London	LSU717	38082	Leicester	LT52WTF	32201	London
LN51GNK	33079	London	LT02NTV	64001	London	LT52WTG	32202	London
LN51GNP	33080	London	LT02NTX	64002	London	LT52WTJ	32203	London
LN51GNU	33081	London	LT02NTY	64003	London	LT52WTK	32204	London
LN51GNV	33082	London	LT02NUA	64004	London	LT52WTL	32205	London
LN51GNX	33083	London	LT02NUB	64005	London	LT52WTM	32206	London
LN51GNY	33096	London	LT02NUC	64006	London	LT52WTN	32207	London
LN51GNZ	33097	London	LT02NUE	64007	London	LT52WTO	32208	London
LN51GOA	33098	London	LT02NUF	64008	London	LT52WTP	32209	London
LN51GOC	33072	London	LT02NUH	64009	London	LT52WTR	32210	London
LN51GOE	33073	London	LT02NUJ	64010	London	LT52WTU	32211	London
LN51GOH	33074	London	LT02NUK	41474	London	LT52WTV	32212	London
LN51GOJ	33075	London	LT02NUM	41475	London	LT52WTW	32213	London
LN51GOK	33076	London	LT02NUO	41476	London	LT52WTX	32214	London
LN51GOP	41794	London	LT02NUP	41477	London	LT52WTY	32215	London
LN51GOU	41795	London	LT02NUU	41478	London	LT52WTZ	32216	London
LN51NRJ	33093	London	LT02NUV	41479	London	LT52WUA	32217	London
LN51NRK	33094	London	LT02NVE	41480	London	LT52WUB	32218	London
LN51NRL	33095	London	LT02NVH	41483	London	LT52WUC	32219	London
LR02LWW	33141	London	LT02NVJ	41484	London	LT52WUD	32220	London
LR02LWX	33142	London	LT02NVK	33123	London	LT52WUE	32221	London
LR02LWY	33143	London	LT02NVL	33122	London	LT52WUG	32222	London
LR02LWZ	33144	London	LT02NVM	33124	London	LT52WUH	32223	London
LR02LXA	33145	London	LT02NVN	33125	London	LT52WUJ	32224	London
LR02LXB	33146	London	LT02NVO	33126	London	LT52WUK	32225	London
LR02LXC	33147	London	LT02NVP	33127	London	LT52WUL	32226	London
LR02LXG	33148	London	LT02NVR	33128	London	LT52WUM	41485	London
LR02LXH	33149	London	LT02NVS	33129	London	LT52WUO	41482	London
LR02LXJ	33150	London	LT02NVU	33116	London	LT52WUP	41481	London
LR02LXK	33151	London	LT02NVV	33115	London	LT52WUR	41486	London
LR02LXL	33152	London	LT02NVW	33114	London	LT52WUV	33244	London
LR02LXM	33153	London	LT02NVX	33113	London	LT52WUW	33245	London
LR02LXN	33154	London	LT02NVY	64011	London	LT52WUX	33246	London

Reg	No	Area	Reg	No	Area	Reg	No	Area
LT52WUY	33247	London	LV52VFY	11068	London	M248VWW	40620	Hampshire
LT52WVA	33248	London	LV52VFZ	11069	London	M249MRW	67249	Midland Red
LT52WVB	33186	London	M101RRJ	40245	Midland Red	M250MRW	67250	Midland Red
LT52WVC	33187	London	M106PKS	20009	Aberdeen	M250VWW	47250	Eastern C
LT52WVD	33188	London	M106RRJ	40250	Hampshire	M251MRW	67251	Midland Red
LT52WVE	33189	London	M109PWN	21109	Wales	M251VWW	47251	Eastern C
LT52WVF	33237	London	M110PWN	21110	Wales	M252MRW	67252	Leicester
LT52WVG	33238	London	M111PWN	21111	Wales	M253MRW	67253	Midland Red
LT52WVH	33239	London	M11AFC	20020	Aberdeen	M253VWU	50255	W Yorkshire
LT52WVJ	33240	London	M137FAE	67337	Somerset &A	M254MRW	67254	Midland Red
LT52WVL	33242	London	M138FAE	67338	Somerset &A	M254VWW	40623	Hampshire
LT52WVM	32249	London	M140FAE	67340	Somerset &A	M255MRW	67255	Midland Red
LT52WVN	32250	London	M141FAE	67341	Somerset &A	M255VWW	40624	W Yorkshire
LT52WVO	32251	London	M142FAE	67342	Somerset &A	M256MRW	67256	Midland Red
LT52WVP	32252	London	M14ABC	51214	Somerset &A	M257VWW	40626	W Yorkshire
LT52WVY	32253	London	M159LNC	50122	Hampshire	M258VWW	40627	Hampshire
LT52WVZ	32254	London	M1GRT	20019	Aberdeen	M259VWW	40628	Hampshire
LT52WWA	32255	London	M201VWW	47201	Eastern C	M260VWW	40629	Hampshire
LT52WWB	32256	London	M202VWW	47202	Eastern C	M263VWW	40632	W Yorkshire
LT52WWC	32257	London	M203VWW	47203	Eastern C	M264SGY	34264	Manchester
LT52WWD	32258	London	M204VWW	40600	W Yorkshire	M265VWW	40634	W Yorkshire
LT52WWE	32259	London	M206VWW	47206	Eastern C	M266VWW	40635	W Yorkshire
LT52WWF	32260	London	M207VWW	47207	Eastern C	M267VWW	40636	W Yorkshire
LT52WWG	32261	London	M208VWW	47208	Eastern C	M281UYD	51281	Hampshire
LT52WWH	32262	London	M209VWW	47209	Eastern C	M290FAE	21090	London
LT52WWJ	32263	London	M210VWW	40602	Eastern C	M301BRL	20441	Devon & C
LT52WWK	32264	London	M211VWW	40603	Eastern C	M302BRL	20442	Devon & C
LT52WWL	32265	London	M212VWW	40604	Glasgow	M303BRL	20443	Devon & C
LT52WWM	32266	London	M215VWW	47215	Eastern C	M305TSF	51305	Somerset &A
LT52WWN	32267	London	M217VWW	47217	Eastern C	M314YOT	46314	Hampshire
LT52WWO	32268	London	M218VWW	47218	Eastern C	M315YOT	46315	Hampshire
LT52WWP	32269	London	M219VWW	47219	Essex	M316YOT	46316	Hampshire
LT52WWR	32270	London	M220VWW	47220	Essex	M317YOT	46317	Hampshire
LT52WWS	32271	London	M221EAF	67301	Midland Red	M318YOT	46318	Hampshire
LT52WWU	32272	London	M221VWW	47221	Essex	M319YOT	46319	Hampshire
LT52WWV	33233	London	M223VWW	47223	Essex	M320YOT	46320	Hampshire
LT52WWX	33234	London	M224VWW	47224	Essex	M321YOT	46321	Hampshire
LT52WWY	33235	London	M225VWW	47225	Essex	M322YOT	46322	Hampshire
LT52WWZ	33236	London	M226VWW	47226	Essex	M323YOT	46323	Hampshire
LT52WXA	64012	Berkshire	M227VWW	47227	Essex	M375YEX	46375	Eastern C
LT52WXB	64013	Berkshire	M228VWU	51228	Wales	M379YEX	46379	Eastern C
LT52WXC	32273	London	M228VWW	47228	Essex	M382KVR	51382	Somerset &A
LT52WXD	32274	London	M229VWW	47229	Essex	M401RVU	34251	Manchester
LT52WXE	32275	London	M231VWW	47231	Eastern C	M401VWW	60939	W Yorkshire
LT52WXF	32276	London	M232VWU	50421	Aberdeen	M402RVU	34252	Manchester
LT52WXG	33229	London	M232VWW	47232	Eastern C	M402UUB	61046	W Yorkshire
LT52WXH	33230	London	M233VWU	50422	Aberdeen	M403RVU	34253	Manchester
LT52WXJ	33231	London	M233VWW	47233	Eastern C	M403UUB	61047	W Yorkshire
LT52WXK	33232	London	M235VWW	40608	W Yorkshire	M403VWW	60941	Bristol
LT52WXL	64014	Berkshire	M236VWW	40609	W Yorkshire	M404RVU	34254	Manchester
LT52WXN	64015	Berkshire	M238MRW	67238	Midland Red	M404UUB	61048	W Yorkshire
LT52WXO	64016	Berkshire	M239MRW	67239	Midland Red	M405RVU	34255	Manchester
LT52WXP	64017	Berkshire	M240MRW	67240	Midland Red	M405UUB	61049	W Yorkshire
LT52XAA	33190	London	M240VWW	40612	W Yorkshire	M405VWW	60943	Somerset &A
LT52XAB	33191	London	M241MRW	67241	Midland Red	M406RVU	34256	Manchester
LT52XAC	33192	London	M241VWW	40613	W Yorkshire	M406VWW	60944	W Yorkshire
LT52XAD	33193	London	M241VYA	51241	Somerset &A	M407RVU	34257	Manchester
LT52XAE	33194	London	M242MRW	67242	Midland Red	M408VWW	60946	Leicester
LT52XAF	33195	London	M242VWW	40614	W Yorkshire	M409VWW	60947	Bristol
LT52XAG	33196	London	M243MRW	67243	Midland Red	M411VWW	60949	Bristol
LT52XAH	33197	London	M243VWU	50252	W Yorkshire	M412VWW	60950	Bristol
LT52XAJ	33198	London	M243VWW	40615	W Yorkshire	M413DEU	20438	Edinburgh
LT52XAK	33199	London	M244MRW	67244	Midland Red	M413VWW	60951	W Yorkshire
LT52XAL	32227	London	M244VWW	40616	Hampshire	M414VWW	60952	Bristol
LT52XAM	32228	London	M245MRW	67245	Midland Red	M415VWW	60953	W Yorkshire
LV52VFW	11066	London	M246VWW	40618	W Yorkshire	M417VHE	40456	S Yorkshire
LV52VFX	11067	London	M248MRW	67248	Midland Red	M417VWW	60955	W Yorkshire

Reg	No	Area	Reg	No	Area	Reg	No	Area
M418VHE	40457	S Yorkshire	M515PNA	60310	Manchester	M736VET	60573	S Yorkshire
M419VHE	40458	S Yorkshire	M516DHU	46616	Bristol	M737VET	60574	S Yorkshire
M419VWW	60957	W Yorkshire	M516RSS	60422	Manchester	M738VET	60575	S Yorkshire
M41FTC	20437	Hampshire	M517DHU	46617	Bristol	M739VET	60576	S Yorkshire
M420CCV	46420	Devon & C	M517PNA	60312	Manchester	M740VET	60577	S Yorkshire
M420VHE	40459	S Yorkshire	M517RSS	60423	Manchester	M765PRS	61371	Glasgow
M421VWW	60959	W Yorkshire	M518PNA	60313	Manchester	M766PRS	61372	Glasgow
M422CCV	46422	Devon & C	M518RSS	60424	Manchester	M767PRS	61373	Glasgow
M422VHE	40461	S Yorkshire	M519PNA	60314	Manchester	M768PRS	61374	Glasgow
M425VHE	40464	S Yorkshire	M519RSS	60425	Manchester	M769PRS	61375	Glasgow
M425VWW	60963	Bristol	M520FFB	46620	Bristol	M770PRS	61376	Glasgow
M426VHE	40465	S Yorkshire	M520PNA	60315	Manchester	M771PRS	61377	Glasgow
M426VWW	60964	Bristol	M520RSS	60426	Manchester	M772PRS	61378	Glasgow
M427VWW	60965	Bristol	M521FFB	46621	Bristol	M773PRS	61379	Glasgow
M428RRN	61370	Glasgow	M521RSS	60427	Manchester	M774PRS	61380	Glasgow
M428VHE	40467	S Yorkshire	M522FFB	46622	Bristol	M775PRS	61381	Glasgow
M428VWW	60966	Bristol	M522RSS	60428	Manchester	M776PRS	61382	Glasgow
M429VHE	40468	S Yorkshire	M523FFB	46623	Bristol	M778PRS	61383	Glasgow
M429VWW	60967	W Yorkshire	M523RSS	60429	Manchester	M779PRS	61384	Glasgow
M430VWW	60968	Somerset &A	M524FFB	46624	Bristol	M780PRS	61385	Glasgow
M431VHE	40470	S Yorkshire	M524RSS	60430	Manchester	M781PRS	61386	Glasgow
M431VWW	60969	Somerset &A	M525FFB	46625	Bristol	M791TCF	64791	Berkshire
M432VHE	40471	S Yorkshire	M526FFB	46626	Bristol	M792TCF	64792	Berkshire
M433VHE	40472	S Yorkshire	M527FFB	46627	Bristol	M793TCF	64793	Berkshire
M433VWW	60971	Bristol	M528FFB	46628	Bristol	M794TCF	64794	Berkshire
M434VWW	60972	Bristol	M529FFB	46629	Bristol	M796MPM	67296	London
M435VWW	60973	Bristol	M530FFB	46630	Bristol	M804UYA	51404	Somerset &A
M436VHE	40475	S Yorkshire	M531FFB	46631	Bristol	M805UYA	51405	Somerset &A
M436VWW	60974	W Yorkshire	M532FFB	46632	Bristol	M810PGM	64810	Berkshire
M437VHE	40476	S Yorkshire	M533FFB	46633	Bristol	M811PGM	64811	Glasgow
M437VWW	60975	Bristol	M534FFB	46634	Bristol	M812PGM	64812	Glasgow
M438VHE	40477	S Yorkshire	M535FFB	46635	Bristol	M817PGM	64817	Berkshire
M439FHW	20439	Hampshire	M536FFB	46636	Bristol	M834DUS	31421	Glasgow
M439VWW	60977	Bristol	M537FFB	46637	Bristol	M835DUS	31422	Glasgow
M440FHW	20440	Hampshire	M538FFB	46638	Bristol	M836DUS	31423	Glasgow
M440VHE	40479	S Yorkshire	M568RMS	62334	Edinburgh	M838DUS	31425	Glasgow
M450VWW	47252	Essex	M569RMS	62335	Edinburgh	M839DUS	31426	Glasgow
M46BEG	51346	Somerset &A	M584ANG	48084	Eastern C	M840DUS	31427	Glasgow
M48BEG	51348	Somerset &A	M585ANG	48085	Eastern C	M841DUS	31428	Glasgow
M501GRY	61149	Manchester	M586ANG	48086	Eastern C	M846DUS	31516	Glasgow
M501PNA	60296	Eastern C	M590ANG	48090	Eastern C	M847DUS	31518	Potteries
M502GRY	61150	Manchester	M610SBA	40185	Eastern C	M848DUS	31522	Potteries
M502PNA	60297	Eastern C	M611SBA	40186	Glasgow	M849DUS	31519	Potteries
M503GRY	61247	Manchester	M612SBA	40187	Eastern C	M858ATC	51558	Somerset &A
M503PNA	60298	Eastern C	M626XWS	67501	Wales	M869ATC	51569	Wales
M504GRY	61151	Manchester	M659VJN	51459	Hampshire	M86MYM	34265	Manchester
M504PNA	60299	Hampshire	M660VJN	51460	Hampshire	M870DYS	48070	Eastern C
M505PNA	60300	Eastern C	M716VET	60553	S Yorkshire	M877PRS	61387	Glasgow
M506GRY	61248	Manchester	M717VET	60554	S Yorkshire	M882BEU	51380	Somerset &A
M507GRY	61249	Manchester	M718VET	60555	S Yorkshire	M918MRW	40448	S Yorkshire
M507PNA	60302	Manchester	M719VET	60556	S Yorkshire	M920TEV	46120	Essex
M508PNA	60303	Manchester	M720VET	60557	S Yorkshire	M922TEV	46122	Essex
M509DHU	46609	Bristol	M721VET	60558	S Yorkshire	M922UYG	34202	Somerset &A
M509GRY	61250	Manchester	M723VET	60560	S Yorkshire	M923TEV	46123	Eastern C
M509PNA	60304	Manchester	M724VET	60561	S Yorkshire	M923UYG	34203	Somerset &A
M510DHU	46610	Bristol	M725VET	60562	S Yorkshire	M925UYG	34205	Somerset &A
M510GRY	61251	Manchester	M726VET	60563	S Yorkshire	M928TEV	46128	Essex
M510PNA	60305	Manchester	M727VET	60564	S Yorkshire	M929TEV	46129	Essex
M511DHU	46611	Bristol	M728VET	60565	S Yorkshire	M92BOU	20436	Devon & C
M511PNA	60306	Eastern C	M729VET	60566	S Yorkshire	M932TEV	46132	Essex
M512PNA	60307	Eastern C	M730VET	60567	S Yorkshire	M936TEV	46136	Essex
M513DHU	46613	Bristol	M731VET	60568	S Yorkshire	M937TEV	46137	Essex
M513PNA	60308	Manchester	M732VET	60569	S Yorkshire	M938TEV	46138	Essex
M514DHU	46614	Bristol	M733VET	60570	S Yorkshire	M939EYS	31429	Glasgow
M514PNA	60309	Eastern C	M734VET	60571	S Yorkshire	M940EYS	31430	Glasgow
M515DHU	46615	Bristol	M735VET	60572	S Yorkshire	M940TEV	46140	Essex

The 2008 First Bus Handbook

M941EYS	31431	Glasgow	MV02VBP	60722	S Yorkshire	MX05CCO	66804	Manchester
M941TEV	46141	Essex	MV02VBT	60723	S Yorkshire	MX05CCU	66805	Manchester
M942EYS	31432	Glasgow	MV02VBU	61148	Leicester	MX05CCV	66806	Manchester
M942TEV	46142	Essex	MV02VBX	66332	Leicester	MX05CCY	66807	Manchester
M943SRE	40109	Potteries	MV02VBY	66333	Leicester	MX05CCZ	66808	Manchester
M943TEV	46143	Essex	MV02VBZ	66334	Leicester	MX05CDE	66809	Manchester
M944SRE	40288	Eastern C	MV02VCA	66335	Leicester	MX05CDF	66810	Manchester
M945SRE	40110	Potteries	MV02VCC	66336	Leicester	MX05CDK	66811	Manchester
M947SRE	40290	Eastern C	MV02VCD	60724	S Yorkshire	MX05CDN	66812	Manchester
M948SRE	40291	Eastern C	MV02VCE	60725	S Yorkshire	MX05CDO	66813	Manchester
M952SRE	40113	Eastern C	MV02VCF	60726	S Yorkshire	MX05CDU	66814	Manchester
M953XVT	40114	Eastern C	MV02VCG	60727	S Yorkshire	MX05CDV	66815	Manchester
M954XVT	40115	Potteries	MV02VCJ	60728	S Yorkshire	MX05CDY	66816	Manchester
M955XVT	40116	Potteries	MV02VCK	60729	S Yorkshire	MX05CDZ	66817	Manchester
M959XVT	40120	Potteries	MV02VCL	60730	S Yorkshire	MX05CEA	66818	Manchester
M960XVT	40121	Potteries	MV02VCM	66337	Leicester	MX05CEF	66819	Manchester
M962XVT	40123	Potteries	MV02VCN	66338	Leicester	MX05CEJ	66820	Manchester
M964XVT	40124	Potteries	MV02VCO	66339	Leicester	MX05CEK	66821	Manchester
M965XVT	40292	Hampshire	MV02VCP	66340	Leicester	MX05CEO	66822	Manchester
M967GDU	66652	W Yorkshire	MV02VCU	66342	Leicester	MX05CEU	66823	Manchester
M968XVT	40126	Potteries	MV02VCW	66343	Leicester	MX05CEV	66824	Manchester
M970XVT	40128	Potteries	MV02VCX	66344	Leicester	MX05CEY	66825	Manchester
M971XVT	40129	Potteries	MV02VCY	66345	Leicester	MX05CFA	66826	Manchester
M972XVT	40130	Potteries	MV02VCZ	66346	Leicester	MX05CFD	66827	Manchester
MA51AET	40323	Manchester	MV02VDA	66347	Leicester	MX05CFE	66828	Manchester
MA51AEU	40324	Manchester	MV02VDC	66348	Leicester	MX05CFG	66829	Manchester
MA51AEV	40325	Manchester	MV02VDD	60731	S Yorkshire	MX05CFJ	66830	Manchester
MA51AEW	40326	Manchester	MV02VDE	60732	S Yorkshire	MX05CFK	66831	Manchester
MH04HCL	68207	Manchester	MV02VDF	60733	S Yorkshire	MX05CFL	66832	Manchester
MH04HCN	68208	Manchester	MV02VDG	60734	S Yorkshire	MX05CFM	66833	Manchester
MH04HCP	68209	Manchester	MV02VDJ	60735	S Yorkshire	MX05CFN	66834	Manchester
MH04HCU	68210	Manchester	MV02VDK	60736	S Yorkshire	MX05CFO	66835	Manchester
ML02OFW	40327	Manchester	MV02VDL	60737	S Yorkshire	MX05CFP	66836	Manchester
ML02OFX	40328	Manchester	MV02VDM	60738	S Yorkshire	MX05CFU	66837	Manchester
ML02OFY	40329	Manchester	MV02VDN	60739	S Yorkshire	MX05CFV	66838	Manchester
ML02OFZ	40330	Manchester	MV02VDO	60740	S Yorkshire	MX05CFY	66839	Manchester
ML02OGA	40331	Manchester	MV02VDP	60741	S Yorkshire	MX05CGE	66840	Manchester
ML02OGB	40332	Manchester	MV02VDR	60742	S Yorkshire	MX05CGF	66841	Manchester
ML02OGC	40333	Manchester	MV02VDT	60743	S Yorkshire	MX05CGG	66842	Manchester
ML02OGD	40334	Manchester	MV02VDX	60744	S Yorkshire	MX05CGK	66843	Manchester
ML02OGE	40335	Manchester	MV02VDY	60745	S Yorkshire	MX05CGO	66844	Manchester
MOD571P	39971	Hampshire	MV02VDZ	66349	Glasgow	MX05CGU	66845	Manchester
MV02VAA	60704	S Yorkshire	MV02VEA	66350	Somerset &A	MX05CGV	66846	Manchester
MV02VAD	60705	S Yorkshire	MV02VEB	66351	Somerset &A	MX05CGY	66847	Manchester
MV02VAE	60706	S Yorkshire	MV02VEF	66352	Somerset &A	MX05CGZ	66848	Manchester
MV02VAF	60707	S Yorkshire	MV02VEH	66353	Somerset &A	MX05CHC	66849	Manchester
MV02VAH	60708	S Yorkshire	MV02VEK	66354	Somerset &A	MX05CHD	66850	Manchester
MV02VAJ	60709	S Yorkshire	MV02VEL	66355	Somerset &A	MX05CHF	66851	Manchester
MV02VAK	60710	S Yorkshire	MV02VEM	66356	Somerset &A	MX05CHG	66852	Manchester
MV02VAM	60711	S Yorkshire	MV06CXB	69138	Manchester	MX05CHH	66853	Manchester
MV02VAO	60712	S Yorkshire	MV06CZG	69136	Manchester	MX05CHJ	66854	Manchester
MV02VAU	60713	S Yorkshire	MV06CZJ	69172	Manchester	MX05CHK	66855	Manchester
MV02VAX	66324	Leicester	MV06CZS	69135	Manchester	MX05CHL	66856	Manchester
MV02VAY	66325	Leicester	MV06CZT	69137	Manchester	MX05CHN	66857	Manchester
MV02VBA	66326	Leicester	MV06DWZ	69173	Manchester	MX05CHO	66858	Manchester
MV02VBB	66327	Leicester	MV06DYU	69206	Manchester	MX05CHV	66859	Manchester
MV02VBC	66328	Leicester	MX04 VML	53074	Devon & C	MX05CHY	66860	Manchester
MV02VBD	66329	Leicester	MX05CBF	66794	Manchester	MX05CHZ	66861	Manchester
MV02VBE	66330	Leicester	MX05CBU	66795	Manchester	MX05CJE	66862	Manchester
MV02VBF	60714	S Yorkshire	MX05CBV	66796	Manchester	MX05CJF	66863	Manchester
MV02VBG	60715	S Yorkshire	MX05CBY	66797	Manchester	MX05CJJ	66864	Manchester
MV02VBJ	60716	S Yorkshire	MX05CCA	66798	Manchester	MX05CJO	66865	Manchester
MV02VBK	60717	S Yorkshire	MX05CCD	66799	Manchester	MX05CJU	66866	Manchester
MV02VBL	60718	S Yorkshire	MX05CCF	66800	Manchester	MX05CJV	66867	Manchester
MV02VBM	60719	S Yorkshire	MX05CCJ	66801	Manchester	MX05CJY	66868	Manchester
MV02VBN	60720	S Yorkshire	MX05CCK	66802	Manchester	MX05CJZ	66869	Manchester
MV02VBO	60721	S Yorkshire	MX05CCN	66803	Manchester	MX05CKA	66870	Manchester

The 2008 First Bus Handbook

Reg	Number	Location	Reg	Number	Location	Reg	Number	Location
MX05CKC	66871	Manchester	MX06YXK	69178	Manchester	MX55FFW	66909	Manchester
MX05CKD	66872	Manchester	MX06YXL	69179	Manchester	MX55FFY	66910	Manchester
MX05CKE	66873	Manchester	MX06YXM	69180	Manchester	MX55FFZ	66911	Manchester
MX05CKF	66874	Manchester	MX06YXN	69181	Manchester	MX55FGA	66912	Manchester
MX05CKJ	66876	Manchester	MX06YXO	69182	Manchester	MX55FGC	66913	Manchester
MX05CKK	66877	Manchester	MX06YXP	69183	Manchester	MX55FGE	66914	Manchester
MX05CKL	66878	Manchester	MX06YXR	69184	Manchester	MX55FGF	66915	Manchester
MX05CKN	66879	Manchester	MX06YXS	69213	Manchester	MX55FGG	66916	Manchester
MX05CKO	66880	Manchester	MX06YXT	69214	Manchester	MX55FGJ	66917	Manchester
MX05CKP	66881	Manchester	MX07 NTV	44901	Devon & C	MX55FGK	66918	Manchester
MX05CLF	66885	Manchester	MX07BPY	37279	Manchester	MX55FGM	66919	Manchester
MX06 AEB	57000	Devon & C	MX07BPZ	37280	Manchester	MX55FGN	66920	Manchester
MX06 BSY	53075	Devon & C	MX07BRF	37281	Manchester	MX55FGO	66921	Manchester
MX06VMW	69165	Manchester	MX07BRV	37282	Manchester	MX55FGP	66922	Manchester
MX06VMZ	69166	Manchester	MX07BRZ	37283	Manchester	MX55FGU	66923	Manchester
MX06VNB	69167	Manchester	MX07BSO	37284	Manchester	MX55FGV	66924	Manchester
MX06VNC	69168	Manchester	MX07BSU	37285	Manchester	MX55FGZ	66925	Manchester
MX06VND	69169	Manchester	MX07BSV	37286	Manchester	MX55FHA	66926	Manchester
MX06VNE	69170	Manchester	MX07BSY	37287	Manchester	MX55FHB	66927	Manchester
MX06VNF	69171	Manchester	MX07BSZ	37288	Manchester	MX55FHC	66928	Manchester
MX06VNK	69174	Manchester	MX07BTE	37289	Manchester	MX55FHD	66929	Manchester
MX06VNM	69156	Manchester	MX07BTF	37290	Manchester	MX55FHE	66930	Manchester
MX06VNN	69157	Manchester	MX07BTO	37291	Manchester	MX55FHF	66931	Manchester
MX06VNO	69158	Manchester	MX07BTU	37292	Manchester	MX55FHG	66932	Eastern C
MX06VNP	69159	Manchester	MX07BTV	37293	Manchester	MX55FHH	66933	Manchester
MX06VNR	69160	Manchester	MX07BTY	37294	Manchester	MX55HHM	66889	Manchester
MX06VNS	69161	Manchester	MX07BTZ	37295	Manchester	MX55HHN	66887	Manchester
MX06VNT	69162	Manchester	MX07BUA	37296	Manchester	MX55HHO	66884	Manchester
MX06VNU	69163	Manchester	MX07BUE	37297	Manchester	MX55HHP	66883	Manchester
MX06VNV	69164	Manchester	MX07BUF	37298	Manchester	MX55HHR	66882	Manchester
MX06VNW	69145	Manchester	MX07BUH	37299	Manchester	MX55LDJ	66892	Manchester
MX06VNY	69146	Manchester	MX07BUJ	37300	Manchester	MX55LDK	66893	Manchester
MX06VNZ	69147	Manchester	MX07BUU	37303	Manchester	MX55LHL	66886	Manchester
MX06VOA	69148	Manchester	MX07BUV	37304	Manchester	MX55NWC	68556	Manchester
MX06VOB	69149	Manchester	MX07BUW	37305	Manchester	MX55NWD	68557	Manchester
MX06VOC	69150	Manchester	MX07BVA	37306	Manchester	MX55NWE	66875	Manchester
MX06VOD	69151	Manchester	MX07BVC	37307	Manchester	MX55NWF	66888	Manchester
MX06VOF	69152	Manchester	MX07BVD	37308	Manchester	MX55NWH	66890	Manchester
MX06VOG	69153	Manchester	MX07BVE	37309	Manchester	MX55NWS	68555	Essex
MX06VOH	69154	Manchester	MX07BVF	37310	Manchester	MX55UAA	66891	Manchester
MX06VOP	69139	Manchester	MX07BVG	37311	Manchester	MX56ACV	69185	Manchester
MX06VOT	69140	Manchester	MX07BVJ	37312	Manchester	MX56ACY	69186	Manchester
MX06VOU	69141	Manchester	MX07BVK	37313	Manchester	MX56ACZ	69187	Manchester
MX06VOV	69142	Manchester	MX07BVL	37314	Manchester	MX56ADO	69188	Manchester
MX06VOY	69143	Manchester	MX54GZA	53143	Manchester	MX56ADU	69189	Manchester
MX06VPA	69144	Manchester	MX54GZB	53144	Manchester	MX56ADV	69190	Manchester
MX06VPC	69203	Manchester	MX54GZC	53145	Manchester	MX56ADZ	69191	Manchester
MX06VPD	69204	Manchester	MX54GZD	53146	Manchester	MX56AEA	69192	Manchester
MX06VPE	69205	Manchester	MX54GZE	53147	Manchester	MX56AEB	69193	Manchester
MX06VPG	69207	Manchester	MX54GZF	53148	Manchester	MX56AEC	69194	Manchester
MX06VPJ	69208	Manchester	MX54GZG	53149	Manchester	MX56AED	69215	Manchester
MX06VPK	69209	Manchester	MX54GZH	53150	Manchester	MX56AEE	69216	Manchester
MX06VPL	69210	Manchester	MX55FFD	66894	Manchester	MX56AEF	69217	Manchester
MX06VPM	69211	Manchester	MX55FFE	66895	Manchester	MX56AEG	69218	Manchester
MX06VPN	69212	Manchester	MX55FFG	66896	Manchester	MX56AEJ	69219	Manchester
MX06VPO	69175	Manchester	MX55FFH	66897	Manchester	MX56AEK	69220	Manchester
MX06VPP	69176	Manchester	MX55FFJ	66898	Manchester	MX56AEL	69221	Manchester
MX06VPR	69195	Manchester	MX55FFK	66899	Manchester	MX56AEM	69222	Manchester
MX06VPT	69196	Manchester	MX55FFL	66900	Manchester	MX56AEN	69223	Manchester
MX06VPU	69197	Manchester	MX55FFM	66901	Manchester	MX56AEO	69224	Manchester
MX06VPV	69198	Manchester	MX55FFO	66902	Manchester	MX56AEP	69225	Manchester
MX06VPW	69199	Manchester	MX55FFP	66903	Manchester	MX56AET	69226	Manchester
MX06VPY	69200	Manchester	MX55FFR	66904	Manchester	MX56AEU	69227	Manchester
MX06VPZ	69201	Manchester	MX55FFS	66905	Manchester	MX56AEV	69228	Manchester
MX06VRC	69202	Manchester	MX55FFT	66906	Manchester	MX56AEW	69229	Manchester
MX06YXJ	69177	Manchester	MX55FFU	66907	Manchester	MX56AEY	69230	Manchester
			MX55FFV	66908	Manchester	MX56AEZ	69231	Manchester

Reg	No	Depot	Reg	No	Depot	Reg	No	Depot
MX56AFA	69232	Manchester	N231KAE	46232	Somerset &A	N304JBV	30549	S Yorkshire
MX56AFE	69233	Manchester	N232WFJ	21132	Wales	N304XAB	47004	Midland Red
MX56AFF	69234	Manchester	N233KAE	46233	Somerset &A	N305JBV	30550	S Yorkshire
MX56AFJ	69235	Manchester	N233WFJ	21133	Wales	N305XAB	47005	Midland Red
MX56AFK	69236	Manchester	N234KAE	46234	Somerset &A	N306JBV	34006	Bristol
MX56AFN	69237	Manchester	N235KAE	46235	Somerset &A	N306XAB	47006	Midland Red
MX56AFO	69238	Manchester	N236KAE	46236	Somerset &A	N307JBV	34007	Bristol
MX56AFU	69239	Manchester	N237KAE	46237	Somerset &A	N307XAB	47007	Midland Red
MX56AFV	69240	Manchester	N238KAE	46238	Somerset &A	N308JBV	34008	Bristol
MX56AFY	69241	Manchester	N239KAE	46239	Somerset &A	N308XAB	47008	Midland Red
MX56AFZ	69242	Manchester	N240KAE	46240	Somerset &A	N309JBV	34009	Bristol
MX56AGO	69243	Manchester	N241CMP	34241	S Yorkshire	N309XAB	47009	Wales
MX56AGU	69244	Manchester	N241KAE	46241	Somerset &A	N310JBV	34010	Bristol
MX57HDZ	37301	Manchester	N242KAE	46242	Somerset &A	N310XAB	47070	Wales
MX57HEJ	37302	Manchester	N243LHT	46243	Somerset &A	N311JBV	30551	S Yorkshire
N3GPD	20499	Devon & C	N244CMP	30553	S Yorkshire	N311XAB	47011	Midland Red
N112EWJ	21112	Wales	N244LHT	46244	Somerset &A	N312JBV	30552	S Yorkshire
N113VWN	21113	Wales	N245LHT	46245	Somerset &A	N312XAB	47012	Wales
N114VWN	21114	Wales	N246LHT	46246	Somerset &A	N313XAB	47013	Midland Red
N115VWN	21115	Wales	N247CKY	60584	Glasgow	N319NHY	21119	Wales
N120OGG	61388	Glasgow	N247CMP	34247	S Yorkshire	N320NHY	21120	Hampshire
N121OGG	61389	Glasgow	N247LHT	46247	Somerset &A	N322NHY	21123	Wales
N122OGG	61390	Glasgow	N248LHT	46248	Somerset &A	N324ECR	46324	Hampshire
N123OGG	61391	Glasgow	N249LHT	46249	Somerset &A	N325ECR	46325	Hampshire
N124OGG	61392	Glasgow	N250LHT	46250	Somerset &A	N326ECR	46326	Hampshire
N125OGG	61393	Glasgow	N269JUM	40638	W Yorkshire	N327ECR	46327	Hampshire
N126OGG	61394	Glasgow	N270JUM	40639	W Yorkshire	N328ECR	46328	Hampshire
N127OGG	61395	Glasgow	N271JUM	40640	W Yorkshire	N329ECR	46329	Hampshire
N128OGG	61396	Glasgow	N272JUM	40641	W Yorkshire	N341EUY	42641	Midland Red
N129OGG	61397	Glasgow	N273JUG	50206	Hampshire	N372CJA	40219	Manchester
N130OGG	61398	Glasgow	N273JUM	40642	W Yorkshire	N373CJA	40220	Manchester
N131OGG	61399	Glasgow	N274JUM	40643	W Yorkshire	N374CJA	40221	Manchester
N132OGG	61400	Glasgow	N275JUM	40644	W Yorkshire	N375CJA	40222	Manchester
N133OGG	61401	Glasgow	N276JUM	40645	W Yorkshire	N376CJA	40223	Manchester
N134OGG	61402	Glasgow	N277CKY	60614	S Yorkshire	N377CJA	40224	Manchester
N135OGG	61403	Glasgow	N277JUM	40646	W Yorkshire	N378CJA	40225	Manchester
N136OGG	61404	Glasgow	N278JUM	40647	W Yorkshire	N379CJA	40226	Manchester
N137OGG	61405	Glasgow	N279JUG	50210	Hampshire	N380CJA	40227	Manchester
N138OGG	61406	Glasgow	N279JUM	40544	S Yorkshire	N381CJA	40228	Manchester
N144BWG	40481	S Yorkshire	N281JUM	40546	S Yorkshire	N382CJA	40229	Manchester
N167 KAF	46267	Devon & C	N284JUG	50215	Hampshire	N383CJA	40230	Manchester
N168 KAF	46268	Devon & C	N284JUM	40649	W Yorkshire	N384CJA	40231	Manchester
N169 KAF	46269	Devon & C	N285JUG	50261	W Yorkshire	N385CRJ	40232	Manchester
N170 KAF	51120	Devon & C	N285JUM	40650	W Yorkshire	N386CRJ	40233	Manchester
N190OGG	61407	Glasgow	N286JUG	50262	W Yorkshire	N406ENW	62299	Edinburgh
N199OGG	61408	Glasgow	N286JUM	40651	W Yorkshire	N407ENW	62295	Edinburgh
N1GRT	20012	Aberdeen	N287JUG	50263	W Yorkshire	N408ENW	62296	Edinburgh
N201VSA	47101	Essex	N287JUM	40652	W Yorkshire	N409ENW	62381	Edinburgh
N202VSA	47102	Essex	N288JUG	50264	W Yorkshire	N410ENW	62382	Edinburgh
N203VSA	47103	Essex	N289JUG	50265	W Yorkshire	N411ENW	62298	Edinburgh
N204VSA	47104	Essex	N289JUM	40654	W Yorkshire	N412ENW	62117	W Yorkshire
N205VSA	47105	Essex	N290JUG	50266	W Yorkshire	N412JBV	34262	Manchester
N206VSA	47106	Essex	N290JUM	40655	W Yorkshire	N413ENW	60132	Potteries
N211WRD	42411	Berkshire	N291JUG	50267	W Yorkshire	N414ENW	60133	Potteries
N212 KBJ	51112	Devon & C	N292JUG	50268	W Yorkshire	N415ENW	60139	Potteries
N212WRD	42412	Berkshire	N292JUM	40657	W Yorkshire	N416ENW	61050	W Yorkshire
N213WRD	40963	W Yorkshire	N293JUG	50269	W Yorkshire	N417ENW	61258	Berkshire
N214WRD	42414	Berkshire	N293JUM	40658	W Yorkshire	N418ENW	61051	W Yorkshire
N215WRD	42415	Berkshire	N294JUM	40659	W Yorkshire	N419ENW	60754	Berkshire
N216WRD	42416	Berkshire	N297JUM	40662	W Yorkshire	N420MWY	60755	Berkshire
N217WRD	42417	Berkshire	N299JUM	40545	S Yorkshire	N421MWY	60756	Berkshire
N226KAE	46226	Somerset &A	N301JBV	30546	S Yorkshire	N422MWY	60757	Berkshire
N227KAE	46227	Somerset &A	N301XAB	47001	Midland Red	N423JBV	34263	Manchester
N228KAE	46228	Somerset &A	N302JBV	30547	S Yorkshire	N423MWY	60758	Berkshire
N229KAE	46229	Somerset &A	N302XAB	47002	Midland Red	N424MWY	62116	W Yorkshire
N22BLU	46230	Devon & C	N303JBV	30548	S Yorkshire	N425MWY	60760	S Yorkshire
N230KAE	46231	Somerset &A	N303XAB	47003	Midland Red	N441BKY	48141	S Yorkshire

The 2008 First Bus Handbook

Reg	Fleet	Depot	Reg	Fleet	Depot	Reg	Fleet	Depot
N441ENW	60979	Bristol	N544WVR	60339	Manchester	N602EBP	47302	Hampshire
N442BKY	48142	S Yorkshire	N545HAE	46645	Bristol	N603APU	20103	Eastern C
N443BKY	40480	S Yorkshire	N546HAE	46646	Bristol	N603EBP	47303	Hampshire
N443ENW	60981	Bristol	N546WVR	60341	Manchester	N603XJM	40297	Hampshire
N445BKY	40482	S Yorkshire	N547HAE	46647	Bristol	N604APU	20104	Eastern C
N446BKY	40483	S Yorkshire	N547LHG	34249	Hampshire	N604EBP	47304	Hampshire
N447BKY	40484	S Yorkshire	N547WVR	60342	Manchester	N604XJM	40298	Hampshire
N448BKY	40485	S Yorkshire	N548HAE	46648	Bristol	N605APU	20105	Eastern C
N449BKY	40486	S Yorkshire	N548WVR	60343	Manchester	N605EBP	47305	Hampshire
N449JUG	60987	Bristol	N549LHU	46649	Bristol	N606APU	20106	Eastern C
N450JUG	60988	Bristol	N549WVR	60344	Manchester	N606EBP	47306	Hampshire
N452JUG	60990	Bristol	N550LHU	46650	Bristol	N607APU	20107	Eastern C
N453JUG	60991	Bristol	N550WVR	60345	Manchester	N607EBP	47307	Hampshire
N454JUG	60992	Bristol	N551LHU	46651	Bristol	N608XJM	40301	Glasgow
N455JUG	60993	Bristol	N551WVR	60346	Manchester	N609APU	20109	Eastern C
N465ETR	46365	Hampshire	N552LHU	46652	Bristol	N609MHB	46709	Wales
N466ETR	46366	Hampshire	N552UCY	46552	Wales	N609XJM	40302	Manchester
N467ETR	46367	Hampshire	N552WVR	60347	Manchester	N610APU	20110	Essex
N472KHU	21127	Wales	N553LHU	46653	Bristol	N610MHB	46710	Wales
N473JUG	61011	Bristol	N553UCY	46553	Wales	N610XJM	40303	Manchester
N474JUG	61012	Bristol	N553WVR	60117	Manchester	N611APU	20111	Eastern C
N475JUG	61013	Midland Red	N554LHU	46654	Bristol	N611MHB	46711	Wales
N476JUG	61014	Somerset &A	N554UCY	46554	Wales	N611XJM	40947	Glasgow
N477JUG	61015	Somerset &A	N554WVR	60348	Manchester	N612APU	20112	Eastern C
N478JUG	61016	Midland Red	N555UCY	46555	Wales	N612MHB	46712	Wales
N500TCC	62268	Edinburgh	N556LHU	46656	Bristol	N614APU	20114	Eastern C
N521WVR	60316	Potteries	N556UCY	46556	Wales	N614MHB	46714	Wales
N522WVR	60317	Potteries	N556WVR	60349	Manchester	N615DWY	47015	Hampshire
N523WVR	60318	Manchester	N557BNF	60350	S Yorkshire	N615MHB	46715	Wales
N524WVR	60319	Manchester	N557EYB	51657	Somerset &A	N615XJM	40903	Glasgow
N525VSA	60431	Manchester	N557LHU	46657	Bristol	N616APU	20116	Eastern C
N525WVR	60320	Manchester	N557UCY	46557	Wales	N616MHB	46716	Wales
N526VSA	60432	Manchester	N558BNF	60351	S Yorkshire	N617APU	20117	Eastern C
N527VSA	60433	Manchester	N558LHU	46658	Bristol	N617XJM	40905	Edinburgh
N527WVR	60322	Manchester	N558UCY	46558	Wales	N618APU	20118	Eastern C
N528LHG	34258	Hampshire	N559BNF	60352	S Yorkshire	N618MHB	46718	Wales
N528VSA	60434	Manchester	N559EYB	51659	Somerset &A	N619APU	20119	Eastern C
N529VSA	60435	Manchester	N559LHU	46659	Bristol	N619CDB	40251	Eastern C
N530VSA	60436	Manchester	N559UCY	46559	Wales	N622CDB	40254	Glasgow
N530WVR	60325	Manchester	N561BNF	60353	S Yorkshire	N622XJM	40951	Glasgow
N531VSA	60437	Manchester	N561EYB	51661	Somerset &A	N624CDB	40256	Eastern C
N532VSA	60438	Manchester	N561UCY	46561	Wales	N624XJM	40909	Edinburgh
N533LHG	34259	Hampshire	N562BNF	60354	S Yorkshire	N625CDB	40257	Eastern C
N533VSA	60439	Manchester	N562LHU	46662	Devon & C	N625GAH	46725	Eastern C
N533WVR	60328	Manchester	N562UCY	46562	Wales	N626GAH	46726	Eastern C
N534VSA	60440	Manchester	N563LHU	46663	Devon & C	N626XJM	40910	Edinburgh
N535VSA	62281	Edinburgh	N563UCY	46563	Wales	N627CDB	40259	Eastern C
N535WVR	60330	Manchester	N564LHU	46664	Devon & C	N630CDB	40262	Hampshire
N536LHG	34260	Manchester	N564UCY	46564	Wales	N633ACF	46733	Hampshire
N536VSA	62283	Edinburgh	N565UCY	46565	Wales	N633CDB	40265	Hampshire
N536WVR	60331	Manchester	N567UCY	46567	Wales	N634ACF	46734	Hampshire
N537WVR	60332	Manchester	N568UCY	46568	Wales	N635ACF	46735	Hampshire
N538VSA	62286	Edinburgh	N572VMS	62339	Edinburgh	N635CDB	40267	Glasgow
N538WVR	60333	Manchester	N573VMS	62340	Edinburgh	N636ACF	46736	Hampshire
N539HAE	46639	Bristol	N574VMS	62341	Edinburgh	N637ACF	46737	Hampshire
N539WVR	60334	Manchester	N579CEH	50095	Wales	N637CDB	40269	Midland Red
N540HAE	46640	Bristol	N580CEH	50096	Wales	N638CDB	40270	Glasgow
N540WVR	60335	Manchester	N581CEH	50097	Wales	N641CDB	40273	Manchester
N541HAE	46641	Bristol	N583WND	51685	Somerset &A	N642CDB	40274	Manchester
N541WVR	60336	Manchester	N584WND	51684	Somerset &A	N645CDB	40277	Manchester
N542HAE	46642	Bristol	N585WND	51688	Somerset &A	N647CDB	40279	Manchester
N542LHG	34261	Hampshire	N586WND	51686	Somerset &A	N648CDB	40280	Manchester
N542WVR	60337	Hampshire	N588CEH	50104	Wales	N650CDB	40282	Manchester
N543HAE	46643	Bristol	N589CEH	50105	Wales	N651CDB	40283	Manchester
N543WVR	60338	Manchester	N601EBP	47301	Hampshire	N652CDB	40284	Midland Red
N544ENW	60982	Bristol	N601XJM	40295	Manchester	N653CDB	40285	Manchester
N544HAE	46644	Bristol	N602APU	20102	Essex	N689WLS	50416	Aberdeen

Reg	No	Location	Reg	No	Location	Reg	No	Location
N68CSC	62400	Edinburgh	N811FLW	46911	Bristol	N949CPU	46149	Essex
N69CSC	62401	Edinburgh	N813FLW	40555	S Yorkshire	N949LSU	61433	Glasgow
N701CPU	40869	W Yorkshire	N814FLW	40549	S Yorkshire	N949SOS	31438	Glasgow
N710GRV	51710	Hampshire	N815FLW	40550	S Yorkshire	N94OGG	61434	Glasgow
N711GRV	51711	Hampshire	N816FLW	40551	S Yorkshire	N950CPU	46150	Essex
N712GRV	51712	Hampshire	N817FLW	40552	S Yorkshire	N950LSU	61435	Glasgow
N713GRV	51713	Hampshire	N821KWS	21121	London	N950SOS	31439	Glasgow
N714GRV	51714	Hampshire	N822KWS	21122	London	N951CPU	46151	Essex
N715GRV	51715	Hampshire	N823APU	46823	Essex	N951LSU	61436	Glasgow
N716GRV	51716	Hampshire	N823FLW	46923	Somerset &A	N951SOS	31440	Glasgow
N717GRV	51717	Hampshire	N824APU	46824	Essex	N952CPU	46152	Essex
N718GRV	51718	Hampshire	N825APU	46825	Essex	N952LSU	61437	Glasgow
N71YNF	40218	Manchester	N825FLW	46925	Somerset &A	N952SOS	31441	Glasgow
N720GRV	51720	Hampshire	N826APU	46826	Essex	N953CPU	46153	Essex
N721GRV	51721	Hampshire	N826FLW	46926	Berkshire	N953LSU	61438	Glasgow
N741CKY	60578	Edinburgh	N827APU	46827	Essex	N953SOS	31442	Glasgow
N742CKY	60579	Edinburgh	N827FLW	46927	Somerset &A	N954CPU	46154	Essex
N743CKY	60580	Glasgow	N828APU	46828	Essex	N954LSU	61439	Glasgow
N744CKY	60581	Edinburgh	N829APU	46829	Essex	N954SOS	31443	Glasgow
N745CKY	60582	Glasgow	N829FLW	46929	Midland Red	N955CPU	46155	Essex
N746CKY	60583	Glasgow	N830APU	46830	Essex	N955LSU	61440	Glasgow
N748CKY	60585	Glasgow	N830FLW	46930	Midland Red	N955SOS	31444	Glasgow
N749CKY	60586	Glasgow	N831FLW	46931	Midland Red	N956CPU	46156	Essex
N750CKY	60587	Glasgow	N832FLW	46932	Midland Red	N956LSU	61441	Glasgow
N751CKY	60588	Glasgow	N863CEH	60097	Potteries	N956SOS	31445	Glasgow
N752CKY	60589	Glasgow	N864CEH	60098	Potteries	N957CPU	46157	Essex
N753CKY	60590	Edinburgh	N866CEH	60100	Potteries	N957LSU	61442	Glasgow
N754CKY	60591	Edinburgh	N883HWS	51583	Hampshire	N957SOS	31446	Glasgow
N755CKY	60592	Edinburgh	N889HWS	51589	Somerset &A	N958CPU	46158	Essex
N756CKY	60593	Glasgow	N890HWS	51590	Somerset &A	N958LSU	61443	Glasgow
N757CKY	60594	Glasgow	N892HWS	51592	Somerset &A	N958SOS	31447	Glasgow
N758CKY	60595	Glasgow	N893HWS	51593	Somerset &A	N959LSU	61444	Glasgow
N759CKY	60596	Glasgow	N894HWS	51594	Somerset &A	N959SOS	31448	Glasgow
N760CKY	60597	Somerset &A	N89OGG	61409	Glasgow	N95OGG	61445	Glasgow
N761CKY	60598	Somerset &A	N902HWS	51602	Somerset &A	N960LSU	61446	Glasgow
N762CKY	60599	Somerset &A	N906HWS	51606	Somerset &A	N960SOS	31449	Glasgow
N763CKY	60600	Somerset &A	N91OGG	61410	Glasgow	N961LSU	61447	Glasgow
N764CKY	60601	Glasgow	N92OGG	61412	Glasgow	N961SOS	31450	Glasgow
N765CKY	60602	S Yorkshire	N930LSU	61413	Glasgow	N962LSU	61448	Glasgow
N766CKY	60603	S Yorkshire	N931LSU	61414	Glasgow	N963LSU	61449	Glasgow
N767CKY	60604	S Yorkshire	N932LSU	61415	Glasgow	N963SOS	31452	Midland Red
N768CKY	60605	S Yorkshire	N933LSU	61416	Glasgow	N964LSU	61450	Glasgow
N769CKY	60606	S Yorkshire	N934LSU	61417	Glasgow	N965LSU	61451	Glasgow
N770CKY	60607	S Yorkshire	N935LSU	61418	Glasgow	N965SOS	31454	Leicester
N771CKY	60608	S Yorkshire	N936LSU	61419	Glasgow	N966LSU	61452	Glasgow
N772CKY	60609	S Yorkshire	N937LSU	61420	Glasgow	N967CPU	46167	Essex
N773CKY	60610	S Yorkshire	N938LSU	61421	Glasgow	N967LSU	61453	Glasgow
N774CKY	60611	S Yorkshire	N939LSU	61422	Glasgow	N967SOS	31456	Essex
N775CKY	60612	S Yorkshire	N93OGG	61423	Glasgow	N968CPU	46168	Essex
N776CKY	60613	S Yorkshire	N940LSU	61424	Glasgow	N968LSU	61454	Glasgow
N778CKY	60615	S Yorkshire	N941LSU	61425	Glasgow	N968SOS	31457	Devon & C
N779CKY	60616	S Yorkshire	N942LSU	61426	Glasgow	N969CPU	46169	Essex
N780CKY	60617	S Yorkshire	N943LSU	61427	Glasgow	N969LSU	61455	Glasgow
N795WAN	64795	Berkshire	N944CPU	46144	Essex	N969SOS	31458	Devon & C
N796WAN	64796	Berkshire	N944LSU	61428	Glasgow	N96OGG	61456	Glasgow
N797WAN	64797	Berkshire	N944SOS	31433	Glasgow	N970CPU	46170	Essex
N798WAN	64798	Berkshire	N945CPU	46145	Essex	N970LSU	61457	Glasgow
N801FLW	46901	Somerset &A	N945SOS	31434	Glasgow	N970SOS	31459	Devon & C
N802FLW	46902	Somerset &A	N946CPU	46146	Essex	N971CPU	46171	Essex
N803FLW	46903	Bristol	N946LSU	61430	Glasgow	N971LSU	61458	Glasgow
N804FLW	46904	Bristol	N946SOS	31435	Glasgow	N971SOS	31460	Devon & C
N805FLW	46905	Bristol	N947CPU	46147	Essex	N972CPU	46172	Essex
N806FLW	46906	Bristol	N947LSU	61431	Glasgow	N972LSU	61459	Glasgow
N807FLW	46907	Bristol	N947SOS	31436	Glasgow	N972SOS	31461	Devon & C
N808FLW	46908	Bristol	N948CPU	46148	Essex	N973EHJ	46173	Essex
N809FLW	46909	Bristol	N948LSU	61432	Glasgow	N973LSU	61460	Glasgow
N810VOD	46440	Devon & C	N948SOS	31437	Glasgow	N973SOS	31462	Essex

Reg	Fleet	Location	Reg	Fleet	Location	Reg	Fleet	Location
N974EHJ	46174	Essex	P127NLW	40176	Potteries	P199TGD	30747	Edinburgh
N974LSU	61461	Glasgow	P128NLW	40177	Potteries	P201NSC	40887	Edinburgh
N975EHJ	46175	Essex	P129NLW	41129	Somerset &A	P201TGD	30748	Edinburgh
N975LSU	61462	Glasgow	P130NLW	41130	Berkshire	P202NSC	40888	Edinburgh
N976EHJ	46176	Essex	P131NLW	41131	Somerset &A	P202TGD	30749	Edinburgh
N976LSU	61463	Glasgow	P132NLW	41132	Somerset &A	P203NSC	40912	Edinburgh
N977EHJ	46177	Essex	P133NLW	41133	Berkshire	P203TGD	30750	Edinburgh
N977LSU	61464	Glasgow	P134NLW	41134	Somerset &A	P204NSC	40913	Edinburgh
N978LSU	61465	Glasgow	P135NLW	41135	Somerset &A	P204TGD	30751	Edinburgh
N979EHJ	46179	Essex	P136NLW	41136	Hampshire	P205NSC	40914	Edinburgh
N979LSU	61466	Glasgow	P137NLW	41137	Hampshire	P206NSC	40915	Edinburgh
N97OGG	61467	Glasgow	P138NLW	40159	Potteries	P207NSC	40916	Edinburgh
N980EHJ	46180	Essex	P139NLW	40160	Wales	P208NSC	40917	Edinburgh
N980LSU	61468	Glasgow	P140NLW	40171	Potteries	P209NSC	40918	Edinburgh
N981EHJ	46181	Essex	P141NLW	40178	Potteries	P20GRT	62266	Glasgow
N981LSU	61469	Glasgow	P142NLW	41142	Wales	P210NSC	40919	Edinburgh
N982EHJ	46182	Essex	P143NLW	41143	Wales	P211NSC	40920	Edinburgh
N982LSU	61470	Glasgow	P144NLW	41144	Wales	P212NSC	40921	Edinburgh
N983EHJ	46183	Essex	P145NLW	41145	Wales	P213HRJ	60140	Manchester
N983LSU	61471	Glasgow	P146NLW	41146	Wales	P213NSC	40922	Edinburgh
N984EHJ	46184	Essex	P148NLW	41148	Wales	P214NSC	40889	Edinburgh
N984LSU	61472	Glasgow	P149NLW	41149	Wales	P215NSC	40923	Wales
N985EHJ	46185	Essex	P150NLW	41150	Wales	P216YSH	40924	Wales
N985LSU	61473	Glasgow	P151NLW	41151	Wales	P217YSH	40925	Wales
N986EHJ	46186	Essex	P152NLW	41152	Wales	P218YSH	40890	Edinburgh
N986LSU	61474	Glasgow	P153NLW	41153	Wales	P223MPU	34223	Potteries
N987EHJ	46187	Essex	P156NLW	41156	Somerset &A	P224MPU	34224	Potteries
N987LSU	61475	Glasgow	P157NLW	41157	Wales	P225MPU	34225	Potteries
N988LSU	61476	Glasgow	P171DMS	62369	Edinburgh	P226MPU	34226	Potteries
N98OGG	61477	Glasgow	P172DMS	62370	Edinburgh	P227MPU	34227	Potteries
NER621	34199	Devon & C	P173DMS	62371	Edinburgh	P228MPU	34228	Potteries
NML623E	39623	Eastern C	P174TGD	34274	Berkshire	P229MPU	34229	Potteries
NTC140Y	34540	Hampshire	P175TGD	34275	Berkshire	P230MPU	34230	Potteries
NTC141Y	34541	Hampshire	P176NAK	20418	Hampshire	P231MPU	34231	Potteries
NTL655	20055	Hampshire	P176TGD	34276	Berkshire	P232MPU	34232	Potteries
NX07DAO	68215	Manchester	P177NAK	20417	Hampshire	P233MPU	34233	Potteries
NX07DAU	68216	Manchester	P177TGD	34277	Berkshire	P234MPU	34234	W Yorkshire
ODZ8911	67311	Midland Red	P178TGD	34278	Berkshire	P235CTA	21135	Wales
ODZ8912	67312	Midland Red	P179LYB	51679	Somerset &A	P236CTA	21136	Wales
ODZ8913	67313	Midland Red	P179TGD	34279	Berkshire	P236MPU	34236	Potteries
ODZ8914	67314	Midland Red	P180TGD	34280	Essex	P237MPU	34237	Potteries
ODZ8915	67315	Midland Red	P181LYB	51880	Somerset &A	P237NLW	42237	Wales
ODZ8916	67316	Somerset &A	P181TGD	30558	Essex	P238MPU	34238	W Yorkshire
ODZ8917	67317	Somerset &A	P182LYB	51682	Somerset &A	P238NLW	42238	Wales
ODZ8918	67318	Midland Red	P182TGD	34282	Essex	P239HMD	34239	S Yorkshire
ODZ8919	67319	Midland Red	P183LYB	51683	Somerset &A	P239NLW	42239	Wales
ODZ8921	67321	Midland Red	P183TGD	30559	London	P240HMD	34240	S Yorkshire
ODZ8922	67322	Midland Red	P184TGD	34284	Essex	P241UCW	34041	Bristol
ODZ8923	67323	Midland Red	P185TGD	34285	Essex	P242HMD	34242	S Yorkshire
ODZ8924	67324	Midland Red	P186TGD	34286	Essex	P242UCW	34042	Bristol
OO06FTR	19006	W Yorkshire	P187TGD	34287	Leicester	P243HMD	30554	S Yorkshire
OWB243	34196	Devon & C	P188TGD	34288	Essex	P243UCW	34043	Bristol
P106MFS	61478	Glasgow	P188UNS	61483	S Yorkshire	P244UCW	34044	Bristol
P107MFS	61479	Glasgow	P189TGD	34289	Midland Red	P245HMD	30555	S Yorkshire
P108MFS	61480	Glasgow	P189UNS	61484	S Yorkshire	P245UCW	34045	Bristol
P109MFS	61481	Glasgow	P190TGD	30560	Essex	P246HMD	34246	S Yorkshire
P113YSH	61482	Potteries	P191TGD	34290	Essex	P246UCW	34046	Bristol
P117NLW	40161	Wales	P191UNS	61486	S Yorkshire	P247OEW	41147	Wales
P118NLW	40165	Potteries	P192TGD	30740	Edinburgh	P247UCW	34047	Bristol
P119NLW	40166	Potteries	P192UNS	61487	S Yorkshire	P248HMD	30556	S Yorkshire
P120NLW	40167	Potteries	P193TGD	30741	Edinburgh	P248UCW	34048	Bristol
P121NLW	40168	Potteries	P193UNS	61488	S Yorkshire	P249HMD	30557	S Yorkshire
P122NLW	40169	Potteries	P194TGD	30742	Edinburgh	P249UCW	34049	Bristol
P123NLW	40170	Potteries	P195TGD	30743	Edinburgh	P250UCW	34050	Bristol
P124NLW	40158	Potteries	P196TGD	30744	Edinburgh	P251PAE	46251	Somerset &A
P125NLW	40172	Potteries	P197TGD	30745	Edinburgh	P251UCW	34051	Bristol
P126NLW	40173	Potteries	P198TGD	30746	Edinburgh	P252PAE	46252	Somerset &A

P252UCW	34052	Bristol	P406MLA	42406	London	P445NEX	43445	Eastern C
P253PAE	46253	Somerset &A	P406PLE	31906	Manchester	P445TCV	42445	Eastern C
P253UCW	34053	S Yorkshire	P407KOW	42507	Hampshire	P446KYC	51746	Somerset &A
P254PAE	46254	Somerset &A	P407MLA	42407	Hampshire	P446NEX	43446	Eastern C
P254UCW	34054	S Yorkshire	P407PLE	30580	Manchester	P446TCV	42446	Eastern C
P255RFL	41155	Wales	P408PLE	30581	Manchester	P447KYC	51747	Somerset &A
P255UCW	34055	S Yorkshire	P409PLE	30582	Manchester	P447NEX	43447	Eastern C
P256PAE	46256	Somerset &A	P410PLE	30583	Manchester	P448KYC	51748	Somerset &A
P257PAE	46257	Somerset &A	P411MLA	47111	Devon & C	P448NEX	43448	Eastern C
P258PAE	46258	Somerset &A	P411PLE	30584	Manchester	P449NEX	43449	Eastern C
P259PAE	46259	Somerset &A	P412PLE	30585	Manchester	P450NEX	43450	Eastern C
P260PAE	46260	Somerset &A	P413MTW	30586	Manchester	P451RPW	43451	Eastern C
P261PAE	46261	Somerset &A	P414MTW	30587	Manchester	P452 SCV	42252	Devon & C
P262PAE	46262	Somerset &A	P415MTW	31915	Manchester	P452JWE	40489	S Yorkshire
P263PAE	46263	Somerset &A	P416MTW	30588	Manchester	P452RPW	43452	Eastern C
P264PAE	46264	Somerset &A	P416NFA	50073	Wales	P453 SCV	42253	Devon & C
P26RFS	23126	Glasgow	P417PVW	31917	Manchester	P453JWE	40490	S Yorkshire
P291KPX	34291	Manchester	P418PVW	31918	Manchester	P453RPW	43453	Eastern C
P292KPX	34292	Manchester	P419PVW	31919	Manchester	P455 SCV	42255	Devon & C
P293KPX	34293	Manchester	P420MEH	50077	Aberdeen	P501LND	40407	Manchester
P294KPX	34294	Manchester	P420PVW	31920	Manchester	P501MNO	67001	Essex
P295KPX	34295	Manchester	P421PVW	31921	Manchester	P502LND	40408	Manchester
P296KPX	34296	Manchester	P422PVW	31922	Manchester	P502MNO	67002	Essex
P2UVG	40724	Glasgow	P423PVW	31923	Manchester	P503LND	40409	Manchester
P301LND	40000	Manchester	P424PVW	31924	Manchester	P503MNO	67003	Essex
P302AUM	42302	Wales	P425PVW	31925	Manchester	P503XSH	62291	Edinburgh
P302LND	40337	Manchester	P426GLS	60761	S Yorkshire	P504LND	40410	Manchester
P303AUM	42303	Wales	P427GLS	60762	S Yorkshire	P504MNO	67004	Essex
P303LND	40338	Manchester	P427ORL	42427	Wales	P504XSH	62292	Edinburgh
P304AUM	42304	Wales	P428GLS	60763	S Yorkshire	P505LND	40411	Manchester
P304LND	40339	Manchester	P428ORL	42428	Wales	P505MNO	67005	Essex
P305AUM	42305	Wales	P429GLS	60764	S Yorkshire	P505XSH	62293	Edinburgh
P305LND	40340	Manchester	P429ORL	42429	Eastern C	P506LND	40412	Manchester
P306LND	40341	Manchester	P430GLS	60134	Potteries	P506MNO	67006	Essex
P307LND	40342	Manchester	P430ORL	42430	Devon & C	P506XSH	62294	Edinburgh
P308LND	40343	Manchester	P431GLS	60765	S Yorkshire	P507LND	40413	Manchester
P309LND	40001	Manchester	P431ORL	42431	Devon & C	P507MNO	67007	Essex
P310LND	40344	Manchester	P432ORL	42432	Devon & C	P508LND	40414	Manchester
P311LND	40345	W Yorkshire	P432YSH	61052	Edinburgh	P508MNO	67008	Essex
P312LND	40346	W Yorkshire	P433NEX	43433	Eastern C	P508VOS	40725	Glasgow
P313LND	40347	Manchester	P433ORL	42433	Devon & C	P509LND	40415	Manchester
P314LND	40348	Manchester	P433YSH	61053	Edinburgh	P509MNO	67009	Essex
P315LND	40349	Manchester	P434NEX	43434	Eastern C	P510LND	40416	Manchester
P316LND	40350	Manchester	P434ORL	42434	Devon & C	P510MNO	67010	Essex
P317LND	40351	Manchester	P435NEX	43435	Eastern C	P510VOS	40726	Glasgow
P318LND	40352	Manchester	P435ORL	42435	Devon & C	P511LND	40417	Manchester
P319LND	40353	Manchester	P435YSH	61055	W Yorkshire	P511MNO	67011	Essex
P320LND	40354	Manchester	P436NEX	43436	Eastern C	P511VOS	40727	Glasgow
P321LND	40355	Manchester	P436ORL	42436	Devon & C	P512LND	40418	Manchester
P322LND	40356	Manchester	P436YSH	61056	W Yorkshire	P512MNO	67012	Essex
P323LND	40357	Manchester	P437NEX	43437	Eastern C	P512VOS	40728	Glasgow
P324LND	40358	Manchester	P437ORL	42437	Devon & C	P513LND	40419	Manchester
P325LND	40359	Manchester	P438NEX	43438	Eastern C	P513MNO	67013	Essex
P330RVG	20120	Eastern C	P438ORL	42438	Devon & C	P513VOS	40729	Glasgow
P401MLA	42401	London	P439NEX	43439	Eastern C	P514LND	40420	Manchester
P401PLE	30579	Manchester	P439ORL	42439	Devon & C	P515LND	40421	Manchester
P402MLA	42402	London	P440NEX	43440	Eastern C	P515VOS	40731	Glasgow
P402PLE	31902	Manchester	P440ORL	42440	Devon & C	P516LND	40422	Manchester
P403MLA	42403	London	P441NEX	43441	Eastern C	P516VOS	40732	Glasgow
P403PLE	31903	Manchester	P441TCV	42441	Eastern C	P517LND	40423	Manchester
P404KOW	42504	Hampshire	P442KYC	51742	Somerset &A	P518LND	40424	Manchester
P404MLA	42404	London	P442NEX	43442	Eastern C	P519LND	40425	Manchester
P404PLE	31904	Manchester	P442TCV	42442	Eastern C	P519TYS	61489	Glasgow
P405KOW	42505	Hampshire	P443KYC	51743	Somerset &A	P520LND	40426	Manchester
P405MLA	42405	London	P443TCV	42443	Eastern C	P520TYS	61490	Glasgow
P405PLE	31905	Manchester	P444TCV	42444	Eastern C	P521LND	40427	Manchester
P406KOW	42506	Hampshire	P445KYC	51745	Somerset &A	P521PRL	20421	Devon & C

The 2008 First Bus Handbook

Reg	No	Location	Reg	No	Location	Reg	No	Location
P521TYS	61491	Glasgow	P546BSS	60447	Manchester	P594WSU	31572	Edinburgh
P522LND	40428	Manchester	P546EFL	34018	Essex	P595WSU	31468	Glasgow
P522TYS	61492	Glasgow	P546RNG	65546	Eastern C	P596WSU	31469	Glasgow
P523LND	40429	Manchester	P546TYS	61516	Glasgow	P597WSU	31470	Glasgow
P523TYS	61493	Glasgow	P547BSS	60448	Manchester	P598WSU	31471	Glasgow
P524LND	40430	Manchester	P547EFL	34057	Manchester	P599WSU	31472	Glasgow
P524TYS	61494	Glasgow	P547RNG	65547	Eastern C	P601WSU	31473	Glasgow
P525LND	40431	Manchester	P547TYS	61517	Glasgow	P602WSU	31474	Glasgow
P525TYS	61495	Glasgow	P548BSS	60449	Manchester	P603WSU	31475	Glasgow
P526LND	40432	Manchester	P548EFL	34058	Manchester	P604WSU	31476	Glasgow
P526TYS	61496	Glasgow	P548RNG	65548	Eastern C	P605WSU	31477	Glasgow
P527LND	40433	Manchester	P548TYS	61518	Glasgow	P606WSU	31478	Glasgow
P527TYS	61497	Glasgow	P549BSS	60450	Manchester	P607WSU	31479	Glasgow
P528HMP	34028	Manchester	P549RNG	65549	Eastern C	P608WSU	31480	Glasgow
P528LND	40434	Manchester	P549TYS	61519	Glasgow	P609WSU	31673	W Yorkshire
P528TYS	61498	Glasgow	P550EFL	34060	Hampshire	P610WSU	31674	W Yorkshire
P529EFL	34019	Manchester	P550RNG	65550	Eastern C	P611WSU	31675	Edinburgh
P529HMP	34029	Manchester	P551EFL	34011	Essex	P612WSU	31676	W Yorkshire
P529LND	40435	Manchester	P552EFL	34012	Essex	P613WSU	31677	W Yorkshire
P529TYS	61499	Glasgow	P553EFL	34013	Essex	P614WSU	31678	Edinburgh
P530EFL	34020	Hampshire	P554EFL	34014	Essex	P615WSU	31679	Edinburgh
P530HMP	34080	Manchester	P556EFL	34056	Essex	P616WSU	31680	Edinburgh
P530LND	40436	Manchester	P559EFL	34059	Hampshire	P617WSU	31481	Glasgow
P530TYS	61500	Glasgow	P561EFL	34061	Manchester	P618WSU	31482	Glasgow
P531HMP	34031	Manchester	P562EFL	34062	Hampshire	P619VDW	46719	Wales
P531TYS	61501	Glasgow	P563EFL	34063	Somerset &A	P619WSU	31483	Glasgow
P532EFL	34082	Manchester	P564EFL	34064	Somerset &A	P620VDW	46720	Wales
P532TYS	61502	Glasgow	P566EFL	34066	Edinburgh	P620WSU	31484	Glasgow
P533EFL	34083	Edinburgh	P567EFL	34067	Edinburgh	P621VDW	46721	Wales
P533HMP	34023	Manchester	P568EFL	34068	Hampshire	P626WSU	40733	Glasgow
P533TYS	61503	Glasgow	P569BTH	42569	Wales	P627CGM	46727	Somerset &A
P534TYS	61504	Glasgow	P569EFL	34069	Manchester	P627WSU	40734	Glasgow
P535EFL	34015	Edinburgh	P570BTH	42570	Wales	P628CGM	46728	Somerset &A
P535HMP	34035	Manchester	P570EFL	34070	Manchester	P628WSU	40872	W Yorkshire
P535TYS	61505	Glasgow	P571BTH	42571	Wales	P629CGM	46729	Somerset &A
P536EFL	34016	Hampshire	P571EFL	34071	Hampshire	P629WSU	40736	Glasgow
P536HMP	34036	Manchester	P572BTH	42572	Wales	P630CGM	46730	Somerset &A
P536TYS	61506	Glasgow	P572EFL	34072	Hampshire	P630WSU	40737	Glasgow
P537HMP	34037	Manchester	P573BTH	42573	Wales	P631CGM	46731	Somerset &A
P537TYS	61507	Glasgow	P573EFL	34073	Edinburgh	P631WSU	40738	Glasgow
P538HMP	34038	Manchester	P574BTH	42574	Wales	P632CGM	40911	Edinburgh
P538TYS	61508	Glasgow	P575BTH	42575	Wales	P632WSU	40739	Glasgow
P539HMP	34039	Manchester	P575DMS	62342	Edinburgh	P633WSU	40740	Glasgow
P539TYS	61509	Glasgow	P575EFL	34075	Edinburgh	P634WSU	40741	Glasgow
P540BSS	60441	Manchester	P576BTH	42576	Wales	P635WSU	40742	Glasgow
P540EFL	34017	Hampshire	P576DMS	62343	Edinburgh	P655UFB	34155	Somerset &A
P540HMP	34040	Manchester	P576EFL	34076	Edinburgh	P656UFB	34156	Somerset &A
P540TYS	61510	Glasgow	P577BTH	42577	Wales	P657UFB	34157	Somerset &A
P541BSS	60442	Manchester	P577DMS	62344	Edinburgh	P658UFB	34158	Somerset &A
P541HMP	34021	Hampshire	P578BTH	42578	Wales	P659UFB	34159	Somerset &A
P541RNG	65541	Eastern C	P578DMS	62345	Edinburgh	P660UFB	34160	Somerset &A
P541TYS	61511	Glasgow	P578EFL	34078	Hampshire	P701HMT	40064	Manchester
P542BSS	60443	Manchester	P579BTH	42579	Wales	P702HMT	40065	Manchester
P542HMP	34022	Hampshire	P579EFL	34079	Hampshire	P702HPU	40871	W Yorkshire
P542RNG	65542	Eastern C	P579RSG	62346	Edinburgh	P703HMT	40066	Manchester
P542TYS	61512	Glasgow	P580BTH	42580	Wales	P703HPU	40879	W Yorkshire
P543BSS	60444	Manchester	P580RSG	62348	Edinburgh	P704HMT	40067	Manchester
P543HMP	34033	Hampshire	P581RSG	62349	Edinburgh	P704HPU	40878	W Yorkshire
P543RNG	65543	Eastern C	P585WSU	31681	Edinburgh	P705HPU	42175	W Yorkshire
P543TYS	61513	Glasgow	P586WSU	31682	Edinburgh	P706HPU	40876	W Yorkshire
P544BSS	60445	Manchester	P587WSU	31683	W Yorkshire	P707HPU	40877	W Yorkshire
P544RNG	65544	Eastern C	P588WSU	31684	Edinburgh	P708HPU	42178	W Yorkshire
P544TYS	61514	Glasgow	P589WSU	31571	Edinburgh	P709HPU	42179	W Yorkshire
P545BSS	60446	Manchester	P590WSU	31685	W Yorkshire	P710HPU	42110	W Yorkshire
P545RNG	65545	Eastern C	P591WSU	31686	W Yorkshire	P711HPU	42181	W Yorkshire
P545TYS	61515	Glasgow	P592WSU	31687	Edinburgh	P722KCR	51722	Hampshire
			P593WSU	31688	Edinburgh	P723KCR	51723	Hampshire

Reg	No	Location	Reg	No	Location	Reg	No	Location
P724KCR	51724	Hampshire	P852VUS	42852	Essex	R132JYG	60799	W Yorkshire
P725KCR	51725	Hampshire	P853VUS	42853	Essex	R133GSF	65533	Glasgow
P726KCR	51726	Hampshire	P854VUS	42854	Essex	R133JYG	60800	W Yorkshire
P727KCR	51727	Hampshire	P855VUS	42855	Essex	R134GSF	65534	Eastern C
P728KCR	51728	Hampshire	P856VUS	40777	Essex	R134JYG	60801	W Yorkshire
P729KCR	51729	Hampshire	P857VUS	42857	Essex	R135GSF	65535	Glasgow
P731NVG	20121	Eastern C	P858VUS	40778	Essex	R135JYG	60802	W Yorkshire
P732NVG	20122	Eastern C	P859VUS	40779	Essex	R136GSF	65536	Glasgow
P733NVG	20123	Eastern C	P860VUS	40780	Glasgow	R136JYG	60803	W Yorkshire
P734NVG	20124	Eastern C	P861VUS	40781	Glasgow	R137GSF	65537	Eastern C
P748XUS	40743	Glasgow	P868MBF	60102	Essex	R137JYG	60804	W Yorkshire
P749XUS	40744	Glasgow	P869MBF	60103	Essex	R138GSF	65538	Eastern C
P750XUS	40745	Glasgow	P870MBF	60104	Essex	R138JYG	60805	W Yorkshire
P751XUS	40746	Glasgow	P875YKS	62402	Edinburgh	R139EHS	31485	Glasgow
P752XUS	40747	Glasgow	P876YKS	62403	Edinburgh	R139GSF	65539	Eastern C
P753XUS	40748	Glasgow	P877YKS	62404	Edinburgh	R139JYG	60806	W Yorkshire
P754XUS	40749	Glasgow	P878YKS	62405	Edinburgh	R140EHS	31670	Edinburgh
P756XUS	40750	Glasgow	P879YKS	62373	Edinburgh	R140GSF	65540	Eastern C
P757XUS	40751	Glasgow	P889TCV	40782	Glasgow	R141EHS	31671	Edinburgh
P758XUS	40752	Glasgow	P890TCV	40783	Glasgow	R141GSF	65521	Eastern C
P759XUS	40753	Glasgow	P908RYO	31828	Hampshire	R142EHS	31672	Edinburgh
P760XUS	40754	Glasgow	P920RYO	31820	Hampshire	R142GSF	65522	Eastern C
P761XHS	61520	S Yorkshire	P921RYO	31821	Hampshire	R143EHS	31486	Glasgow
P761XUS	40755	Glasgow	P925RYO	31825	Hampshire	R143GSF	65523	Eastern C
P762XHS	61521	S Yorkshire	P926RYO	31826	Hampshire	R144EHS	31487	Glasgow
P762XUS	40756	Glasgow	P930RYO	31830	Hampshire	R144GSF	65524	Eastern C
P763XHS	61522	S Yorkshire	P944RWS	20454	Hampshire	R145EHS	31488	Glasgow
P764XHS	61523	S Yorkshire	P945RWS	20455	Somerset &A	R145GSF	65525	Eastern C
P765XHS	20125	Eastern C	P946RWS	20456	Somerset &A	R146EHS	31489	Glasgow
P766XHS	20126	Eastern C	P973MBF	40131	Potteries	R146GSF	65526	Eastern C
P767XHS	20127	Eastern C	P974MBF	40132	Potteries	R147EHS	31490	Glasgow
P768XHS	20128	Eastern C	P975MBF	40133	Potteries	R147GSF	65527	Eastern C
P769XHS	20129	Eastern C	P976MBF	40134	Potteries	R148EHS	31491	Glasgow
P771XHS	20131	Eastern C	PSU627	20016	Aberdeen	R148GSF	65528	Eastern C
P807YUM	40757	Glasgow	PSU628	20017	Aberdeen	R149EHS	31492	Glasgow
P808YUM	40758	Glasgow	PSU629	20018	Aberdeen	R149GSF	65529	Eastern C
P809YUM	40759	Glasgow	R1 TRU	20471	Devon & C	R150EHS	31493	Glasgow
P810YUM	40760	Glasgow	R10LCB	60160	Manchester	R150GSF	65530	Glasgow
P812YUM	40762	Glasgow	R110GSF	61524	Glasgow	R151EHS	31494	Glasgow
P813YUM	40763	Glasgow	R112GSF	61525	Glasgow	R151GSF	65531	Eastern C
P814YUM	40764	Glasgow	R114GSF	61526	Glasgow	R152EHS	31200	Glasgow
P815YUM	40765	Glasgow	R115GSF	61527	Potteries	R152GSF	65532	Eastern C
P816YUM	40766	Glasgow	R116GSF	61528	Potteries	R153EHS	31495	Glasgow
P817YUM	40767	Glasgow	R117GSF	61529	Potteries	R153GSF	61542	Potteries
P818AWT	64808	W Yorkshire	R118GSF	61530	Potteries	R154GSF	62359	Edinburgh
P818YUM	40768	Glasgow	R119GSF	61531	Potteries	R155GSF	62398	Edinburgh
P819YUM	40870	W Yorkshire	R120FUP	42620	Wales	R156GSF	62360	Edinburgh
P822YUM	40770	Glasgow	R120GSF	61532	Glasgow	R157GSF	62361	Edinburgh
P823YUM	40771	W Yorkshire	R121FUP	42621	Wales	R158GSF	61543	Glasgow
P824YUM	40874	W Yorkshire	R121GSF	61533	Potteries	R158TLM	41158	Wales
P825YUM	40773	Glasgow	R122FUP	42622	Wales	R159GSF	61544	Glasgow
P826YUM	42626	Wales	R122GSF	61534	Glasgow	R159TLM	41159	Wales
P827YUM	40875	W Yorkshire	R123GSF	61535	Glasgow	R160GSF	61545	Glasgow
P828FEF	34128	Hampshire	R124GSF	61244	Potteries	R160TLM	41160	Wales
P828YUM	40697	Edinburgh	R125GSF	61536	Potteries	R161GSF	61546	Glasgow
P829FEF	34129	Hampshire	R126GSF	61243	Potteries	R162GSF	61547	Glasgow
P829YUM	40774	Glasgow	R127GSF	61245	Potteries	R162TLM	41162	Wales
P830FEF	34130	Hampshire	R128GSF	61537	Glasgow	R163GSF	61548	Glasgow
P830YUM	40775	Glasgow	R129GSF	61538	Potteries	R163TLM	41163	Wales
P831YUM	40776	Glasgow	R130FUP	42630	Somerset &A	R164GSF	61549	Glasgow
P832YUM	40698	Edinburgh	R130GSF	61539	Glasgow	R164TLM	41164	Wales
P833YUM	42633	Wales	R131FUP	42631	Wales	R165GSF	61550	Glasgow
P834YUM	42634	Somerset &A	R131GSF	61540	Glasgow	R165TLM	41165	Hampshire
P835YUM	40701	Edinburgh	R131JYG	60798	W Yorkshire	R166GSF	61551	Potteries
P836YUM	42636	Hampshire	R132FUP	42632	Wales	R166TLM	41166	Hampshire
P844OAH	43444	Eastern C	R132GSF	61541	Potteries	R167GSF	61552	Glasgow

Reg	No	Location	Reg	No	Location	Reg	No	Location
R167TLM	41167	Wales	R213TLM	41213	Glasgow	R242SBA	40368	Manchester
R168GSF	61553	Potteries	R214MSA	42214	Wales	R243ERE	50033	Potteries
R168TLM	41168	Wales	R214SBA	60141	Manchester	R243SBA	40369	Manchester
R169GSF	61554	Potteries	R214TLM	41214	Glasgow	R244SBA	40370	Manchester
R169TLM	41169	Berkshire	R215MSA	42215	Wales	R245ERE	50035	Potteries
R170GSF	61555	Potteries	R215SBA	60142	Manchester	R245SBA	40371	Manchester
R170TLM	41170	Berkshire	R215TLM	41215	Glasgow	R246ERE	50036	Potteries
R171GSF	61556	Potteries	R216MSA	42216	Wales	R246SBA	40372	Manchester
R171TLM	41171	Wales	R216SBA	60143	Manchester	R247SBA	40373	Potteries
R172GSX	61557	Potteries	R216TLM	41216	Glasgow	R248ERE	50038	Potteries
R172TLM	41172	Berkshire	R217MSA	42217	Midland Red	R248SBA	40374	Manchester
R173GSX	61159	Potteries	R217SBA	60144	Manchester	R249SBA	40375	Potteries
R173TLM	41173	Wales	R217TLM	41217	Glasgow	R250SBA	40376	Potteries
R174GSX	61234	Potteries	R218MSA	42218	Wales	R251SBA	40377	Potteries
R174TLM	41174	Berkshire	R218SBA	60145	Manchester	R252SBA	40378	Potteries
R175GSX	61158	Potteries	R218TLM	41218	Glasgow	R253SBA	40379	Potteries
R175TLM	41175	Berkshire	R219GFS	40926	Edinburgh	R254ERE	50044	Potteries
R175VWN	21145	Wales	R219MSA	42219	Midland Red	R254SBA	40380	Manchester
R176GSX	60456	Potteries	R219SBA	60146	Manchester	R255ERE	50045	Potteries
R176HUG	30808	W Yorkshire	R219TLM	41219	Glasgow	R255SBA	40381	Manchester
R176TLM	41176	Berkshire	R220GFS	40927	Edinburgh	R256ERE	50046	Potteries
R176VWN	21146	Wales	R220MSA	42220	Midland Red	R256SBA	40382	Manchester
R177GSX	60135	Potteries	R220SBA	60147	Manchester	R257DVF	65557	Eastern C
R177TLM	41177	Wales	R220TLM	41220	Edinburgh	R257ERE	50047	Potteries
R177VWN	21147	Wales	R221GFS	40928	Edinburgh	R257SBA	40383	Potteries
R178GSX	60131	Potteries	R221MSA	42221	Somerset &A	R258DVF	65558	Eastern C
R178TLM	41178	Wales	R221SBA	60148	Manchester	R258ERE	50048	Potteries
R178VWN	21148	Wales	R221TLM	41221	Glasgow	R258SBA	40384	Manchester
R179GSX	60136	Potteries	R222MSA	42222	Somerset &A	R259SBA	40385	Manchester
R179TLM	41179	Wales	R223GFS	40929	Edinburgh	R260SBA	40388	Manchester
R180TLM	41180	Wales	R223SBA	60149	Manchester	R261SBA	40387	Manchester
R181TLM	41181	Wales	R224GFS	40891	Wales	R262SBA	40386	Manchester
R182TLM	41182	Wales	R224TLM	41224	Glasgow	R263SBA	40389	Manchester
R183TLM	41183	Wales	R225GFS	40930	Edinburgh	R264SBA	40390	Manchester
R184TLM	41184	Wales	R225TLM	41225	Glasgow	R265SBA	40391	Manchester
R185TLM	41185	Wales	R226GFS	40931	Edinburgh	R266SBA	40392	Manchester
R186TLM	41186	Wales	R226SBA	40940	Edinburgh	R267SBA	40393	Manchester
R187TLM	41187	Wales	R226TLM	41226	Glasgow	R268SBA	40394	Manchester
R188TLM	41188	Wales	R227GFS	40932	Edinburgh	R269SBA	40395	Manchester
R190TLM	41190	Wales	R227SBA	40941	Edinburgh	R270SBA	40396	Manchester
R191VLD	41191	Wales	R227TLM	41227	Glasgow	R271SBA	40397	Manchester
R192VLD	41192	Wales	R228GFS	40933	Edinburgh	R272SBA	40398	Manchester
R193VLD	41193	Wales	R228SBA	40942	Edinburgh	R273SBA	40399	Manchester
R194VLD	41194	Wales	R228TLM	41228	Glasgow	R274SBA	40400	Manchester
R195GSX	61558	Glasgow	R229GFS	40934	Edinburgh	R275SBA	40401	Manchester
R195VLD	41195	Wales	R229SBA	40943	Edinburgh	R276SBA	40402	Manchester
R196VLD	41196	Wales	R229TLM	41229	London	R277LGH	31877	Hampshire
R201TLM	41201	Glasgow	R230SBA	40944	Edinburgh	R277SBA	40403	Manchester
R202TLM	41202	Glasgow	R230TLM	41230	London	R278LGH	31878	Hampshire
R203TLM	41203	Glasgow	R231SBA	40945	Edinburgh	R278SBA	40404	Manchester
R204TLM	41204	Glasgow	R232ERE	50022	Potteries	R279SBA	40405	Manchester
R205TLM	41205	Glasgow	R232SBA	40901	Edinburgh	R280SBA	40406	Manchester
R206LKS	31638	Edinburgh	R232TLM	41232	London	R288GHS	40784	Hampshire
R206TLM	41206	Glasgow	R233ERE	50023	Potteries	R289GHS	40785	Hampshire
R207MSA	42207	Wales	R233SBA	40946	Edinburgh	R290GHS	40786	Hampshire
R208MSA	42208	Wales	R233TLM	41233	London	R291GHS	40787	Hampshire
R208TLM	41208	Glasgow	R234SBA	40360	Manchester	R292GHS	40788	Hampshire
R209MSA	42209	Wales	R234TLM	41234	London	R293GHS	40789	S Yorkshire
R209TLM	41209	Glasgow	R235ERE	50025	Potteries	R294GHS	40790	Hampshire
R210MSA	42210	Wales	R235SBA	40361	Manchester	R295GHS	40791	Hampshire
R210TLM	41210	Glasgow	R236SBA	40362	Manchester	R296GHS	40792	Hampshire
R211GSF	61559	Glasgow	R237SBA	40363	Manchester	R297AYB	21097	Wales
R211MSA	42211	Wales	R238SBA	40364	Manchester	R297GHS	40793	Hampshire
R211TLM	41211	Glasgow	R239SBA	40365	Manchester	R298AYB	21098	Wales
R212MSA	42212	Wales	R240SBA	40366	Manchester	R298GHS	40794	Hampshire
R212TLM	41212	Glasgow	R241LGH	31841	Somerset &A	R299AYB	21099	Wales
R213MSA	42213	Wales	R241SBA	40367	Potteries	R299GHS	40795	Hampshire

Reg	No	Location	Reg	No	Location	Reg	No	Location
R2LCB	60152	Manchester	R340HYG	60933	W Yorkshire	R438ALS	60075	Potteries
R301GHS	40796	Glasgow	R341HYG	40868	W Yorkshire	R438ULE	31938	Manchester
R301LKS	31569	Edinburgh	R341SUT	61561	Glasgow	R439ALS	60076	Potteries
R302GHS	40797	Glasgow	R342HYG	40706	Edinburgh	R439ULE	31939	Manchester
R302LKS	31634	Edinburgh	R342SUT	61562	Glasgow	R440ALS	60077	Potteries
R303GHS	40798	Glasgow	R343GHS	60030	Glasgow	R440ULE	31940	Manchester
R303LKS	31635	Edinburgh	R343HYG	40708	Edinburgh	R441ALS	60078	Potteries
R304GHS	40799	Glasgow	R343SUT	61563	Potteries	R441ULE	31941	Manchester
R304JAF	20404	Edinburgh	R344GHS	60130	Essex	R442ALS	60079	Potteries
R304LKS	31636	Edinburgh	R344SUT	61564	Glasgow	R442ULE	31942	Manchester
R305GHS	40800	Glasgow	R345GHS	60129	Glasgow	R443ALS	62300	Edinburgh
R305JAF	20405	Edinburgh	R345SUT	61565	Glasgow	R443ULE	31943	Manchester
R305LKS	31637	Edinburgh	R346GHS	60031	Essex	R445ALS	62302	Edinburgh
R307GHS	40801	Glasgow	R346LGH	31846	Somerset &A	R445ULE	31945	Manchester
R307LKS	31639	Edinburgh	R346SUT	60011	Potteries	R446ALS	62303	Edinburgh
R308GHS	40722	Glasgow	R404HYG	50386	Glasgow	R446ULE	31946	Manchester
R308JAF	20408	Devon & C	R405WWR	50299	Hampshire	R447ALS	62304	Edinburgh
R308LKS	31640	Edinburgh	R408WPX	42508	Hampshire	R447CCV	42447	Eastern C
R309GHS	40802	Glasgow	R409WPX	42509	Hampshire	R447ULE	31947	Manchester
R309LKS	31641	Edinburgh	R410WPX	42510	Hampshire	R448ALS	62305	Edinburgh
R310GHS	40803	Glasgow	R411WPX	42511	Hampshire	R448CCV	42448	Eastern C
R310JAF	20410	Devon & C	R412WPX	42512	Hampshire	R448ULE	31948	Manchester
R310LKS	31642	Edinburgh	R413WPX	42513	Hampshire	R449CCV	42449	Devon & C
R311GHS	40804	Glasgow	R414WPX	42514	Hampshire	R449JSG	61063	W Yorkshire
R311LKS	31643	Edinburgh	R415WPX	41515	Hampshire	R449ULE	31949	Manchester
R312GHS	40805	Midland Red	R416VPU	52596	Devon & C	R450CCV	42450	Eastern C
R312LKS	31644	Edinburgh	R416WPX	41516	Hampshire	R450JSG	61064	W Yorkshire
R313GHS	40806	Glasgow	R416YMS	31648	Edinburgh	R450ULE	31950	Manchester
R313LKS	31645	Edinburgh	R417VPU	52597	Devon & C	R451CCV	42451	Eastern C
R314GHS	40807	Glasgow	R417WPX	41517	Hampshire	R451JSG	61065	W Yorkshire
R314LKS	31646	Edinburgh	R417YMS	31649	Edinburgh	R452CCV	42452	Devon & C
R315GHS	40808	Glasgow	R418VPU	52598	Devon & C	R452JSG	61066	W Yorkshire
R315LKS	31647	Edinburgh	R418WPX	41518	Hampshire	R453JFS	61067	W Yorkshire
R317GHS	40809	Glasgow	R418YMS	31650	Edinburgh	R454CCV	42454	Devon & C
R319GHS	40810	Glasgow	R419WPX	41519	Hampshire	R454JFS	61068	W Yorkshire
R321GHS	40811	Glasgow	R419YMS	31651	Edinburgh	R455CCV	42455	Devon & C
R322GHS	40812	Glasgow	R420WPX	42520	Hampshire	R455JFS	61069	W Yorkshire
R322TLM	41222	Glasgow	R420YMS	31652	Edinburgh	R456CCV	42456	Devon & C
R324GHS	40813	Glasgow	R421WPX	42521	Hampshire	R456JFS	61070	W Yorkshire
R324HYG	40703	Edinburgh	R421YMS	31653	Edinburgh	R457CCV	42457	Devon & C
R326GHS	62146	Aberdeen	R422WPX	42522	Hampshire	R457JFS	61071	W Yorkshire
R326HYG	40666	W Yorkshire	R422YMS	31570	Edinburgh	R458BNG	40881	W Yorkshire
R327GHS	62147	Aberdeen	R423WPX	42523	Hampshire	R458CCV	42458	Eastern C
R327HYG	40900	Edinburgh	R423YMS	31654	Edinburgh	R458JFS	61072	W Yorkshire
R329GHS	62148	Aberdeen	R424WPX	42524	Hampshire	R459BNG	43459	Eastern C
R329HYG	40667	W Yorkshire	R425WPX	42525	Hampshire	R459CCV	42459	Devon & C
R330GHS	62156	Aberdeen	R426SOY	31926	Manchester	R459JFS	61073	W Yorkshire
R330HYG	40179	Potteries	R426WPX	42526	Hampshire	R460BNG	43460	Eastern C
R331GHS	62157	Aberdeen	R427ULE	31927	Manchester	R460CCV	42460	W Yorkshire
R331HYG	40668	W Yorkshire	R427WPX	42527	Hampshire	R460JFS	61074	W Yorkshire
R332GHS	62158	Aberdeen	R428ULE	31928	Manchester	R460VOP	66100	Somerset &A
R332HYG	40669	W Yorkshire	R429ULE	31929	Manchester	R461BNG	43461	Eastern C
R334GHS	62159	Aberdeen	R430PSH	40935	Wales	R461CCV	42461	Devon & C
R334HYG	40867	W Yorkshire	R430ULE	31930	Manchester	R461JFS	61075	W Yorkshire
R335GHS	62160	Aberdeen	R431PSH	40163	Potteries	R462BNG	43462	Eastern C
R335HYG	40164	Potteries	R432PSH	40681	W Yorkshire	R462CCV	42462	Devon & C
R336GHS	62161	Aberdeen	R432ULE	31932	Manchester	R462JFS	61076	W Yorkshire
R336HYG	60929	W Yorkshire	R433PSH	40936	Edinburgh	R463CAH	43463	Eastern C
R336LGH	31836	Hampshire	R433ULE	31933	Manchester	R463CCV	42463	Devon & C
R337GHS	62162	Aberdeen	R434GSF	61054	Essex	R463JFS	61077	W Yorkshire
R337HYG	60930	W Yorkshire	R434PSH	40937	Edinburgh	R464CAH	43464	Eastern C
R338GHS	61560	Manchester	R434ULE	31934	Manchester	R464CCV	42464	Devon & C
R338HYG	60931	W Yorkshire	R435ULE	31935	Manchester	R464JFS	61078	W Yorkshire
R339GHS	61241	Manchester	R436ULE	31936	Manchester	R465CAH	43465	Eastern C
R339HYG	60932	W Yorkshire	R437GSF	61057	Essex	R466CAH	43466	Eastern C
R340GHS	61240	Manchester	R437ULE	31937	Manchester	R467CAH	43467	Eastern C

The 2008 First Bus Handbook

Reg	No	Location	Reg	No	Location	Reg	No	Location
R468CAH	43468	Eastern C	R588SBA	62142	Manchester	R630CVR	60385	Manchester
R469CAH	43469	Eastern C	R588SWN	42588	Wales	R630JUB	30810	W Yorkshire
R470CAH	43470	Eastern C	R589BMS	62352	Edinburgh	R631CVR	60386	Manchester
R471CAH	43471	Eastern C	R589SBA	62143	Manchester	R631DUS	40814	Glasgow
R472CAH	43472	Eastern C	R589SWN	42589	Wales	R631JUB	30811	W Yorkshire
R473CAH	43473	Eastern C	R590BMS	62353	Edinburgh	R632CVR	60387	Manchester
R474CAH	43474	Eastern C	R590SWN	42590	Wales	R632DUS	40815	Glasgow
R476CAH	43476	Eastern C	R591BMS	62354	Edinburgh	R632JUB	30812	W Yorkshire
R477CAH	43477	Eastern C	R591SBA	62145	Aberdeen	R633CVR	60388	Manchester
R478CAH	43478	Eastern C	R591SWN	42591	Wales	R633DUS	40816	Glasgow
R483EDW	52483	Glasgow	R592SWN	42592	Wales	R633JUB	30813	W Yorkshire
R486EDW	52486	Glasgow	R593SWN	42593	Wales	R633VLX	41633	Hampshire
R489EDW	52489	Glasgow	R594SWN	42594	Wales	R634CVR	60856	W Yorkshire
R4LCB	60154	Manchester	R595SWN	42595	Wales	R634DUS	40817	Glasgow
R501CNP	52501	Midland Red	R596SWN	42596	Wales	R634JUB	30814	W Yorkshire
R501NPR	52601	Hampshire	R597SWN	42597	Wales	R634VLX	41634	Hampshire
R502CNP	52502	Midland Red	R598SWN	42598	Wales	R636CVR	60858	W Yorkshire
R502NPR	52602	Hampshire	R599SWN	42599	Wales	R636DUS	40818	Glasgow
R503CNP	52503	Midland Red	R5LCB	60155	Manchester	R636HYG	30816	W Yorkshire
R503NPR	52603	Hampshire	R606JUB	30786	W Yorkshire	R636JUB	30815	W Yorkshire
R504CNP	52504	Midland Red	R607JUB	30787	W Yorkshire	R636VLX	41636	Hampshire
R504NPR	52604	Hampshire	R608JUB	30788	W Yorkshire	R637CVR	60859	W Yorkshire
R505NPR	52605	Hampshire	R608YCR	40880	W Yorkshire	R637DUS	40819	Glasgow
R506NPR	52606	Hampshire	R609JUB	30789	W Yorkshire	R637HYG	30817	W Yorkshire
R507NPR	52607	Hampshire	R609YCR	42109	Hampshire	R637VLX	41637	Essex
R508NPR	52608	Hampshire	R610JUB	30790	W Yorkshire	R638CVR	60860	W Yorkshire
R519BMS	62306	Edinburgh	R610YCR	42180	Hampshire	R638DUS	40820	Glasgow
R521BMS	62308	Edinburgh	R611JUB	30791	W Yorkshire	R638HYG	30818	W Yorkshire
R522BMS	62384	Edinburgh	R611YCR	42111	Hampshire	R638VLX	41638	Hampshire
R524BMS	62310	Edinburgh	R612JUB	30792	W Yorkshire	R639CVR	60861	S Yorkshire
R544ALS	62301	Edinburgh	R612YCR	42112	Hampshire	R639HYG	30819	W Yorkshire
R551CNG	65551	Eastern C	R613JUB	30793	W Yorkshire	R639VLX	41639	Wales
R552CNG	65552	Eastern C	R613YCR	42113	Hampshire	R640CVR	60862	S Yorkshire
R553CNG	65553	Eastern C	R614JUB	30794	W Yorkshire	R640HYG	30820	W Yorkshire
R554CNG	65554	Eastern C	R614YCR	42114	Hampshire	R640VLX	41640	Essex
R556CNG	65556	Eastern C	R615JUB	30795	W Yorkshire	R641CVR	60863	W Yorkshire
R571YNC	60361	Manchester	R615YCR	42115	Hampshire	R641DUS	40821	S Yorkshire
R572SBA	60362	Manchester	R616JUB	30796	W Yorkshire	R641HYG	30821	W Yorkshire
R573SBA	60363	Manchester	R616YCR	42116	Hampshire	R641VLX	41641	Hampshire
R574SBA	60364	Manchester	R617JUB	30797	W Yorkshire	R642CVR	60864	Hampshire
R575SBA	60365	Manchester	R617YCR	42117	Hampshire	R642DUS	40822	Hampshire
R576SBA	60366	Manchester	R618JUB	30798	W Yorkshire	R642HYG	30822	W Yorkshire
R577SBA	60367	Manchester	R618YCR	42118	Hampshire	R642TLM	41642	Essex
R578SBA	60368	Manchester	R619JUB	30799	W Yorkshire	R643CVR	60865	W Yorkshire
R579SBA	60369	Manchester	R619YCR	42119	Hampshire	R643DUS	40823	Hampshire
R580SBA	60370	Manchester	R620JUB	30800	W Yorkshire	R643HYG	30823	W Yorkshire
R581SBA	60371	Manchester	R620YCR	42120	Hampshire	R643TLM	41643	Hampshire
R581SWN	42581	Wales	R621CVR	60376	Manchester	R644CVR	60766	Eastern C
R582SBA	60372	Manchester	R621JUB	30801	W Yorkshire	R644DUS	40824	Hampshire
R582SWN	42582	Wales	R621YCR	42121	Hampshire	R644HYG	30824	W Yorkshire
R582YMS	62393	Edinburgh	R622CVR	60377	Manchester	R644TLM	41644	Essex
R583SBA	60373	Manchester	R622JUB	30802	Potteries	R645CVR	60389	Manchester
R583SWN	42583	Wales	R622YCR	42122	Hampshire	R645DUS	40825	Hampshire
R583YMS	62394	Edinburgh	R623CVR	60378	Manchester	R645HYG	30825	W Yorkshire
R584SBA	62215	Manchester	R623JUB	30803	Potteries	R645TLM	41645	Essex
R584SWN	43584	Wales	R623YCR	42123	Hampshire	R646CVR	60390	Manchester
R584YMS	62395	Edinburgh	R624CVR	60379	Manchester	R646DUS	40826	Hampshire
R585SBA	62216	Manchester	R624JUB	30804	Potteries	R646HYG	30826	Edinburgh
R585SWN	42585	Wales	R625CVR	60380	Manchester	R646TLM	41646	Hampshire
R585YMS	62396	Edinburgh	R625JUB	30805	Potteries	R647CVR	60391	Manchester
R586SBA	62217	Manchester	R626CVR	60381	Manchester	R647DUS	40827	Hampshire
R586SWN	42586	Wales	R626JUB	30806	Potteries	R647HYG	30827	Edinburgh
R587BMS	62350	Edinburgh	R627CVR	60382	Manchester	R647TLM	41647	Essex
R587SBA	62218	Manchester	R627JUB	30807	Potteries	R648CVR	60392	Manchester
R587SWN	42587	Wales	R629CVR	60384	Manchester	R648HYG	30828	Edinburgh
R588BMS	62351	Edinburgh	R629JUB	30809	W Yorkshire	R649CVR	60393	Manchester

Reg	Fleet	Location	Reg	Fleet	Location	Reg	Fleet	Location
R649HYG	30829	Edinburgh	R710BAE	42710	Bristol	R881HRF	60115	Potteries
R649TLM	41649	London	R710VLA	41010	Essex	R882ENF	60151	Manchester
R650CVR	60394	Manchester	R711BAE	42711	Bristol	R8LCB	60158	Manchester
R650HYG	30830	Edinburgh	R711VLA	41011	Essex	R901BOU	66101	S Yorkshire
R650TLM	41650	Essex	R712BAE	42712	Bristol	R902BOU	66102	Somerset &A
R651CVR	60395	Manchester	R712DJN	43712	Essex	R903BOU	66103	Somerset &A
R651HYG	30831	Edinburgh	R712VLA	41012	Essex	R904BOU	66104	Somerset &A
R651TLM	41651	Essex	R713BAE	42713	Wales	R905BOU	66105	Somerset &A
R652HYG	30832	Edinburgh	R713DJN	43713	Essex	R906BOU	66106	Somerset &A
R652TLM	41652	Wales	R713VLA	41013	Essex	R907BOU	66107	Somerset &A
R653HYG	30833	Edinburgh	R714BAE	42714	Wales	R908BOU	66108	Somerset &A
R653TLM	41653	Essex	R714DJN	43714	Essex	R909BOU	66109	Somerset &A
R654CVR	60383	Manchester	R714VLA	41014	Essex	R910BOU	66110	Somerset &A
R654DUS	31496	Glasgow	R715BAE	42715	Wales	R912BOU	66112	S Yorkshire
R655CVR	60857	W Yorkshire	R715DJN	43715	Essex	R913BOU	66113	S Yorkshire
R655DUS	31497	Glasgow	R715VLA	41015	Essex	R914BOU	66114	S Yorkshire
R656DUS	31498	Glasgow	R716BAE	42716	Wales	R915BOU	66115	Somerset &A
R657DUS	31499	Glasgow	R716DJN	43716	Essex	R916BOU	66116	Somerset &A
R658DUS	31500	Glasgow	R716VLA	41016	Essex	R917BOU	66117	Somerset &A
R659DUS	31501	Glasgow	R717BAE	42717	Wales	R918BOU	66118	Somerset &A
R661DUS	31503	Glasgow	R717DJN	43717	Essex	R918WOE	31818	W Yorkshire
R661NHY	34161	Bristol	R717VLA	41017	Essex	R919BOU	66119	S Yorkshire
R662DUS	31504	Glasgow	R718BAE	42718	Bristol	R920COU	66120	Somerset &A
R662NHY	34162	Bristol	R718DJN	43718	Essex	R921WOE	31760	W Yorkshire
R663DUS	31505	Glasgow	R719DJN	43719	Essex	R922WOE	31761	W Yorkshire
R663NHY	34163	Bristol	R719RAD	42719	Bristol	R923WOE	31762	W Yorkshire
R664DUS	40828	Glasgow	R720DJN	43720	Essex	R924WOE	31763	W Yorkshire
R664NHY	34164	Bristol	R721DJN	43721	Essex	R925WOE	31764	W Yorkshire
R665DUS	40829	Glasgow	R722HHK	60934	W Yorkshire	R926WOE	31765	W Yorkshire
R667DUS	40830	Glasgow	R723HHK	60935	W Yorkshire	R927WOE	31805	W Yorkshire
R668DUS	40831	Glasgow	R724HHK	60936	W Yorkshire	R928WOE	31806	W Yorkshire
R669DUS	40832	Glasgow	R725HHK	60937	W Yorkshire	R929WOE	31807	W Yorkshire
R670DUS	40833	Midland Red	R726HHK	60938	W Yorkshire	R930WOE	31766	W Yorkshire
R671DUS	40834	Glasgow	R757DYS	40842	Glasgow	R931WOE	31767	W Yorkshire
R672DUS	40835	Somerset &A	R758DYS	40843	S Yorkshire	R932YOV	31768	W Yorkshire
R673DUS	40836	Wales	R759DYS	40844	S Yorkshire	R933YOV	31769	W Yorkshire
R674DUS	40837	Midland Red	R781WKW	60618	S Yorkshire	R934YOV	31770	W Yorkshire
R675DUS	40838	Midland Red	R782WKW	60619	S Yorkshire	R935YOV	31771	W Yorkshire
R676DUS	40839	Glasgow	R783WKW	60620	S Yorkshire	R936YOV	31808	W Yorkshire
R677DUS	40840	Glasgow	R784WKW	60621	S Yorkshire	R937YOV	31772	W Yorkshire
R678DUS	40841	S Yorkshire	R785WKW	60622	S Yorkshire	R938YOV	31773	W Yorkshire
R680DPW	43480	Eastern C	R787WKW	60624	S Yorkshire	R939YOV	31774	W Yorkshire
R681DPW	43481	Eastern C	R788WKW	60625	S Yorkshire	R940YOV	31775	W Yorkshire
R682DPW	43482	Eastern C	R789WKW	60626	S Yorkshire	R943LHT	20459	Bristol
R683DPW	43483	Eastern C	R790WKW	60627	S Yorkshire	R977NVT	40135	Potteries
R684DPW	43484	Eastern C	R7LCB	60157	Manchester	R978NVT	40136	Potteries
R685DPW	43485	Eastern C	R810NVT	60052	Potteries	R979NVT	40137	Potteries
R686DPW	43486	Eastern C	R811NVT	60053	Potteries	R980NVT	40138	Potteries
R687DPW	43487	Eastern C	R812NVT	60054	Potteries	R981NVT	40139	Potteries
R688DPW	43488	Eastern C	R813HWS	20457	Hampshire	R9LCB	60159	Manchester
R689DPW	43489	Eastern C	R814HWS	20458	Bristol	RA04 YGX	54601	Devon & C
R6LCB	60156	Manchester	R835VLX	41635	Hampshire	RA04 YHS	54602	Devon & C
R701BAE	42701	Bristol	R841DVF	20141	Eastern C	RD51FKV	68001	Berkshire
R702BAE	42702	Bristol	R842DVF	20142	Eastern C	RD51FKW	68002	Berkshire
R703BAE	42703	Bristol	R844YLC	31944	Manchester	RD51FKZ	68003	Berkshire
R704BAE	42704	Bristol	R853TFJ	52653	Devon & C	RD51FLA	68004	Berkshire
R705BAE	42705	Bristol	R86XHL	60623	S Yorkshire	RG51FWZ	41403	London
R705VLA	41005	Essex	R871ERE	60105	Potteries	RG51FZA	41404	London
R706BAE	42706	Bristol	R872ERE	60106	Potteries	RG51FZB	41405	London
R706VLA	41006	Essex	R873ERE	60107	Potteries	RG51FZC	41406	London
R707BAE	42707	Bristol	R874ERE	60108	Potteries	RG51FZD	41407	London
R707VLA	41007	Essex	R875ERE	60109	Potteries	RG51FZE	41408	London
R708BAE	42708	Bristol	R876ERE	60110	Potteries	RG51FZF	41409	London
R708VLA	41008	Essex	R877ERE	60111	Potteries	RG51FZH	41410	London
R709BAE	42709	Bristol	R878ERE	60112	Potteries	RIL1053	21053	Somerset &A
R709VLA	41009	Essex	R879HRF	60113	Potteries	RIL1069	66511	Somerset &A
			R880HRF	60114	Potteries	RX54AOV	68511	Hampshire

172

Reg	No	Location	Reg	No	Location	Reg	No	Location
RX54AOY	68512	Hampshire	S236KLM	41236	London	S353NPO	66153	Hampshire
RX54OGZ	68522	Berkshire	S237KLM	41237	London	S354MFP	60007	Potteries
S101CSG	61137	Potteries	S238KLM	41238	London	S354NPO	66154	Hampshire
S101TNB	60081	Potteries	S239KLM	41239	London	S355MFP	60008	Potteries
S102CSG	65602	Berkshire	S240CSF	40893	Edinburgh	S355XCR	66155	Hampshire
S102TNB	60118	Potteries	S240KLM	41240	London	S356MFP	60004	Potteries
S103CSG	61138	Potteries	S241CSF	40892	Wales	S356XCR	66156	Hampshire
S103TNB	60013	Potteries	S241KLM	41241	London	S357MFP	60082	Potteries
S104CSG	61139	Potteries	S242CSF	40894	Edinburgh	S357XCR	66157	Hampshire
S104TNB	60014	Potteries	S242KLM	41242	London	S358MFP	60010	Potteries
S105CSG	61140	Potteries	S243CSF	40895	Edinburgh	S358XCR	66158	Hampshire
S105TNB	60128	Potteries	S243KLM	41243	London	S359MFP	61141	Potteries
S106CSG	61291	Glasgow	S244CSF	40938	Edinburgh	S359XCR	66159	Hampshire
S106TNB	60015	Potteries	S244KLM	41244	London	S360MFP	61142	Potteries
S107CSG	61292	Glasgow	S245CSF	40939	Wales	S360XCR	66160	Hampshire
S107TNB	60119	Potteries	S245KLM	41245	London	S361MFP	61143	Potteries
S108CSG	61293	Glasgow	S246CSF	40174	Potteries	S361XCR	66161	Hampshire
S108TNB	60161	Potteries	S246KLM	41246	London	S362XCR	66162	Hampshire
S109CSG	61294	Glasgow	S247CSF	40175	Potteries	S363XCR	66163	Hampshire
S109TNB	60162	Berkshire	S247KLM	41247	London	S372SUX	40957	Devon & C
S110CSG	61295	Glasgow	S248CSF	40896	Edinburgh	S374SUX	40034	Devon & C
S110TNB	60163	Berkshire	S248KLM	41248	London	S375SUX	40035	Devon & C
S111FML	10000	Manchester	S249CSF	40897	Edinburgh	S376SUX	40036	Devon & C
S112TNB	60165	Berkshire	S250CSF	40898	Edinburgh	S377SUX	40037	Devon & C
S113CSG	61298	Glasgow	S251CSF	40899	Edinburgh	S378SUX	40038	Devon & C
S113TNB	60166	Berkshire	S253JLP	41253	London	S389SUX	40039	Devon & C
S114CSG	61299	Glasgow	S254JLP	41254	London	S406GUB	50300	Hampshire
S114TNB	60167	Berkshire	S255JLP	41255	London	S407GUB	50301	Devon & C
S115CSG	61300	Glasgow	S256JLP	41256	London	S409GUB	50303	Hampshire
S115TNB	60168	Berkshire	S259AFA	50049	Potteries	S410GUB	50304	Devon & C
S116CSG	61017	Glasgow	S264AFA	50054	Potteries	S412GUB	50306	Devon & C
S116JTP	66126	Eastern C	S265AFA	50055	Potteries	S413GUB	50307	Devon & C
S116RKG	21150	Wales	S266AFA	50056	Potteries	S422LLO	34222	S Yorkshire
S117CSG	61018	Glasgow	S267AFA	50057	Potteries	S443BSG	60080	Potteries
S117JTP	66127	Hampshire	S268AFA	50058	Potteries	S445BSG	61059	W Yorkshire
S118CSG	61019	Glasgow	S269AFA	50059	Potteries	S446BSG	61060	W Yorkshire
S118JTP	66128	Hampshire	S270AFA	50060	Potteries	S447BSG	61061	W Yorkshire
S119CSG	61020	Glasgow	S301EWU	50270	Hampshire	S448BSG	61062	W Yorkshire
S119JTP	66129	Hampshire	S302EWU	50271	Hampshire	S451SLL	31951	Manchester
S120JTP	66130	Hampshire	S303EWU	50272	Hampshire	S452SLL	31952	Manchester
S121JTP	66121	Hampshire	S304EWU	50273	Eastern C	S453SLL	31953	Manchester
S122UOT	66122	Hampshire	S305EWU	50274	Eastern C	S454SLL	31954	Manchester
S140AGR	40873	W Yorkshire	S306EWU	50275	W Yorkshire	S474TJX	40961	Devon & C
S197KLM	41197	Wales	S311SCV	20411	Wales	S508UAK	40513	S Yorkshire
S198KLM	41198	Wales	S312SCV	20412	Devon & C	S509UAK	40514	S Yorkshire
S199KLM	41199	Wales	S313SCV	20413	Devon & C	S510UAK	40515	S Yorkshire
S206LLO	34206	S Yorkshire	S314SRL	20144	Devon & C	S511UAK	40516	S Yorkshire
S207LLO	34207	S Yorkshire	S315SRL	20145	Devon & C	S512UAK	40517	S Yorkshire
S208LLO	34208	S Yorkshire	S334TJX	40958	Devon & C	S513RWP	52513	Hampshire
S209LLO	34209	S Yorkshire	S335TJX	40959	Devon & C	S513UAK	40518	S Yorkshire
S210LLO	34210	S Yorkshire	S337TJX	40688	Devon & C	S514UAK	40519	S Yorkshire
S211CSG	61296	Glasgow	S338TJX	40960	Devon & C	S515RWP	52515	Devon & C
S211LLO	34211	S Yorkshire	S340WYB	52640	Somerset &A	S515UAK	40520	S Yorkshire
S212LLO	34212	S Yorkshire	S341EWU	40670	Potteries	S516UAK	40521	S Yorkshire
S213LLO	34213	S Yorkshire	S342EWU	42642	Wales	S517RWP	52517	Hampshire
S214LLO	34214	S Yorkshire	S343EWU	42643	Berkshire	S517UAK	40522	S Yorkshire
S215LLO	34215	London	S343SUX	40033	Devon & C	S518UAK	40523	S Yorkshire
S216LLO	34216	London	S344EWU	42644	Berkshire	S519RWP	52519	Devon & C
S217LLO	34217	S Yorkshire	S345EWU	40671	W Yorkshire	S519UAK	40524	S Yorkshire
S218LLO	34218	London	S347MFP	60009	Potteries	S520UAK	40525	S Yorkshire
S219LLO	34219	S Yorkshire	S348MFP	60012	Potteries	S520UMS	62383	Edinburgh
S220GKS	61021	Glasgow	S350MFP	60006	Potteries	S521UAK	40526	S Yorkshire
S220KLM	41200	Somerset &A	S351MFP	60005	Potteries	S522UAK	40527	S Yorkshire
S220LLO	34220	S Yorkshire	S351NPO	66151	Hampshire	S523RWP	52523	Devon & C
S221LLO	34221	S Yorkshire	S352NPO	66152	Hampshire	S523UAK	40528	S Yorkshire
S235KLM	41235	London	S353MFP	60083	Potteries	S523UMS	62309	Edinburgh

Reg	No	Area	Reg	No	Area	Reg	No	Area
S524UAK	40529	S Yorkshire	S636XCR	42136	Hampshire	S676SVU	60819	W Yorkshire
S525UAK	40530	S Yorkshire	S637XCR	42137	Hampshire	S677AAE	34177	Somerset &A
S525UMS	62311	Edinburgh	S638XCR	42138	Hampshire	S677SNG	42777	Devon & C
S526RWP	52526	Devon & C	S639XCR	42139	Hampshire	S677SVU	60820	W Yorkshire
S526UAK	40531	S Yorkshire	S640XCR	42140	Hampshire	S678AAE	34178	Somerset &A
S526UMS	62312	Edinburgh	S641XCR	42141	Hampshire	S679AAE	34179	Somerset &A
S527UAK	40532	S Yorkshire	S642XCR	42142	Hampshire	S679SNG	42779	Devon & C
S528RWP	52528	Devon & C	S644BSG	61058	W Yorkshire	S680AAE	34180	Somerset &A
S528UAK	40533	S Yorkshire	S651RNA	60164	Berkshire	S680BFS	61235	Potteries
S529RWP	52529	Devon & C	S652RNA	60396	Manchester	S680SNG	42780	Devon & C
S529UAK	40534	S Yorkshire	S652SNG	42752	Devon & C	S681AAE	34181	Bristol
S530UAK	40535	S Yorkshire	S653RNA	60397	Manchester	S681BFS	61237	Potteries
S531UAK	40536	S Yorkshire	S653SNG	42754	Devon & C	S682AAE	34182	Bristol
S532RWP	52532	Devon & C	S654FWY	30834	W Yorkshire	S682BFS	61157	Potteries
S532UAK	40537	S Yorkshire	S654NUG	30238	W Yorkshire	S683AAE	34183	Bristol
S533RWP	52533	Hampshire	S654RNA	60398	Manchester	S683BFS	61238	Potteries
S533UAK	40538	S Yorkshire	S655FWY	30835	W Yorkshire	S683SNG	42783	Devon & C
S534RWP	52534	Devon & C	S655NUG	30239	W Yorkshire	S684AAE	34184	Bristol
S534UAK	40539	S Yorkshire	S655RNA	60399	Manchester	S684BFS	61160	Potteries
S535RWP	52535	Devon & C	S656FWY	30836	W Yorkshire	S684SNG	42784	Devon & C
S535UAK	40540	S Yorkshire	S656NUG	30240	W Yorkshire	S685AAE	34185	Bristol
S536RWP	52536	Devon & C	S656RNA	60400	Manchester	S685BFS	60137	Potteries
S536UAK	40541	S Yorkshire	S657FWY	30837	W Yorkshire	S686AAE	34186	Bristol
S537UAK	40542	S Yorkshire	S657NUG	30241	W Yorkshire	S686BFS	61246	Potteries
S538UAK	40543	S Yorkshire	S657RNA	60767	Eastern C	S687AAE	34187	Bristol
S540RWP	52540	Devon & C	S657SNG	42757	Devon & C	S687BFS	61577	Glasgow
S547RWP	52547	Devon & C	S658FWY	30838	W Yorkshire	S688AAE	34188	Somerset &A
S549 SCV	43809	Devon & C	S658NUG	30242	W Yorkshire	S688BFS	61144	Potteries
S550JSE	61567	Glasgow	S658RNA	60807	Eastern C	S689AAE	34189	Somerset &A
S550RWP	52550	Devon & C	S658SNG	42758	Devon & C	S689BFS	61239	Potteries
S551JSE	61568	Glasgow	S659FWY	30839	W Yorkshire	S690AAE	34190	Somerset &A
S551RWP	52551	Devon & C	S659NUG	30243	W Yorkshire	S690BFS	61145	Potteries
S551WAT	42551	Eastern C	S659RNA	60808	Eastern C	S691AAE	34191	Somerset &A
S552JSE	61569	Glasgow	S659SNG	42759	Devon & C	S691BFS	61578	Glasgow
S552RWP	52552	Devon & C	S660NUG	30244	W Yorkshire	S692BFS	61579	Glasgow
S553JSE	61570	Glasgow	S660RNA	60809	W Yorkshire	S693BFS	61580	Glasgow
S553RWP	52553	Somerset &A	S661NUG	30245	W Yorkshire	S694BFS	61581	Glasgow
S554JSE	61571	Glasgow	S661RNA	60810	W Yorkshire	S696BFS	61582	Glasgow
S554RWP	52554	Bristol	S662NUG	30246	W Yorkshire	S697BFS	61583	Glasgow
S555JSE	61572	Glasgow	S662RNA	60811	W Yorkshire	S698BFS	61584	Glasgow
S556JSE	61573	Glasgow	S663NUG	30247	W Yorkshire	S699BFS	61585	Glasgow
S556RWP	52556	Devon & C	S663RNA	60812	Eastern C	S701BFS	61586	Glasgow
S557JSE	61574	Glasgow	S664RNA	60813	Eastern C	S720AFB	42720	Bristol
S557RWP	52557	Devon & C	S664SNG	42764	Devon & C	S721AFB	42721	Bristol
S558JSE	61575	Glasgow	S665AAE	34165	Somerset &A	S722AFB	42722	Bristol
S558RWP	52558	Hampshire	S665RNA	60814	Eastern C	S723AFB	42723	Bristol
S559JSE	61576	Glasgow	S667AAE	34167	Somerset &A	S724AFB	42724	Bristol
S559RWP	52559	Hampshire	S667RNA	60815	W Yorkshire	S725AFB	42725	Bristol
S560JSE	60222	Potteries	S668AAE	34168	Somerset &A	S729TWC	43729	Essex
S560RWP	52560	Hampshire	S668RNA	60816	W Yorkshire	S730TWC	43730	Essex
S561JSE	60215	Potteries	S668SVU	60401	Manchester	S731TWC	43731	Essex
S562RWP	52562	Devon & C	S669AAE	34169	Somerset &A	S732TWC	43732	Essex
S564RWP	52564	Somerset &A	S669SVU	60402	Manchester	S733TWC	43733	Essex
S569TPW	65569	Eastern C	S670AAE	34170	Somerset &A	S734TWC	43734	Essex
S570TPW	65570	Eastern C	S670SVU	60403	Manchester	S735TWC	43735	Essex
S624KTP	42124	Hampshire	S671AAE	34171	Somerset &A	S736TWC	43736	Essex
S625KTP	42125	Hampshire	S671SVU	60404	Manchester	S737TWC	43737	Essex
S626KTP	42126	Hampshire	S672AAE	34172	Somerset &A	S738TWC	43738	Essex
S627KTP	42127	Hampshire	S672SNG	42772	Devon & C	S753SNG	42753	Devon & C
S628KTP	42128	Hampshire	S672SVU	62118	W Yorkshire	S764RNE	40002	Devon & C
S629KTP	42129	Hampshire	S673AAE	34173	Somerset &A	S765RNE	40042	Potteries
S630KTP	42130	Hampshire	S673SNG	42773	Devon & C	S766RNE	40003	Potteries
S631KTP	42131	Hampshire	S673SVU	62214	Aberdeen	S791RWG	66191	Manchester
S632KTP	42132	Hampshire	S674AAE	34174	Somerset &A	S792RWG	66192	Manchester
S633KTP	42133	Hampshire	S675AAE	34175	Somerset &A	S793RWG	66193	Manchester
S634KTP	42134	Hampshire	S675SVU	60818	W Yorkshire	S794RWG	66194	Manchester
S635XCR	42135	Hampshire	S676AAE	34176	Somerset &A	S795RWG	66195	Manchester

The 2008 First Bus Handbook

Reg	No.	Location	Reg	No.	Location	Reg	No.	Location
S796RWG	66196	Hampshire	SA02BZE	61588	Glasgow	SF06GYJ	69078	Glasgow
S797RWG	66197	Hampshire	SA02BZF	61589	Glasgow	SF06GYK	69079	Glasgow
S798RWG	66198	Hampshire	SA02BZG	61590	Glasgow	SF06GYN	69080	Glasgow
S799RWG	66199	Hampshire	SA02BZH	61591	Glasgow	SF06GYO	69081	Glasgow
S801RWG	66201	Hampshire	SA02BZJ	61592	Glasgow	SF06GYP	69082	Glasgow
S802RWG	66202	Hampshire	SA02BZK	61593	Glasgow	SF06GYR	69083	Glasgow
S803RWG	66203	Hampshire	SA02BZL	61594	Glasgow	SF06GYS	69084	Glasgow
S804RWG	66204	Hampshire	SA02BZM	61595	Glasgow	SF06GYT	69085	Glasgow
S805RWG	66205	Hampshire	SA02BZN	61596	Glasgow	SF06GYU	69086	Glasgow
S806RWG	66206	Somerset &A	SA02BZP	40845	Glasgow	SF06GYV	69087	Glasgow
S807RWG	66207	Somerset &A	SA02BZR	40846	Glasgow	SF06GYW	69088	Glasgow
S808RWG	61288	W Yorkshire	SA02BZS	40847	Glasgow	SF06GYX	69089	Glasgow
S809RWG	61289	W Yorkshire	SA02BZT	40848	Glasgow	SF06GYY	69090	Glasgow
S810RWG	60628	W Yorkshire	SA52DVR	31506	Glasgow	SF06GYZ	69091	Glasgow
S811RWG	60629	S Yorkshire	SA52DVT	31507	Glasgow	SF06GZA	69092	Glasgow
S812RWG	60630	S Yorkshire	SA52DVU	31508	Glasgow	SF06GZB	69093	Glasgow
S813AEH	60055	Potteries	SA52DVV	31509	Glasgow	SF06GZC	69094	Glasgow
S813RWG	60631	S Yorkshire	SA52DVW	31510	Glasgow	SF06GZD	69095	Glasgow
S814AEH	60056	Potteries	SA52DVX	31511	Glasgow	SF06GZE	69096	Glasgow
S814RWG	60632	S Yorkshire	SA52DVZ	31513	Glasgow	SF06GZG	69097	Glasgow
S815AEH	60057	Potteries	SA52DWC	31514	Glasgow	SF06GZH	69098	Glasgow
S816AEH	60058	Potteries	SA52DWD	31515	Glasgow	SF06GZJ	69099	Glasgow
S817AEH	60059	Potteries	SF04HXW	69295	Glasgow	SF06GZK	69100	Glasgow
S817KPR	42817	Hampshire	SF04HXX	69296	Glasgow	SF06GZL	69101	Glasgow
S818AEH	60060	Potteries	SF04ZPE	69297	Glasgow	SF06GZM	69102	Glasgow
S818KPR	42818	Hampshire	SF04ZPG	69298	Glasgow	SF06GZN	69103	Glasgow
S819AEH	60061	Potteries	SF05KUH	10183	Glasgow	SF06GZO	69104	Glasgow
S819KPR	42819	Hampshire	SF05KUJ	53202	Glasgow	SF06GZP	69105	Glasgow
S820AEH	60062	Potteries	SF05KUK	53203	Glasgow	SF06GZR	69106	Glasgow
S820KPR	42820	Hampshire	SF05KWY	42877	Wales	SF06GZS	69107	Glasgow
S821AEH	60063	Potteries	SF05KWZ	42878	Wales	SF06GZT	69108	Glasgow
S821KPR	42821	Hampshire	SF05KXA	42879	Wales	SF06GZV	69109	Glasgow
S822KPR	42822	Hampshire	SF05KXB	42880	Wales	SF06GZX	69111	Glasgow
S823KPR	42823	Hampshire	SF05KXC	42881	Wales	SF06GZY	69112	Glasgow
S824WYD	42824	Somerset &A	SF05KXD	42882	Wales	SF06GZZ	69113	Glasgow
S825WYD	42825	Somerset &A	SF05KXE	42883	Wales	SF06HAA	69114	Glasgow
S826TCL	50391	Glasgow	SF05KXH	42884	Wales	SF06HAE	69115	Glasgow
S830TCL	50395	Glasgow	SF05KXJ	42885	Glasgow	SF06HAO	69116	Glasgow
S863LRU	52573	Somerset &A	SF05KXK	42886	Glasgow	SF06HAU	69117	Glasgow
S864LRU	52574	Somerset &A	SF05KXL	42887	Glasgow	SF06HAX	69118	Glasgow
S867NOD	52567	Devon & C	SF05KXM	42888	Glasgow	SF06HBA	69119	Glasgow
S868NOD	52568	Devon & C	SF05XDT	20498	Devon & C	SF06HBB	69120	Glasgow
S869NOD	52569	Devon & C	SF06GXG	69039	Glasgow	SF06HBC	69121	Glasgow
S870NOD	52570	Devon & C	SF06GXH	69059	Glasgow	SF07FCC	37188	Glasgow
S871NOD	52571	Devon & C	SF06GXJ	69038	Glasgow	SF07FCD	37189	Glasgow
S924AKS	31655	Edinburgh	SF06GXK	69040	Glasgow	SF07FCE	37190	Glasgow
S925AKS	31656	Edinburgh	SF06GXL	69041	Glasgow	SF07FCG	37191	Glasgow
S926AKS	31657	Edinburgh	SF06GXM	69057	Glasgow	SF07FCJ	37192	Glasgow
S928AKS	31659	Edinburgh	SF06GXN	69058	Glasgow	SF07FCL	37199	Glasgow
S929AKS	31660	Edinburgh	SF06GXO	69060	Glasgow	SF07FCM	37201	Glasgow
S930AKS	31661	Edinburgh	SF06GXP	69061	Glasgow	SF07FCO	37202	Glasgow
S931AKS	31662	Edinburgh	SF06GXR	69062	Glasgow	SF07FCP	37166	Glasgow
S932AKS	31663	Edinburgh	SF06GXS	69063	Glasgow	SF07FCV	37167	Glasgow
S933AKS	31664	Edinburgh	SF06GXT	69064	Glasgow	SF07FCX	37168	Glasgow
S934AKS	31665	Edinburgh	SF06GXU	69065	Glasgow	SF07FCY	37169	Glasgow
S935AKS	31666	Edinburgh	SF06GXV	69072	Glasgow	SF07FCZ	37170	Glasgow
S936AKS	31667	Edinburgh	SF06GXW	69073	Glasgow	SF07FDA	37171	Glasgow
S937AKS	31668	Edinburgh	SF06GXY	69075	Glasgow	SF07FDC	37172	Glasgow
S938AKS	31669	Edinburgh	SF06GXZ	69076	Glasgow	SF07FDD	37173	Glasgow
S955RWP	52555	Hampshire	SF06GYA	69077	Glasgow	SF07FDE	37174	Glasgow
S979JLM	43800	Essex	SF06GYB	69066	Glasgow	SF07FDG	37175	Glasgow
S992UJA	10001	Manchester	SF06GYC	69067	Glasgow	SF07FDJ	37176	Glasgow
S993UJA	10002	Manchester	SF06GYD	69068	Glasgow	SF07FDK	37177	Glasgow
S994UJA	10003	Manchester	SF06GYE	69069	Glasgow	SF07FDL	37178	Glasgow
S995UJA	10004	Manchester	SF06GYG	69070	Glasgow	SF07FDM	37179	Glasgow
SA02BZD	61587	Glasgow	SF06GYH	69071	Glasgow	SF07FDN	37180	Glasgow

SF07FDO	37181	Glasgow	SF54OTE	32564	Glasgow	SF55UAG	69014	Glasgow
SF07FDP	37182	Glasgow	SF54OTG	32565	Glasgow	SF55UAH	69015	Glasgow
SF07FDU	37183	Glasgow	SF54OTH	32566	Glasgow	SF55UAJ	69016	Glasgow
SF07FDV	37184	Glasgow	SF54OTJ	32567	Glasgow	SF55UAK	69017	Glasgow
SF07FDX	37185	Glasgow	SF54OTK	32568	Glasgow	SF55UAL	69018	Glasgow
SF07FDY	37186	Glasgow	SF54OTL	32569	Glasgow	SF55UAM	69019	Glasgow
SF07FDZ	37187	Glasgow	SF54OTN	32571	Glasgow	SF55UAN	69020	Glasgow
SF07FEG	37193	Glasgow	SF54OTP	32572	Glasgow	SF55UAO	69021	Glasgow
SF07FEH	37194	Glasgow	SF54OTR	32573	Glasgow	SF55UAP	69022	Glasgow
SF07FEJ	37195	Glasgow	SF54OTT	32574	Glasgow	SF55UAR	69023	Glasgow
SF07FEK	37196	Glasgow	SF54OTU	32575	Glasgow	SF55UAS	69024	Glasgow
SF07FEM	37197	Glasgow	SF54OTV	32576	Glasgow	SF55UAT	69025	Glasgow
SF07FEO	37198	Glasgow	SF54OTW	32577	Glasgow	SF55UAU	69026	Glasgow
SF07FEP	37200	Glasgow	SF54OTX	32578	Glasgow	SF55UAV	69027	Glasgow
SF07FET	37203	Glasgow	SF54OTY	32579	Glasgow	SF55UAW	69028	Glasgow
SF07FEU	37204	Glasgow	SF54OTZ	32580	Glasgow	SF55UAX	69029	Glasgow
SF51YAA	61597	Glasgow	SF54OUA	32581	Glasgow	SF55UAY	69030	Glasgow
SF51YAD	61598	Glasgow	SF54OUB	32582	Glasgow	SF55UAZ	69031	Glasgow
SF51YAE	61599	Glasgow	SF54OUC	32583	Glasgow	SF55UBA	69032	Glasgow
SF51YAG	61600	Glasgow	SF54OUD	32584	Glasgow	SF55UBB	69042	Glasgow
SF51YAH	61601	Glasgow	SF54OUE	32585	Glasgow	SF55UBC	69043	Glasgow
SF51YAJ	61602	Glasgow	SF54OUG	32586	Glasgow	SF55UBD	69044	Glasgow
SF51YAK	61603	Glasgow	SF54OUH	32587	Glasgow	SF55UBE	69045	Glasgow
SF51YAO	61604	Glasgow	SF54OUJ	32588	Glasgow	SF55UBG	69046	Glasgow
SF51YAU	61605	Glasgow	SF54OUK	32589	Glasgow	SF55UBH	69047	Glasgow
SF51YAV	61606	Glasgow	SF54OUL	32590	Glasgow	SF55UBJ	69048	Glasgow
SF51YAW	61607	Glasgow	SF54OUM	32591	Glasgow	SF55UBK	69049	Glasgow
SF51YAX	61608	Glasgow	SF54OUN	32592	Glasgow	SF55UBL	69050	Glasgow
SF51YAY	61609	Glasgow	SF54THV	32593	Glasgow	SF55UBM	69051	Glasgow
SF51YBA	61610	Glasgow	SF54THX	32594	Glasgow	SF55UBN	69052	Glasgow
SF51YBB	61611	Glasgow	SF54THZ	32595	Glasgow	SF55UBO	69053	Glasgow
SF51YBC	61612	Glasgow	SF54TJO	32596	Glasgow	SF55UBP	69054	Glasgow
SF51YBD	61613	Glasgow	SF54TJU	32597	Glasgow	SF55UBR	69055	Glasgow
SF51YBE	61614	Glasgow	SF54TJV	32598	Glasgow	SF55UBS	69056	Glasgow
SF51YBG	61615	Glasgow	SF54TJX	32599	Glasgow	SF55UBT	69033	Glasgow
SF51YBH	61616	Glasgow	SF54TJY	32600	Glasgow	SF55UBU	69034	Glasgow
SF51YBJ	61617	Glasgow	SF54TJZ	32601	Glasgow	SF55UBV	69035	Glasgow
SF51YBK	61618	Glasgow	SF54TKA	32602	Glasgow	SF55UBW	69036	Glasgow
SF51YBL	61619	Glasgow	SF54TKC	32603	Glasgow	SF55UBX	69037	Glasgow
SF51YBM	61620	Glasgow	SF54TKD	32604	Glasgow	SF56GYP	66988	Glasgow
SF51YBN	61621	Glasgow	SF54TKE	32605	Glasgow	SF56GYR	66989	Glasgow
SF51YBO	61622	Glasgow	SF54TKJ	32606	Glasgow	SF56GYS	66990	Glasgow
SF51YBP	61623	Glasgow	SF54TKK	32607	Glasgow	SF56GYT	66991	Glasgow
SF51YBR	61624	Glasgow	SF54TKN	32609	Glasgow	SF57MKA	37205	Glasgow
SF51YBS	61625	Glasgow	SF54TKO	32608	Glasgow	SF57MKC	37206	Glasgow
SF51YBT	61626	Glasgow	SF54TKT	32610	Glasgow	SF57MKD	37207	Glasgow
SF54OSD	32543	Glasgow	SF54TKU	32611	Glasgow	SF57MKG	37208	Glasgow
SF54OSE	32544	Glasgow	SF54TKV	32612	Glasgow	SF57MKJ	37209	Glasgow
SF54OSG	32545	Glasgow	SF54TKX	32613	Glasgow	SF57MKK	37210	Glasgow
SF54OSJ	32546	Glasgow	SF54TKY	32614	Glasgow	SF57MKL	37211	Glasgow
SF54OSK	32547	Glasgow	SF54TKZ	32615	Glasgow	SF57MKM	37212	Glasgow
SF54OSL	32548	Glasgow	SF54TLJ	32616	Glasgow	SF57MKN	37213	Glasgow
SF54OSM	32549	Glasgow	SF54TLK	32617	Glasgow	SF57MKO	37214	Glasgow
SF54OSN	32550	Glasgow	SF54TLN	32618	Glasgow	SF57MKP	37215	Glasgow
SF54OSO	32551	Glasgow	SF54TLO	32619	Glasgow	SF57MKU	37216	Glasgow
SF54OSP	32552	Glasgow	SF54TLU	32620	Glasgow	SF57MKV	37217	Glasgow
SF54OSR	32553	Glasgow	SF54TLX	32621	Glasgow	SF57MKX	37218	Glasgow
SF54OSU	32554	Glasgow	SF54TLY	32622	Glasgow	SF57MKZ	37219	Glasgow
SF54OSV	32555	Glasgow	SF54TLZ	32623	Glasgow	SF57MLE	37220	Glasgow
SF54OSW	32556	Glasgow	SF54TMO	32624	Glasgow	SF57MLJ	37221	Glasgow
SF54OSX	32557	Glasgow	SF54TMU	32625	Glasgow	SF57MLK	37222	Glasgow
SF54OSY	32558	Glasgow	SF54TMV	32626	Glasgow	SF57MLL	37223	Glasgow
SF54OSZ	32559	Glasgow	SF55TXA	68564	Glasgow	SF57MLN	37224	Glasgow
SF54OTA	32560	Glasgow	SF55TXB	68565	Glasgow	SF57MLO	37225	Glasgow
SF54OTB	32561	Glasgow	SF55TXC	68566	Glasgow	SF57MLU	37226	Glasgow
SF54OTC	32562	Glasgow	SF55UAD	69012	Glasgow	SF57MLV	37227	Glasgow
SF54OTD	32563	Glasgow	SF55UAE	69013	Glasgow	SH51MHM	40849	Glasgow

Reg	Fleet	Depot	Reg	Fleet	Depot	Reg	Fleet	Depot
SH51MHN	40850	Glasgow	SK57ADV	69259	Edinburgh	SN05HXA	36011	Edinburgh
SH51MHO	40723	Glasgow	SK57ADX	69260	Edinburgh	SN05HXB	36012	Edinburgh
SH51MHU	40851	Glasgow	SK57ADZ	69261	Edinburgh	SN06AHK	65754	Edinburgh
SH51MHV	40852	Glasgow	SK57AEA	69262	Edinburgh	SN51MSU	62354	Edinburgh
SH51MHX	40853	Glasgow	SK57AEB	69263	Edinburgh	SN51MSV	62355	Edinburgh
SH51MHY	61627	Glasgow	SK57AEC	69264	Edinburgh	SN51MSX	62358	Edinburgh
SH51MHZ	61628	Glasgow	SMK717F	39717	Eastern C	SN51MSY	62357	Edinburgh
SH51MJE	61629	Glasgow	SN03CLX	65757	Glasgow	SN51UXX	65665	Essex
SH51MJF	61630	Glasgow	SN03CLY	65758	Glasgow	SN51UXY	65666	Essex
SH51MJY	40854	Glasgow	SN03LGG	43901	Wales	SN51UXZ	65667	Essex
SH51MKF	61631	Glasgow	SN03LGJ	43902	Wales	SN51UYA	65668	Essex
SH51MKG	61632	Glasgow	SN03LGK	43903	Wales	SN51UYB	65669	Essex
SH51MKJ	61633	Glasgow	SN03WLD	42482	Essex	SN51UYC	65670	Essex
SH51MKK	61634	Glasgow	SN03WLK	42483	Essex	SN51UYD	65671	Essex
SH51MKL	61635	Glasgow	SN03WLW	42484	Essex	SN51UYE	65672	Essex
SH51MKM	40855	Glasgow	SN03WME	42487	Essex	SN51UYG	65673	Essex
SH51MKN	40856	Glasgow	SN03WMJ	62411	Edinburgh	SN51UYH	65674	Essex
SH51MKO	40857	Glasgow	SN03WMM	42485	Essex	SN51UYJ	65675	Essex
SH51MKP	40858	Glasgow	SN03WMU	62412	Edinburgh	SN51UYK	65676	Essex
SJ03DNY	40965	Glasgow	SN03WMX	42486	Essex	SN51UYL	65677	Essex
SJ03DOA	40966	Glasgow	SN04CKX	65701	Edinburgh	SN53ESU	43837	Wales
SJ03DOH	50460	Glasgow	SN04CKY	65700	Edinburgh	SN53ESV	43836	Wales
SJ03DPE	50461	Glasgow	SN04CLF	65702	Edinburgh	SN53ETD	43839	Wales
SJ03DPF	50462	Glasgow	SN04CNK	65703	Edinburgh	SN53ETE	43840	Wales
SJ03DPN	50463	Glasgow	SN04EFY	43843	Edinburgh	SN53ETF	43841	Wales
SJ03DPU	50464	Glasgow	SN04EFZ	43844	Edinburgh	SN53KHH	65693	Edinburgh
SJ03DPV	50465	Glasgow	SN05DZO	42933	Devon & C	SN53KHJ	65694	Edinburgh
SJ03DPX	50466	Glasgow	SN05DZP	42934	Devon & C	SN53KHK	65695	Edinburgh
SJ03DPY	50467	Glasgow	SN05DZR	42935	Devon & C	SN53KHL	65696	Edinburgh
SJ03DPZ	50468	Glasgow	SN05DZS	42936	Devon & C	SN53KHM	65697	Edinburgh
SJ51DHD	61636	Glasgow	SN05DZT	42937	Devon & C	SN53KHO	65698	Edinburgh
SJ51DHE	61637	Eastern C	SN05DZU	42558	Devon & C	SN53KHP	65699	Edinburgh
SJ51DHF	61638	Glasgow	SN05DZV	42559	Devon & C	SN53KJX	42488	Essex
SJ51DHG	61639	Glasgow	SN05DZW	42560	Devon & C	SN53KJY	42489	Essex
SJ51DHK	61640	Glasgow	SN05DZX	42561	Devon & C	SN53KJZ	42876	Devon & C
SJ51DHL	61641	Glasgow	SN05DZY	42562	Devon & C	SN53KKA	42871	Devon & C
SJ51DHM	61642	Glasgow	SN05DZZ	42563	Devon & C	SN53KKB	42872	Devon & C
SJ51DHN	61643	Glasgow	SN05EAA	42924	Devon & C	SN53KKC	42873	Devon & C
SJ51DHO	61644	Glasgow	SN05EAC	42925	Devon & C	SN53KKD	42874	Devon & C
SJ51DHP	61645	Glasgow	SN05EAE	42926	Devon & C	SN53KKE	42875	Devon & C
SJ51DHV	61646	Glasgow	SN05EAF	42927	Devon & C	SN53KKY	67600	Midland Red
SJ51DHX	61647	Glasgow	SN05EAG	42928	Devon & C	SN54KDF	65708	Edinburgh
SJ51DHZ	61648	Glasgow	SN05EAJ	42929	Devon & C	SN54KDJ	65709	Edinburgh
SJ51DJD	61649	Glasgow	SN05EAM	42930	Devon & C	SN54KDK	65710	Edinburgh
SJ51DJE	61650	Glasgow	SN05EAO	42931	Devon & C	SN54KDO	65711	Edinburgh
SJ51DJF	61651	Glasgow	SN05EAP	42932	Devon & C	SN54KDU	65712	Edinburgh
SJ51DJK	61652	Glasgow	SN05HEJ	43849	Devon & C	SN54KDV	65713	Edinburgh
SJ51DJO	61653	Glasgow	SN05HWD	36023	Edinburgh	SN54KDX	65714	Edinburgh
SJ51DJU	61654	Glasgow	SN05HWE	36022	Edinburgh	SN54KDZ	65715	Edinburgh
SJ51DJX	61656	Glasgow	SN05HWF	36020	Edinburgh	SN54KEJ	65716	Edinburgh
SJ51DJY	61657	Glasgow	SN05HWG	36018	Edinburgh	SN54KEK	65717	Edinburgh
SJ51DJZ	61306	Glasgow	SN05HWH	36019	Edinburgh	SN54KEU	65718	Edinburgh
SJ51DKA	61658	Glasgow	SN05HWJ	36017	Edinburgh	SN54KFA	65719	Edinburgh
SJ51DKD	61659	Glasgow	SN05HWK	36014	Edinburgh	SN54KFC	65720	Edinburgh
SJ51DKE	61660	Glasgow	SN05HWL	36013	Edinburgh	SN54KFD	65721	Edinburgh
SJ51DKF	61661	Glasgow	SN05HWM	36016	Edinburgh	SN54KFE	65722	Edinburgh
SJ51DKK	61662	Glasgow	SN05HWO	36015	Edinburgh	SN54KFF	65723	Edinburgh
SJ51DKL	61663	Glasgow	SN05HWP	36021	Edinburgh	SN55CXE	43848	Hampshire
SJ51DKN	61664	Glasgow	SN05HWR	36024	Edinburgh	SN55CXF	43846	Hampshire
SK02ZYG	65755	Glasgow	SN05HWS	36025	Edinburgh	SN55CXH	43845	Hampshire
SK02ZYH	65756	Glasgow	SN05HWT	36028	Edinburgh	SN55CXJ	43847	Hampshire
SK07JVN	69254	Edinburgh	SN05HWU	36026	Edinburgh	SN55HDZ	32669	Edinburgh
SK07JVO	69255	Edinburgh	SN05HWV	36027	Edinburgh	SN55HEJ	32670	Edinburgh
SK07JVP	69256	Edinburgh	SN05HWW	36007	Edinburgh	SN55HEU	32671	Edinburgh
SK57ADO	69257	Edinburgh	SN05HWX	36008	Edinburgh	SN55HEV	32672	Edinburgh
SK57ADU	69258	Edinburgh	SN05HWY	36009	Edinburgh	SN55HFA	32673	Edinburgh
			SN05HWZ	36010	Edinburgh	SN55HFB	32674	Edinburgh

SN55HFC	32675	Edinburgh	SV05DXH	10160	Aberdeen	T160BBF	40007	Potteries
SN55HFD	32676	Edinburgh	SV05DXJ	10161	Aberdeen	T161BBF	40008	Potteries
SN55HFE	32677	Edinburgh	SV05DXK	10162	Aberdeen	T162BBF	40009	Potteries
SN55HFF	32678	Edinburgh	SV05DXL	10163	Aberdeen	T163BBF	40010	Potteries
SN55HFG	32679	Edinburgh	SV05DXM	10164	Aberdeen	T164BBF	40011	Potteries
SN55HFH	32680	Edinburgh	SV05DXO	10165	Aberdeen	T165BBF	40012	Somerset &A
SN55HFJ	32681	Edinburgh	SV05DXP	10166	Aberdeen	T166BBF	40682	Potteries
SN55HFK	32682	Edinburgh	SV05DXR	10167	Aberdeen	T167BBF	40683	Potteries
SN55HFL	32683	Edinburgh	SV05DXS	10168	Aberdeen	T168BBF	40013	Potteries
SN55JVA	65750	Edinburgh	SV05DXT	10169	Aberdeen	T2TRU	20472	Devon & C
SN55JVC	65751	Edinburgh	SV05DXU	10170	Aberdeen	T20TVL	53402	Devon & C
SN55JVD	65752	Edinburgh	SV05DXW	10171	Aberdeen	T211VWU	10028	W Yorkshire
SN55JVE	65753	Edinburgh	SV05DXX	10172	Aberdeen	T255GUG	60822	W Yorkshire
SN55JVG	65742	Edinburgh	SV05DXY	10173	Aberdeen	T257JLD	41257	London
SN55JVH	65743	Edinburgh	SV06GRF	69110	Aberdeen	T259JLD	41259	London
SN55JVJ	65744	Edinburgh	SV06GRK	69122	Aberdeen	T261JLD	41261	London
SN55JVK	65745	Edinburgh	SV06GRU	69123	Aberdeen	T263JLD	41263	London
SN55JVL	65746	Edinburgh	SV06GRX	69124	Aberdeen	T264JLD	41264	London
SN55JVM	65747	Edinburgh	SV07EHB	69125	Aberdeen	T265JLD	41265	London
SN55JVO	65748	Edinburgh	SV07EHC	69126	Aberdeen	T266JLD	41266	London
SN55JVP	65749	Edinburgh	SV07EHD	69127	Aberdeen	T267JLD	41267	Berkshire
SN55KKE	36029	Edinburgh	SV07EHE	69128	Aberdeen	T268JLD	41268	London
SN55KKF	36030	Edinburgh	SV07EHF	69129	Aberdeen	T269JLD	41269	London
SN57HCP	37135	Edinburgh	SV07EHG	69130	Aberdeen	T270JLD	41270	London
SN57HCU	37136	Edinburgh	SV07EHH	69131	Aberdeen	T271JLD	41271	London
SN57HCV	37137	Edinburgh	SV07EHJ	69132	Aberdeen	T272JLD	41272	London
SN57HCX	37138	Edinburgh	SV07EHK	69133	Aberdeen	T273JLD	41273	London
SN57HCY	37139	Edinburgh	SV07EHL	69134	Aberdeen	T274JLD	41274	London
SN57HCZ	37140	Edinburgh	SV08 FHA	69351	Aberdeen	T275JLD	41275	London
SN57HDA	37141	Edinburgh	SV08 FHB	69352	Aberdeen	T276JLD	41276	London
SN57HDC	37142	Edinburgh	SV08 FHC	69353	Aberdeen	T277JLD	41277	London
SN57HDD	37143	Edinburgh	SV08 FHD	69354	Aberdeen	T278JLD	41278	London
SN57HDE	37144	Edinburgh	SV08 FHE	69355	Aberdeen	T279JLD	41279	London
SN57HDF	37145	Edinburgh	SV08 FHF	69356	Aberdeen	T280JLD	41280	London
SN57HDG	37266	Edinburgh	SV08 FHG	69357	Aberdeen	T281JLD	41281	London
SN57HDH	37133	Edinburgh	SV54CFY	68518	Aberdeen	T282JLD	41282	London
SN57HDJ	37134	Edinburgh	SV54CFZ	68519	Aberdeen	T283JLD	41283	London
SN57HZX	69292	Edinburgh	SV54FRZ	23401	Aberdeen	T284JLD	41284	London
SN57HZY	69293	Edinburgh	SV54FTA	23402	Aberdeen	T285JLD	41285	London
SN57HZZ	69294	Edinburgh	SV57EYH	69265	Aberdeen	T286JLD	41286	London
SN57JAO	37267	Edinburgh	SV57EYJ	69266	Aberdeen	T287JLD	41287	London
SN57JAU	37268	Edinburgh	SV57EYK	69267	Aberdeen	T288JLD	41288	London
SN57JBE	37269	Edinburgh	T101VWU	10018	W Yorkshire	T289JLD	41289	London
SN57JBO	37270	Edinburgh	T101XDE	21151	Wales	T291JLD	41291	Devon & C
SN57JBU	37271	Edinburgh	T102VWU	10019	W Yorkshire	T292JLD	41292	London
SN57JBV	37272	Edinburgh	T102XDE	21152	Wales	T293JLD	41293	London
SN57JBX	37273	Edinburgh	T103VWU	10020	W Yorkshire	T294JLD	41294	London
SN57JBZ	69281	Edinburgh	T103XDE	21153	Aberdeen	T295JLD	41295	London
SN57JCJ	69282	Edinburgh	T104JBC	20304	Devon & C	T296JLD	41296	London
SN57JCO	69283	Edinburgh	T104VWU	10021	W Yorkshire	T297JLD	41297	London
SN57JCU	69284	Edinburgh	T105JBC	20305	Devon & C	T298JLD	41298	London
SN57JCV	69285	Edinburgh	T105VWU	10022	W Yorkshire	T299JLD	41299	London
SN57JCX	69286	Edinburgh	T106JBC	20306	Devon & C	T301JLD	41301	London
SN57JCY	69287	Edinburgh	T106VWU	10023	W Yorkshire	T302JLD	41302	London
SN57JCZ	69288	Edinburgh	T107VWU	10024	W Yorkshire	T303JLD	41303	London
SN57JDF	69289	Edinburgh	T108VWU	10025	W Yorkshire	T304JLD	41304	London
SN57JDJ	69290	Edinburgh	T109VWU	10026	W Yorkshire	T305JLD	41305	London
SN57JDK	69291	Edinburgh	T110VWU	10027	W Yorkshire	T306JLD	41306	London
SN57MSU	69280	Edinburgh	T12 TRU	43812	Devon & C	T307VYG	40558	Glasgow
SSU821	62250	Edinburgh	T154OUB	60821	W Yorkshire	T308VYG	40559	Glasgow
SV05DXA	10154	Aberdeen	T156OUB	60823	W Yorkshire	T309VYG	40560	Glasgow
SV05DXC	10155	Aberdeen	T157BBF	40004	Somerset &A	T310AHY	20460	Bristol
SV05DXD	10156	Aberdeen	T157OUB	60824	W Yorkshire	T310VYG	40561	Glasgow
SV05DXE	10157	Aberdeen	T158BBF	40005	Somerset &A	T311VYG	40562	Glasgow
SV05DXF	10158	Aberdeen	T158OUB	60825	W Yorkshire	T312VYG	40563	Glasgow
SV05DXG	10159	Aberdeen	T159BBF	40006	Somerset &A	T313VYG	40564	Manchester

The 2008 First Bus Handbook

Reg	Fleet	Location	Reg	Fleet	Location	Reg	Fleet	Location
T314VYG	40565	Manchester	T506JNA	10005	Manchester	T731REU	42731	Somerset &A
T315VYG	40566	Manchester	T507JNA	10006	Manchester	T735JGB	62935	Glasgow
T316VYG	40567	Manchester	T509JNA	10008	Manchester	T736JGB	62936	Glasgow
T317VYG	40568	Manchester	T510JNA	10009	Manchester	T77 TRU	53206	Devon & C
T318VYG	40569	Manchester	T511JNA	10010	Manchester	T801LLC	32801	London
T32 JCV	42232	Devon & C	T512JNA	10011	Manchester	T801RHW	48201	Devon & C
T336ALR	41336	London	T513JNA	10012	Manchester	T802LLC	32802	Devon & C
T337ALR	41337	London	T514JNA	10013	Manchester	T803LLC	32803	Devon & C
T338ALR	41338	London	T562BSS	60216	Potteries	T804LLC	32804	London
T339ALR	41339	London	T563BSS	60217	Manchester	T805LLC	32805	Glasgow
T34JCV	42234	Devon & C	T564BSS	60218	Manchester	T806LLC	32806	London
T340ALR	41340	London	T565BSS	60219	Berkshire	T807LLC	32807	London
T341ALR	41341	London	T566BSS	60220	Edinburgh	T808LLC	32808	Devon & C
T342ALR	41342	London	T567BSS	60221	Edinburgh	T809LLC	32809	London
T343ALR	41343	London	T576JNG	65576	Eastern C	T810LLC	32810	London
T344ALR	41344	London	T577JNG	65577	Eastern C	T811LLC	32811	Glasgow
T346EUB	40672	W Yorkshire	T578JNG	65578	Eastern C	T812LLC	32812	Devon & C
T347EUB	40673	W Yorkshire	T579JNG	65579	Eastern C	T813LLC	32813	London
T348EUB	40674	W Yorkshire	T580JNG	65580	Eastern C	T814LLC	32814	London
T349EUB	40675	W Yorkshire	T622SEJ	42322	Wales	T815LLC	32815	London
T35 JCV	42235	Devon & C	T623SEJ	42323	Wales	T815MAK	60633	S Yorkshire
T350EUB	40676	W Yorkshire	T624SEJ	42324	Wales	T816LLC	32816	London
T351EUB	40677	W Yorkshire	T625SEJ	42325	Wales	T816MAK	60634	S Yorkshire
T352EUB	40678	W Yorkshire	T626SEJ	42326	Wales	T817LLC	32817	Devon & C
T353EUB	40679	W Yorkshire	T627SEJ	42327	Wales	T817MAK	60635	S Yorkshire
T354EUB	40680	W Yorkshire	T628SEJ	42328	Wales	T818LLC	32818	London
T356VWU	42656	Berkshire	T629SEJ	42329	Wales	T818MAK	60636	S Yorkshire
T359VWU	42659	Berkshire	T630SEJ	42330	Wales	T819LLC	32819	Devon & C
T364NUA	40153	Potteries	T631SEJ	42331	Wales	T819MAK	60637	S Yorkshire
T365NUA	40154	Potteries	T632SEJ	42332	Wales	T820JBL	65620	Berkshire
T366NUA	42841	Somerset &A	T633SEJ	42333	Wales	T820LLC	32820	Glasgow
T367NUA	42842	Somerset &A	T634SEJ	42334	Wales	T820MAK	60638	S Yorkshire
T368NUA	42843	Somerset &A	T635SEJ	42335	Wales	T821JBL	65621	Berkshire
T369NUA	42844	Somerset &A	T636SEJ	42336	Wales	T821LLC	32821	Glasgow
T370NUA	42845	Somerset &A	T637SEJ	42337	Wales	T821MAK	60639	S Yorkshire
T371NUA	40030	Potteries	T64BHY	20424	Wales	T822JBL	65622	Berkshire
T372NUA	40155	Potteries	T650SSF	65650	Essex	T822LLC	32822	London
T373NUA	42673	Berkshire	T651SSF	65651	Essex	T822MAK	60640	S Yorkshire
T375NUA	40721	Berkshire	T652SSF	65652	Essex	T822SFS	60064	Potteries
T421GUG	61022	Glasgow	T653SSF	65653	Essex	T823JBL	65623	Berkshire
T422GUG	61023	Glasgow	T654SSF	65654	Essex	T823LLC	32823	Glasgow
T423GUG	61024	Glasgow	T660VWU	30840	W Yorkshire	T823MAK	60641	S Yorkshire
T424GUG	61025	Glasgow	T661VWU	30841	W Yorkshire	T823SFS	60065	Potteries
T425GUG	61026	Glasgow	T662VWU	30842	W Yorkshire	T824JBL	65624	Berkshire
T426GUG	61027	Glasgow	T663VWU	30843	W Yorkshire	T824LLC	32824	Glasgow
T427GUG	61028	Glasgow	T664VWU	30844	W Yorkshire	T824MAK	60642	S Yorkshire
T428GUG	61029	W Yorkshire	T665VWU	30845	W Yorkshire	T824SFS	60066	Potteries
T429GUG	61030	W Yorkshire	T701JLD	20201	Essex	T825JBL	65625	Berkshire
T430GUG	61031	W Yorkshire	T701PND	40437	Manchester	T825LLC	32825	Glasgow
T430JLD	41300	London	T702JLD	20202	Essex	T825MAK	60643	S Yorkshire
T431GUG	61032	W Yorkshire	T702PND	40438	Manchester	T825SFS	60067	Potteries
T432GUG	61033	W Yorkshire	T703JLD	20203	Essex	T826AFX	42826	Hampshire
T456JDT	40493	S Yorkshire	T703PND	40439	Manchester	T826LLC	32826	Glasgow
T457JDT	40494	S Yorkshire	T704JLD	20204	Aberdeen	T826MAK	60644	S Yorkshire
T458JDT	40495	S Yorkshire	T704PND	40440	Manchester	T826SFS	60068	Potteries
T459JDT	40496	S Yorkshire	T705JLD	20205	Aberdeen	T827AFX	42827	Hampshire
T460JDT	40497	S Yorkshire	T705PND	40441	Manchester	T827LLC	32827	Glasgow
T461JDT	40498	S Yorkshire	T706JLD	20206	Aberdeen	T827MAK	60645	S Yorkshire
T462JDT	40499	S Yorkshire	T706PND	40442	Manchester	T827SFS	60069	Potteries
T463JDT	40500	S Yorkshire	T707JLD	20207	Aberdeen	T828AFX	42828	Hampshire
T464JDT	40501	S Yorkshire	T707PND	40443	Manchester	T828LLC	32828	Glasgow
T465JDT	40502	S Yorkshire	T708PND	40444	Manchester	T828MAK	60646	S Yorkshire
T469JCV	42469	Devon & C	T726REU	42726	Potteries	T828SFS	60070	Potteries
T470JCV	42470	Devon & C	T727REU	42727	Potteries	T829AFX	42829	Hampshire
T471JCV	42471	Devon & C	T728REU	42728	Hampshire	T829LLC	32829	Glasgow
T472YTT	42472	Devon & C	T729REU	42729	Somerset &A	T829MAK	60647	S Yorkshire
T473YTT	42473	Devon & C	T730REU	42730	Somerset &A	T829SFS	60071	Potteries

Reg	No	Location	Reg	No	Location	Reg	No	Location
T830LLC	32830	Glasgow	T867ODT	60685	S Yorkshire	TT03 TRU	42860	Devon & C
T830MAK	60648	S Yorkshire	T868KLF	32868	London	TT04 TRU	20556	Devon & C
T830RYC	42830	Somerset &A	T868ODT	60686	S Yorkshire	TT05 TRU	20557	Devon & C
T831LLC	32831	Glasgow	T869ODT	60687	S Yorkshire	TT06 NEX	20559	Devon & C
T831MAK	60649	S Yorkshire	T870KLF	32870	London	TT54 TVL	53404	Devon & C
T831RYC	42831	Somerset &A	T870ODT	60688	S Yorkshire	TT55 TRU	20558	Devon & C
T832LLC	32832	Glasgow	T871KLF	32871	London	TU04 TRU	53204	Devon & C
T832MAK	60650	S Yorkshire	T871ODT	60689	S Yorkshire	TX06 NEX	20560	Devon & C
T833LLC	32833	Glasgow	T872ODT	60690	S Yorkshire	UHW661	20050	Devon & C
T833MAK	60651	S Yorkshire	T873KLF	32873	London	UKT552	34198	Devon & C
T834LLC	32834	Glasgow	T873ODT	60691	S Yorkshire	UWB183	20052	Devon & C
T834MAK	60652	S Yorkshire	T874ODT	60692	S Yorkshire	V112LVH	10029	W Yorkshire
T835LLC	32835	Glasgow	T875KLF	32875	London	V113LVH	10030	W Yorkshire
T835MAK	60653	S Yorkshire	T875ODT	60693	S Yorkshire	V114LVH	10031	W Yorkshire
T836LLC	32836	Glasgow	T876KLF	32876	London	V115LVH	10032	W Yorkshire
T836MAK	60654	S Yorkshire	T876ODT	60694	S Yorkshire	V116FSF	61667	Glasgow
T837LLC	32837	Glasgow	T877ODT	60695	S Yorkshire	V117FSF	61668	Glasgow
T837MAK	60655	S Yorkshire	T878KLF	32878	London	V118FSF	61669	Glasgow
T838LLC	32838	London	T878ODT	60696	S Yorkshire	V119FSF	61670	Glasgow
T838MAK	60656	S Yorkshire	T879KLF	32879	London	V120FSF	61671	Glasgow
T839LLC	32839	London	T879ODT	60697	S Yorkshire	V122DND	60174	Potteries
T839MAK	60657	S Yorkshire	T880KLF	32880	London	V122FSF	61672	Glasgow
T840LLC	32840	London	T880ODT	60698	S Yorkshire	V124DND	60176	Potteries
T840MAK	60658	S Yorkshire	T881KLF	32881	London	V125DND	60177	Potteries
T841LLC	32841	London	T881ODT	60699	S Yorkshire	V126DND	60178	Edinburgh
T841MAK	60659	S Yorkshire	T882ODT	60700	S Yorkshire	V127DND	60179	Edinburgh
T842LLC	32842	London	T883KLF	32883	London	V128DND	60180	Edinburgh
T842MAK	60660	S Yorkshire	T883ODT	60701	S Yorkshire	V129DND	60181	Edinburgh
T843LLC	32843	London	T884KLF	32884	London	V130DND	60182	Edinburgh
T843MAK	60661	S Yorkshire	T884ODT	60702	S Yorkshire	V131DND	60183	Potteries
T844LLC	32844	London	T885KLF	32885	London	V132DND	60184	Potteries
T844MAK	60662	S Yorkshire	T889KLF	34089	S Yorkshire	V133DND	60185	Potteries
T845LLC	32845	London	T890KLF	34090	S Yorkshire	V133ESC	61034	W Yorkshire
T845MAK	60663	Manchester	T891KLF	34091	S Yorkshire	V134DND	60186	Edinburgh
T846LLC	32846	Devon & C	T892KLF	34092	S Yorkshire	V134ESC	61035	W Yorkshire
T846MAK	60664	S Yorkshire	T893KLF	34093	S Yorkshire	V135DND	60187	Edinburgh
T847LLC	32847	London	T894KLF	34094	S Yorkshire	V135ESC	61036	W Yorkshire
T847MAK	60665	S Yorkshire	T895KLF	34095	S Yorkshire	V136DND	60188	Edinburgh
T848LLC	32848	Glasgow	T896KLF	34096	S Yorkshire	V136ESC	61037	W Yorkshire
T848MAK	60666	S Yorkshire	T897KLF	34097	S Yorkshire	V137DND	60189	Potteries
T849LLC	32849	London	T898KLF	34098	S Yorkshire	V137ESC	61038	W Yorkshire
T849MAK	60667	S Yorkshire	T899KLF	34099	S Yorkshire	V138DND	60190	Potteries
T850LLC	32850	London	T901KLF	34101	S Yorkshire	V138ESC	61039	W Yorkshire
T850MAK	60668	S Yorkshire	T902KLF	34102	S Yorkshire	V139DND	60191	Edinburgh
T851LLC	32851	London	T903KLF	34103	S Yorkshire	V139ESC	61040	W Yorkshire
T851MAK	60669	S Yorkshire	T904KLF	34104	S Yorkshire	V140DND	60192	Edinburgh
T852LLC	32852	London	T905KLF	34105	S Yorkshire	V140ESC	61041	W Yorkshire
T852MAK	60670	S Yorkshire	T906KLF	34106	S Yorkshire	V141DND	60193	Potteries
T853LLC	32853	London	T907KLF	34107	S Yorkshire	V141ESC	61042	W Yorkshire
T853MAK	60671	S Yorkshire	T916SSF	60169	Potteries	V142DND	60173	Potteries
T854KLF	32854	London	T917SSF	60170	Potteries	V142ESC	61043	Glasgow
T854MAK	60672	S Yorkshire	T918SSF	60171	Potteries	V143ESC	61044	Glasgow
T855MAK	60673	S Yorkshire	T919SSF	60172	Potteries	V154LUA	42654	Berkshire
T856MAK	60674	S Yorkshire	T948UEU	20428	Wales	V221GLS	61673	Glasgow
T857MAK	60675	S Yorkshire	T982LBF	40140	Potteries	V307GBY	41307	London
T858MAK	60676	S Yorkshire	T983LBF	40141	Potteries	V308GBY	41308	London
T859MAK	60677	S Yorkshire	T984LBF	40142	Potteries	V309GBY	41309	London
T860MAK	60678	S Yorkshire	T985LBF	40143	Potteries	V310GBY	41310	London
T861MAK	60679	S Yorkshire	T986LBF	40144	Potteries	V311GBY	41311	London
T862MAK	60680	S Yorkshire	T987LBF	40145	Potteries	V312GBY	41312	London
T863MAK	60681	S Yorkshire	T988KLF	34088	S Yorkshire	V313GBY	41313	London
T864KLF	32864	London	T990KLF	34100	S Yorkshire	V314GBY	41314	London
T864MAK	60682	S Yorkshire	TJI4838	34195	Devon & C	V315GBY	41315	London
T865KLF	32865	London	TL54 TVL	53403	Devon & C	V316GBY	41316	London
T865ODT	60683	S Yorkshire	TO54 TRU	53401	Devon & C	V317GBY	41317	London
T866KLF	32866	London	TPL 762X	22062	Devon & C	V318GBY	41318	London
T866ODT	60684	S Yorkshire	TSU651	20029	Aberdeen	V319GBY	41319	London

The 2008 First Bus Handbook

Reg	No	Location	Reg	No	Location	Reg	No	Location
V320GBY	41320	London	V603GGB	10103	Glasgow	V857HBY	32857	London
V322GBY	41322	London	V604GGB	10104	Glasgow	V858HBY	32858	London
V323GBY	41323	London	V605GGB	10105	Glasgow	V859HBY	32859	London
V324GBY	41324	London	V606GGB	10106	Glasgow	V860HBY	32860	London
V325GBY	41325	London	V607GGB	10107	Glasgow	V861HBY	32861	London
V326GBY	41326	London	V608GGB	10108	Glasgow	V862HBY	32862	London
V327GBY	41327	London	V609GGB	10109	Glasgow	V863HBY	32863	London
V328GBY	41328	London	V610GGB	10110	Glasgow	V867HBY	32867	London
V329GBY	41329	London	V676FPO	42376	Glasgow	V869HBY	32869	London
V330DBU	60175	Potteries	V69GEH	40156	Potteries	V872HBY	32872	London
V330GBY	41330	Somerset &A	V701FFB	32701	Bristol	V874HBY	32874	London
V331GBY	41331	Somerset &A	V71GEH	40304	Potteries	V877HBY	32877	London
V332GBY	41332	Somerset &A	V721UVY	60828	W Yorkshire	V882HBY	32882	London
V334GBY	41334	Somerset &A	V732FAE	42732	Bristol	V886HBY	32886	London
V335GBY	41335	Somerset &A	V733FAE	42733	Bristol	V887HBY	32887	London
V345DLH	41345	London	V734FAE	42734	Bristol	V889HLH	32889	London
V346DLH	41346	London	V735FAE	42735	Bristol	V890HLH	32890	London
V347DLH	41347	London	V736FAE	42736	Bristol	V891HLH	32891	London
V348DLH	41348	London	V737FAE	42737	Bristol	V892HLH	32892	London
V349DLH	41349	Edinburgh	V738FAE	42738	Bristol	V893HLH	32893	London
V34ESC	62391	Edinburgh	V739GPU	43739	Essex	V894HLH	32894	London
V350DLH	41350	London	V740GPU	43740	Essex	V895HLH	32895	London
V351DLH	41351	London	V741GPU	43741	Essex	V896HLH	32896	London
V356DLH	41356	London	V742GPU	43742	Essex	V897HLH	32897	London
V356DVG	43356	Eastern C	V743GPU	43743	Essex	V898HLH	32898	London
V357DLH	41357	Edinburgh	V744GPU	43744	Essex	V899HLH	32899	London
V357DVG	43357	Eastern C	V759UVY	60826	W Yorkshire	V988GBF	40146	Potteries
V358DVG	43358	Eastern C	V760UVY	60827	W Yorkshire	V988HLH	32888	London
V359DLH	41359	Edinburgh	V762UVY	60829	W Yorkshire	V989GBF	40147	Potteries
V359DVG	43359	Eastern C	V763UVY	60830	W Yorkshire	V990HLH	32900	London
V35ESC	62392	Edinburgh	V764UVY	60831	W Yorkshire	VJT738	34193	Devon & C
V360DVG	43360	Eastern C	V765UVY	60832	W Yorkshire	VOO273	34200	Devon & C
V362CNH	65662	Edinburgh	V767UVY	60834	W Yorkshire	VU02PKX	53040	Midland Red
V363CNH	65663	Edinburgh	V768UVY	60835	W Yorkshire	VU02PKY	53041	Midland Red
V364CNH	65664	Edinburgh	V769UVY	60836	W Yorkshire	VU03YJT	53042	Midland Red
V368KLG	41068	Potteries	V770UVY	60837	W Yorkshire	VU03YJV	53043	Midland Red
V369KLG	41069	Potteries	V771UVY	60838	W Yorkshire	VU03YJW	53044	Midland Red
V370KLG	41070	Potteries	V772UVY	60839	W Yorkshire	VU03YJX	53045	Midland Red
V371KLG	41071	Potteries	V773UVY	60840	W Yorkshire	VU03YJY	53046	Midland Red
V372KLG	41072	Potteries	V801KAF	53001	Devon & C	VU03YJZ	53047	Midland Red
V373KLG	41073	Potteries	V802EFB	48202	Hampshire	VU03YKB	53048	Midland Red
V374KLG	41074	Potteries	V802KAF	53002	Devon & C	VU03YKC	53049	Midland Red
V41DTE	40180	Potteries	V803EFB	48203	Hampshire	VU03YKD	53050	Midland Red
V421HBY	41321	London	V803KAF	53003	Devon & C	VU03YKE	53051	Midland Red
V42DTE	40181	Potteries	V804EFB	48204	Hampshire	VX05JWW	42894	Midland Red
V430GTW	52580	Hampshire	V805EFB	48205	Hampshire	VX05LVS	67652	Midland Red
V431GTW	52581	Hampshire	V806EFB	48206	Hampshire	VX05LVT	67653	Midland Red
V433GTW	52583	Hampshire	V807EFB	48207	Hampshire	VX05LVU	67654	Midland Red
V433HBY	41333	Somerset &A	V808EFB	48208	Hampshire	VX05LVV	67655	Midland Red
V434GTW	52584	Essex	V809EFB	48209	Hampshire	VX05LVW	67656	Midland Red
V435GTW	52585	Essex	V810EFB	48210	Bristol	VX05LVY	67657	Midland Red
V43DTE	40182	Potteries	V826FSC	65626	Essex	VX05LVZ	67658	Midland Red
V470GBF	40157	Potteries	V827FSC	65627	Essex	VX05LWA	68549	W Yorkshire
V472GBF	40305	Potteries	V828FSC	65628	Essex	VX05LWC	67659	Midland Red
V527ESH	62385	Edinburgh	V829FSC	65629	Essex	VX05LWD	67660	Midland Red
V528ESH	62386	Edinburgh	V830FSC	65630	Essex	VX05LWE	67661	Midland Red
V529ESH	62387	Edinburgh	V830GBF	60072	Potteries	VX05LWF	67662	Midland Red
V530ESH	62388	Edinburgh	V831FSC	65631	Essex	VX05LWG	67663	Midland Red
V531ESH	62389	Edinburgh	V831GBF	60073	Potteries	VX05LWH	67664	Midland Red
V532ESH	62390	Edinburgh	V832DYD	42832	Somerset &A	VX53OEN	53059	Midland Red
V586DVF	65586	Eastern C	V832FSC	65632	Essex	VX53OEO	53060	Midland Red
V587DVF	65587	Eastern C	V832GBF	60074	Potteries	VX53OEP	53061	Midland Red
V588DVF	65588	Eastern C	V833DYD	42833	Somerset &A	VX53OER	53062	Midland Red
V589DVF	65589	Eastern C	V834DYD	42834	Somerset &A	VX53OET	53063	Midland Red
V590DVF	65590	Eastern C	V835DYD	42835	Somerset &A	VX53OEU	53064	Midland Red
V601GGB	10044	Glasgow	V855HBY	32855	London	VX53OEV	53058	Midland Red
V602GGB	10045	Glasgow	V856HBY	32856	London	VX53VJV	67601	Midland Red

Reg	No	Operator	Reg	No	Operator	Reg	No	Operator
VX53VJZ	67602	Midland Red	W304JND	60226	Manchester	W356RJA	60278	Manchester
VX53VKA	67603	Midland Red	W307DWX	50276	Devon & C	W357RJA	60279	Manchester
VX53VKB	67604	Midland Red	W307JND	60229	Manchester	W358RJA	60280	Manchester
VX54MOV	67631	Midland Red	W308DWX	50277	Hampshire	W358VLN	41370	London
VX54MPE	67632	Midland Red	W308JND	60230	Manchester	W359RJA	60281	Manchester
VX54MPF	67633	Midland Red	W309DWX	50278	Hampshire	W361RJA	60262	Manchester
VX54MPO	67634	Midland Red	W309JND	60231	Manchester	W362RJA	60272	Manchester
VX54MPU	67635	Midland Red	W311DWX	50280	Manchester	W362VLN	41362	London
VX54MPV	67636	Midland Red	W311JND	60233	Manchester	W363RJA	60255	Manchester
VX54MPY	67637	Midland Red	W312DWX	50281	W Yorkshire	W363VLN	41363	London
VX54MPZ	67638	Midland Red	W312JND	60234	Manchester	W364EOW	66164	Hampshire
VX54MRO	67639	Midland Red	W313DWX	50282	W Yorkshire	W364RJA	60282	Manchester
VX54MRU	67640	Midland Red	W313JND	60235	Manchester	W365EOW	66165	Hampshire
VX54MRV	67641	Midland Red	W314DWX	50283	W Yorkshire	W365RJA	60267	Manchester
VX54MSO	67643	Midland Red	W314JND	60236	Manchester	W365VLN	41365	London
VX54MSU	67644	Midland Red	W315DWX	50284	W Yorkshire	W366EOW	66166	Somerset &A
VX54MSY	67645	Midland Red	W315JND	60237	Manchester	W366RJA	60277	Manchester
VX54MTE	67646	Midland Red	W317DWX	50286	W Yorkshire	W366VLN	41366	London
VX54MTF	67647	Midland Red	W317JND	60239	Manchester	W367EOW	66167	Somerset &A
VX54MTJ	67648	Midland Red	W319DWX	50288	W Yorkshire	W367VLN	41367	London
VX54MTK	67649	Midland Red	W319JND	60241	Manchester	W368EOW	66168	Hampshire
VX54MTO	67650	Midland Red	W322DWX	50291	W Yorkshire	W368VLN	41368	London
VX54MTU	67651	Midland Red	W322JND	60244	Manchester	W369EOW	66169	Hampshire
VX54MTV	33401	Midland Red	W324DWX	50293	W Yorkshire	W369VLN	41369	London
VX54MTY	33402	Midland Red	W324JND	60246	Manchester	W371EOW	66171	Somerset &A
VX54MTZ	33403	Midland Red	W326DWX	50295	W Yorkshire	W371VLN	41371	London
VX54MUA	33404	Midland Red	W326JND	60248	Manchester	W372EOW	66172	Somerset &A
VX54MUB	33405	Midland Red	W327DWX	50296	Midland Red	W372VLN	41372	London
VX54MUC	42889	Midland Red	W327JND	60249	Manchester	W373EOW	66173	Somerset &A
VX54MUO	42890	Midland Red	W329DWX	50279	Wales	W374EOW	66174	Somerset &A
VX54MUP	42891	Midland Red	W329JND	60251	Manchester	W376EOW	66176	Hampshire
VX54MUU	42892	Midland Red	W331DWX	50290	W Yorkshire	W376VLN	41376	London
VX54MUV	42893	Midland Red	W331JND	60252	Manchester	W377EOW	66177	Hampshire
W116CWR	10033	Glasgow	W331RJA	60253	Manchester	W377VLN	41377	London
W117CWR	10034	Glasgow	W332DWX	50287	W Yorkshire	W378EOW	66178	Somerset &A
W118CWR	10035	W Yorkshire	W332JND	60232	Manchester	W378JNE	60247	Manchester
W119CWR	10036	W Yorkshire	W332RJA	60254	Manchester	W378VLN	41378	London
W122CWR	10037	W Yorkshire	W334DWX	50289	W Yorkshire	W379EOW	66179	Hampshire
W122DWX	10039	W Yorkshire	W334JND	60238	Manchester	W379JNE	60250	Manchester
W124DWX	10041	W Yorkshire	W334RJA	60256	Manchester	W379VLN	41379	London
W126DWX	10043	W Yorkshire	W335DWX	50294	W Yorkshire	W381EOW	66181	Hampshire
W127DWX	10038	W Yorkshire	W335JND	60227	Manchester	W3FAL	10048	Aberdeen
W128DWX	10040	W Yorkshire	W335RJA	60257	Manchester	W4 TRU	56000	Devon & C
W129DWX	10042	W Yorkshire	W336DWX	50285	W Yorkshire	W422SRP	32062	Leicester
W131WPO	10131	Glasgow	W336JND	60228	Manchester	W425SRP	32065	Leicester
W132VLO	32950	Glasgow	W336RJA	60258	Manchester	W425VLO	41725	London
W132WPO	10132	Glasgow	W337DWX	50292	W Yorkshire	W431CWX	34111	Somerset &A
W133VLO	41720	London	W337JND	60242	Manchester	W432CWX	34112	Somerset &A
W133WPO	10133	Glasgow	W337RJA	60259	Manchester	W433CWX	34113	Somerset &A
W142PSH	60194	Potteries	W338DWX	53028	Somerset &A	W434CWX	34114	Somerset &A
W179BVP	60283	Manchester	W338JND	60240	Manchester	W435CWX	34108	Somerset &A
W213XBD	32053	Leicester	W338RJA	60260	Manchester	W436CWX	34109	Somerset &A
W214XBD	32054	Leicester	W339JND	60245	Manchester	W437CWX	34110	Somerset &A
W215XBD	32055	Leicester	W339RJA	60261	Manchester	W473SVT	40014	Potteries
W216XBD	32056	Leicester	W341JND	60243	Manchester	W474SVT	40015	Potteries
W217XBD	32057	Leicester	W342RJA	60264	Manchester	W475SVT	40016	Potteries
W218XBD	32058	Leicester	W343RJA	60265	Manchester	W476SVT	40017	Potteries
W219XBD	32059	Leicester	W344RJA	60266	Manchester	W477SVT	40018	Potteries
W221XBD	32061	Leicester	W346RJA	60268	Manchester	W478SVT	40019	Potteries
W223XBD	32063	Leicester	W347RJA	60269	Manchester	W49WDS	62949	Glasgow
W224XBD	32064	Leicester	W348RJA	60270	Manchester	W4FAL	10049	Aberdeen
W2FAL	10047	Aberdeen	W349RJA	60271	Manchester	W52WDS	62952	Glasgow
W3 TRU	20473	Devon & C	W351RJA	60273	Manchester	W577RFS	62170	Aberdeen
W301JND	60223	Manchester	W352RJA	60274	Manchester	W578RFS	62171	Aberdeen
W302JND	60224	Manchester	W353RJA	60275	Manchester	W579RFS	62172	Aberdeen
W303JND	60225	Manchester	W354RJA	60276	Manchester	W581RFS	62173	Aberdeen

Reg	No.	Location	Reg	No.	Location	Reg	No.	Location
W582RFS	62174	Aberdeen	W706CWR	30851	W Yorkshire	W759DWX	30904	S Yorkshire
W583RFS	62175	Aberdeen	W706PHT	32706	Bristol	W761DWX	30906	W Yorkshire
W584RFS	62176	Aberdeen	W707CWR	30852	W Yorkshire	W762DWX	30907	W Yorkshire
W585RFS	62184	Aberdeen	W707PHT	32707	Bristol	W766HBT	60833	W Yorkshire
W586RFS	62185	Aberdeen	W708CWR	30853	W Yorkshire	W768DWX	30913	W Yorkshire
W587RFS	62186	Aberdeen	W708PHT	32708	Bristol	W769DWX	30914	W Yorkshire
W588RFS	62187	Aberdeen	W709CWR	30854	W Yorkshire	W771DWX	30875	S Yorkshire
W589RFS	62188	Aberdeen	W709RHT	32709	Devon & C	W771KBT	30916	W Yorkshire
W591RFS	62189	Aberdeen	W711CWR	30856	W Yorkshire	W772DWX	30885	W Yorkshire
W591SNG	65591	Glasgow	W711RHT	32711	Devon & C	W772KBT	30917	W Yorkshire
W592RFS	62190	Aberdeen	W712CWR	30857	W Yorkshire	W773DWX	30895	W Yorkshire
W592SNG	65592	Glasgow	W712RHT	32712	Devon & C	W773KBT	30918	W Yorkshire
W593RFS	62205	Aberdeen	W713CWR	30858	W Yorkshire	W774DWX	30900	Eastern C
W593SNG	65593	Glasgow	W713RHT	32713	Devon & C	W774KBT	30919	W Yorkshire
W594RFS	62206	Aberdeen	W714CWR	30859	W Yorkshire	W776DWX	30905	W Yorkshire
W594SNG	65594	Edinburgh	W714RHT	32714	Devon & C	W776KBT	30921	W Yorkshire
W595RFS	62207	Aberdeen	W715CWR	30860	W Yorkshire	W778DWX	30910	W Yorkshire
W595SNG	65595	Edinburgh	W715RHT	32715	Devon & C	W787KBT	30920	W Yorkshire
W596RFS	62208	Aberdeen	W716CWR	30861	W Yorkshire	W788KBT	30922	W Yorkshire
W596SNG	65596	Glasgow	W716RHT	32716	Devon & C	W7FAL	10052	Aberdeen
W597RFS	62209	Aberdeen	W717CWR	30862	W Yorkshire	W801DWX	60841	W Yorkshire
W597SNG	65597	Edinburgh	W717RHT	32717	Devon & C	W801EOW	32031	Hampshire
W598RFS	62210	Aberdeen	W718CWR	30863	W Yorkshire	W801PAE	32001	Bristol
W598SNG	65598	Edinburgh	W718ULL	41718	London	W802DWX	60842	W Yorkshire
W599RFS	62211	Aberdeen	W719CWR	30864	W Yorkshire	W802EOW	32032	Hampshire
W599SNG	65599	Edinburgh	W719ULL	41719	London	W802PAE	32002	Bristol
W5FAL	10050	Aberdeen	W721CWR	30866	W Yorkshire	W803DWX	60843	W Yorkshire
W601PAF	48261	Devon & C	W721ULL	41721	London	W803EOW	32033	Hampshire
W601RFS	62219	Aberdeen	W722CWR	30867	W Yorkshire	W803PAE	32003	Bristol
W601SNG	65601	Edinburgh	W722ULL	41722	London	W804DWX	60844	W Yorkshire
W602PAF	48262	Devon & C	W723CWR	30868	W Yorkshire	W804EOW	32034	Hampshire
W602RFS	62220	Aberdeen	W723PSF	61674	Edinburgh	W804PAE	32004	Bristol
W603PAF	48263	Devon & C	W723ULL	41723	London	W804PAF	53004	Devon & C
W603RFS	62221	Aberdeen	W724CWR	30869	W Yorkshire	W805DWX	60845	W Yorkshire
W604PAF	48264	Devon & C	W724ULL	41724	London	W805EOW	32035	Hampshire
W604RFS	62222	Aberdeen	W726CWR	30870	W Yorkshire	W805PAE	32005	Bristol
W605PAF	48265	Devon & C	W726DWX	30871	S Yorkshire	W805PAF	53005	Devon & C
W605RFS	62223	Aberdeen	W726ULL	41726	London	W806DWX	60846	W Yorkshire
W606PAF	48266	Devon & C	W727DWX	30872	S Yorkshire	W806EOW	32036	Hampshire
W607PAF	48267	Devon & C	W727ULL	41727	London	W806PAE	32006	Bristol
W607RFS	62225	Aberdeen	W728DWX	30873	S Yorkshire	W806PAF	53006	Devon & C
W608PAF	48268	Devon & C	W728VLO	41728	London	W807DWX	60847	W Yorkshire
W608RFS	62226	Aberdeen	W729DWX	30874	S Yorkshire	W807EOW	32037	Hampshire
W609PAF	48269	Devon & C	W731DWX	30876	S Yorkshire	W807PAE	32007	Bristol
W609RFS	62227	Aberdeen	W732DWX	30877	S Yorkshire	W807PAF	53007	Devon & C
W667CWT	30855	W Yorkshire	W733DWX	30878	S Yorkshire	W808DWX	60848	W Yorkshire
W668CWT	30865	W Yorkshire	W734DWX	30879	S Yorkshire	W808EOW	32038	Hampshire
W681RNA	62204	Aberdeen	W735DWX	30880	S Yorkshire	W808PAE	32008	Bristol
W681ULL	41681	London	W736DWX	30881	W Yorkshire	W808PAF	53008	Devon & C
W682RNA	62212	Aberdeen	W737DWX	30882	W Yorkshire	W809DWX	60849	W Yorkshire
W682ULL	41682	London	W738DWX	30883	W Yorkshire	W809EOW	32039	Hampshire
W683RNA	62213	Aberdeen	W739DWX	30884	W Yorkshire	W809PAE	32009	Bristol
W683ULL	41683	London	W741DWX	30886	Eastern C	W809PAF	53009	Devon & C
W684ULL	41684	London	W742DWX	30887	Eastern C	W809VMA	42350	Hampshire
W685ULL	41685	London	W743DWX	30888	Eastern C	W811DWX	60850	W Yorkshire
W686ULL	41686	London	W744DWX	30889	Eastern C	W811EOW	32041	Hampshire
W687ULL	41687	London	W745DWX	30890	W Yorkshire	W811PAE	32011	Bristol
W6FAL	10051	Aberdeen	W746DWX	30891	W Yorkshire	W811PAF	53011	Devon & C
W701CWR	30846	W Yorkshire	W747DWX	30892	W Yorkshire	W811PFB	48211	Bristol
W702CWR	30847	W Yorkshire	W748DWX	30893	W Yorkshire	W812DWX	60851	W Yorkshire
W702PHT	32702	Bristol	W751DWX	30896	W Yorkshire	W812EOW	32042	Hampshire
W703CWR	30848	W Yorkshire	W752DWX	30897	W Yorkshire	W812PAE	32012	Bristol
W703PHT	32703	Bristol	W753DWX	30898	W Yorkshire	W812PAF	53012	Devon & C
W704CWR	30849	W Yorkshire	W754DWX	30899	W Yorkshire	W812PFB	48212	Bristol
W704PHT	32704	Bristol	W756DWX	30901	Eastern C	W813DWX	60852	W Yorkshire
W705CWR	30850	W Yorkshire	W757DWX	30902	Eastern C	W813EOW	32043	Hampshire
W705PHT	32705	Bristol	W758DWX	30903	W Yorkshire	W813PAE	32013	Bristol

W813PAF	53013	Devon & C	W927VLN	32927	London	WK06 AFV	43853	Devon & C
W813PFB	48213	Bristol	W928VLN	32928	London	WK52 LZA	54502	Devon & C
W814DWX	60853	W Yorkshire	W929VLN	32929	London	WK52 WTV	43811	Devon & C
W814EOW	32044	Hampshire	W931ULL	32931	Glasgow	WK52SVU	20528	Devon & C
W814PAE	32014	Bristol	W933JNF	43833	Berkshire	WK52SVV	20529	Devon & C
W814PAF	53014	Devon & C	W934JNF	43834	Berkshire	WK52SYE	32755	Devon & C
W814PFB	48214	Bristol	W934ULL	32934	Glasgow	WK56 ABZ	44500	Devon & C
W815DWX	60854	W Yorkshire	W935JNF	43835	Berkshire	WLT408	31517	Glasgow
W815EOW	32045	Hampshire	W935ULL	32935	Glasgow	WLT659	41406	London
W815PAE	32015	Bristol	W936ULL	32936	Glasgow	WLT741	31520	Glasgow
W815PAF	53015	Devon & C	W937ULL	32937	Glasgow	WLT770	31521	Glasgow
W815PFB	48215	Bristol	W939ULL	32939	Glasgow	WLT976	31523	Glasgow
W816DWX	60855	W Yorkshire	W941ULL	32941	Glasgow	WM03BXP	20535	Devon & C
W816EOW	32046	Hampshire	W942ULL	32942	Glasgow	WM03BYD	20303	Bristol
W816PAE	32016	Bristol	W946ULL	32946	Glasgow	WM04NYV	23205	Wales
W816PFB	48216	Bristol	W947ULL	32947	Glasgow	WM04NYW	23206	Wales
W817PAE	32017	Bristol	W948ULL	32948	Glasgow	WM04NZU	23208	Devon & C
W817PFB	48217	Bristol	W949ULL	32949	Glasgow	WM04PHK	23207	Wales
W818PAE	32018	Bristol	W951ULL	32951	Glasgow	WR03YZL	32279	Bristol
W818PFB	48218	Bristol	W952ULL	32952	Glasgow	WR03YZM	32280	Bristol
W819PAE	32019	Bristol	WA05UNE	20352	Devon & C	WR03YZN	32281	Bristol
W819PFB	48219	Bristol	WA05UNF	20353	Devon & C	WR03YZP	32282	Bristol
W821PAE	32021	Bristol	WA05UNG	20351	Devon & C	WR03YZS	32283	Bristol
W821PFB	48221	Bristol	WA54OLN	32759	Devon & C	WR03YZT	32284	Bristol
W822PAE	32022	Bristol	WA54OLO	32756	Devon & C	WR03YZU	32285	Bristol
W822PFB	48222	Bristol	WA54OLP	32757	Devon & C	WR03YZV	32286	Bristol
W823PAE	32023	Bristol	WA54OLR	32760	Devon & C	WR03YZW	32287	Bristol
W823PFB	48223	Bristol	WA54OLT	32758	Devon & C	WR03YZX	32288	Bristol
W824PAE	32024	Bristol	WA56FTK	33414	Devon & C	WR03ZBC	32291	Bristol
W824PFB	48224	Bristol	WA56FTN	33415	Devon & C	WR03ZBD	32292	Bristol
W825PFB	48225	Devon & C	WA56FTO	33416	Devon & C	WSU481	38122	Leicester
W826PFB	48226	Devon & C	WA56FTP	33417	Devon & C	WSV408	20416	Devon & C
W827PFB	48227	Devon & C	WA56FTT	33418	Devon & C	WU02KVE	30564	S Yorkshire
W828PFB	48228	Devon & C	WA56FTU	33419	Devon & C	WU02KVF	30565	S Yorkshire
W829PFB	48229	Devon & C	WA56FTV	42946	Devon & C	WU02KVG	30566	S Yorkshire
W831PFB	48231	Devon & C	WA56FTX	42947	Devon & C	WU02KVH	30567	S Yorkshire
W832PFB	48232	Devon & C	WA56FTY	42948	Devon & C	WU02KVJ	30568	S Yorkshire
W833PFB	48233	Devon & C	WA56FTZ	42969	Devon & C	WU02KVK	30569	S Yorkshire
W834PFB	48234	Devon & C	WA56FUB	33411	Devon & C	WU02KVL	30570	S Yorkshire
W840VLO	32940	Glasgow	WA56FUD	33412	Devon & C	WU02KVM	30571	S Yorkshire
W895VLN	32910	London	WA56FUE	33413	Devon & C	WU02KVO	30572	S Yorkshire
W896VLN	32911	London	WA56OAN	42940	Devon & C	WU02KVP	30573	S Yorkshire
W897VLN	32920	London	WA56OAO	42941	Devon & C	WU02KVR	30574	S Yorkshire
W898VLN	32925	London	WA56OAP	42942	Devon & C	WU02KVS	30575	S Yorkshire
W899VLN	32930	London	WA56OAS	42943	Devon & C	WU02KVT	30576	S Yorkshire
W901VLN	32901	London	WA56OAU	42944	Devon & C	WU02KVV	30577	S Yorkshire
W902VLN	32902	London	WA56OAV	42945	Devon & C	WU02KVW	30578	S Yorkshire
W903VLN	32903	London	WJ55CRX	32761	Devon & C	WV02EUP	20514	Somerset &A
W904VLN	32904	London	WJ55CRZ	32762	Devon & C	WV02EUR	20515	Somerset &A
W905VLN	32905	London	WJ55CSF	32763	Devon & C	WV02EUT	20516	Somerset &A
W906VLN	32906	London	WJ55CSO	32764	Devon & C	WV02EUU	20517	Somerset &A
W907VLN	32907	London	WJ55CSU	32765	Devon & C	WV52AKY	20533	Bristol
W908VLN	32908	London	WJ55CSV	32766	Devon & C	WV52FAM	20521	Wales
W909VLN	32909	London	WJ55CTE	32767	Devon & C	WV52FAO	20522	Devon & C
W912VLN	32912	London	WJ55CTF	32768	Devon & C	WV52FCX	20523	Devon & C
W913VLN	32913	London	WK02 XLT	54501	Devon & C	WV52HSX	20524	Devon & C
W914VLN	32914	London	WK02TYD	48270	Devon & C	WV52HTT	20530	Devon & C
W915VLN	32915	London	WK02TYF	48271	Devon & C	WV52HVE	20531	Devon & C
W916VLN	32916	London	WK02TYH	48272	Devon & C	WV52HVF	20532	Devon & C
W917VLN	32917	London	WK02UMA	20518	Devon & C	WV52KTJ	20525	Somerset &A
W918VLN	32918	London	WK02UMB	20519	Devon & C	WV52KTK	20526	Somerset &A
W919VLN	32919	London	WK02UMC	20520	Devon & C	WV52KTL	20527	Somerset &A
W921VLN	32921	London	WK03EKW	20537	Devon & C	WX03ZFG	20534	Wales
W922VLN	32922	London	WK03EKX	20536	Devon & C	WX05OZF	20307	Bristol
W923VLN	32923	London	WK06 AEE	43850	Devon & C	WX05RRV	53802	Somerset &A
W924VLN	32924	London	WK06 AEF	43851	Devon & C	WX05RRY	53803	Somerset &A
W926VLN	32926	London	WK06 AFU	43852	Devon & C	WX05RRZ	53804	Somerset &A

Reg	Fleet	Depot	Reg	Fleet	Depot	Reg	Fleet	Depot
WX05RSO	53805	Somerset &A	WX06ONB	42967	Bristol	WX55TZS	66955	Somerset &A
WX05RSU	53806	Somerset &A	WX06ONC	42968	Bristol	WX55TZT	66956	Somerset &A
WX05RSV	53807	Somerset &A	WX51AJU	20511	Bristol	WX55TZU	66957	Eastern C
WX05RSY	53808	Somerset &A	WX51AJV	20510	Bristol	WX55TZV	66958	Somerset &A
WX05RSZ	53809	Somerset &A	WX51AJY	20512	Wales	WX55TZW	66959	Eastern C
WX05RTO	53810	Somerset &A	WX51AKY	20513	Wales	WX55TZY	66960	Somerset &A
WX05RTU	53811	Somerset &A	WX53PFG	20541	Devon & C	WX55TZZ	66961	Somerset &A
WX05RTV	53812	Somerset &A	WX53PFJ	20540	Devon & C	WX55UAA	66934	Somerset &A
WX05RTZ	53813	Somerset &A	WX53UKK	32289	Bristol	WX55UAB	66935	Somerset &A
WX05RUA	53814	Somerset &A	WX53UKL	32290	Bristol	WX55UAC	66936	Somerset &A
WX05RUC	53815	Somerset &A	WX53WEW	20543	Wales	WX55UAD	66937	Somerset &A
WX05RUJ	53816	Somerset &A	WX53WFA	20542	Wales	WX55VHK	37001	Bristol
WX05RUO	53817	Somerset &A	WX53WFP	20544	Wales	WX55VHL	37002	Bristol
WX05RUR	53818	Somerset &A	WX53WGF	20547	Devon & C	WX55VHM	37003	Bristol
WX05RUU	53819	Somerset &A	WX53WGG	20546	Devon & C	WX55VHN	37004	Bristol
WX05RUV	53820	Somerset &A	WX53WGJ	20545	Devon & C	WX55VHO	37005	Bristol
WX05RUW	42895	Somerset &A	WX54XCM	66727	Somerset &A	WX55VHP	37006	Bristol
WX05RUY	42896	Somerset &A	WX54XCN	66728	Somerset &A	WX55VHR	37007	Bristol
WX05RVA	42897	Somerset &A	WX54XCO	66729	Somerset &A	WX55VHT	37008	Bristol
WX05RVC	42898	Somerset &A	WX54XCP	66730	Somerset &A	WX55VHU	37009	Bristol
WX05RVE	42899	Somerset &A	WX54XCR	66731	Somerset &A	WX55VHV	37010	Bristol
WX05RVF	42900	Somerset &A	WX54XCT	66732	Somerset &A	WX55VHW	37011	Bristol
WX05RVJ	42901	Somerset &A	WX54XCU	66733	Somerset &A	WX55VHY	37012	Bristol
WX05RVK	42902	Somerset &A	WX54XCV	66734	Somerset &A	WX55VHZ	37013	Bristol
WX05RVL	42903	Somerset &A	WX54XCW	66735	Somerset &A	WX55VJA	37014	Bristol
WX05RVM	42904	Somerset &A	WX54XCY	66736	Somerset &A	WX55VJC	37015	Bristol
WX05RVN	42905	Somerset &A	WX54XCZ	66737	Somerset &A	WX55VJD	37016	Bristol
WX05RVO	42906	Somerset &A	WX54XDA	66716	Somerset &A	WX55VJE	37017	Bristol
WX05RVP	42907	Somerset &A	WX54XDB	66718	Somerset &A	WX55VJF	37018	Bristol
WX05RVR	42908	Somerset &A	WX54XDC	66719	Somerset &A	WX55VJG	37019	Bristol
WX05RVT	42909	Somerset &A	WX54XDD	66717	Somerset &A	WX55VJJ	37020	Bristol
WX05RVU	42910	Somerset &A	WX54XDE	66721	Somerset &A	WX56HJZ	32684	Somerset &A
WX05RVV	42911	Somerset &A	WX54XDF	66720	Somerset &A	WX56HKA	32685	Somerset &A
WX05RVW	42912	Somerset &A	WX54XDG	66724	Somerset &A	WX56HKB	32686	Somerset &A
WX05RVY	42913	Somerset &A	WX54XDH	66723	Somerset &A	WX56HKC	32687	Somerset &A
WX05RVZ	42914	Somerset &A	WX54XDJ	66725	Somerset &A	WX56HKD	32688	Somerset &A
WX05RWE	42915	Somerset &A	WX54XDK	66726	Somerset &A	WX56HKE	32689	Somerset &A
WX05RWF	42916	Somerset &A	WX54XDL	66722	Somerset &A	WX56HKF	32690	Somerset &A
WX05SVD	42938	Bristol	WX54ZHM	20300	Bristol	WX56HKG	32691	Somerset &A
WX05SVE	42939	Bristol	WX54ZHN	20301	Bristol	WX57HJO	37315	Somerset &A
WX05UAF	32636	Somerset &A	WX54ZHO	20302	Bristol	WX57HJU	37316	Somerset &A
WX05UAG	32637	Somerset &A	WX55HVZ	10174	Somerset &A	WX57HJV	37317	Somerset &A
WX05UAH	32638	Somerset &A	WX55HWA	10175	Somerset &A	WX57HJY	37318	Bristol
WX05UAJ	42552	Somerset &A	WX55HWB	10176	Somerset &A	WX57HJZ	37319	Bristol
WX05UAK	42553	Somerset &A	WX55HWC	10177	Somerset &A	WX57HKA	37320	Bristol
WX05UAL	42554	Somerset &A	WX55HWD	10178	Somerset &A	WX57HKB	37321	Bristol
WX05UAM	42555	Somerset &A	WX55HWE	10179	Somerset &A	WX57HKC	37322	Bristol
WX05UAN	42556	Somerset &A	WX55HWF	10180	Somerset &A	WX57HKD	37323	Bristol
WX05UAO	42557	Somerset &A	WX55HWG	10181	Somerset &A	WX57HKE	37324	Bristol
WX06OMF	42949	Bristol	WX55HWH	10182	Somerset &A	WX57HKF	37325	Bristol
WX06OMG	42950	Bristol	WX55TYZ	66938	Somerset &A	WX57HKG	37326	Bristol
WX06OMH	42951	Bristol	WX55TZA	66939	Somerset &A	WX57HKH	37327	Bristol
WX06OMJ	42952	Bristol	WX55TZB	66940	Somerset &A	WX57HKJ	37328	Bristol
WX06OMK	42953	Bristol	WX55TZC	66941	Somerset &A	WX57HKK	37329	Bristol
WX06OML	42954	Bristol	WX55TZD	66942	Somerset &A	WX57HKL	37330	Bristol
WX06OMM	42955	Bristol	WX55TZE	66943	Somerset &A	WX57HKM	37331	Bristol
WX06OMO	42956	Bristol	WX55TZF	66944	Somerset &A	WX57HKN	37332	Bristol
WX06OMP	42957	Bristol	WX55TZG	66945	Somerset &A	WX57HKO	37333	Bristol
WX06OMR	42958	Bristol	WX55TZH	66946	Somerset &A	WX57HKP	37334	Bristol
WX06OMS	42959	Bristol	WX55TZJ	66947	Somerset &A	WX57HKT	37335	Bristol
WX06OMT	42960	Bristol	WX55TZK	66948	Somerset &A	WX57HKU	37336	Bristol
WX06OMU	42962	Bristol	WX55TZL	66949	Somerset &A	WX57HKV	37337	Bristol
WX06OMV	42961	Bristol	WX55TZM	66950	Eastern C	WX57HKW	37338	Bristol
WX06OMW	42963	Bristol	WX55TZN	66951	Somerset &A	WX57HKY	37339	Bristol
WX06OMY	42964	Bristol	WX55TZO	66952	Somerset &A	WX57HKZ	37340	Bristol
WX06OMZ	42965	Bristol	WX55TZP	66953	Somerset &A	WX57HLA	37341	Bristol
WX06ONA	42966	Bristol	WX55TZR	66954	Somerset &A	WX57HLC	37342	Bristol

Reg	No	Location	Reg	No	Location	Reg	No	Location
WX57HLD	37343	Bristol	X304JGE	66234	Glasgow	X501JLO	41690	London
WX57HLE	37344	Bristol	X351VWT	30931	W Yorkshire	X502BFJ	32752	Devon & C
WX57HLF	37345	Bristol	X352VWT	30932	W Yorkshire	X502JLO	41700	London
WX57HLG	37346	Bristol	X353VWT	30933	W Yorkshire	X503BFJ	32753	Devon & C
WX57HLH	37347	Bristol	X354VWT	30934	W Yorkshire	X503JLO	41730	London
WX57HLJ	37348	Bristol	X356VWT	30935	W Yorkshire	X504BFJ	32754	Devon & C
WX57HLK	37349	Bristol	X357VWT	30936	W Yorkshire	X504JLO	41740	London
WX57HLM	37350	Bristol	X358VWT	30937	W Yorkshire	X506HLR	41755	London
WX57HLN	37351	Bristol	X359VWT	30938	W Yorkshire	X507HLR	41760	London
WX57HLO	37352	Bristol	X381HLR	41381	London	X508HLR	41765	London
WX57HLP	37353	Bristol	X382HLR	41382	London	X509HLR	41770	London
WX57HLR	37354	Bristol	X383HLR	41383	London	X511HLR	41775	London
WX57HLU	37355	Bristol	X384HLR	41384	London	X512HLR	41777	London
WX57HLV	37356	Bristol	X385HLR	41385	London	X513HLR	41780	London
WX57HLW	37357	Bristol	X386HLR	41386	London	X514HLR	41786	London
WX57HLY	37358	Bristol	X387HLR	41387	London	X578RJW	32052	London
WX57HLZ	37359	Bristol	X388HLR	41388	London	X601NSS	62122	Aberdeen
X103NSS	31560	Aberdeen	X389HLR	41389	London	X602NSS	62123	Aberdeen
X104NSS	31561	Aberdeen	X391HLR	41391	London	X603NSS	62124	Aberdeen
X132NSS	31558	Aberdeen	X392HLR	41392	London	X604NSS	62125	Aberdeen
X134FPO	10134	Glasgow	X393HLR	41393	London	X605NSS	62126	Aberdeen
X136FPO	10136	Glasgow	X394HLR	41394	London	X606NSS	62127	Aberdeen
X136NSS	31562	Aberdeen	X395HLR	41395	London	X606RFS	62224	Aberdeen
X137FPO	10137	Glasgow	X396HLR	41396	London	X607NSS	62128	Aberdeen
X137NSS	31563	Aberdeen	X397HLR	41397	London	X608NSS	62129	Aberdeen
X138FPO	10138	Glasgow	X398HLR	41398	London	X609NSS	62130	Aberdeen
X139FPO	10139	Glasgow	X399HLR	41399	London	X611HLT	32955	London
X141FPO	10141	Glasgow	X401CSG	10017	Manchester	X611NBU	40445	Manchester
X142FPO	10142	Glasgow	X401HLR	41401	London	X611NSS	62132	Aberdeen
X143FPO	10143	Glasgow	X402HLR	41402	London	X611OBN	40308	Manchester
X144FPO	10144	Glasgow	X424UMS	61675	Glasgow	X612HLT	32960	London
X146FPO	10146	Glasgow	X425UMS	61676	Glasgow	X612NSS	62133	Aberdeen
X191HFB	20461	W Yorkshire	X426UMS	61677	Glasgow	X612OBN	40309	Manchester
X192HFB	20462	W Yorkshire	X427UMS	61678	Glasgow	X613HLT	32970	London
X193HFB	20463	Essex	X429UMS	61679	Glasgow	X613NSS	62134	Aberdeen
X194HFB	20464	W Yorkshire	X431UMS	61680	Glasgow	X613OBN	40310	Manchester
X201HAE	43821	Somerset &A	X432UMS	61681	Glasgow	X614HLT	32980	London
X202HAE	43822	Somerset &A	X433UMS	61682	Glasgow	X614NSS	62135	Aberdeen
X203HAE	43823	Somerset &A	X434UMS	61683	Glasgow	X614OBN	40311	Manchester
X238AMO	42338	Berkshire	X435UMS	61684	Glasgow	X615NSS	62136	Aberdeen
X239AMO	42339	Berkshire	X436UMS	61685	Glasgow	X615OBN	40312	Manchester
X241AMO	42341	Berkshire	X437UMS	61686	Glasgow	X616NSS	62137	Aberdeen
X242AMO	42342	Berkshire	X438UMS	61687	Glasgow	X616OBN	40313	Manchester
X243AMO	42343	Berkshire	X439UMS	61688	Glasgow	X617NSS	62138	Aberdeen
X244AMO	42344	Berkshire	X441UMS	61689	Glasgow	X617OBN	40314	Manchester
X246AMO	42346	Berkshire	X442UMS	61690	Glasgow	X618NSS	62139	Aberdeen
X247AMO	42347	Berkshire	X443UMS	61691	Glasgow	X618OBN	40315	Manchester
X253USH	60196	Potteries	X445UMS	61692	Glasgow	X619NSS	62140	Aberdeen
X256USH	60199	Edinburgh	X446UMS	61693	Glasgow	X619OBN	40316	Manchester
X257USH	60201	Potteries	X447UMS	61694	Glasgow	X621NSS	62149	Aberdeen
X261USH	60205	Potteries	X448UMS	61695	Glasgow	X622NSS	62150	Aberdeen
X265USH	60209	Manchester	X449UMS	61696	Glasgow	X623NSS	62151	Aberdeen
X266USH	60210	Manchester	X451UMS	61697	Glasgow	X624NSS	62152	Aberdeen
X269USH	60213	Manchester	X452UMS	61698	Glasgow	X627OBN	40317	Manchester
X271USH	60200	Potteries	X453UMS	61699	Glasgow	X683ADK	62182	Aberdeen
X272USH	60204	Edinburgh	X454UMS	61700	Glasgow	X684ADK	62183	Aberdeen
X289FFA	40020	Potteries	X457UMS	61701	Glasgow	X685ADK	62191	Aberdeen
X291FFA	40021	Potteries	X458UMS	61702	Glasgow	X686ADK	62192	Aberdeen
X292FFA	40022	Potteries	X459UMS	61703	Glasgow	X687ADK	62193	Somerset &A
X293FFA	40023	Potteries	X461UMS	61704	Glasgow	X688ADK	62194	Somerset &A
X294FFA	40024	Potteries	X474SCY	42474	Devon & C	X688HLF	41688	London
X295FFA	40025	Potteries	X475SCY	42475	Devon & C	X689ADK	62195	Aberdeen
X296FFA	40026	Potteries	X476SCY	42476	Devon & C	X689HLF	41689	London
X297FFA	40027	Potteries	X477NSS	62153	Aberdeen	X691ADK	62196	Aberdeen
X298FFA	40028	Potteries	X477SCY	42477	Devon & C	X692ADK	62197	Aberdeen
X299FFA	40029	Potteries	X478SCY	42478	Devon & C	X693ADK	62198	Aberdeen
X303JGE	66233	Glasgow	X501BFJ	32751	Devon & C	X694ADK	62199	Aberdeen

The 2008 First Bus Handbook

Reg	No	Location	Reg	No	Location	Reg	No	Location
X695ADK	62200	Aberdeen	X794NWR	30926	W Yorkshire	Y344XBN	60198	Edinburgh
X696ADK	62201	Aberdeen	X795NWR	30927	W Yorkshire	Y346NLF	32982	London
X697ADK	62202	Aberdeen	X796NWR	30928	W Yorkshire	Y346XBN	60202	Potteries
X697HLF	41697	London	X797NWR	30929	W Yorkshire	Y347XBN	60208	Potteries
X698ADK	62203	Aberdeen	X798NWR	30930	W Yorkshire	Y352AUY	42352	Midland Red
X698HLF	41698	London	X79HLR	41400	London	Y353AUY	42353	Midland Red
X699ADK	60405	Manchester	X856UOK	30561	S Yorkshire	Y354AUY	42354	Midland Red
X699HLF	41699	London	X857UOK	30562	S Yorkshire	Y356AUY	42356	Midland Red
X69NSS	62131	Aberdeen	X858UOK	30563	S Yorkshire	Y393RTD	40447	Manchester
X729HLF	41729	London	X944NSO	62141	Aberdeen	Y394RTD	40446	Manchester
X731HLF	41731	London	X954HLT	32954	London	Y445CUB	60876	W Yorkshire
X732HLF	41732	London	X956HLT	32956	London	Y446CUB	60877	W Yorkshire
X733HLF	41733	London	X957HLT	32957	London	Y447CUB	60878	W Yorkshire
X734HLF	41734	London	X958HLT	32958	London	Y449CUB	60880	W Yorkshire
X735HLF	41735	London	X959HLT	32959	London	Y451CUB	60881	W Yorkshire
X736HLF	41736	London	X961HLT	32961	London	Y5 TRU	20475	Devon & C
X737HLF	41737	London	X962HLT	32962	London	Y546XNW	53034	S Yorkshire
X738HLF	41738	London	X963HLT	32963	London	Y547XNW	53035	S Yorkshire
X741HLF	41741	London	X964HLT	32964	London	Y597KNE	60197	Edinburgh
X742HLF	41742	London	X965HLT	32965	London	Y598KNE	60206	Manchester
X743HLF	41743	London	X966HLT	32966	London	Y626RSA	62154	Aberdeen
X744HLF	41744	London	X967HLT	32967	London	Y627RSA	62155	Aberdeen
X745HLF	41745	London	X968HLT	32968	London	Y628RSA	62163	Aberdeen
X746JLO	41746	London	X969HLT	32969	London	Y629RSA	62164	Aberdeen
X747JLO	41747	London	X971HLT	32971	London	Y631RSA	62166	Aberdeen
X748JLO	41748	London	X972HLT	32972	London	Y632RSA	62167	Aberdeen
X749VUA	30894	W Yorkshire	X973HLT	32973	London	Y632RTD	60203	Edinburgh
X751JLO	41751	London	X974HLT	32974	London	Y633RSA	62168	Aberdeen
X752HLR	41752	London	X975HLT	32975	London	Y633RTD	60212	Manchester
X753HLR	41753	London	X977HLT	32977	London	Y634RSA	62169	Aberdeen
X754HLR	41754	London	X978HLT	32978	London	Y634RTD	60214	Manchester
X756HLR	41756	London	X981HLT	32981	London	Y635RSA	62177	Aberdeen
X757HLR	41757	London	X991FFA	40148	Potteries	Y636RSA	62178	Aberdeen
X758HLR	41758	London	X992FFA	40149	Potteries	Y637RSA	62179	Aberdeen
X759HLR	41759	London	X993FFA	40150	Potteries	Y638RSA	62180	Aberdeen
X761HLR	41761	London	X994FFA	40151	Potteries	Y639RSA	62181	Aberdeen
X762HLR	41762	London	X995FFA	40152	Potteries	Y642AVV	10152	Somerset &A
X763HLR	41763	London	XDZ5911	31811	W Yorkshire	Y643AVV	10153	Somerset &A
X763VUA	30908	W Yorkshire	XDZ5912	31812	W Yorkshire	Y644AVV	10151	Somerset &A
X764HLR	41764	London	XDZ5913	31813	W Yorkshire	Y661UKU	60703	S Yorkshire
X764VUA	30909	W Yorkshire	XDZ5914	31814	W Yorkshire	Y701RSA	62165	Aberdeen
X766HLR	41766	London	XDZ5915	31815	W Yorkshire	Y774TNC	60406	S Yorkshire
X766VUA	30911	W Yorkshire	XDZ5916	31816	W Yorkshire	Y794XNW	30939	W Yorkshire
X767HLR	41767	London	XFF283	20053	Devon & C	Y795XNW	30940	W Yorkshire
X767VUA	30912	W Yorkshire	Y1 EDN	42801	Devon & C	Y796XNW	30941	W Yorkshire
X768HLR	41768	London	Y147ROT	10147	Glasgow	Y797XNW	30942	W Yorkshire
X769HLR	41769	London	Y148ROT	10148	Glasgow	Y798XNW	30943	W Yorkshire
X771HLR	41771	London	Y149ROT	10149	Glasgow	Y901KND	40318	Manchester
X771NSO	31559	Aberdeen	Y151ROT	10015	Glasgow	Y902KND	40319	Manchester
X772HLR	41772	London	Y152ROT	10016	Glasgow	Y903KND	40320	Manchester
X773HLR	41773	London	Y181BGB	66281	Glasgow	Y904KND	40321	Manchester
X774HLR	41774	London	Y182BGB	66282	Glasgow	Y905KND	40322	Manchester
X776HLR	41776	London	Y2 EDN	42802	Devon & C	Y932NLP	32990	London
X778HLR	41778	London	Y223NLF	32976	London	Y933NLP	32999	London
X779HLR	41779	London	Y224NLF	32979	London	Y934NLP	33000	London
X779VUA	30915	W Yorkshire	Y251HHL	50232	S Yorkshire	Y937CSF	62232	S Yorkshire
X781HLR	41781	London	Y252HHL	50233	S Yorkshire	Y938CSF	62245	Somerset &A
X782HLR	41782	London	Y253HHL	50234	S Yorkshire	Y939CSF	62242	Somerset &A
X783HLR	41783	London	Y254HHL	50235	S Yorkshire	Y941CSF	62231	Manchester
X784HLR	41784	London	Y256HHL	50236	S Yorkshire	Y942CSF	62233	Manchester
X785HLR	41785	London	Y301RTD	61705	Glasgow	Y943CSF	62234	S Yorkshire
X787HLR	41787	London	Y302RTD	61706	Glasgow	Y944CSF	62236	Manchester
X788HLR	41788	London	Y303RTD	61707	Glasgow	Y945CSF	62237	S Yorkshire
X78HLR	41390	London	Y304RTD	61708	Glasgow	Y946CSF	62235	S Yorkshire
X791NWR	30923	W Yorkshire	Y307RTD	61709	Glasgow	Y947CSF	62238	Somerset &A
X792NWR	30924	W Yorkshire	Y343XBN	60195	Edinburgh	Y948CSF	62239	S Yorkshire
X793NWR	30925	W Yorkshire	Y344NLF	32983	London	Y949CSF	62240	S Yorkshire

Reg	No	Location	Reg	No	Location	Reg	No	Location
Y949RTD	61710	Glasgow	YJ04FYG	32437	W Yorkshire	YJ05VVT	66775	W Yorkshire
Y951CSF	62241	Manchester	YJ04FYH	32438	W Yorkshire	YJ05VVU	66776	W Yorkshire
Y952CSF	62244	S Yorkshire	YJ04FYK	32439	W Yorkshire	YJ05VVW	66777	W Yorkshire
Y953CSF	62243	S Yorkshire	YJ04FYL	32440	W Yorkshire	YJ05VVX	66778	W Yorkshire
Y961XBU	60207	Manchester	YJ04FYM	32441	W Yorkshire	YJ05VVY	66779	W Yorkshire
Y962XBU	60211	Manchester	YJ04FYN	32442	W Yorkshire	YJ05VVZ	66780	W Yorkshire
Y984NLP	32984	London	YJ04FYP	32443	W Yorkshire	YJ05VWA	68545	W Yorkshire
Y985NLP	32985	London	YJ04FYR	32444	W Yorkshire	YJ05VWB	68544	W Yorkshire
Y986NLP	32986	London	YJ04FYS	32445	W Yorkshire	YJ05VWC	68543	W Yorkshire
Y987NLP	32987	London	YJ04FYT	32446	W Yorkshire	YJ05VWE	32540	W Yorkshire
Y988NLP	32988	London	YJ04FYU	32447	W Yorkshire	YJ05VWF	32541	W Yorkshire
Y989NLP	32989	London	YJ04FYV	32448	W Yorkshire	YJ05VWG	32539	W Yorkshire
Y991NLP	32991	London	YJ04FYW	32449	W Yorkshire	YJ05VWH	32542	W Yorkshire
Y992NLP	32992	London	YJ04FYX	32450	W Yorkshire	YJ05XOP	53140	Hampshire
Y993NLP	32993	London	YJ04FYY	32451	W Yorkshire	YJ06FYS	53824	W Yorkshire
Y994NLP	32994	London	YJ04FYZ	32452	W Yorkshire	YJ06FYT	53825	W Yorkshire
Y995NLP	32995	London	YJ04FZA	32453	W Yorkshire	YJ06WTV	68628	W Yorkshire
Y996NLP	32996	London	YJ04FZB	32454	W Yorkshire	YJ06WTW	68627	W Yorkshire
Y997NLP	32997	London	YJ04FZC	32455	W Yorkshire	YJ06WTX	68626	W Yorkshire
Y998NLP	32998	London	YJ04FZD	32456	W Yorkshire	YJ06WTY	68629	W Yorkshire
YA05SOJ	66792	W Yorkshire	YJ04FZE	32457	W Yorkshire	YJ06WTZ	68630	W Yorkshire
YA05SOU	66790	W Yorkshire	YJ04FZF	32458	W Yorkshire	YJ06WUA	68631	W Yorkshire
YA54WBK	68528	W Yorkshire	YJ04FZG	32459	W Yorkshire	YJ06XEK	68640	W Yorkshire
YA54WBL	68527	W Yorkshire	YJ04FZH	32460	W Yorkshire	YJ06XEL	68641	W Yorkshire
YA54WBN	68530	W Yorkshire	YJ04FZK	32461	W Yorkshire	YJ06XFR	68608	W Yorkshire
YA54WBO	68529	W Yorkshire	YJ04FZL	32462	W Yorkshire	YJ06XFS	68607	W Yorkshire
YG02DGY	60926	W Yorkshire	YJ04FZM	32463	W Yorkshire	YJ06XKK	37021	W Yorkshire
YG02DGZ	60909	W Yorkshire	YJ04FZN	32464	W Yorkshire	YJ06XKL	37022	W Yorkshire
YG02DHA	60908	W Yorkshire	YJ04FZP	32465	W Yorkshire	YJ06XKM	37023	W Yorkshire
YG02DHC	60927	W Yorkshire	YJ04FZR	32466	W Yorkshire	YJ06XKN	37024	W Yorkshire
YG02DHE	60924	Eastern C	YJ04FZS	32467	W Yorkshire	YJ06XKO	37025	W Yorkshire
YG02DHF	60923	W Yorkshire	YJ04FZT	32468	W Yorkshire	YJ06XKP	37026	W Yorkshire
YG02DHJ	60922	W Yorkshire	YJ04FZU	32469	W Yorkshire	YJ06XKS	37027	W Yorkshire
YG02DHK	60902	W Yorkshire	YJ04FZV	32470	W Yorkshire	YJ06XKT	37028	W Yorkshire
YG02DHL	60904	W Yorkshire	YJ04FZX	32471	W Yorkshire	YJ06XKU	37029	W Yorkshire
YG02DHM	60903	Eastern C	YJ04FZY	32472	W Yorkshire	YJ06XKV	37030	W Yorkshire
YG02DHN	60906	W Yorkshire	YJ04FZZ	32473	W Yorkshire	YJ06XKW	37031	W Yorkshire
YG02DHO	60905	Eastern C	YJ05 XNV	53205	Devon & C	YJ06XKX	37032	W Yorkshire
YG02DHP	40592	W Yorkshire	YJ05 XOR	53154	Devon & C	YJ06XKY	37033	W Yorkshire
YG02DHU	60928	W Yorkshire	YJ05KNV	66754	W Yorkshire	YJ06XKZ	37034	W Yorkshire
YG02DHV	60907	W Yorkshire	YJ05KNW	66755	W Yorkshire	YJ06XLA	37035	W Yorkshire
YG02DHX	40599	W Yorkshire	YJ05KNX	66756	W Yorkshire	YJ06XLB	37036	W Yorkshire
YG02DHY	40593	W Yorkshire	YJ05KNY	66757	W Yorkshire	YJ06XLC	37037	W Yorkshire
YG02DJY	50297	Wales	YJ05KNZ	66758	W Yorkshire	YJ06XLD	37038	W Yorkshire
YG02DJZ	50298	Wales	YJ05KOB	66750	W Yorkshire	YJ06XLE	37039	W Yorkshire
YG02DKO	60914	W Yorkshire	YJ05KOD	66751	W Yorkshire	YJ06XLF	37040	W Yorkshire
YG02DKU	60916	W Yorkshire	YJ05KOE	66752	W Yorkshire	YJ06XLG	37041	W Yorkshire
YG02DKV	60917	W Yorkshire	YJ05KOH	66753	W Yorkshire	YJ06XLH	37042	W Yorkshire
YG02DKX	40598	W Yorkshire	YJ05VUW	32538	W Yorkshire	YJ06XLK	32692	W Yorkshire
YG02DKY	40597	W Yorkshire	YJ05VUX	32537	W Yorkshire	YJ06XLL	32693	W Yorkshire
YG02DLD	60912	W Yorkshire	YJ05VUY	32532	W Yorkshire	YJ06XLM	32694	W Yorkshire
YG02DLE	40596	W Yorkshire	YJ05VVA	66759	W Yorkshire	YJ06XLN	32695	W Yorkshire
YG02DLF	40595	W Yorkshire	YJ05VVB	66760	W Yorkshire	YJ06XLO	32696	W Yorkshire
YG02DLJ	60918	W Yorkshire	YJ05VVC	66761	W Yorkshire	YJ06XLP	32697	W Yorkshire
YG02DLK	40594	W Yorkshire	YJ05VVD	66762	W Yorkshire	YJ06XLR	19012	W Yorkshire
YG02DLN	60921	W Yorkshire	YJ05VVE	66763	W Yorkshire	YJ06XLS	19013	W Yorkshire
YG02DLO	60911	W Yorkshire	YJ05VVF	66764	W Yorkshire	YJ06XLT	37043	W Yorkshire
YG02DLU	60920	W Yorkshire	YJ05VVG	66765	W Yorkshire	YJ06XLU	37044	W Yorkshire
YG02DLV	48273	Devon & C	YJ05VVH	66766	W Yorkshire	YJ06XLV	37045	W Yorkshire
YG02DLX	60919	W Yorkshire	YJ05VVK	66767	W Yorkshire	YJ06XLW	37046	W Yorkshire
YG02DLY	60913	W Yorkshire	YJ05VVL	66768	W Yorkshire	YJ06XLX	37047	W Yorkshire
YG02DLZ	60915	W Yorkshire	YJ05VVM	66769	W Yorkshire	YJ06XLY	37048	W Yorkshire
YJ04FYB	32432	W Yorkshire	YJ05VVN	66770	W Yorkshire	YJ06XLZ	37049	W Yorkshire
YJ04FYC	32433	W Yorkshire	YJ05VVO	66771	W Yorkshire	YJ06XMA	37050	W Yorkshire
YJ04FYD	32434	W Yorkshire	YJ05VVP	66772	W Yorkshire	YJ06XMB	37051	W Yorkshire
YJ04FYE	32435	W Yorkshire	YJ05VVR	66773	W Yorkshire	YJ06XMC	37052	W Yorkshire
YJ04FYF	32436	W Yorkshire	YJ05VVS	66774	W Yorkshire	YJ06XMD	37053	W Yorkshire

The 2008 First Bus Handbook

Reg	Fleet	Area
YJ06XME	37054	W Yorkshire
YJ06XMF	37055	W Yorkshire
YJ06XMG	37056	W Yorkshire
YJ06XMH	37057	W Yorkshire
YJ06XMK	37058	W Yorkshire
YJ06XMM	37060	W Yorkshire
YJ06XMO	37061	W Yorkshire
YJ06XMP	37062	W Yorkshire
YJ07EHO	53907	W Yorkshire
YJ07EHP	53908	W Yorkshire
YJ07EHR	53909	W Yorkshire
YJ07LVL	19019	W Yorkshire
YJ07LVM	19020	W Yorkshire
YJ07LVN	19021	W Yorkshire
YJ07LVO	19022	W Yorkshire
YJ07LVR	19023	W Yorkshire
YJ07LVS	19024	W Yorkshire
YJ07LVT	19025	W Yorkshire
YJ07LVU	19026	W Yorkshire
YJ07LVV	19027	W Yorkshire
YJ07LVW	19028	W Yorkshire
YJ07LVX	19031	Luton Airport
YJ07LWC	66995	W Yorkshire
YJ07LWD	66996	W Yorkshire
YJ07LWE	66997	W Yorkshire
YJ07LWF	66998	W Yorkshire
YJ07WFM	69245	W Yorkshire
YJ07WFN	69246	W Yorkshire
YJ07WFO	69247	W Yorkshire
YJ07WFP	69248	W Yorkshire
YJ07WFR	69249	W Yorkshire
YJ07WFS	69250	W Yorkshire
YJ07WFT	69251	W Yorkshire
YJ07WFU	69252	W Yorkshire
YJ07WFV	69253	W Yorkshire
YJ07WFW	69270	W Yorkshire
YJ07WFX	69271	W Yorkshire
YJ07WFY	69272	W Yorkshire
YJ07WFZ	69273	W Yorkshire
YJ07WGA	69274	W Yorkshire
YJ08 CDE	69329	W Yorkshire
YJ08 CDF	69330	W Yorkshire
YJ08 CDK	69331	W Yorkshire
YJ08 CDN	69332	W Yorkshire
YJ08 CDO	69333	W Yorkshire
YJ08 CDU	69334	W Yorkshire
YJ08 CDV	69335	W Yorkshire
YJ08 CDX	69336	W Yorkshire
YJ08 CDY	69337	W Yorkshire
YJ08 CDZ	69338	W Yorkshire
YJ08 CEA	69339	W Yorkshire
YJ08 CEF	69340	W Yorkshire
YJ08 CEK	69341	W Yorkshire
YJ08 CEN	69342	W Yorkshire
YJ08 CEO	69343	W Yorkshire
YJ08 CEU	69344	W Yorkshire
YJ08 CEV	69345	W Yorkshire
YJ08 CEX	69346	W Yorkshire
YJ08 CEY	69347	W Yorkshire
YJ08 CFA	69348	W Yorkshire
YJ08 CFD	69349	W Yorkshire
YJ08 CFE	69350	W Yorkshire
YJ08 GVZ	37087	W Yorkshire
YJ08 GWA	37088	W Yorkshire
YJ08 GWC	37089	W Yorkshire
YJ08 GWD	37090	W Yorkshire
YJ08 GWE	37091	W Yorkshire
YJ08 GWF	37092	W Yorkshire
YJ08 GWG	37093	W Yorkshire
YJ08 GWK	37094	W Yorkshire
YJ08 GWL	37095	W Yorkshire
YJ08 GWM	37096	W Yorkshire
YJ08 GWN	37097	W Yorkshire
YJ08 GWO	37098	W Yorkshire
YJ08 GWP	37099	W Yorkshire
YJ08 GWU	37100	W Yorkshire
YJ08 GWV	37101	W Yorkshire
YJ08 GWW	37102	W Yorkshire
YJ08 GWX	69299	W Yorkshire
YJ08 GWY	69300	W Yorkshire
YJ08GVE	37071	W Yorkshire
YJ08GVF	37072	W Yorkshire
YJ08GVG	37073	W Yorkshire
YJ08GVK	37074	W Yorkshire
YJ08GVL	37075	W Yorkshire
YJ08GVM	37076	W Yorkshire
YJ08GVN	37077	W Yorkshire
YJ08GVO	37078	W Yorkshire
YJ08GVP	37079	W Yorkshire
YJ08GVR	37080	W Yorkshire
YJ08GVT	37081	W Yorkshire
YJ08GVU	37082	W Yorkshire
YJ08GVV	37083	W Yorkshire
YJ08GVW	37084	W Yorkshire
YJ08GVX	37085	W Yorkshire
YJ08GVY	37086	W Yorkshire
YJ51PZT	60882	W Yorkshire
YJ51PZU	60883	W Yorkshire
YJ51PZV	60884	W Yorkshire
YJ51PZW	60885	S Yorkshire
YJ51PZX	60886	S Yorkshire
YJ51PZY	60887	S Yorkshire
YJ51PZZ	40570	Devon & C
YJ51RAU	30964	W Yorkshire
YJ51RAX	30965	W Yorkshire
YJ51RCO	30959	W Yorkshire
YJ51RCU	30955	W Yorkshire
YJ51RCV	30956	W Yorkshire
YJ51RCX	30957	W Yorkshire
YJ51RCZ	30958	W Yorkshire
YJ51RDO	30954	W Yorkshire
YJ51RDU	30960	W Yorkshire
YJ51RDV	30961	W Yorkshire
YJ51RDX	30962	W Yorkshire
YJ51RDY	30963	W Yorkshire
YJ51RDZ	60888	S Yorkshire
YJ51REU	60894	S Yorkshire
YJ51RFE	60895	W Yorkshire
YJ51RFF	60896	W Yorkshire
YJ51RFK	60910	W Yorkshire
YJ51RFL	60899	W Yorkshire
YJ51RFN	60900	W Yorkshire
YJ51RFO	60901	W Yorkshire
YJ51RFX	60898	W Yorkshire
YJ51RFY	60897	W Yorkshire
YJ51RFZ	40587	W Yorkshire
YJ51RGO	40588	W Yorkshire
YJ51RGU	40589	W Yorkshire
YJ51RGV	40590	W Yorkshire
YJ51RGX	40591	W Yorkshire
YJ51RGY	60893	S Yorkshire
YJ51RGZ	60891	S Yorkshire
YJ51RHE	60889	S Yorkshire
YJ51RHF	60892	S Yorkshire
YJ51RHK	60890	S Yorkshire
YJ51RHO	40577	W Yorkshire
YJ51RHU	40578	W Yorkshire
YJ51RHV	40579	W Yorkshire
YJ51RHX	40580	Devon & C
YJ51RHY	40581	Devon & C
YJ51RHZ	40582	Devon & C
YJ51RJO	40583	Devon & C
YJ51RJU	40584	Devon & C
YJ51RJV	40585	Devon & C
YJ51RJX	40586	Devon & C
YJ51RKO	40571	W Yorkshire
YJ51RKU	40572	W Yorkshire
YJ51RKV	40573	W Yorkshire
YJ51RPY	30944	W Yorkshire
YJ51RPZ	30945	W Yorkshire
YJ51RRO	30946	W Yorkshire
YJ51RRU	30947	W Yorkshire
YJ51RRV	30948	W Yorkshire
YJ51RRX	30949	W Yorkshire
YJ51RRY	30950	W Yorkshire
YJ51RRZ	30951	W Yorkshire
YJ51RSO	30952	W Yorkshire
YJ51RSU	30953	W Yorkshire
YJ51RSV	40574	W Yorkshire
YJ51RSX	40575	W Yorkshire
YJ51RSY	40576	W Yorkshire
YJ53HVC	66700	W Yorkshire
YJ54BSV	53201	Glasgow
YJ54BVA	53301	W Yorkshire
YJ54BVB	53302	W Yorkshire
YJ54BVC	53303	W Yorkshire
YJ54UXF	53821	W Yorkshire
YJ54UXG	53822	W Yorkshire
YJ54XTO	32503	W Yorkshire
YJ54XTP	32504	W Yorkshire
YJ54XTR	32505	W Yorkshire
YJ54XTT	32506	W Yorkshire
YJ54XTU	32507	W Yorkshire
YJ54XTV	32508	W Yorkshire
YJ54XTW	32509	W Yorkshire
YJ54XTX	32510	W Yorkshire
YJ54XTZ	32511	W Yorkshire
YJ54XUA	32512	W Yorkshire
YJ54XUB	32513	W Yorkshire
YJ54XUC	32514	W Yorkshire
YJ54XUD	32515	W Yorkshire
YJ54XUE	32516	W Yorkshire
YJ54XUF	32517	W Yorkshire
YJ54XUG	32518	W Yorkshire
YJ54XUH	32519	W Yorkshire
YJ54XUK	32520	W Yorkshire
YJ54XUM	32521	W Yorkshire
YJ54XUN	32522	W Yorkshire
YJ54XUO	32523	W Yorkshire
YJ54XUP	32524	W Yorkshire
YJ54XUR	32525	W Yorkshire
YJ54XUT	32526	W Yorkshire
YJ54XUU	32527	W Yorkshire
YJ54XUV	32528	W Yorkshire
YJ54XUW	32529	W Yorkshire
YJ54XUX	32530	W Yorkshire
YJ54XUY	32531	W Yorkshire
YJ54XVA	32533	W Yorkshire
YJ54XVB	32534	W Yorkshire
YJ54XVC	32535	W Yorkshire
YJ54XVD	32536	W Yorkshire

Reg	No.	Area	Reg	No.	Area	Reg	No.	Area
YJ54XVM	66738	W Yorkshire	YK04EZH	66715	W Yorkshire	YK07FTU	68676	W Yorkshire
YJ54XVN	66739	W Yorkshire	YK04EZJ	66711	W Yorkshire	YK07FTY	68678	W Yorkshire
YJ54XVO	66740	W Yorkshire	YK04EZL	66712	W Yorkshire	YK07FTZ	68679	W Yorkshire
YJ54XVP	66741	W Yorkshire	YK04EZM	66714	W Yorkshire	YK07FUA	68680	W Yorkshire
YJ54XVR	66742	W Yorkshire	YK04KWR	53801	Hampshire	YK07FUB	68681	W Yorkshire
YJ54XVT	66743	W Yorkshire	YK05 CDN	53826	Devon & C	YK07FUD	68677	W Yorkshire
YJ54XVU	66744	W Yorkshire	YK05 CDO	53827	Devon & C	YK53GXJ	66701	W Yorkshire
YJ54XVW	66745	W Yorkshire	YK05FJE	66784	W Yorkshire	YK53GXL	66702	W Yorkshire
YJ54XVX	66746	W Yorkshire	YK05FJF	66783	W Yorkshire	YK53GXM	66703	W Yorkshire
YJ54XVY	66747	W Yorkshire	YK05FJJ	66781	W Yorkshire	YK53GXN	66704	W Yorkshire
YJ54XVZ	66748	W Yorkshire	YK05FLB	66782	W Yorkshire	YK53GXO	66705	W Yorkshire
YJ54XWA	66749	W Yorkshire	YK05FLC	66786	W Yorkshire	YK53GXP	66706	W Yorkshire
YJ54YCO	68515	W Yorkshire	YK05FOP	66791	W Yorkshire	YK53GXR	66707	W Yorkshire
YJ54YCP	68516	W Yorkshire	YK05FOT	66789	W Yorkshire	YK53GXT	66708	W Yorkshire
YJ55BJE	64501	Wales	YK05FOU	66788	W Yorkshire	YK53GXU	66709	W Yorkshire
YJ55BJF	64502	Wales	YK05FOV	66787	W Yorkshire	YK53GXV	66710	W Yorkshire
YJ55BJK	64503	Wales	YK05FPA	66785	W Yorkshire	YK54ENL	69001	W Yorkshire
YJ55CAO	68546	W Yorkshire	YK06AOU	19001	W Yorkshire	YK54ENM	69002	W Yorkshire
YJ55CAU	68548	W Yorkshire	YK06ATO	68642	W Yorkshire	YK54ENN	69003	W Yorkshire
YJ55CAV	68547	W Yorkshire	YK06ATU	19003	W Yorkshire	YK54ENO	69004	W Yorkshire
YJ55YGU	53823	W Yorkshire	YK06ATV	19002	W Yorkshire	YK54ENP	69000	W Yorkshire
YJ55ZZY	68601	W Yorkshire	YK06ATX	19005	W Yorkshire	YK54GZD	68523	W Yorkshire
YJ56EAA	19014	W Yorkshire	YK06ATY	19007	W Yorkshire	YK54GZE	68524	W Yorkshire
YJ56EAC	19015	W Yorkshire	YK06ATZ	19008	W Yorkshire	YK55AAE	68602	W Yorkshire
YJ56EAE	19016	W Yorkshire	YK06AUA	19010	W Yorkshire	YK55AAF	68611	W Yorkshire
YJ56EAF	19017	W Yorkshire	YK06AUC	19011	W Yorkshire	YK55AAJ	68603	W Yorkshire
YJ56EAG	19018	W Yorkshire	YK06AUL	19009	W Yorkshire	YK55AAN	68610	W Yorkshire
YJ56LJA	68649	W Yorkshire	YK06CZY	68644	W Yorkshire	YK55AUA	68612	W Yorkshire
YJ56LJC	68650	W Yorkshire	YK06CZZ	68643	W Yorkshire	YK55AUC	68613	W Yorkshire
YJ56LJE	68651	W Yorkshire	YK06DAA	68646	W Yorkshire	YK55AUE	68614	W Yorkshire
YJ56LJF	68652	W Yorkshire	YK06DAO	68647	W Yorkshire	YK55AUF	68615	W Yorkshire
YJ56LJK	68653	W Yorkshire	YK06DNN	68638	W Yorkshire	YK55AUH	68616	W Yorkshire
YJ56LJL	68655	W Yorkshire	YK06DNO	68633	W Yorkshire	YK55AUN	68604	W Yorkshire
YJ56LJN	68654	W Yorkshire	YK06DNU	68632	W Yorkshire	YK55AUO	68605	W Yorkshire
YJ56LJY	68664	W Yorkshire	YK06DTZ	68639	W Yorkshire	YK55AUP	68606	W Yorkshire
YJ56LJZ	68665	W Yorkshire	YK06DYH	68636	W Yorkshire	YK55AUU	68609	W Yorkshire
YJ56LKA	68666	W Yorkshire	YK06DYJ	68635	W Yorkshire	YK55AVB	68617	W Yorkshire
YJ56LKC	68667	W Yorkshire	YK06EHE	68648	W Yorkshire	YK55AVC	68618	W Yorkshire
YJ56LKD	68668	W Yorkshire	YK06EHL	68637	W Yorkshire	YK55AVD	68619	W Yorkshire
YJ56LKE	68663	W Yorkshire	YK06EHM	68634	W Yorkshire	YK55AVE	68620	W Yorkshire
YJ56LLG	68656	W Yorkshire	YK06EKT	19029	W Yorkshire	YK55AVF	68621	W Yorkshire
YJ56LLK	68657	W Yorkshire	YK06FHC	68645	W Yorkshire	YK55AVG	68622	W Yorkshire
YJ56LLM	68658	W Yorkshire	YK07AYA	37103	W Yorkshire	YK55AVJ	68623	W Yorkshire
YJ56LLN	68659	W Yorkshire	YK07AYB	37104	W Yorkshire	YK55AVL	68624	W Yorkshire
YJ56LLO	68660	W Yorkshire	YK07AYC	37105	W Yorkshire	YK55AVM	68625	W Yorkshire
YJ56LMX	68669	W Yorkshire	YK07AYD	37106	W Yorkshire	YK55ENM	53905	W Yorkshire
YJ56LNA	68662	W Yorkshire	YK07AYE	37107	W Yorkshire	YK55ENN	53906	W Yorkshire
YJ56LNC	68661	W Yorkshire	YK07AYF	37108	W Yorkshire	YK55ENR	53904	W Yorkshire
YJ56LRL	68672	W Yorkshire	YK07AYG	37109	W Yorkshire	YK57CJF	37125	W Yorkshire
YJ56LRN	68671	W Yorkshire	YK07AYH	37110	W Yorkshire	YK57CJJ	37126	W Yorkshire
YJ56LRU	68670	W Yorkshire	YK07AYJ	37111	W Yorkshire	YK57CJO	37127	W Yorkshire
YJ56WGA	68674	W Yorkshire	YK07AYL	37112	W Yorkshire	YK57CJU	37128	W Yorkshire
YJ56WGC	68673	W Yorkshire	YK07AYM	37113	W Yorkshire	YK57CJV	37129	W Yorkshire
YJ56ZMU	68675	W Yorkshire	YK07AYN	37114	W Yorkshire	YK57CJX	37130	W Yorkshire
YJ57VTV	68685	W Yorkshire	YK07AYO	37115	W Yorkshire	YK57CJY	37131	W Yorkshire
YJ57VVA	68686	W Yorkshire	YK07AYP	37116	W Yorkshire	YK57CJZ	37132	W Yorkshire
YJ57VYX	68684	W Yorkshire	YK07AYS	37117	W Yorkshire	YK57EZS	37063	W Yorkshire
YJ57VYY	68687	W Yorkshire	YK07AYT	37118	W Yorkshire	YK57EZU	37065	W Yorkshire
YJ57YSK	69268	W Yorkshire	YK07AYU	37119	W Yorkshire	YK57EZW	37067	W Yorkshire
YJ57YSL	69269	W Yorkshire	YK07AYV	37120	W Yorkshire	YK57EZX	37068	W Yorkshire
YJ57YSM	69276	W Yorkshire	YK07AYW	37121	W Yorkshire	YK57EZZ	37069	W Yorkshire
YJ57YSN	69275	W Yorkshire	YK07AYX	37122	W Yorkshire	YK57FAA	37070	W Yorkshire
YJ57YSO	69277	W Yorkshire	YK07AYY	37123	W Yorkshire	YK57FCL	66999	W Yorkshire
YJ57YSP	69278	W Yorkshire	YK07AYZ	37124	W Yorkshire	YK57FOM	68688	W Yorkshire
YJ57YSR	69279	W Yorkshire	YK07FTP	68682	W Yorkshire	YM52UVK	61214	Edinburgh
YK04EZG	66713	W Yorkshire	YK07FTT	68683	W Yorkshire	YM52UVL	61215	Edinburgh

The 2008 First Bus Handbook

YM52UVN	61216	Edinburgh	YN05HCX	65731	Potteries	YN08LCP	37237	S Yorkshire
YM52UVO	61217	Edinburgh	YN05HCY	65732	Potteries	YN08LCT	37238	S Yorkshire
YM52UVP	61218	Edinburgh	YN05HCZ	65733	Potteries	YN08LCU	37239	S Yorkshire
YM52UVR	61219	Edinburgh	YN05HGA	36006	Hampshire	YN08LCV	37240	S Yorkshire
YM52UVS	61220	Edinburgh	YN05WKC	65734	Potteries	YN08LCW	37241	S Yorkshire
YM52UVT	61221	Edinburgh	YN05WKD	65735	Potteries	YN08LCY	37242	S Yorkshire
YM52UVU	61222	Edinburgh	YN05WKE	65736	Potteries	YN08LCZ	37243	S Yorkshire
YM52UVW	61223	Edinburgh	YN05WKF	65737	Potteries	YN08LDA	37244	S Yorkshire
YM52UVZ	61224	Edinburgh	YN05WKG	65738	Potteries	YN08LDC	37245	S Yorkshire
YM52UWA	61225	Edinburgh	YN05WKH	65739	Potteries	YN08LDD	37278	S Yorkshire
YM52UWB	61226	Edinburgh	YN05WKJ	65740	Potteries	YN53EFE	31787	S Yorkshire
YM52UWD	61227	Edinburgh	YN05WKK	65741	Potteries	YN53EFF	31788	S Yorkshire
YM52UWF	61228	Edinburgh	YN06CGU	23321	Bristol	YN53EFG	31789	S Yorkshire
YM52UWG	61229	Edinburgh	YN06CGV	23322	Bristol	YN53EFH	31790	S Yorkshire
YM52UWH	61230	Edinburgh	YN06CGX	23323	Bristol	YN53EFJ	31791	S Yorkshire
YM52UWJ	61231	Edinburgh	YN06CGY	23324	Bristol	YN53EFK	31792	S Yorkshire
YM52UWK	61232	Edinburgh	YN06CGZ	23325	Bristol	YN53EFL	31793	S Yorkshire
YM52UWN	61233	Edinburgh	YN06TDO	65028	Essex	YN53EFM	31794	S Yorkshire
YN03ZVW	53151	Hampshire	YN06TDU	65029	Essex	YN53EFO	31795	S Yorkshire
YN03ZVX	50407	W Yorkshire	YN06TDV	65030	Essex	YN53EFP	31796	S Yorkshire
YN03ZVY	50408	W Yorkshire	YN06TDX	65031	Essex	YN53EFR	31797	S Yorkshire
YN04AJU	23013	Berkshire	YN06TDZ	65032	Essex	YN53EFT	31798	S Yorkshire
YN04AJV	23015	Berkshire	YN06UPZ	37146	Eastern C	YN53EFU	31799	S Yorkshire
YN04AJX	23014	Berkshire	YN06URA	37147	S Yorkshire	YN53EFV	31800	S Yorkshire
YN04GLV	36005	Hampshire	YN06URB	37148	S Yorkshire	YN53EFW	31801	S Yorkshire
YN04GME	65705	Potteries	YN06URC	37149	S Yorkshire	YN53EFX	31802	S Yorkshire
YN04GMF	65706	Potteries	YN06URD	37150	S Yorkshire	YN53EFZ	31803	S Yorkshire
YN04GMG	65707	Potteries	YN06URE	37151	S Yorkshire	YN53EGC	31804	S Yorkshire
YN04GNU	65704	Hampshire	YN06URF	37152	S Yorkshire	YN53ELJ	50319	W Yorkshire
YN04GNV	36001	Hampshire	YN06URG	37153	S Yorkshire	YN53ELO	50318	W Yorkshire
YN04GNX	36002	Hampshire	YN06URH	37154	S Yorkshire	YN53EOA	31776	S Yorkshire
YN04GNY	36003	Hampshire	YN06URJ	37155	S Yorkshire	YN53EOB	31777	S Yorkshire
YN04GNZ	36004	Hampshire	YN06WME	65033	Potteries	YN53EOC	31778	S Yorkshire
YN04LWV	55003	Wales	YN06WMF	65034	Potteries	YN53EOD	31779	S Yorkshire
YN04LWW	55004	Wales	YN06WMG	65035	Potteries	YN53EOE	31780	S Yorkshire
YN04YHW	23202	Bristol	YN06WMJ	65036	Potteries	YN53EOF	31781	S Yorkshire
YN04YHX	23203	Bristol	YN06WMK	65037	Potteries	YN53EOG	31782	S Yorkshire
YN04YHY	23201	Bristol	YN06WML	65038	Potteries	YN53EOH	31783	S Yorkshire
YN04YHZ	23204	Bristol	YN06WMM	65039	Potteries	YN53EOJ	31784	S Yorkshire
YN04YJC	65001	Potteries	YN06WMO	65040	Potteries	YN53EOK	31785	S Yorkshire
YN04YJD	65002	Potteries	YN06WMP	65041	Potteries	YN53EOL	31786	S Yorkshire
YN04YJE	65003	Potteries	YN06WMT	65042	Potteries	YN53VBT	56001	Aberdeen
YN04YJF	65004	Potteries	YN07MKD	37246	S Yorkshire	YN53VBU	56002	Essex
YN04YJG	65005	Potteries	YN07MKE	37247	S Yorkshire	YN53VBV	56003	Essex
YN05GYA	12001	Manchester	YN07MKF	37248	S Yorkshire	YN53YHH	55000	Wales
YN05GYB	12002	Manchester	YN07MKG	37249	S Yorkshire	YN54 JSX	25654	Devon & C
YN05GYC	12005	Manchester	YN07MKJ	37250	S Yorkshire	YN54APF	23021	Bristol
YN05GYD	12006	Manchester	YN07MKK	37251	S Yorkshire	YN54APK	23020	Bristol
YN05GYE	12007	Manchester	YN07MKL	37252	S Yorkshire	YN54APO	23016	London
YN05GYF	12008	Manchester	YN07MKM	37253	S Yorkshire	YN54APU	23017	London
YN05GYG	12009	Manchester	YN07MKO	37254	S Yorkshire	YN54APV	23018	London
YN05GYH	12003	Manchester	YN07MKP	37255	S Yorkshire	YN54APX	23019	Bristol
YN05GYJ	12004	Manchester	YN07MKV	37256	S Yorkshire	YN54NXM	23301	Bristol
YN05GYK	12010	Manchester	YN07MKZ	37258	S Yorkshire	YN54NXO	23308	Bristol
YN05GYO	12011	Manchester	YN07MLE	37259	S Yorkshire	YN54NXR	23309	Bristol
YN05GYP	12014	Manchester	YN07MLF	37260	S Yorkshire	YN54NXT	23310	Bristol
YN05GYR	12015	Manchester	YN07MLJ	37261	S Yorkshire	YN54NXU	23302	Bristol
YN05GYS	12016	Manchester	YN07MLK	37262	S Yorkshire	YN54NXV	23303	Bristol
YN05GYT	12017	Manchester	YN07MLL	37263	S Yorkshire	YN54NXW	23304	Bristol
YN05GYU	12013	Manchester	YN07MLO	37264	S Yorkshire	YN54NXX	23305	Bristol
YN05GYV	12012	Manchester	YN07MLU	37265	S Yorkshire	YN54NXY	23306	Bristol
YN05GYW	12018	Manchester	YN07SYJ	19033	Luton Airport	YN54NXZ	23307	Bristol
YN05HCL	65027	Potteries	YN08LCJ	37229	S Yorkshire	YN54NYR	23311	Bristol
YN05HCO	65727	Potteries	YN08LCK	37230	S Yorkshire	YN54NYT	23312	Bristol
YN05HCP	65728	Potteries	YN08LCL	37231	S Yorkshire	YN54NYU	23313	Bristol
YN05HCU	65729	Potteries	YN08LCM	37234	S Yorkshire	YN54NYV	23314	Bristol
YN05HCV	65730	Potteries	YN08LCO	37235	S Yorkshire	YN54NZA	65006	Hampshire

Reg	No	Location	Reg	No	Location	Reg	No	Location
YN54NZC	65007	Hampshire	YR02UVU	50239	S Yorkshire	YU52VXX	61205	S Yorkshire
YN54NZD	65008	Hampshire	YR52VEH	65679	Essex	YU52VXY	61206	S Yorkshire
YN54NZE	65009	Hampshire	YR52VEK	65680	Essex	YU52VXZ	61207	S Yorkshire
YN54NZF	65010	Hampshire	YR52VEL	65681	Essex	YU52VYA	61208	S Yorkshire
YN54NZG	65011	Hampshire	YR52VEP	65682	Essex	YU52VYB	61209	S Yorkshire
YN54NZH	65012	Hampshire	YR52VEU	65683	Essex	YU52VYC	61210	S Yorkshire
YN54NZJ	65013	Hampshire	YR52VEY	65684	Essex	YU52VYD	61211	S Yorkshire
YN54NZK	65014	Hampshire	YR52VFO	65685	Essex	YU52VYE	31129	S Yorkshire
YN54NZM	65015	Hampshire	YS03ZKA	62406	Essex	YU52VYF	31130	S Yorkshire
YN54NZO	65016	Hampshire	YS03ZKB	62407	Essex	YU52VYG	31131	S Yorkshire
YN54NZP	65017	Hampshire	YS03ZKC	65686	Essex	YU52VYH	31132	S Yorkshire
YN54NZR	65018	Hampshire	YS03ZKD	62409	Essex	YU52VYJ	31133	S Yorkshire
YN54NZT	65019	Hampshire	YS03ZKE	62408	Essex	YU52VYK	31134	S Yorkshire
YN54NZU	65020	Hampshire	YS03ZKF	62410	Essex	YU52VYL	31135	S Yorkshire
YN54NZV	65021	Hampshire	YS03ZKG	65687	Essex	YU52VYM	32278	Bristol
YN54NZW	65022	Hampshire	YS03ZKH	65688	Essex	YU52VYN	31137	S Yorkshire
YN54NZX	65023	Hampshire	YS03ZKJ	65689	Essex	YU52VYO	31138	S Yorkshire
YN54NZY	65024	Hampshire	YS03ZKK	65690	Essex	YU52VYP	31139	S Yorkshire
YN54NZZ	65025	Hampshire	YS03ZKL	65691	Essex	YU52VYR	31140	S Yorkshire
YN54OCK	65026	Potteries	YS03ZKM	65692	Essex	YU52VYS	31141	S Yorkshire
YN55PXF	23315	Bristol	YS51JVA	61135	Berkshire	YU52VYT	31142	W Yorkshire
YN55PXG	23316	Bristol	YS51JVD	62228	Aberdeen	YU52VYV	31143	W Yorkshire
YN55PXH	23317	Bristol	YS51JVE	68005	Berkshire	YU52VYX	31144	W Yorkshire
YN55PXJ	23318	Bristol	YS51JVH	68006	Berkshire	YU52VYY	31145	W Yorkshire
YN55PXK	23319	Bristol	YS51JVK	61136	Berkshire	YU52VYZ	31146	W Yorkshire
YN55PXL	23320	Bristol	YT51EZW	50237	S Yorkshire	YU52VZA	31147	W Yorkshire
YN56NHE	57001	Essex	YT51EZX	50238	S Yorkshire	YU52VZA	31148	S Yorkshire
YN56NHF	57002	Essex	YU52VXH	61192	S Yorkshire	YV03UBA	23008	Berkshire
YN57BVU	20321	Wales	YU52VXJ	61193	S Yorkshire	YV03UBB	23009	Berkshire
YN57BVV	20322	Wales	YU52VXK	61194	S Yorkshire	YV03UBC	23010	Berkshire
YN57BVW	20323	Wales	YU52VXL	61195	S Yorkshire	YV03UBD	23011	Berkshire
YN57BVX	20324	Wales	YU52VXM	61196	S Yorkshire	YV03UBE	23012	Berkshire
YN57BVY	20325	Wales	YU52VXN	61197	S Yorkshire	YV03UOU	40976	S Yorkshire
YN57BVZ	20326	Wales	YU52VXO	61198	S Yorkshire	YV03UOW	40975	S Yorkshire
YN57BWU	20327	Wales	YU52VXP	61199	S Yorkshire	YV03UOX	40974	S Yorkshire
YN57RJU	37228	S Yorkshire	YU52VXR	61200	S Yorkshire	YV03UOY	40973	S Yorkshire
YN57RJZ	37232	S Yorkshire	YU52VXS	61201	S Yorkshire	YX05AVV	56501	Aberdeen
YN57RKA	37233	S Yorkshire	YU52VXT	61202	S Yorkshire			
YN57RKJ	37236	S Yorkshire	YU52VXV	61203	S Yorkshire			
YP02ABN	65678	Essex	YU52VXW	61204	S Yorkshire			

ISBN 9781904875185

© Published by *British Bus Publishing Ltd, July 2008*

British Bus Publishing Ltd, 16 St Margaret's Drive, Telford, TF1 3PH
Telephone: 01952 255669 - Facsimile: 01952 222397

www.britishbuspublishing.co.uk